Luminos is the Open Access monograph publishing program from UC Press. Luminos provides a framework for preserving and reinvigorating monograph publishing for the future and increases the reach and visibility of important scholarly work. Titles published in the UC Press Luminos model are published with the same high standards for selection, peer review, production, and marketing as those in our traditional program. www.luminosoa.org

The publisher gratefully acknowledges the generous support of the Sue Tsao Endowment Fund in Chinese Studies of the University of California Press Foundation.

Taiwan and China

Taiwan and China

Fitful Embrace

―――

Edited by

Lowell Dittmer

UNIVERSITY OF CALIFORNIA PRESS

University of California Press, one of the most distinguished university presses in the United States, enriches lives around the world by advancing scholarship in the humanities, social sciences, and natural sciences. Its activities are supported by the UC Press Foundation and by philanthropic contributions from individuals and institutions. For more information, visit www.ucpress.edu.

University of California Press

Oakland, California

Suggested citation: Dittmer, Lowell (ed.). *Taiwan and China: Fitful Embrace*. Oakland: University of California Press, 2017. doi: https://doi.org/10.1525/luminos.38

Library of Congress Cataloging-in-Publication Data

Names: Dittmer, Lowell, editor.
Title: Taiwan and China : fitful embrace / edited by Lowell Dittmer.
Description: Oakland, California : University of California Press, [2017] | Includes bibliographical references and index. |
Identifiers: LCCN 2017016677 (print) | LCCN 2017019352 (ebook) | ISBN 9780520968707 (ebook) | ISBN 9780520295988 (pbk. : alk. paper)
Subjects: LCSH: Taiwan—Relations—China. | China—Relations—Taiwan. | Chinese reunification question, 1949- | Taiwan--Politics and government—21st century. | China--Politics and government—21st century.
Classification: LCC DS799.63.C6 (ebook) | LCC DS799.63.C6 T25 2017 (print) | DDC 327.51051249--dc23
LC record available at https://lccn.loc.gov/2017016677

26 25 24 23 22 21 20 19 18 17

10 9 8 7 6 5 4 3 2 1

CONTENTS

ACC   ASEAN-China Center
AFTA   ASEAN-China Free Trade Area
AIIB   Asian Infrastructure Investment Bank
ANZTEC   Agreement between New Zealand and the Separate Customs Terri-
            tory of Taiwan, Penghu, Kinmen and Matsu on Economic Coop-
            eration
APEC   Asia Pacific Economic Cooperation
APROC   Asia-Pacific Regional Operations Center
ARATS   Association for Relations Across the Taiwan Straits
ARF   ASEAN Regional Forum
ASEAN   Association of Southeast Asian Nations
ASL   Anti-Secession Law
ASTEP   Agreement between Singapore and the Separate Customs Territory
            of Taiwan, Penghu, Kinmen and Matsu on Economic Partnership
A2AD   Anti-Access Area Denial
BFA   Boao Forum for Asia
BOP   balance-of-power
CAFTA   China-ASEAN Free Trade Agreement
CCP   Chinese Communist Party
COC   Code of Conduct in the South China Sea
CPCCC   Chinese People's Political Consultative Conference
CSTA   Cross-Strait Service Trade Agreement
DOC   Declaration on the Conduct of Parties in the South China Sea
DPP   Democratic Progressive Party

EAS	East Asia Summit
ECFA	Economic Cooperation Framework Agreement
FDI	foreign direct investment
FIE	foreign-invested enterprise
FPEZ	Free Economic Pilot Zone
FTA	free trade agreement
GMS	Greater Mekong Subregion
IC	integrated circuit
ICBM	intercontinental ballistic missile
ICT	information and communications technology
IMF	International Monetary Fund
IR	international relations
ITRI	Industry Technology Research Institute
KMT	Kuomintang
MIRV	multiple independently retargeted vehicle
OBM	own-brand manufacture
OBOR	One Belt, One Road
ODM	original design manufacture
OEM	original equipment manufacture
PAP	People's Action Party (Singapore)
P3 CEP	Pacific Three Closer Economic Partnership
P4	Trans-Pacific Strategic Economic Partnership (aka TPSEP)
PLA	People's Liberation Army
PRC	People's Republic of China
RCEP	Regional Comprehensive Economic Partnership
RMB	renminbi
ROC	Republic of China
SASAC	State-Owned Assets Supervision and Administration Commission
SEF	Straits Exchange Foundation
SLBM	submarine-launched missile
SMEs	small and medium enterprises
SOE	state-owned enterprise
SPIL	Silicon Precision Industries Co.
TAC	Treaty of Amity and Cooperation in Southeast Asia
TAO	Taiwan Affairs Office
TFT-LCD	thin-film-transistor liquid-crystal-display
TPP	Trans-Pacific Partnership
TPTS	Taiwan Public Television Service
TSMC	Taiwan Semiconductor Manufacturing Company

Introduction

Lowell Dittmer

China's contentious relation to Taiwan began when the People's Republic of China (PRC) was founded in October 1949 and the defeated Kuomintang (KMT) set up an exile regime on the island two months later. Without now delving into the rich legal and historical complexities, suffice it to say that the island's autonomous sovereignty has been in contention ever since, initially because of the KMT's stubborn insistence that it continued to represent not just Taiwan but all of China, and later, when the tables had turned, because Taiwan refused to cede sovereignty to the now dominant power that had arisen on the other side of the Strait. At this writing, the election of a Democratic Progressive Party (DPP) government under Tsai Ing-wen in January 2016 brings the island to a new inflection point. For, like the Chen Shui-bian administration in 2000–2008, the incoming DPP regime would really prefer to drop all claim to be part of the Chinese mainland and to embrace political independence. Of course they dare not say this in so many words because it would infuriate Beijing, which continues to insist that there is one China, that Taiwan is a part of it, and that any assertion otherwise by Taiwan constitutes an illegal attempt at secession that Beijing has the legal right to prevent by force. China would prefer that contingency not to arise. Its use of force against Taiwan would result in great damage to the lives and property of people with whom mainlanders share a Chinese ancestry (compatriots in an ethnic or cultural sense, *tongbao*) whom the PRC aims to return to the motherland's embrace and possibly to the mainland as well. Chinese military forces still respect the striking power of Taiwan's armed forces and wish to avoid the possibility of US intervention to defend the island's sovereignty (even though the United States no longer formally recognizes that sovereignty). Such escalation could well cause great harm to China, to

Taiwan, and indeed to the United States. In other words, the Taiwan Strait remains an international flash point, one of the few places in the world that could unleash war between two great powers, both of which are nuclear weapon states.

But one of the things that makes Taiwan so politically difficult and so intellectually fascinating is that it poses not merely a security problem but a nexus of interrelated puzzles. The following chapters focus in turn on three of its aspects. The first is "national identity." This is a problem that Taiwan should not be permitted to have, according to mainland critics, because it is not even a nation. Yet Taiwanese do share a sense of collective identity that is widely perceived there as distinct, which they seek to preserve and profess to be willing to fight for. This has greatly complicated Beijing's quest to promote reunification, particularly after the post-1979 shift from a focus on "armed liberation" to a focus on peaceful reunion, for to be peaceful it must also be voluntary. The second aspect of the problem is socioeconomic. The post-1979 shift to peaceful reunification was premised on the assumption that through "three direct links"—postal, transportation, and trade—the embittered gulf dividing the two peoples at the Strait could eventually be bridged. While the "three links" met with an immediate "three nos" (no contact, no compromise, no negotiation) from the Chiang Ching-kuo regime, Beijing nevertheless persevered by accommodating "three indirect links" (mainly via Hong Kong), and these informal connections, unsuccessfully repressed but ultimately tolerated by the Taiwan authorities, have proved surprisingly robust, paving the way for their formalization in 2008. Yet communication has not exactly blossomed into fraternal love. The third dimension of the problem is political-strategic. This has both national and international aspects. Nationally, what do China and Taiwan expect of their future relationship—what adjustments will each demand of the other in terms of structural political changes, or what nonchanges will each tolerate—and how do they plan to effect such changes? Internationally, how will reunification be achieved—or, how can Taiwan's autonomy be preserved—in the prevailing balance of power, and what impact will either outcome have on that balance?

NATIONAL IDENTITY

A sense of national identity has long been conceived by political scientists to be a vital part of nation building, as it instills loyalty and participatory zeal in an ethnoreligiously heterogeneous citizenry and a sense of collective coherence and international affiliation or direction in the nation-state. At the same time, in extreme cases it can drive blind and ultimately self-destructive international ambitions. The Chinese sense of identity with regard to Taiwan and other peripheral regions has been fairly stable, even spanning both Nationalist and communist revolutionary eras: the understanding is that all of these areas should be assimilated into the motherland as soon and as fully as possible, making minimal allowance for ethnolinguistic differences.[1] In contrast, the sense of national identity in Taiwan has varied greatly over time, recurrently tending to destabilize the relationship. Taiwan attained provincial status in the Qing Empire only ten years before being forfeited to Japan as part of the Shimonoseki peace settlement at the end of the first Sino-Japanese War in 1895, thenceforth remaining a Japanese colony for the next fifty years. Upon occupying the island after 1945, the Nationalist forces reintroduced a Chinese identity for it, initially as a backward outpost of the lost republic but after loss of the civil war as temporary capital of a government in exile. While there had been resistance to the Japanese occupation regime, it seems to have been less than in the contemporaneous Korean colony, and postcolonial Taiwan has also remained friendlier to Japan than either South or North Korea, affiliating Taiwan during the Cold War into a US-Japan-Taiwan security network. All these identity adjustments were superimposed from the top down on a relatively passive populace.

With the introduction of democracy in the twilight years of the Chiangs' reign at the end of the 1980s, the evolution of national identity on the island was stimulated by diverse impulses, including a scrambled international scene at the end of the Cold War, an attractive offer for peaceful reunification from the mainland, and the aspirations of the newly enfranchised Taiwanese electorate. As Yi-huah Jiang, former premier of the Republic of China and professor of political science at Taiwan University, indicates in chapter 2 of this volume, the overall thrust of Taiwan's evolving identity tended to be "modernist." Drawing on the pattern-variable distinction between ascribed and achieved identities, he shows how the primordial division, a "subethnic" split between original inhabitants of the island (*benshengren*) and the wave of Chinese who fled the mainland at the end of the civil war (*waishengren*), has gradually faded over time. This is evinced not only in the growing number of citizens who answer the survey question "I am" with "Taiwanese" (as opposed to "Chinese" or "both") but in more refined survey instruments of his own devising that measure identity in terms of various constructed variables. And this corresponds with a "future nation preference" shifting ever more toward independence and away from any interest in reunification. All this is quite contrary to the preferences of the mainland, of course, which is thereby incentivized to reconsider its option to resort to force if Taiwan moves toward formal independence. Yet ironically Jiang finds that while majority preferences have shifted toward independence they are not strongly held: only a small percentage would still pursue independence in the face of a credible threat of force. The Taiwanese electorate is pragmatic, willing to subordinate ideal preferences to political survival. Hence the consistent majority preference for "no independence, no reunification" (*bu du bu tong*). In view of the fairly invariant attachment to a cross-Strait status quo, Jiang argues that the more relevant issue is not identity but the interpretation of "one China." If the PRC and ROC agree that, despite the existence of two governments that claim to be "China," there is only one China in the world, who is its legitimate representative, and what repercussions do differing interpretations of "one China" have for policy and diplomacy? In other words, the essential question is one of sovereignty: Who rules?

In chapter 3, one of the few extant studies of the evolution of national identity in Taiwan during the Ma Ying-jeou era, Jean-Pierre Cabestan arrives at the rather startling finding that despite a landslide victory for this Nationalist president in 2008, followed by rapid and successful moves toward reconciliation with the mainland, the Taiwan electorate's interest in reunification has only waned. And this, he argues, is not because the "Blue" camp (a coalition of parties, most predominantly the KMT and the People First Party, that takes a softer position toward the PRC, supporting a reunification that is often envisioned as long-deferred and as dependent on the PRC's fulfillment of many conditions, as well as an increase in ties with the mainland) simply avoided an unpopular issue. To the contrary, the Nationalists made a concerted drive during their eight-year control of both executive and legislative branches to reverse the DPP's foregoing "de-Sinification" movement and restore faith in "one China," interpreted as the Republic of China (ROC) on Taiwan. Cross-Strait trade and investment increased, regular discussions were resumed between the Taiwan's Straits Exchange Foundation (SEF) and China's Association for Relations Across the Taiwan Straits (ARATS), resulting in some two dozen agreements, most prominently the "three direct links" and the 2010 Economic Cooperation Framework Agreement (ECFA), and mainland tourism and investment in the island was for the first time permitted. Having already passed a law against "secession," Beijing downplayed its invasion threats and agreed and adhered to a diplomatic truce, permitting Taiwan to make trade agreements with New Zealand and Singapore that it could have blocked and to participate informally in the World Health Association. The mainland authorities even agreed to negotiate cultural exchanges and some form of peace treaty with the island. But after initially expressing interest the Ma leadership opted not to pursue these. And the attempt to move ahead toward further economic integration in a Cross-Strait Service Trade Agreement (CSTA), after being bilaterally agreed on, was blocked in the Legislative Yuan, where the KMT held a commanding majority.

The PRC authorities must have been quite perplexed that a relationship they had so carefully nurtured and that seemed to be making excellent economic progress could so swiftly unravel. How could this be? Cabestan points to a number of unnoticed flaws with cross-Strait détente. First and foremost, increasing economic linkages with the mainland did not prove to be quite the panacea that had been advertised. Exports constitute about 70 percent of Taiwan's GDP, some 40 percent of which go to China or Hong Kong. But PRC growth has been decelerating since 2010 for a number of reasons, none of which have much to do with Taiwan, nor have the island's other trade partners made a very impressive recovery from the global financial crisis, so export growth stalled. There is a perception (only weakly supported by available evidence) that the growth that has occurred has been more unequally distributed (to businesses with mainland investments) than before. The economic "gifts" bestowed by the PRC, such as "early harvest" post-ECFA trade arrangements, tend to be discounted in Taiwan for having ulterior political motives (which China has never denied). The student-led, anti-CSTA "Sunflower Movement" that occupied the legislature several weeks in the spring of 2014 seems to have been surprisingly successful in mobilizing mass support, especially among the young people ironically most likely to seek jobs on the mainland. It seems that the more economic integration succeeds, the greater the tendency to mobilize national identity as a counterweight.

Chapter 4, by Shu Keng and Emmy Ruihua Lin of the Shanghai University of Finance and Economics, takes on one of the key pieces of this puzzle, namely the political opinions of the growing number (currently estimated at over a million) of Taiwanese businesspeople or *taishang* who move to the mainland on a more or less permanent basis to pursue their livelihoods. On the basis of an extensive (452 respondents) survey of Taiwan sojourners in Dongguan and the Shanghai region, Keng and Lin indeed find many changes: these Taiwanese are happy to assimilate to mainland culture, to marry Chinese spouses and have children, and to set up their own business associations, even schools. Their attitudes toward the mainland do change as well: they are more likely to vote "Blue," less likely to endorse Taiwan independence (the percentage sinks drastically, from 25.8 percent to 3.5 percent), and more likely to be open to future reunification (the percentage more than doubles, from 9.9 percent to 21.4 percent). The puzzle is that despite all these adaptations they are not inclined to give up their Taiwanese identity. They even continue to prefer independence to reunification, by a wide (if reduced) margin. Why? Keng and Lin attribute the resilience of Taiwan identities to *taishang* mobility: because they can quickly and easily return, they continue to view Taiwan as "home." There may be other answers as well to this underresearched and methodologically elusive question. Class may be a factor—living standards remain much higher in Taiwan than on the mainland (even though sojourners typically still draw Taiwanese salaries). And sojourners tend to limit their assimilation, forming their own clubs, social networks, schools, and communities on the mainland. Finally, politics—though ideology is played down, and Taiwan's democracy is often derided in China as chaotic and corrupt—may play a role. It may take generations (e.g., children of Taiwan-Chinese marriages) for full identity convergence to occur.

The Chinese insist that the mainland population should also have a voice in the future of Taiwan, and although this is often disputed on the island, in view of the PRC's looming economic and military power it seems inevitable that it will. In chapter 5, Gang Lin of Shanghai Jiaotong University and Weixu Wu of Tsinghua University bring a perceptive Chinese perspective to the issue. Understandably, while Taiwanese intellectuals tend to focus on national identity as "constructed," the mainland preference is to view it as primordial—as Chinese president Xi Jinping put it in his 2015 Singapore meeting with Ma Ying-jeou, "No force can pull us apart because we are brothers who are still connected by our flesh even if our bones are broken, we are a family in which blood is thicker than water." Mainlanders invoke a shared culture, again viewed not as malleable but as primordial: the path-dependent culture laid down by Confucianism, which the People's Republic now honors along with Taiwan. The future is also evoked as a sentimental basis for togetherness: the two peoples constitute a "community of cross-Strait shared destinies." The complex issue of institutional integration (i.e., mutual structural adjustments) is postponed with the "one country, two systems" formula that assures Taiwan even more latitude than Hong Kong's Special Administrative Region for the next fifty years. Successful integration of *taishang* into mainland society supposedly illustrates the potential for integration without institutional convergence. At the same time Chinese tacitly concede the weakness of their approach, noting that civil identity has fallen behind ethnic identity as a force for reunification. The possibility that the People's Democracy might at some future point usefully emulate Taiwan-style structural reforms is rarely entertained (and never officially).

Mainland views of the Taiwan issue are difficult to research because public opinion polling on that sensitive topic is not permitted, no doubt because Beijing's hopes for peaceful reunification could well be derailed by an outburst of Chinese nationalism. In chapter 6, Rou-lan Chen thus tackles the even more volatile but still uncensored issue of the Senkaku Islands, known in Taiwan (to which they are closest, some 43.5 miles away) as Diaoyu Tai and on the mainland as Diaoyu Dao. Japan surveyed the eight tiny uninhabited islets, declared them *terra nullius*, and annexed them under the jurisdiction of Okinawa prefecture in 1895; ever since their occupation by the United States from 1945 to 1971 they have been under Japanese control. Since the discovery of potential subsurface hydrocarbon deposits in the area in 1968, Japanese sovereignty has been disputed by both Taiwan and the PRC. Beijing's claim to the islets is subsidiary to its claim to Taiwan, as it contends (despite Tokyo's claims to the contrary) that they were part of the "unequal" Shimonoseki treaty ceding Taiwan to Japan. Although the islets are also claimed by Taiwan (much to China's satisfaction), their parallel provenance and proximity make them a politically accessible synecdoche for China's claim to Taiwan, and as such a polemical target of China's nationalistic "raging youth" (*fen qing*). Chen analyzes this politically articulate subsection of Chinese civil society through a sample of over a thousand contributions to a quasi-official Internet bulletin board called the Strong Nation Forum. In a fascinating psycho-political analysis of these data, she finds that the outraged nationalism provoked by the issue symptomizes deep ambivalence in China's younger generation. Their rage is directed partly against Japan, for claiming property that rightfully belongs to China, but also against the Chinese Communist Party (CCP) leadership for responding with such weakness and timidity to this violation of national sovereignty. This sense of nationalist outrage, which has upon occasion taken the form of mass demonstrations and even collective vandalism, may be traced to the massive expansion of the education system since 1999, the decay of established institutions of collective identity (e.g., the Communist Youth League), rising expectations after several decades of double-digit growth, and limited job opportunities for young people. Whatever the socioeconomic reagents, it seems to be a recurrent pattern of explosive youthful activism.

POLITICAL ECONOMY

In chapter 7, Chih-shian Liou begins our discussion of political economic connections with a comparative analysis of state-owned enterprise (SOE) in China and Taiwan. As an isomorphic component of Leninist "commanding heights" state-led developmentalism on both sides of the Strait, the SOE provides a useful point of departure. Though SOEs in China and Taiwan have the same origin, they have since undergone diverging trajectories. In the PRC they have been ideologically identified with socialism and thus favored with subsidies, preferred bank loan terms, merger and acquisition opportunities, initial public offerings, and stock market listings, and, in a number of "pillar" or strategic industries, they have been protected from market competition. Though subject to a series of reforms since the 1990s, SOEs continue to enjoy de facto soft budget constraints, while the directors are appointed by the Organization Department of the CCP Central Committee and have ministerial rank. The state has tried to make SOEs "national champions" able to compete with multinational corporations globally, thanks to which the second- and third-largest corporations in the world (Sinopec and China National Petroleum Corporation, respectively) are both SOEs. Though SOEs in 1978 made up three-quarters of China's GDP and have shriveled to only about one-quarter of that today, they are likely to remain in a privileged upstream industrial position under CCP control. In Taiwan, on the other hand, while SOEs played a key role in the early industrialization stage, privatization policy was introduced in the late 1980s. Thus, while SOEs accounted for 35.2 percent of capital formation in 1961, by 2001 they accounted for only about 9 percent. In contradistinction to Japan, South Korea, and China, Taiwan's growth has been led by small and medium enterprises (SMEs), usually family controlled. The pioneering dimension of Liou's analysis relates this comparative analysis to the dynamics of cross-Strait economic relations. Depending on the ideological emphasis at the time, SOEs are politically preferred to foreign-invested enterprises (FIEs), and this will tend to crowd out Taiwan-invested capital on the mainland. Growing cross-Strait economic interdependence, Liou points out, also raises the issue of trade externality: "In general trade among allies generates a positive security externality while trade among nonallies generates a negative security externality." Finally, there is the issue of economic asymmetry: the proportion of Chinese trade with Taiwan is much smaller than the proportion of Taiwan's trade with China (over 30 percent), meaning Taiwan is more dependent on China than vice versa. To deepen bilateral economic integration the mainland has consistently permitted an imbalance of payments very much in Taiwan's favor, also making the China-Taiwan trade relations more valuable to Taiwan than to the PRC.

Chapter 8, by Chung-min Tsai of National Cheng Chi University, focuses squarely on cross-Strait trade and investment and its impact on politics. Trade and investment, he finds, have increased inexorably over time, giving rise to Chinese confidence that economic integration must eventually lead, in accordance with neofunctional (and Marxist) logic, to political integration. In Taiwan's case, trade was soon followed by investment, and as investment increased it pulled in related trade. There were four big waves of Taiwan investment in China: (1) in the late 1980s, after the appreciation of Taiwan's currency priced Taiwan out of American markets and the government removed constraints on capital outflow; (2) 1992–94, after Deng's "southern voyage" inaugurating a new wave of liberal economic reform and coinciding with the Singapore talks; (3) in the early 2000s, during the world high-tech recession, when Taiwan's computer industry moved to the mainland to remain price competitive; and (4) post-2010, following the signing of the ECFA with its "early harvest" enticements. As the connection thrived, Taiwan capital has moved from labor-intensive assembly to high-tech production, from south to north and from east to west, from a more general export orientation to a focus on the China market. What is perhaps surprising is that the nexus between economics and politics has certainly not gone unnoticed in Taiwan, and politicians opposed to unification, such as Lee Teng-hui and Chen Shui-bian, have taken steps to arrest its development.

And what has been the impact of politics on economic integration? Attempts under Lee Teng-hui's presidency to "go slow" (*jieji yongren*) on investment in the mainland and divert it to Southeast Asia may have had some temporary impact in the wake of the 1995–96 missile crisis. But the Asian financial crisis (1997–98) then scared *taishang* out of Southeast Asia, and in the early 2000s the mainland eased foreign direct investment (FDI) regulations. For their part, Chinese attempts to co-opt *taishang* seem to have had some effect on voting patterns (most vote "Blue"), but not on policy making in Taiwan. Though the evidence is not entirely clear, Tsai concludes that the impact of political pressure (by either side) on trade and investment has been negligible. Economic transactions actually increased following the 2000 election of DPP leader Chen Shui-bian (because of the high-tech crash) and decreased following the 2008 election of KMT leader Ma Ying-jeou (because of the global financial crisis)—in each case, economic considerations trumped political.

Still, the prospects for the economic relationship going forward are decidedly mixed: election of a DPP leadership will not incentivize PRC political cooperation, mainland wages have been escalating, Beijing has been trying to upgrade its own national champions at the expense of competing foreign enterprises, and of course there has been an overall slowdown of GDP growth. Taiwan faces the contradictory pull of mainland jobs and opportunities departing the island while leaving an antimainland political backlash behind. In 2015 the United States was Taiwan's largest export destination by country, as trade with China slumped because their expanding domestic supply chain decreased demand for Taiwanese components.[2] Meanwhile, encouraged by the PRC leadership to "go out" (*zuo chuqu*) and acquire brands and expertise abroad, mainland enterprises have invested some $1.3 billion in the Taiwan market, where they received a mixed popular reception. Recent attempts by the state-owned chip maker and IT giant Tsinghua Unigroup to shell out $2 billion for substantial stakes in two Taiwan chip-packaging companies, Silicon Precision Industries Co. (SPIL) and ChipMOS Technologies Inc., have raised eyebrows in business and political circles on the island, for example.

In chapter 9, Tse-Kang Leng of the Academia Sinica in Taiwan focuses specifically on information technology (IT), the Silicon Island's leading strategic sector since the 1990s, constituting 30 percent of its exports. According to the original conception of the cross-Strait division of labor in Taiwan's industrial policy, the technology-intensive crown jewels were to be kept at home while labor-intensive assembly work was downloaded to the mainland. But that plan went overboard in the high-tech crash of the early 2000s, when Taiwan's laptop industry relocated to keep prices competitive—if one left, the rest had to follow or see their prices undercut by the one that left. Despite its ever growing importance, the cross-Strait nexus is only part of Taiwan's globalization. Taiwan is part of a tangle of value-added chains in which the upstream is largely in the United States and Japan while the downstream (assembly and export) is located on the mainland. Taiwan has found its niche in the middle, in ODM (original design manufacture) and OEM (original equipment manufacture) production. This niche is, however, endangered by competition from Japanese and Korean firms like Samsung upstream, while the Chinese plan is to move up from downstream by co-opting or buying or otherwise displacing Taiwanese OEM producers and semiconductor fabrication plants and forming a "red supply chain." To avoid being squeezed out, Taiwan firms have been attempting to move upstream from OEM to OBM (original brand manufacture), that is, to control the entire chain including the brand, as in Acer laptops or HTM smart phones. But this is a challenge amid stiff international competition, and it remains to be seen whether Taiwan firms can master the logistic and network requirements. Taiwan must simultaneously "handle the two situations" of international commercial competition and domestic security (in which industrial leadership and technological innovation have also become securitized).

In chapter 10, by You-tien Hsing, professor of geography and chair of the Center for China Studies at the University of California at Berkeley, we shift focus from the economic to the social dimension of cross-Strait relations. Hsing focuses on the proliferation and political organization of social media, which has emerged as a functional complement and sometime nemesis to industrial expansion on the island. Taiwanese businesspeople have sometimes tended to charge ahead oblivious of negative externalities such as high-tech or petrochemical pollution (in which they are hardly unique), creating fertile ground for social entrepreneurs and informal media networks such as PeoPo to harness "not in my back yard" (NIMBY) sentiments. And these have sometimes had major impact. Indeed, this has been one of the factors facilitating the wholesale exodus of externality-freighted production facilities such as Foxconn to the mainland, where environmental activism is less problematic. In this sense, Taiwan's democratic social entrepreneurialism might be said to make an ironic contribution to cross-Strait economic integration. China for its part, with the largest number of netizens and social media users on the planet, has also experienced electronically enhanced political involvement. Netizens have been active in fighting unfair land expropriations, pollution, corruption, health care abuses, and foreign investors. They have, for example, engaged in spontaneously assembled "human flesh searches" that use the Internet to identify and harass demonstrably corrupt officials, and in some cases (e.g., the 1986 anti-Japan demonstrations) have used social media to organize public protest. The widespread political use of social media has been particularly impressive in view of the state's various efforts to steer or suppress it, making the public context quite different from Taiwan's in that standing networks such as PeoPo cannot be established without state links. But Taiwan also has developed more politically acceptable contributions to cross-Strait civil society. The Tzu Chi organization, a Buddhist charity and one of the largest philanthropic organizations in the world, is based in Taiwan but is also fully functional on the mainland, where it propagates quasi-socialist values, does not endorse electoral democracy or market capitalism, and constitutes no threat to the state in either Taiwan or the PRC.

POLITICAL STRATEGY

Taiwan is in an unusual position in that its number one threat to national security is also its leading trade partner and investment recipient. In chapter 11, Yu-Shan Wu of Taiwan National University and Academia Sinica places Taiwan's unusual but not unique position in a strategic theoretical framework for comparative analysis, focusing on the recent security dilemma of Ukraine. Ukraine also has close historical, cultural and economic ties with a much larger neighbor, the Russian

Federation, which under Putin has moved to strengthen those ties. Ukraine attempted to resist Russian encroachments by balancing them against the European Union's expansionist ambitions. Ukrainian resistance was however complicated by a precarious domestic balance of power between one leadership faction (i.e., Yulia Tymoshenko) tilting toward affiliation with the EU and another (i.e., Viktor Yanukovich) tilting toward Russia's rival Eurasian Union. When this delicate balance collapsed in the Euromaidan demonstrations (and their suppression) and the flight of Yanukovich, Russia employed thinly disguised military force to reassert its predemocratic hegemony. Taiwan's strategic position is in many relevant respects analogous. True, Taiwan has had a much longer period of effective independence from China (over a century), and, like England, it is a maritime state facing a continental power across a defensible body of water (the Taiwan Strait). But like Ukraine, Taiwan has close historical, cultural, and economic ties to a much more powerful neighbor, which has asserted even more explicitly than Russia its claim to sovereignty over the island and its legal right to take it by force. Like Ukraine, Taiwan seeks to balance China's claims against an American informal and ambiguous pledge of security support without denying its historical, cultural, and economic ties to the mainland—that is, to "hedge." Was Ukraine's failure one of refusing to commit or of trying to commit to both sides at once? Is Ukraine's current embattled situation Taiwan's future? Of course no one knows the future, but the thrust of the Ukraine experience suggests that the position of a relatively weak "pivot" balancing two great powers becomes highly tenuous if relations between the wings polarize, leading each to pressure the pivot to "choose sides."

Chapters 12 and 13 focus on the other two angles of Taiwan's strategic triangle. With regard to American policy, we see an awkward gap between formal diplomatic ties and informal security commitments. In accordance with a "one-China policy" that required states to officially recognize only the ROC or the PRC, Washington recognizes the PRC as the one and only China; it dropped both its former defense alliance and its diplomatic recognition of Taiwan in January 1979. The United States and China have built their relationship upon recognition supplemented by three communiqués (1972, 1979, and 1982), reinforced by a booming bilateral trade and investment relationship, and the relationship has resulted in important strategic agreements on specific issues such as nuclear proliferation and climate control. Yet the United States has hedged by inserting into its recognition documents a provision for continued sale of weaponry to a Taiwan it no longer formally recognizes and by a law (the Taiwan Relations Act) implying continuing (if ambiguous) security protection and upgrading the informal relationship. In chapter 12, Ping-Kuei Chen, Scott L. Kastner, and William L. Reed debate the proposition put forth by some critics of American China policy that this is not only ambiguous but inconsistent and surely detrimental to closer Sino-American cooperation, that the United States should hence rescind its informal security commitment to Taiwan, and that, since it has already withdrawn from its defense alliance and diplomatic relationship with Taiwan it should withdraw as well the last symbol of support, weapons sales. In this exercise in rational futurology that conceives of "independence" and "reunification" as the authors do, it may indeed be correct that if the United States stopped selling weapons morale in Taiwan could collapse and the leaders would become more willing to reunite with the mainland on Beijing's terms—a result that would damage the US regional strategic position and its reputation for honoring security commitments. But Chen, Kastner, and Reed argue that inasmuch as this is only one possible scenario and not necessarily the most likely one, it would be risky for the United States to rescind weapon sales and for China to apply sanctions to force it to do so. Why? First, cessation of weapons sales would not necessarily make Taiwan more willing to submit to the mainland or make the United States more willing to allow the island to be overrun by force—after all, the United States had no formal security commitment to Korea when it intervened to resist a North Korean attack in the summer of 1950 (an alliance was agreed in 1953), or to South Vietnam in 1964. For the United States to halt weapon sales would make Taiwan a weaker and a more vulnerable target for PRC coercion, but it would also make Taiwan a more sympathetic victim for the Americans to rescue in the face of an unprovoked attack, as the futility of self-defense against an overwhelmingly superior adversary would be immediately apparent. Taiwan's reactions are not necessarily based on rational calculation of the power balance, and American reactions are not entirely predictable on the basis of paper commitments.

Whereas American defense of the cross-Strait status quo is aimed at avoiding destabilizing uncertainties, China is betting on statistical probabilities: it is growing faster and stronger and is confident that time is on its side. Yet China is also wary of destabilizing collateral damage (let alone war with the United States) and would very much prefer peaceful reunification. According to Jing Huang of the Lee Kuan Yew Institute at the National University of Singapore, the Chinese have relied upon both carrots (socioeconomic integration) and sticks (the ultimate threat of overwhelming force). But since carrots have thus far proved inconclusive and the use of threats of force has had negative side effects in terms of mobilizing an antimainland backlash in Taiwan and degrading Chinese soft power abroad, Beijing has shifted from demanding reunification within a defined time span to proscribing movement toward independence. Under Hu Jintao and Xi Jinping, Beijing's prime emphasis has not been sticks or new carrots but a gradual constriction of diplomatic and political space: "boxing Taiwan in," as Huang puts it, so that Taiwan eventually realizes that it has no rational way out but through Beijing. This gradual attrition strategy must be delicately nuanced, giving Taiwan enough space to avoid a negative backlash and encourage pro-China sentiment but not enough to set back the isolation strategy or give the island the illusion it could break out from it. Under Xi Jinping this subtle balance has tended to shift, like Chinese foreign policy generally, to a slightly more assertive stance, for example in his reaffirmation of "one country, two systems," or his emphasis on "one China" over "differing interpretations." This harder line may become still harder during the forthcoming Tsai Ing-wen era. Yet overall the strategy might be said to have been at least a quasi-success in that it has won the limited approval of the "Blue" camp and the industrial interests with a stake in the mainland economy, the tolerance of the United States, and an overwhelming diplomatic united front in international diplomacy. But as the Sunflower Movement and the results of the January 2016 election illustrate, just because Taiwan is trapped does not necessarily mean they love their trapper.

Taiwan in the 1990s looked to Southeast Asia as a possible way out, as chapter 14, by Samuel Ku of National Kaohsiung University, notes in his interesting account, partly because the revaluation of the currency (under American pressure) squeezed exports and partly because it wanted to lessen its excessive economic dependency on the mainland. Although the island lost its last battles for diplomatic recognition against the PRC in Indonesia and Singapore in 1990 and Brunei in 1991, Lee Teng-hui's "vacation diplomacy" helped maintain informal friends and business contacts there, and Taiwan has established Taiwan affairs offices in all Southeast Asian countries to facilitate trade, investment, and travel. As of 2010, the Association of Southeast Asian Nations (ASEAN) was Taiwan's second-largest trade partner after the PRC, with US$93.64 billion in trade by 2014 (15.9 percent of Taiwan's total trade). While China's involvement in the Indochina wars and a number of other Southeast Asian "national liberation struggles" alienated Southeast Asian governments during the Maoist period, China announced a "good neighbor policy" in 1990, and in the early 1990s it signed the Treaty of Amity and Cooperation (TAC) and joined the ASEAN Regional Forum (ARF), then attended ASEAN Plus Three meetings promoting north-south collaboration and the East Asian Summit. The real breakthrough for China came during the Asian financial crisis (1997–98), when it made generous loans to Thailand and Indonesia while the International Monetary Fund (IMF) imposed strict austerity conditions on its bailout packages. In 2001 the Boao Asia Forum was established to facilitate informal pan-Asian "track two" diplomacy, and in 2010 the China-ASEAN Free Trade Agreement (CAFTA) came into effect, the largest such free trade agreement in the world, quickly catapulting China to the leading position among most ASEAN trade partners. With its launch of the Asian Infrastructure Investment Bank in 2014 and its proposal, in 2013, of the boldly visionary "One Silk Road Economic Belt and one Twenty-First-Century Maritime Silk Road," an initiative to establish economic corridors connecting China with other countries in Central Asia, West Asia, Southeast Asia, and Europe, China appears to be moving not only to further expand its influence in the region but to claim entrepreneurial leadership. Yet at the same time China's maritime territorial claims over the South China Sea and its increasingly forcible efforts to enforce them have not been welcomed by any Southeast Asian nation. In the face of China's economic and diplomatic initiatives, Taiwan under Ma Ying-jeou abandoned Chen Shui-bian's vigorous but ultimately failing "scorched-earth" competition with the mainland in favor of a nonconfrontational survival strategy that tacked somewhat closer to PRC positions. While Taiwan might have expected to benefit from the backlash against China's overbearing regional presence, Taiwan's position is compromised by the fact that its maritime territorial claims are identical to those of the PRC (indeed, based on the same "eleven-dash-line" 1947 map). Taiwan under Ma adopted an ambiguous policy, attempting to differentiate its gentler enforcement policy from the mainland's without relinquishing its sovereignty claims. At the same time the *taishang*, as ethnic Chinese alongside an economically influential ethnic minority in Southeast Asia, seek to ride the coattails of the mainland in private business ventures as well as the Asian Infrastructure Investment Bank and the Maritime Silk Road.

CONCLUSION

Taiwan, just when it seemed to have put the endlessly nettlesome cross-Strait problem to rest after a decade of cordial and constructive relations, appears to have resurrected it with the landslide defeat of its political sponsors. President Tsai Ing-wen has made clear her preference for no trouble with the mainland, and perhaps she will have none. But even on the off chance that this turns out to be true, the election itself says a great deal. While the results still need to be sorted out thematically in terms of the distribution of voter dissatisfaction with the Ma regime (clearly leadership failure must play a large part: e.g., Wang Jin-pyng), a portion of that discontent must be attributed to cross-Strait policy, if only because that took such a central place in the Ma agenda. Tsai's presidency must logically be seen to mark a deliberate departure from Ma's cross-Strait policy: otherwise she would not have so steadfastly refused to sign on to the status quo of the "1992 Consensus"— one China Constitution; one China, differing interpretations; no immediate reunification, no independence, and no use of force. Thus we stand at the threshold of a brave new era.

If Tsai maintains her current position of refusing to endorse the 1992 Consensus but "promoting communication, no provocations and no accidents," and holds to her statement that "we will not be provocative, and hope the two sides can sit down and talk in a rational manner," Beijing may not resort to the various economic and diplomatic weapons in its armory, which it cannot easily impose without damage to its own interests.[3] That would allow the relationship to glide down to a more stagnant phase in which high-level cross-Strait communications are *faute de mieux* limited to the CCP-KMT Forum. But the relationship even in the best case is apt to be fragile and suspicious.

NOTES

1. See Bill Chou, "New Bottle, Old Wine: China's Governance of Hong Kong in View of Its Policies in the Restive Borderlands," *Journal of Current Chinese Affairs* 44, no. 4 (2015): 177–209.

2. Enru Lin, "Export Orders Down by 4.4 Percent in '15, Economics Ministry," *China Post* (Taipei), January 21, 2016, www.chinapost.com.tw/taiwan/business/2016/01/21/456639/Export-orders.htm.

3. *Hong Kong Economic Times*, December 28, 2015, and Taiwan.cn [Beijing], December 25, 2015, quoted in Willy Lam, "After the Election: The Future of Cross-Strait Relations," *China Brief* 16, no. 1 (January 12, 2016), www.jamestown.org/programs/chinabrief/single/?tx_ttnews%5Btt_news%5D=44971&tx_ttnews%5BbackPid%5D=25&cHash=1ed4b9f61c57e3c8de0d90ae99be0109#.VqvH3HqAMi8.

National Identity

2

Taiwan's National Identity and Cross-Strait Relations

Yi-huah Jiang

The situation of the Taiwan Strait has remained one of the most worrisome flash points on the globe since the Second World War. Even in the aftermath of the collapse of the Soviet bloc, the possibility of a military confrontation between communist China and the United States still remains. The 1995–96 missile-test crisis following former president Lee Teng-hui's visit to the United States was a testimony to how sensitive cross-Strait relations were and how flammable the political situation could become overnight.

In the past eight years (2008–16), cross-Strait relations were relatively peaceful compared to how they had been under former president Chen Shui-bian (2000–2008). This peaceful coexistence was primarily a result of President Ma Ying-jeou's mainland policy, which replaced "confrontation" with "engagement," implemented the "three direct links" (postal, transportation, and trade) between mainland China and Taiwan, and successfully procured the Economic Cooperation Framework Agreement (ECFA) and another twenty bilateral agreements with mainland China, covering areas that ranged from trade promotion to crime prevention, food safety, environmental protection, and transportation cooperation.

Nevertheless, Ma's mainland policy was fiercely criticized by the Democratic Progressive Party (DPP) and was frequently denigrated as a betrayal of Taiwan's real interests. The critics accused Ma's government and the Nationalist Party (the Kuomintang, KMT) of "selling Taiwan to China" on the grounds that the KMT was a prounification party, and Ma himself never identified with Taiwan. The accusation, though emotional and exaggerated, had its political effect among those who did not benefit from his mainland policy. The general discontent with that policy, together with the poor performance of the government and nasty intraparty cleavages (first between Ma and Wang Jin-pyng, then between Eric Chu and Hung Shiu-chu), resulted in the unprecedented defeat of the KMT in the 2014 local elections and the 2016 presidential election.

The DPP's landslide victory in the 2016 election may become a turning point in the long-term development of cross-Strait relations. The DPP has traditionally favored a de jure Taiwan independence policy, and the newly elected president, Ms. Tsai Ing-wen, is generally regarded as a careful but uncompromising advocate of the independence cause. She was the drafter of former Republic of China (ROC) president Lee Teng-hui's "two states" concept (*liang guo lun*) and was a strong supporter of Chen Shui-bian's "one country on each side [of the Taiwan Strait]" (*yi bian yi guo*) concept, both of which describe Taiwan and China as two different countries and counter the notion of a single China. During the presidential election, Tsai asserted that most Taiwanese do not identify themselves with China and that "most youths are naturally inclined to Taiwan independence." Whether Tsai's policy toward mainland China will change Ma's legacy and what the consequences will be for cross-Strait relations (and East Asian security) deserve a thorough examination.

Issues of national identity and unification/independence are always conceived as critical in Taiwanese politics and cross-Strait relations. This chapter first explains the meaning of national identity in the context of Taiwanese politics, examines the different ways of measuring national identity in Taiwan, and shows that no matter which measurement is adopted, Taiwanese identification has risen precipitately in the past two decades. I then focus on the "one-China principle," an issue that I think more important and worthy of attention than the issue of national identity or the unification/independence choice. Finally I analyze what the scenarios of cross-Strait relations will be after the 2016 election, keeping in mind that cross-Strait relations are not merely bilateral, since they involve Taiwan, mainland China, and the United States in a strategic triangle relationship, and conclude with suggestions for improving cross-Strait relations.

CHANGING NATIONAL IDENTIFICATION IN TAIWAN

Theories of nationalism and national identity have been extensively discussed in Taiwan in recent decades.[1] Roughly speaking, there are two major schools concerning the meaning of a nation: the modernist and the primordial. The modernist school argues that the nation is a modern political construction arising in the process of state building. Since the global system of nation-states was formed no earlier than the seventeenth century, the modernists argue that the concepts of nation, nationalism, and national identity are all very novel socially constructed forms. On the other hand, the primordial school maintains that although the nation-state system is a modern phenomenon the nation has an antecedent objective existence that summons people's loyalty and identity, mostly on the bases of shared history, myth, genealogical relations, or religious belief, long before the modern state learns how to mobilize its citizens in the name of a fatherland.[2]

Most Taiwanese scholars tend to buy the modernist argument and see the "Taiwanese people" as a modern social construction emerging in the process of decolonization and democratization. They tend to agree on the following points: (1) A nation is an aggregate of persons who associate with each other by common descent, language, religion, or history, although the sense of communion may be imagined rather than actual. (2) National identity is a feeling that one has toward one's imagined community, the fundamental features of which include a homeland, a people, a common historical memory, and a common public culture. (3) Taiwanese identity is the source of Taiwanese nationalism and the Taiwanese nationalist movement, which pursues the political goal of Taiwanese independence.[3] As the building of a nation-state is usually described as the highest accomplishment of nationalism, Taiwanese nationalist scholars have little hesitation in accepting nationalism as a doctrine that holds that "the political and the national unit should be congruent," as Ernest Gellner succinctly puts it.[4]

Three different methods of measuring Taiwanese national identity are designed and widely employed in Taiwan. The first targets the consciousness of being Taiwanese as a distinct concept from that of being Chinese. The second addresses Taiwanese people's attitude toward unification with mainland China or a de jure independence of the island state. The third examines the extent to which respondents consider themselves to be Taiwanese nationalists or Chinese nationalists. I will analyze all the three methods in order and will argue that none proves a perfect measurement, though each serves a specific function in understanding Taiwanese people's collective consciousness.

Let us begin with the most popular method of understanding Taiwan's national identity—considering oneself Taiwanese versus Chinese. It is assumed that those who declare themselves to be Taiwanese only are identified with a political community called Taiwan; those who declare themselves to be Chinese only have a Chinese national identity; and those who say they are both Taiwanese and Chinese have a dual national identity.

According to a systematic survey conducted by the Election Study Center at National Chengchi University, the self-identity of Taiwan's residents has shifted spectacularly from a predominantly Chinese identity in the early years of democratization to a prevailing Taiwanese identity in Ma's second term of presidency. As figure 1 indicates, in the early 1990s nearly 25.5 percent of those polled by this survey answered that they perceived themselves as exclusively Chinese. The percentage dropped to 10.6 percent in 2001 at the beginning of Chen Shui-bian's administration and stood at only 3 percent in 2016. On the other hand, those who considered themselves exclusively Taiwanese rose dramatically from 17.6 percent

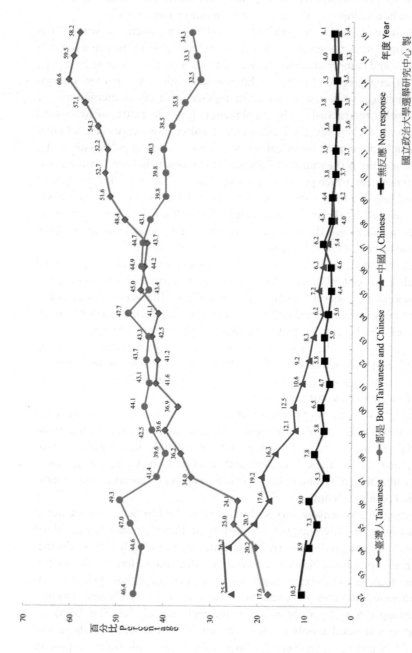

FIGURE 1. Changes in the Taiwanese/Chinese Identity of Taiwanese as tracked in surveys by the Election Study Center, National Chengchi University (1992–2016).

SOURCE: Hui-ling Chen, "Taiwanese/Chinese Identification Trend Distribution in Taiwan (1992/06~2016/12)," Election Study Center, National Chengchi University, August 24, 2016, http://esc.nccu.edu.tw/course/news.php?Sn=166.

in 1992 to 41.6 percent in 2001, and to 59.3 percent in 2016. That is to say, nearly two-thirds of Taiwan's population identify themselves exclusively Taiwanese now, and a great portion of this increase occurred during Ma Ying-jeou's administration. The proportion who regarded themselves as both Taiwanese and Chinese also dropped steadily from 46.4 percent to 33.6 percent in the same period.[5]

I have pointed out elsewhere that the classification of Taiwanese/Chinese/both is not an effective measurement of Taiwan's national identity, although it reveals some important information about the shift of the collective self-consciousness of Taiwanese. One major reason is that the term *Chinese* (*Zhongguoren*) is ambiguous in Mandarin. It can be used to designate a person who identifies with Chinese culture without referring to any specific body politic, or it can be understood to designate a person who identifies with either the ROC or the PRC. When a person responds to the question "Are you a Chinese or a Taiwanese?" with the answer "I am a Chinese," there is no way to determine whether he or she is referring to cultural identity or political identity. People living in mainland China, Taiwan, Hong Kong, or even oversea Chinese communities will have no difficulty regarding themselves as "Chinese" if they are thinking in cultural or ethnical terms. If we understand Chinese identity in cultural terms, as many scholars did when they cited the poll, then the category of "being Chinese" cannot be understood to be the people who identify with the PRC, and the category of being "both Chinese and Taiwanese" cannot be described as dual national identity or confusion of national identity. The latter may be simply an expression of one's multiple cultural affinities rather than one's political identity.[6]

The second approach to understand Taiwanese people's identity is to survey their attitude toward unification and independence. It is assumed that if a person prefers unification with mainland China to Taiwanese independence, he or she should be regarded a person with Chinese national identity. The opposite would describe a person with a Taiwanese national identity. The research team of the Election Study Center further divided the binary unification/independence option into a six-option classification. The result is shown in figure 2.

If we put the "independence as soon as possible" and "maintain status quo, move toward independence" together, put the "unification as soon as possible" and "maintain status quo, move toward unification" together, and put the "maintain status quo indefinitely" and "maintain status quo, decide at later date" together, we find that people in favor of independence rose from over 11 in 1994 to almost 23 percent in 2016. Those in favor of unification declined steadily from 20 percent in 1994 to slightly over 10 percent in 2016. Those favoring the status quo also rose from around 48 percent in 1994 to almost 60 percent in 2016, remaining the greatest share of the population in the past two decades.[7]

The survey is important for our understanding of Taiwanese's preferences on the issue of "unification/independence," but it is more about Taiwanese people's

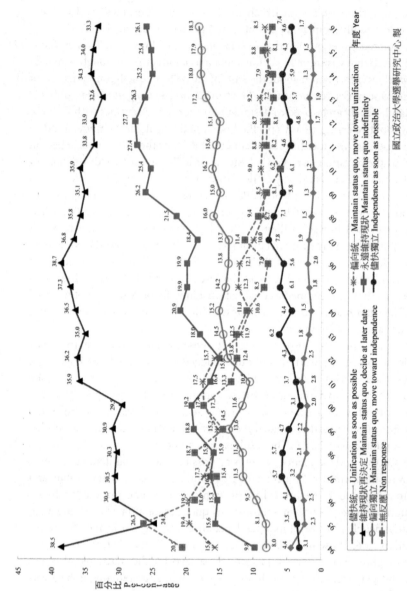

FIGURE 2. Changes in the unification-independence stances of Taiwanese as tracked in surveys by the Election Study Center, National Chengchi University (1994–2016).

SOURCE: Hui-ling Chen, "Taiwan Independence vs. Unification with the Mainland Trend Distribution in Taiwan (1992/06~2016/12)," Election Study Center, National Chengchi University, http://esc.nccu.edu.tw/course/news.php?Sn=167.

choice of the future than an expression of their national identity. These two questions are closely related but different. Especially when more than 60 percent of the respondents answer that they prefer the status quo, it is difficult to say what kind of national identity "the status quo" means.[8] I will come back to the diverse interpretations of "the status quo" later.

The problem with the previous two methods has been noticed by many scholars. Wu Naiteh argues that national identity as conceived in the unification/independence choice can be influenced by unfavorable, external political circumstances, and people will accordingly modify their attitude to a more pragmatic standpoint for the short term. To explore the hidden, long-term view of national identity, he designed a questionnaire with two key questions: (1) If a Taiwanese independence would not precipitate a war, then would you agree that Taiwan should become an independent country? (2) If Taiwan and China were to become comparably developed economically, socially, and politically, would you agree that the two sides of the Taiwan Strait should be united into one country?[9]

Wu classifies those who say "yes" to the first question but "no" to the second as "Taiwanese nationalists" (those who pursue independence under favorable conditions and refuse to unify with China even if the latter becomes as well developed as Taiwan). The respondents who say "no" to the first question but "yes" to the second are classified as "Chinese nationalists" (those who expect unification under a favorable situation but oppose Taiwanese independence even if no war will happen). Those who say "yes" to both questions are described by Wu as "pragmatists," while those who say "no" to both questions are termed "conservatives" (table 1).

From their survey, Shen and Wu discovered that the proportion of Taiwanese nationalists rose considerably from 9.3 percent in 1992 to 27.7 percent in 2005 but seemed to stop short of a 30 percent ceiling. On the other hand, the proportion of Chinese nationalists declined steadily from 38 percent in 1992 to 13 percent in 2005. The trend of a rising Taiwanese identity and a declining Chinese identity is consistent with the findings of the other two methods discussed above. What bothered Shen and Wu, however, was that there has always been a significantly large group of pragmatists who "are willing to accept an independent Taiwan if their security is not endangered, and they are likewise willing to accept unification with China if there are no negative economic or political repercussions." Their proportion was 25 percent in 1992 and 30 percent in 2005, with a peak of nearly 40 percent in 1996, when cross-Strait relations reached the most dangerous point since the 1950s. Shen and Wu could not tell whether these pragmatists had a dual national identity or no particular national identity at all, so they decided to leave this puzzle for further study.[10]

I think Wu's questionnaire is helpful in trying to identify those who clearly and strongly wish to pursue their nationalist cause, either independence or unification. Yet it would be more convincing if Wu could add two more questions to it: (3) If a

TABLE 1   Taiwanese national identities (a simplified version of Wu and Shen's original classification
of national identities in Taiwan, 1992–2005)

	Accept unification if no disparity between Taiwan and China	Reject unification even if no disparity between Taiwan and China
Accept Taiwanese independence if no war happens	Pragmatists	Taiwanese Nationalists
Reject Taiwanese independence even if no war happens	Chinese Nationalists	Conservatives

SOURCES: Shiau-chi Shen and Nai-teh Wu, "Ethnic and Civic Nationalisms: Two Roads to the Formation of a Taiwanese Nation," in The "One China" Dilemma, ed. Peter C. Y. Chow (New York: Palgrave Macmillan, 2008), 122.

Taiwanese independence would precipitate a war, then would you agree that Taiwan should become an independent country? (4) If Taiwan and China were not to become comparably developed economically, socially, and politically, would you agree that the two sides of the Taiwan Strait should be united into one country? It is only with a combination of (1) and (4) can we identify the real Chinese nationalists (those who reject independence even if no war happens and who want to unify with China even if the political, social, and economic conditions across the Strait cannot be compatible), and only with a combination of (2) and (3) can we identify the real Taiwanese nationalists (those who reject unification even if conditions across the Strait are similar and who are determined to pursue independence even if it will cause a war).[11]

The real problem, however, is that Shen and Wu's survey still cannot explain the existence of a substantial number of "pragmatic" respondents and instead beats around the bush by looking for the principled "nationalists." If the so-called pragmatists have stayed the greatest portion of the whole population for decades, isn't it a clear indication that the questionnaire itself may be misleading in the inquiry concerning national identity? It is a good questionnaire to detect the degree of a respondent's determination to seek independence or unification but not a satisfactory measurement of one's national identity. For instance, one might have no doubt about one's political identity with the ROC but refuse to fight for Taiwanese independence or refuse to unify with mainland China under unfavorable conditions, and we could not say that this person did not have a political identity. After all, "having an identity" is different from "having a strong identity."

For this reason, I have suggested another method of investigating Taiwan's national identity. Liu I-chou suggested many years ago that we should try to understand people's national identity according to their perception of the territory of their country and who their compatriots are. The questions based on this line of thinking would be: (1) Do you think that the territory of your country includes mainland China or only Taiwan? (2) Do you think that your compatriots include those living in mainland China or only those living in Taiwan? Those who recognize only Taiwanese territory and compatriots as their own have a Taiwanese (or ROC) national identity. By contrast, those who include mainland China in their territory and mainland Chinese as their compatriots have a Greater Chinese national identity.[12]

When Liu administered this questionnaire to Taiwan residents in 1998, about 77 percent of respondents had a Taiwanese identity, and about 9 percent had a Greater Chinese identity. The rest were of mixed identity or did not answer. Unfortunately, the questionnaire was not readministered in ensuing years.[13] My conjecture is that, after more than a decade of increasing Taiwanese consciousness, the proportion of those with a Taiwanese national identity has grown even greater and now probably makes up more than 85 percent of the population, while the proportion of those with a Greater Chinese national identity may now be less than 5 percent. Liu's measure is the most appropriate way to describe the national identity of Taiwanese people. The large majority of Taiwanese who identify themselves with the country existing on the island may differ among themselves in their cultural and ethnic identity (their sense of being Taiwanese or Chinese or both), or in their ideas as to whether Taiwan should pursue de jure independence or unify with mainland China in the future), or in the degree of their patriotism regarding the ROC (or Taiwan), but they identify with the ROC (or Taiwan) in the strictly political sense. The few who identify with mainland China (or a greater China) should be respected, as long as they abide by the constitution and laws of the ROC.

In other words, national identity in Taiwan is not as divisive an issue as many scholars imagine or describe if we understand the concept correctly. Taiwanese may differ in their sense of cultural belonging, ethnic origins, political choices, or determination to pursue their ideals, just as they differ on public policy issues, taste of food and clothes, style of entertainment, obsession with sport, philosophy of life, and so on. But as a popular Taiwanese writer once remarked, "Taiwan is one hundred percent a country. If it is not a country, what is a country?"[14] Most controversies arise not from the question of whether Taiwan is a country but from the question of whether it should be called "the Republic of China" or simply "Taiwan." In other words, what makes the issue of Taiwan's national identity complicated is not its boundary, population, or sovereignty but dispute over the "one-China" principle, to which we now turn.

THE "ONE-CHINA" PROBLEM

As noted in the previous section, some measures of national identity in Taiwan do not exactly reflect what they are purported to measure. The classification of "Taiwanese/Chinese/both" helps us realize how two different and overlapping cultures affect Taiwanese's self-perception, but it cannot be translated into a political identity that corresponds to a specific territory and sovereignty. The classification of unification/independence/status quo tells us what kind of political future Taiwanese want, but that wish makes sense only under the precondition that Taiwan is a political entity that can make the choice. The questionnaire combining "independence if no war" and "unification if China well developed" explores the factors that Taiwanese might consider when they face the choice of independence or unification. It may help us distinguish moderate nationalists from unyielding nationalists, but it is not a measurement of national identity per se.

If we stick to the core meaning of national identity (namely, a sense of belonging to a specific sovereign territory and a group of people with common life experience), it becomes clear that Taiwanese do know where their country is and who their compatriots are. A few do not agree with the overwhelming majority on this issue, but this is not a big problem. Taiwanese people may be divided on the issue of independence or unification, yet they are fully aware of their national identity. In other words, national identity is not a real issue in Taiwan. It is, unfortunately, many politicians' favorite means of political mobilization during elections.

Unification/independence is not a real issue either. The KMT is frequently described as prounification and the DPP as proindependence. That is true if we assume that they are faithful to their party platforms and that their candidates are arguing against each other for no other reason but the cause of unification or independence. Nevertheless, as all opinion polls show, more than 60 percent of Taiwanese want to maintain the status quo; and only about 24 percent favor an independence policy, and only 9 percent of them favor a unification policy. Aware of public opinion, neither the KMT nor the DPP has declared that it would implement a clear policy of unification or independence. On the contrary, both parties are busy persuading the people that they will do better than the other in maintaining the status quo. Politicians who do not adhere to the status quo but promote independence or unification are either targeting a specific electorate out of political calculation or committing political suicide.

If national identity is not a serious problem, and unification/independence is not an urgent choice, then what makes Taiwanese politics so turbulent and antagonistic? The answer has to do with the challenge of the "one-China policy" coming from the Chinese Communist Party (CCP) in mainland China.

Ever since 1949, when the CCP crushed the KMT in the civil war and forced the Nationalist government retreat to Taiwan, the communist government has declared that the People's Republic of China (PRC) is the only legitimate representative of China in the world; at the same time the defeated Nationalist government has maintained that it is the only legal representative of China. In the following decades, Beijing has consistently insisted on a "one-China principle," based on the premises that (1) there is only one China in the world; (2) Taiwan is part of China;

and (3) the PRC is the only legitimate government to represent China. Springing from this principle, is an insistence on the policy that all countries seeking to establish diplomatic relations with the PRC must terminate official relations with the ROC. These countries must recognize the PRC as the only legitimate representative of mainland China and Taiwan, or at least acknowledge its claim on the issue.

The "one-China policy" is a zero-sum game between the PRC and the ROC. Whenever a country recognizes the legal status of the PRC, the ROC immediately cuts its diplomatic relations with that country, and vice versa. The policy also forces Taiwan gradually to adopt a defensive position in the international arena because it cannot afford to compete with China politically or economically.

Taiwan is fully aware of its difficult international situation under the isolation strategy of China. Particularly after the ban on cross-Strait tours was lifted in the late 1980s, the ROC found that there was no way of avoiding negotiation with the PRC with regard to administrative affairs. But when the PRC faced severe international sanctions as a result of the Tiananmen Square incident and saw pro-independence forces gaining strength in Taiwan, it felt a need to adjust its Taiwan policy. That was the background for the "1992 Consensus" reached between the Straits Exchange Foundation (SEF, representing Taiwan) and the Association for Relations Across the Taiwan Straits (ARATS, representing mainland China).

The most important point of the 1992 Consensus is that the ROC and the PRC agree that there is only one China but also agree that each side can have its own interpretation of what "one China" means, so that they can go on to do functional work without being influenced by controversy about sovereignty. The announcement of the SEF on November 3, 1992, read as follows: "In the Hong Kong talks, the ARATS insisted that both parties should make 'public statements' on the issue of 'one China.' With the authorization from the Mainland Affairs Council, the SEF is agreeable to an oral statement of their respective interpretations. As to the content of this oral statement, we will express it in line with the Guidelines for National Unification and the resolution on the meaning of 'one China' adopted by the National Unification Council on August 1, 1992."[15] This is the famous "one China, differing interpretations" (*yizong gebiao*) formula for dealing with the "one-China principle" asserted by Beijing: the ROC is willing to accept the principle that there is only one China in order to process cross-Strait affairs, but it reserves the right to interpret what "one China" means and, not surprisingly, sees itself rather than the PRC as the "one China."

The SEF's announcement was soon echoed by the ARATS, which declared: "The SEF officially has notified the ARATS that it received consent from the authorities concerned in Taiwan to 'an oral statement of their respective interpretations.' The ARATS fully respects and accepts the SEF's suggestion. . . . Now the ARATS wishes to inform the SEF of the salient points of its oral statement: Both sides of the Taiwan Strait insist on the one China principle and strive for national unification; however, the meaning of 'one China' shall not be involved in cross-Strait talks of a functional nature."[16] For reasons that we cannot elaborate here, the 1992 Consensus was not honored from 1993 to 2008.[17] When Chen Shui-bian came to power in 2000, he even denied the existence of such a consensus. However, Ma Ying-jeou decided to resume the talks between the SEF and the ARATS on the basis of the 1992 Consensus after he was elected as the president in 2008. From then on, the new principle of "one China, differing interpretations" played a very important role in stabilizing cross-Strait relations and made possible the signing of twenty-one agreements between the two sides.

The 1992 Consensus was celebrated by the KMT as a milestone in the development of cross-Strait relations. It was also acknowledged in Assistant Secretary of State James Kelly's testimony before the US Congress and in Chairman Hu Jintao's telephone conversation with President George W. Bush.[18] However, DPP leaders have either refused to recognize the existence of the consensus, refused to concede its legitimacy, or refused to agree that the consensus is good for Taiwan.

Those who claim that there is no 1992 Consensus say that the concept is a fiction made up by the former deputy minister of mainland affairs Su Qi. And if they do acknowledge something like a consensus reached by the two sides, they say it is not legitimate because it refers to a "one-China principle," which can only mean that Taiwan is part of China. They understand very well that the Nationalist government insists on the ROC being the "one China," but they do not believe that the consensus leaves any room for Taiwan to interpret "one China" differently. They think mainland China will monopolize the interpretation because it is much more powerful and resourceful than Taiwan in the international community.[19]

The official statement of Tsai Ing-wen in 2000, who served as the minister of the Mainland Affairs Council during Chen Shui-bian's administration, was very typical of the DPP's position on this issue: "The so-called 'one China, differing interpretations' is only a usage by our side to describe the process of the meeting. It is a way of description that the new government can accept, but it does not mean that we have accepted Beijing's 'one-China principle.'"[20] In 2003, she reinforced her stand on the issue by emphasizing that the ROC and the PRC did not belong to each other. "One side, one country," she emphasized, "is a statement of fact."

When Tsai ran for president in 2012, she tried to eliminate Taiwanese people's Chinese identity by promoting Taiwanese identity as its substitute. She maintained: "The Republic of China is an exile (alien) government, which rules Taiwan at the moment. The Chineseness of the ROC must be relocated from a subjective status to an objective status, and yields to Taiwaneseness." She also tried to persuade the general public to think of the cross-Strait relation in a novel way: "There is no 1992 Consensus. What I propose is to create a Taiwan consensus to replace the 1992 Consensus, which would be ratified by legislation and a referendum. This new consensus should then form the basis for negotiations with the PRC."

Tsai lost the 2012 presidential election. Many political analysts believe that her failure to prove the feasibility of the Taiwanese Consensus was a salient, if not the most important, reason. It explains why she decided not to employ the terminology again during the 2016 presidential campaign. Yet she has been as unwavering as before on the issue of the 1992 Consensus. With the prospect that the DPP might win both the 2014 local elections and the 2016 general election, she was confident enough to believe that even the PRC would yield to her view about the 1992 Consensus afterwards. She said in an interview: "Whoever has power, different parties will shift their direction toward those with power. The DPP's biggest challenge is to do well in this year's local elections. If we do well, even China will shift in the direction of the DPP. If they feel that the DPP has the best chance of winning in 2016, they will automatically create the conditions for that."[21]

With this confidence, Tsai was ready to appeal to the majority who favored the status quo without endorsing the 1992 Consensus. Her successful strategy in the 2016 presidential election was to replace the unwelcome "Taiwan Consensus" with the popular "maintaining the status quo" but not to discuss what "the status quo" actually meant. In her speech at the Center for Strategic and International Studies on June 3, 2016, she repeated that maintaining the status quo "serves the best interest of all parties concerned," and she vowed to be "committed to a consistent, predictable, and sustainable relationship with China." She also emphasized that, if elected, she would "push for the peaceful and stable development of cross-Strait relations in accordance with the will of the Taiwanese people and *the existing ROC constitutional order*" (my italics). Nevertheless, when asked by the audience to elaborate her views on the issue and explain how her thesis could be reconciled with the DPP's independence platform, she refused to explain further and only asked them to carefully read her speech again.[22]

Maintaining the status quo, as we point out in the previous section, has remained the favorite option of the majority in Taiwan. However, "the status quo" can mean different things to different people. Some think the status quo is a country called the Republic of China, which agrees with mainland China that both sides can interpret their concept of China respectively. Some think the status quo is a separate country called Taiwan, which has never agreed with China regarding the idea that there is only "one China" under which they should be subsumed. As Ma Ying-jeou reiterated several times, the status quo for most Taiwanese is a peaceful cross-Strait relationship created by his policy of three nos—"no unification, no independence, and no use of military force" under the framework of the ROC constitution. It is also a result of cross-Strait dialogues based on the 1992 Consensus (namely, "one China, differing interpretations"). If Tsai Ing-wen's "status quo" was similar to the status quo that Ma created, he would be very glad to have the leader of the opposition party follow his own mainland policy.[23] Unfortunately, Tsai is clear that she will not accept the 1992 Consensus or agree that Taiwan and

TABLE 2   Different players' conception of the "one-China principle"

	China	KMT	USA	DPP
There is only one China in the world.	X	X	X	X
Taiwan is part of China.	X	X	X	
"China" can be interpreted differently.	?	X		
China is represented by the PRC.	X		X	X
China is represented by the ROC.		X		
Taiwan is not part of China.				X
China and Taiwan are two countries.				X

the mainland belong to the same China, even though that is the frame of the ROC constitution. She is going to change the status quo and pretend that she does not.

Tsai now acknowledges that there was a talk between the two sides of the Taiwan Straits in 1992, but she still does not acknowledge that a consensus was reached by the two sides. This minor revision of her original position on the 1992 Consensus appeared shortly before Election Day and reappeared in her inaugural address on May 20, 2016. She asserted, "There was a bilateral summit in 1992 as a matter of historical fact and there was a mutual cognizance of 'seeking common ground while shelving differences.'" Nevertheless, she refused to concede that the "common ground" was the 1992 Consensus or "one China, different interpretations," let alone the idea that Taiwan is or will be part of China, no matter what "China" means. Beijing responded immediately that this was not the answer "to the examination" (i.e., not the right answer), but apparently the CCP is willing to wait until Tsai changes her mind in the near future.

Before we end this section, it may be helpful to illuminate different players' position regarding the "one-China" question (table 2): From this table, we can see how that four concerned actors (China, USA, KMT, DPP) can agree on the unspecified statement that "there is only one China in the world," while still differing dramatically on the related components of the "one-China" question. It also explains why the simple statement "There is only one China in the world" cannot be easily developed into either a "one-China policy," a "one-China principle," a "one-China framework," or any terminology that includes "one China." In Taiwan, the really divisive issue is not national identity nor the choice of unification or independence but the meaning and implications of "one China."

PROSPECTS OF CROSS-STRAIT RELATIONS

The problem of cross-Strait relations is never restricted to Taiwan and mainland China alone. It involves the PRC, the ROC, and the United States, and within the

ROC it is an issue of contention between the KMT and the DPP. Therefore, it can be described as a strategic triangular relationship concerning four key players. Understanding this complex issue requires considering the position of each player, as well as players' interactions and chains of reaction.

In international relations theory, the interaction between the PRC, the Soviet Union (later, Russia) and the United States is regarded as a typical "great strategic triangle," while the interaction between Beijing, Taipei, and Washington can be conceived as a small strategic triangle. It is a triangular relation because the ROC needs the United States to resist the political and military pressure of the PRC, the PRC needs the United States' tacit support to prevent the ROC from seeking de jure independence, and the United States wants the PRC and the ROC to constrain their hostility[24] Furthermore, the small strategic triangle is unbalanced in that the power and influence of the PRC and the United States are disproportionally superior to the ROC's. As Yu-shan Wu points out, when the power between two actors is asymmetrical, the interpretation and prediction of the two actors' moves should also be adjusted correspondingly. Power asymmetry also affects other variables, such as motivation for economic integration, probability of military confrontation, shifts in national identity, strategy of electoral campaigns, and so forth.[25]

With this framework in mind, we may now begin to analyze what the four actors pursue and avoid with regard to cross-Strait relations. The PRC wishes to complete its unification enterprise in the twenty-first century, especially under the guideline of Chairman Xi Jinping's "Chinese Dream" of attaining wealth, power, and modernization for China as a whole. The PRC realizes that more and more Taiwanese are embracing a Taiwanese consciousness and favoring independence, even though maintaining the status quo still remains the majority's priority for the moment. To keep Taiwan from moving forward to de jure independence, the PRC is keen to reach a political agreement between the two sides that formally acknowledges the principle that there is only one China in the world and that both the mainland and Taiwan are parts of China. But when Ma's government was politically challenged after the intraparty conflict with Speaker Wang in 2013 and the turbulence of the Sunflower Movement in 2014, it virtually lost the momentum to negotiate any political agreement with mainland China, whether a "framework of peace agreement" or a "mechanism for military mutual trust." With the DPP's overwhelming victory in the 2016 election, the best result the PRC can expect is to secure the 1992 Consensus and assent to the principle of "one China" in no more than a vague sense. If this minimum expectation cannot be fulfilled, Xi Jinping may have to consider other options. It is not to the PRC's advantage to confront the United States when China has many more important goals to achieve, but the Taiwan independence issue is too serious to be neglected. Xi definitely does not want to become the leader in Chinese history who loses Taiwan: this would be a devastating blow to his own political life and the legitimacy of the CCP.

The challenge, therefore, is to secure US cooperation in preventing the DPP from nullifying the 1992 Consensus.

In the KMT, former president Ma and his political allies believe that the 1992 Consensus (in the sense of "one China, differing interpretations") is the best policy for cross-Strait relations. However, the current chair, Ms. Hung Hsiu-chu, obviously has a quite different conception of cross-Strait relations. Hung accuses the DPP of pushing for Taiwanese independence in the name of democracy and predicts that this will "bring threats to national security, make Taiwan even more isolated, cause economic stagnation, and fuel hatred in society." Yet she was not satisfied with the current "one China, differing interpretations" policy either. She asserted that the best policy for cross-Strait relations should be "one China, same interpretation" (*yizhong tongbiao*) and said Taiwan should sign a peace agreement with mainland China on the precondition that the ROC constitution be upheld and the will of the people respected.[26] Hung's statement is generally viewed as supportive of unification and immediately causes suspicion and criticism among the KMT politicians who feel more comfortable with Ma's "three nos." To ease intraparty opposition, Hung argues that her policy is merely "enhancing" the 1992 Consensus rather than "replacing" it. Nevertheless, it is becoming more and more clear that she is not going to continue Ma's policy. Her move toward unification will help the DPP appear more like an advocate of the status quo. How Beijing will react to Hung's proposal is yet to be seen.

As for the DPP, Tsai Ing-wen's major challenge is to persuade the Taiwanese people, the PRC, and the United States that she will not pursue de jure Taiwan independence during her presidential term. What she needs to accomplish on this tough question is to find a subtle balance between the DPP's "Taiwanese Independence Platform" (which proposes the drafting of a new constitution and the establishment of a Republic of Taiwan) and the general public's concern about the risk of war if the DPP pursues Taiwanese independence or amends some critical articles of the current constitution. Tsai's repeated announcement of "maintaining the status quo" is an attempt to assure the people that she will neither pursue outright independence nor try to amend the ROC constitution in favor of independence. Nonetheless, her DPP supporters (especially the "fundamentalists," or hard-liners on the independence issue) will complain that there is no difference between her position and Ma's. Ever since her inauguration, she has been careful not to challenge mainland China directly, but her consistent denial of the 1992 Consensus, her shifting position on the South China Sea controversy, her apathy toward the Chinese victims who died in a mysterious bus accident in Taiwan, her appointment of several proindependence grand justices to the Supreme Court, and her tacit support of the Hong Kong independence movement all make the CCP suspect her sincerity about maintaining the status quo. As many cross-Strait relation experts observe, Tsai is pursuing Taiwanese independence under the (temporary) cover of the ROC, a strategy that may satisfy the United States but cannot win the trust of China.

Finally, the role of the United States is always essential. In the small strategic triangle of Beijing-Taipei-Washington, the United States seems more like a pivot than merely a partner. The US stake in this issue is to maintain peaceful and stable cross-Strait relations, without any unexpected unilateral political or military moves. The missile-test crisis of 1996 was solved by the deployment of American aircraft carrier battle groups in this region. The "one country on each side" controversy and independence referendum initiated by Chen Shui-bian was rebuked by the US government. From the way Washington has interfered and managed various crises in the past, it is clear that the United States prefers a no-surprise, low-risk status quo in this region. To date, the United States seems to welcome Taiwan and the mainland to continue dialogue on the basis of Beijing's assertion that there is only one China and that only one government can legitimately represent it, and to insist that the solution to cross-Strait antagonism must be peaceful. It does not support any unilateral action to seek Taiwanese independence; neither does it publicly endorse the 1992 Consensus or the "one China, differing interpretations" policy. However, as the rise of a powerful China becomes more and more threatening, many observers begin to wonder if the United States will change its position and encourage Taiwan to keep a greater distance from China. Some DPP leaders actually think that even if Taiwan moves toward independence, the US response may change from that of 2002–4 simply because the United States and the PRC have so many conflicts of interest in the East China Sea and the South China Sea. Yet for the very same reason the PRC may urge the United States to clarify its position on "one China" in the years to come. As Huang Jing indicates, Xi Jinping has consistently maintained that Taiwan is a core interest of China, and he will not allow Taiwan to be the bargaining chip in negotiations over the PRC's new relationship with the United States.[27] After so many years' experience of interaction, Beijing has become increasingly convinced that the United States is reliable about "not supporting Taiwanese independence."[28] What remains to be seen is the extent to which the PRC will tolerate the United States' taking advantage of anti-China sentiment among the Taiwanese and tacitly endorsing the DPP's assertion that Taiwan is not part of China. From Washington's perspective, continuing its support of cross-Strait dialogue on the basis of the 1992 Consensus means stability in the East Asia, but Taiwan may become more tied to mainland China. On the other hand, encouraging a new cross-Strait policy without the 1992 Consensus opens up some novel strategic possibilities for relations between the United States and its East Asian associates, but it also involves the risk of Beijing's retaliation. Washington's judgment and decision on this issue will be of great significance for the future development in this region.

Cross-Strait relations are very complicated and unpredictable. When Ma Ying-jeou was elected as Taiwan's president, he was determined to improve relations with mainland China and successfully reached dozens of agreements between the two sides. The scenario during his first term of presidency was so rosy that some scholars even speculated about the possibility of drafting a peace agreement between the PRC and the ROC.[29] Yet only a couple of years later the Taiwanese people expressed their deep worry and suspicion about the pace of cross-Strait rapprochement.[30]

In the past eight years, cross-Strait relations stayed relatively peaceful and stable compared with the period of 2000–2008 because the two sides could carry out constructive dialogues and cooperation under the 1992 Consensus. But now that the DPP has regained political power, commentators have begun to consider the unpleasant possibility of military confrontation. As Scott L. Kastner reminds us, "It is possible to imagine a number of future events—ranging from a return of the DPP to power in Taiwan, to continued growth in Taiwan-centric identity despite deepening cross-Strait economic integration, to a period of economic malaise in the PRC—that could lead to renewed pessimism in Beijing about long-term trends in the Taiwan Strait." If any of these scenarios comes true, a "preventive war fought to alter unfavorable long-term trends" cannot be excluded.[31] Although Kastner thinks there are reasons to be optimistic about the future of cross-Strait relations in the short to medium term, he admits that the current détente requires continual careful management.[32]

What will happen if the Tsai administration continues to reject the 1992 Consensus? This is a difficult question to answer. The PRC has many tools to compel the DPP back to the "one-China" track, including diplomatic, economic, political, and military measures. Diplomatically, the PRC can carry out a surprise attack on Taiwan by asking several countries to immediately cut official relations with Taiwan or by withdrawing its support of Taiwan's participation in international organizations.[33] Economically, the PRC can tighten the financial supply of Taiwanese enterprises doing business with China, restrict importation of Taiwanese goods and services to China, or trim down the quota of Chinese tourists visiting Taiwan. Politically, it can cancel all cross-Strait negotiations, meetings, academic cooperation, sporting events, and cultural exchanges. Militarily, it can fire missiles again over the island, perform military operations around Taiwan's harbors, intrude into the Air Defense Identification Zone, or send aircraft carriers and naval vessels to patrol in the Taiwan Strait. These measures may prove counterproductive and arouse more anger and resentment than fear among Taiwanese people, but it could be hard for the PRC to act differently.

Some of the measures will hurt Taiwan only, others may make the United States nervous and give it no choice but to respond with similar measures. The situation may not deteriorate into a comprehensive war between China and the United

States (and its East Asia allies), but a certain kind of political deadlock or military confrontation is not altogether impossible. Since Tsai's inauguration, China seems to be exercising a gradual escalation strategy of putting pressure on Taiwan, rather than employing all its tools at hand. It is unlikely that China will use its military power against Taiwan as long as Tsai avoids any explicit policy of Taiwan independence, yet there is no sign of China's concession to Tsai's rejection of the 1992 Consensus either. A new détente may be the best description of cross-Strait relations in years to come.

CONCLUSION

The national identity of Taiwan and its impact on cross-Strait relations might seem to be a "domestic" issue of Taiwan, or at most a bilateral issue between Taiwan and China. But as I have shown, this problem has a much more far-reaching effect than is apparent at first glance. It not only reflects the positions of different parties in Taiwan on the unification/independence question but also concerns the realization of Xi Jinping's "Chinese Dream." It does not merely involve the United States in the sense of consolidating a maritime alliance against China but also bears on the structural transformation of superpowers in the twenty-first century.[34] If we do not pay enough attention to the political consequences of a seemingly "domestic" issue of a small island country, we will not be able to cope with one of the most difficult challenges East Asia faces now.

National identity is an equivocal concept in political theory. Sometimes it means one's sense of belonging to a specific ethnic or cultural community; sometimes it means one's self-identity as a member of a particular state. Nationalist scholarship tends to combine the two elements in order to portray or predict the formation of a nation-state, but such a move is not warranted because consciousness of a cultural group is not always consistent with identity of a political community. To presuppose that the political unit and the cultural unit should be congruent is a misleading starting point in the study of national identity.

All three of the popular methods of measuring national identity in Taiwan— the Chinese/Taiwanese/both identity measure, the unification/independence measure, and the "Chinese Nationalist versus Taiwanese Nationalist" measure— reveal important information about the collective consciousness of Taiwanese, but none of these adequately describe the political identity of the people living on the island. I therefore recommend a fourth method that is frequently ignored in Taiwan studies: the method of assessing how respondents delineate their compatriots and homeland. Measuring in this way, we find that Taiwan's national identity is not as divisive an issue as many scholars or politicians describe. The people of Taiwan may differ at being Chinese or Taiwanese, and they may disagree about their political future (to unify with China or seek independence), but most of them favor the status quo (neither unification nor independence), and perhaps more than 85 percent of them have a clear identity as to which country they belong to.

But although national identity per se is not a real or pressing issue in Taiwan, the question of how to deal with the one-China principle embedded in the 1992 Consensus *is* a real problem. Ma's government successfully signed twenty-one agreements with mainland China on the basis of the 1992 Consensus during his administration. The DPP endorses the signed agreements but refuses to negotiate with the PRC any more on the precondition of the 1992 Consensus. The DPP's new mainland policy and the CCP's reaction will affect stability in East Asia and destabilize further the already edgy PRC-US relationship.

There are several possible ways to ease tensions across the Taiwan Strait. One would be to convince Tsai Ing-wen and the DPP that it would be good for Taiwan to maintain cross-Strait relations on the basis of the 1992 Consensus, but Xi Jinping or the PRC would need to acknowledge the "differing interpretations" part of the consensus in addition to its favorite "one-China" part. In this case, Tsai might be able to maintain the status quo by adhering to the name of ROC. Another possibility would be for the United States and the PRC to finally agree that the 1992 Consensus is not the only formula for securing peace and stability in the Taiwan Strait, and for Tsai to provide an innovative, practicable, and convincing new policy. This would mean the end of the era of the 1992 Consensus and the beginning of a new age whose direction no one can predict at the moment. The third solution would be to invite all concerned parties to deliberate on the changing meaning of "one China" and to figure out if any better definition or interpretation could satisfy the purposes of all parties. It is difficult to say which solution would produce the best possible outcome. But all concerned parties should do their best to prevent the escalation of political tension and to secure sustainable peace among peoples.

NOTES

1. Some of the most influential scholarly works on nationalism in Taiwan are E. J. Hobsbawn, *Nations and Nationalism since 1780: Programme, Myth, Reality* (Cambridge: Cambridge University Press, 1990); Benedict Anderson, *Imagined Communities: Reflections on the Origin and Spread of Nationalism,* 2nd ed. (London: Verso, 1991); Anthony D. Smith, *National Identity* (Reno: University of Nevada Press, 1991). Important Taiwanese scholarship includes Zhang Maugui, ed., *Zuqun guanxi yu guojia rentong* [Ethnic relations and national identity] (Taipei: Yueqiang, 1993); Lin Jialung and Zheng Yongnian, eds., *Minzu zhuyi yu liangan guanxi* [Nationalism and cross-Strait relations] (Taipei: New Naturalism, 2001); and Hsiau A-chin, *Chonggo Taiwan: Dangdai minzuzhuyi de wenhua zhengzhi* [Reconstructing Taiwan: The cultural politics of contemporary nationalism] (Taipei: Linking, 2012).

2. For further discussion of the different approaches to nationalism, see John Breuilly, "Approaches to Nationalism," in *Mapping the Nation,* ed. Gopal Balakrishnan (London: Verso, 1996), 149–59, and Anthony D. Smith, *The Nation in History: Historiographical Debates about Ethnicity and Nationalism* (Hanover, NH: University Press of New England, 2000), 27–51.

3. See Yi-huah Jiang, "Is Taiwan a Nation? On the Current Debate over Taiwanese National Identity and National Recognition," in *The Dignity of Nations: Equality, Competition, and Honor in East*

Asian Nationalism, ed. Sechin Y. S. Chien and John Fitzgerald (Hong Kong: Hong Kong University Press, 2006), 141–64.

4. Earnest Gellner, *Nations and Nationalism* (Ithaca, NY: Connell University Press, 1983), 1.

5. Hui-ling Chen, "Taiwanese/Chinese Identification Trend Distribution in Taiwan (1992/06~2016/12)," Election Study Center, National Chengchi University, August 24, 2016, http://esc. nccu.edu.tw/course/news.php?Sn=166. See also Chu Yun-han, "Navigating between China and the United States: Taiwan's Politics of Identity," in *Taiwanese Identity in the Twenty-First Century: Domestic, Regional and Global Perspectives*, ed. Gunter Schubert and Jens Damm (London: Routledge, 2011), 141–48, with an emphasis on the change during Chen Shui-bian's administration, and Christopher R. Hughes, "Revisiting Identity Politics under Ma Ying-jeou," in *Political Changes in Taiwan under Ma Ying-jeou: Partisan Conflict, Policy Choices, External Constraints and Security Challenges*, ed. Jean-Pierre Cabestan and Jacques deLisle (London: Routledge, 2014), 130–32, with an emphasis on developments during Ma's administration.

6. See Jiang Yi-huah, "Xin guojia yundong xia de Taiwan rentong" [Taiwanese identity in the movement to create a new country], in Lin Jialung and Zheng Yongnian, *Minzu zhuyi yu liangan guanxi*, 202–3. A similar problem also occurs on the part of "being Taiwanese." Jean-Pierre Cabestan, in chapter 3 of this book, reminds us that the survey of the Chinese/Taiwanese identity "has a major weakness: it does not make any distinction between cultural and political identities."

7. Hui-ling Chen, "Taiwan Independence vs. Unification with the Mainland Trend Distribution in Taiwan (1992/06~2016/12)," Election Study Center, National Chengchi University, http://esc.nccu.edu. tw/course/news.php?Sn=167. See also Chen Luhui and Geng Shu, "Taiwan minzhong tongdu lichang de chixu yu bianqian" [The continuity and change of Taiwanese people's attitude toward unification/ independence], in *Chong xin jian shi zheng bian zhong de liang an guan xi li lun* [Revisiting theories on cross-Strait relations], ed. Bao Zonghe and Wu Yushan, 2nd ed. (Taipei: Wunan Press, 2012), for a more detailed analysis of different generations' stance on this issue. Needless to say, the composition of those preferring the status quo has changed dramatically over time. Many supporters of the status quo come from former unification supporters, while many who used to maintain the status quo have become independence supporters.

8. See Jiang Yi-huah, *Ziiu zhui, minzu zhui yu guojia rentong* [Liberalism, nationalism, and national identity] (Taipei: Yangzhi Press, 1998), 217–21; Jiang Yi-huah, "Xin guojia yundong xia de Taiwan rentong," 203–5. To further explore what "maintaining the status quo" means, many scholars have tried to add more conditional questionnaires; see Ching-hsin Yu, "National Identity in Taiwan: A Revisit," paper presented at the Second World Congress of Taiwan Studies, School of Oriental and African Studies (SOAS), University of London, June 18–20, 2015.

9. For the following discussion, see Wu Nai-teh, "Shengji yishi, zhengzhi zhichi he guojia rentong" [Provincial consciousness, political support and national identity], in Zhang Maugui, *Zuqun guanxi yu guojia rentong*; Shiau-chi Shen and Nai-teh Wu, "Ethnic and Civic Nationalisms: Two Roads to the Formation of a Taiwanese Nation," in *The "One China" Dilemma*, ed. Peter C. Y. Chow (New York: Palgrave Macmillan, 2008), 120–24.

10. Shen and Wu, "Ethnic and Civic Nationalisms," 123–24. Yun-han Chu offers a similar analysis but interestingly terms the four categories "principled believers in independence," "principled believers in unification," "open-minded rationalists," and "strong believers in the status quo." See Yun-han Chu, "Taiwan's National Identity Politics and the Prospect of Cross-Strait Relations," *Asian Survey* 44, no. 4 (July/August 2004): 504–6.

11. See Jiang Yi-huah, *Ziiu zhui*, 172. See also Yu, "National Identity."

12. See Liu I-chou, "Taiwan minzhong de guojia rentong: Yige xinde celiang fangfa" [National identity of Taiwanese people: A new measurement], paper presented at the annual meeting of the Chinese Political Science Association, Taipei, 1998.

13. Qualitative research through focus group interviews has been conducted, but further investigation is needed; see Yu, "National Identity."

14. Fang Chou, *Yu zhongguo wuguan* [Nothing to do with China] (New Taipei City: Baqiwuhua, 2014), 34.

15. Su Qi and Cheng Ankuo, eds., *"Yige zhongguo, gezhi biaoshu": Gongshi de shishi* [One China, differing interpretations: A historical account of the 1992 Consensus], 2nd ed. (Taipei: National Policy Foundation, 2011), 203–4. The resolution of the National Unification Council reads: "Both sides of the Taiwan Strait uphold the principle that there is but one China. However, the two sides hold different interpretations of that principle."

16. Ibid., 204.

17. For detailed background on this, see Su Qi, preface to ibid., v–xii.

18. Su Qi and Cheng Ankuo, *"Yige zhongguo,"* 16–17. James Kelly's testimony runs as follows: "The 1990s ushered in a decade of incremental consensus-building. Both sides agreed in 1992 that there was one China, but left each side free to express their interpretation of the concept."

19. For an interesting defense of denial and criticism of the 1992 Consensus in the Pan-Green coalition (the proindependence alliance formed in Taiwan after the 2000 elections between the DPP, the Taiwan Solidary Union, and the Taiwan Independence Party), see Wu Jiemin, "Zhongguo insu yu liangan gongmin shehui duihua" [The China factor and dialogues between civil society across the Strait], in *Wenming de huhuan: xunzhao liangan heping de jichu* [Civility and peace dialogue], ed. Tsen Guoxiang and Xu Siqin (New Taipei City: Zuoan wenhua, 2012), 280–88.

20. Quoted in Su Qi and Cheng Ankuo, *"Yige zhongguo,"* 82. The statement is actually a reversal of President Chen's earlier statement that the DPP government was willing to negotiate with China on the basis of the 1992 Consensus.

21. Sara Wu, Jung-Shin Ho, and Hsiao-Wen Wang, "Tsai Ing-wen: Election Win Will Shift China toward DPP," *Commonwealth* magazine, July 10, 2014.

22. Tsai Ing-wen, "Taiwan Meeting the Challenges Crafting a Model of New Asian Value," June 4, 2015, Center for Strategic and International Studies, Washington, DC, http://csis.org/event/tsai-ing-wen-2016.

23. For Ma's speech on his mainland policy, see "President Ma's Speech Reaffirms the 1992 Consensus," Central News Agency, April 29, 2015, www.cna.com.tw/news/firstnews/201504290149-1.aspx.

24. See Lowell Dittmer, "Triangular Diplomacy amid Leadership Transition," in Chow, *"One China" Dilemma*, 179.

25. See Yu-Shan Wu, "Under the Shadow of a Rising China: Convergence towards Hedging and the Peculiar Case of Taiwan," in *Globalization and Security Relations across the Taiwan Strait: In the Shadow of China*, ed. Ming-chin Monique Chu and Scott L. Kastner (London: Routledge, 2015), 25–36; Wu Yu-shan, "Quanli buduichen yu liangan guanxi ianjiu" [Power asymmetry and cross-Strait relations studies], in Bao Zonghe and Wu Yu-shan, *Chong xin jian shi zheng bian zhong de liang an guan xi li lun*, 31–60; see also Yu-Shan Wu's chapter 11 in this volume.

26. Shih Hsiu-chuan and Alison Hsiao, "KMT's Hung Criticizes DPP over Independence," *Taipei Times*, June 11, 2015, www.taipeitimes.com/News/front/archives/2015/06/11/2003620411.

27. See Huang Jing's chapter 13 in this volume.

28. Chu, "Taiwan's National Identity Politics," 494.

29. See Phillip C. Saunders and Scott L. Kastner, "Envisioning a China-Taiwan Peace Agreement," in *New Thinking about the Taiwan Issue: Theoretical Insights into Its Origins, Dynamics, and Prospects*, ed. Jean-Marc F. Blanchard and Dennis V. Hickey (London: Routledge, 2012), 153–71.

30. T. Y. Wang, Su-feng Cheng, Ching-hsin Yu, and Lu-huei Chen, "Structural Realism and Liberal Pluralism: An Assessment of Ma Ying-jeou's Cross-Strait Policy," in Blanchard and Hickey, *New Thinking*, 142.

31. Scott L. Kastner, "Rethinking the Prospects for Conflict in the Taiwan Strait," in Chu and Kastner, *Globalization and Security Relations*, 50–52.

32. See Ping-Kuei Chen, Scott Kastner, and William Reed's chapter 12 in this volume.

33. China allowed Taiwan's low-profile participation in the 2016 World Health Assembly but canceled Taiwan's right to participate in the 2016 International Civil Aviation Organization meeting. It closed the door of the World Health Organization in 2017. In addition, two countries, São Tomé and Príncipe and Panama, have terminated their diplomatic relations with Taiwan and shifted to the PRC since Tsai's coming to power.

34. See Chu, "Taiwan's National Identity Politics," 484–512, for a similar reminder of the significance of the "domestic issue" for regional security. See also Chu Yun-han, *Gaosi zaiyun: Yige zhishifenzi dui ershiyi shiji de sikao* [Lofty thoughts on the cloud: An intellectual's reflection on the twenty-first century] (Taipei: Commonwealth, 2015), 29–35, 144–47, for a more detailed analysis of the transformation of the regional order in East Asia.

3

Changing Identities in Taiwan under Ma Ying-jeou

Jean-Pierre Cabestan

Since the beginning of Taiwan's democratization in the late 1980s, identities on the island have fundamentally changed. Then, most citizens of the Republic of China (ROC), Taiwan's official name, considered themselves as Chinese, and only a minority considered themselves as Taiwanese. The latter segment of the society was concentrated in and around the newly formed and legalized opposition group, the Democratic Progressive Party (DPP). Today, the situation has reversed: fewer than 5 percent of ROC citizens regard themselves as Chinese, between 60 and 70 percent see themselves as Taiwanese, and the rest claim a double identity, both Taiwanese and Chinese. In other words, all political forces, including the Kuomintang (KMT), which for a long time enjoyed a dominant and in reality one-party status and dreamed of reunifying China under its rule, have "Taiwanized." However, many ROC citizens would readily admit that they are politically Taiwanese but culturally Chinese, suggesting that, as in many modern societies, multiple identities are getting more common and do not necessarily generate social or political tensions. Only the most militant of the proindependence, or "Green," Taiwanese would try to draw a clear line between Chinese and Taiwanese cultures, emphasizing the distinctiveness and specificity of the latter.

At the same time, after Ma Ying-jeou's election as Taiwan president and the KMT's return to power in 2008, Ma, the KMT, and what is called in Taiwan the "Blue camp" (*fanlanjun*, a coalition of the KMT, the People First Party [PFP], the New Party [CNP], and the Minkuotang [MKT]) embarked on an attempt to restore a more traditional Chinese and ROC political and cultural identity, both as a way to facilitate the rapprochement that they had initiated with the People's Republic of China (PRC) and as a strategy to weaken their political opponents, the independence-leaning forces called the "Green camp" (*fanlüjun*) in general and the DPP in particular. Simultaneously, economic and social relations across the Taiwan Strait have rapidly developed, multiplying interactions between ROC and PRC citizens.

These two trends can nurture opposite consequences: they can help bridge the gap between mainland Chinese and Taiwanese and persuade the latter that, after all, not much separates them from the former; but, they can also help expose or underscore differences between both societies, and, in a protective reaction observed elsewhere, convince most Taiwanese that while they may share with PRC citizens some cultural features, such as the (written) language, they belong to a very different socioeconomic environment and polity.

My hypothesis is that the Taiwanese political or civic identity, closely linked to the island's democratization and democratic life, will continue to consolidate. The Spring 2014 Sunflower Movement, the KMT's landslide defeat in the late November 2014 local elections, and, more importantly, Tsai Ing-wen's victory and the DPP's return to power (and for the first time control of the Legislative Yuan) since 2016 have all illustrated this trend. Simultaneously, we are witnessing a diversification of ways to be Taiwanese, leading some to associate their identity with the local culture, the building of a new Taiwanese nation, and even the quest for formal independence from China and others to accommodate Taiwanese people's identity with a democratized, sovereign, and de facto independent ROC on Taiwan.

CHANGING POLITICAL IDENTITIES IN TAIWAN BEFORE 2008: A BRIEF OVERVIEW

We start this section with some broad and well-known trends: National Chengchi University's Election Study Center, one of the most respected and reliable opinion poll organizations on the island, tells us that in June 2016 59.3 percent of the interviewees considered themselves Taiwanese, as opposed to 17.6 percent in 1992 and 43.7 percent in 2008; 3.4 percent of them see themselves as Chinese (25.5 percent in 1992 and 4.1 percent in 2008); and 33.6 percent of them view themselves as both Taiwanese and Chinese (46.4 percent in 1992 and 44.7 percent in 2008).[1]

The first, most obvious conclusion from this survey is that Taiwanese identity now dominates the society, completely sidelining Chinese identity. The second is that, stable and dominant until 2008, the group of Taiwanese claiming a double identity has started to decrease since Ma Ying-jeou was elected, raising some doubts about the efficacy of the KMT's attempt to "resinicize" the island. But the third conclusion—often overlooked—is that in 1992, at the beginning of Taiwan's democratization, people claiming a Chinese identity were already a minority that would weaken rather rapidly in the middle of the same decade, becoming the smallest group, behind the people who saw themselves as only Taiwanese, as early as 1995 (20.7 percent against 25.0 percent). In other words, when Taiwan was still at the dawn of democracy, nearly half of the island population had a double identity and almost two-thirds saw themselves either as both Taiwanese and Chinese or as simply Taiwanese.

It is true that, while informative, this kind of survey has a major weakness: it does not make any distinction between cultural and political identities.[2] However, from the beginning the emergence of Taiwanese identity has been both a political or civic and a cultural phenomenon. It originated as a response to the February 28 Massacre (an uprising against the KMT-led government in Taiwan in 1947 that was violently suppressed by the ROC military and resulted in an estimated ten thousand deaths) as well as the KMT's policy forbidding and punishing Taiwanese students' use of their native language at school (mainly Hokkien or Minnan, known in Taiwanese as *Tâi-oân-oê* or *Tâi-gí*)[3] and more broadly to the disconnect, imposed by the civil war in 1949, between the ROC's "one-China" principle or legal fiction and the Taiwanese geocultural reality. While political activists like Peng Ming-min claimed as early as the 1960s a Taiwanese identity closely linked to their democratization demands, in the 1970s the rise of this identity was also a cultural phenomenon of "nativization" (*bentuhua*), particularly in literature and arts, that took shape in reaction to the KMT-inspired dominant traditional Chinese culture and cultural production. In the political realm, in spite of martial law, the KMT itself had no other choice but to get "Taiwanized" (66 percent of its members were Taiwanese in 1986), a process that would reach its leadership in 1986 (when mainlander domination of its powerful Central Standing Committee dropped to 55 percent, then two years later dropped to 48 percent), just before President Chiang Ching-kuo legalized the DPP and lifted martial law (1987), initiating Taiwan's democratic transition. In the local and (partial) national elections that have been allowed to take place since the early 1950s (with an increase of the seats for national elections starting in 1969), opposition (or *dangwai*) candidates were more and more often inclined to use Taiwanese as opposed to Mandarin during their campaigns, contributing to promoting a politico-cultural identity that the KMT then continued, if not to ignore, to actively downplay. And since the 1970s, in Taiwan's scholarly and intellectual community and later in the general public, there has been a growing awareness of the ethnic diversity of the island, leading to the construction of the concept of "subethnic" groups (*zuqun*) to characterize its major components: the Hoklo (*fulao*) or South Fujian immigrants (70 percent of the population), the Hakka (*kejiaren*, 15 percent), the mainlanders (*waishengren*, 13 percent), and the aborigines (*shandiren* and after democratization the various groups of *yuanzhumin*, 2 percent).[4] Over the same period, more Taiwanese have given themselves another definition of their Chineseness, accepting the epithet *huaren* or ethnic Chinese but not *zhongguoren* (Chinese), which has become clearly associated with PRC citizenship. In other words, cultural identity and cultural identity debates in Taiwan are closely linked to democratization and have always been highly politicized. As a result, for a long time Taiwanese surveys on identity have been understood by both the interviewees and the public to have a dominant political or, to be more accurate, civic dimension: in other words, they have been indicative of the emergence of a new Taiwanese national "civic identity."[5]

Another issue, more contentious, is whether there is a direct relationship between identity and nation, between political identity and national identity, and between Taiwanese identity and the quest for Taiwan's de jure or de facto independence. This relationship is obvious: as Christopher Hughes has argued, a "civic nationalism" has taken shape in Taiwan.[6] But the nature and content of the nation that has been under construction since democratization and even since 1949 and the split of China into two separate states can still be understood differently.[7] Taiwanese civic and national identities sometimes converge, notably for those who favor formal independence or a permanent separation from China, but sometimes diverge, for those who prefer to keep the ROC constitutional envelope or "order," to use an expression proposed by President Tsai Ing-wen in her inauguration speech in May 2016, or even the "one-China" (ROC) principle as defined in the KMT's inspired formula "one China, differing interpretations."[8] And as we shall see below, the gap between the aspiration to build a distinct and new Taiwanese nation and the geopolitical reality and political options that can be contemplated is widening. Hence the constant ambiguities and limitations of Taiwan nationalism.[9] Said differently, in Taiwan more than in any other place and because of well-known international constraints, the relationship between identity and nationalism has remained complicated.[10]

Identity politics have been widely studied in Taiwan. This chapter is not the place to present or review this rich literature. Suffice it to say that, because of Taiwan's unusual history, diverse subethnic composition, ill-recognized statehood and international status, and long domination by the 1.5 million mainlanders or "outsiders" (*waishengren*, who arrived in 1945–50, as opposed to Taiwan's "natives" or *benshengren*), democratization has had a direct impact both on the central role played by identity politics and on the rapid consolidation of Taiwanese civic—and to a large extent national—identity. Consequently, since the early 1990s, identity politics has influenced all parties. For the KMT, it has induced a painful metamorphosis, playing a role in the new internal fractures that took shape under Lee Teng-hui (1988–2000) between the then "mainstream faction" (*zhuliupai*), which supported the president's Taiwanization process, and the "nonmainstream faction" (*feizhuliupai*), which included leaders as General Hau Pei-tsun, prime minister from 1990 to 1993. The latter wished to keep the party's strong Chinese identity and mainland traditions (such as the "Huangpu spirit," a spirit of unity and cooperation among parties and factions for the good of the country as a whole).[11] One of the disputes of this period concerned the revision of history textbooks and the

publication of the series "Get to Know Taiwan" (*Renshi Taiwan*).[12] In his first term
as KMT chair, Lee Teng-hui kept a balance between his desire to promote Taiwan's
identity, uniqueness, and statehood and the need to compromise with the more
conservative leaders of his party.[13] Launched in 1993, Taiwan's United Nations bid
was a good example of the middle road then adopted: Taiwan proposed to return
to the UN under the name of ROC rather than Taiwan, as the DPP would have
preferred. And in its 1994 white paper on cross-Strait relations, the Taiwanese government stuck to the idea that there was only one Chinese nation (*guojia*) while
asking Beijing to recognize that it was divided into two "political entities" (*zhengzhi shiti*).

But after his reelection by the whole Taiwanese electorate in 1996, Lee gradually
moved away from this path: in 1999, he advocated a (quasi) two-state approach
to cross-Strait relations that clearly indicated a priority given to the building of a
Taiwanese nation distinct not only from the PRC but also in reality from China.
In doing so, he was trying both to rein in the DPP's growing popularity by co-
opting its issue and to move the KMT in the direction he wished. This change
affected many KMT leaders, including Ma Ying-jeou, who declared in 1998 as he
was running for Taipei mayor that, in spite of his mainland origin, he was a "new
Taiwanese" (*xin Taiwanren*). In any event, it is interesting to note that the proportion of ROC citizens who defined themselves as only Taiwanese increased from
25 percent in 1995 to 39.6 percent in 1999, while Chinese identity dropped even
lower (from 20.7 percent in 1995 to 12.1 percent) and dual identity remained rather
stable (42.5 percent in 1995 versus 47 percent in 1999).[14]

The DPP underwent an easier but no less ambiguous evolution. As we know,
since its establishment in 1986, the main opposition party was united around the
goal to democratize Taiwan but was divided about its quest for formal independence. Then the Formosa faction (*meilidao*) was seen as more moderate and ready
to operate within the ROC framework than the New Tide faction (*xin chaoliu*),
which wanted to create a new nation, the Republic of Taiwan. Eventually, all DPP
factions agreed in 1999 to adopt a self-determination platform that clearly denied
that Taiwan was part of China but at the same time accepted faute de mieux the
ROC institutions and the formula "ROC = Taiwan." In other words, by the end of
the 1990s, the consolidation of Taiwanese identity favored the emergence of a new
Taiwanese national identity and even nationalism that would pave the way for
DPP candidate Chen Shui-bian's victory in the 2000 presidential election.[15]

The KMT defeat in the 2000 election constituted a turning point in Taiwan's
identity politics. Once in power, Chen Shui-bian pushed the ROC's Taiwanization
further: he added "Taiwan" to the ROC passport, insisted after 2002 on the island's separate statehood ("one country on each side of the Strait," or *yibian yiguo*)
and promoted a new historical narrative and all sorts of cultural activities that
underscored Taiwan's distinct identity, particularly its non-Chinese or aboriginal

dimensions. For instance, he tried to propagate Shi Ming (Su Beng)'s interpretation of Taiwan's history as a four-hundred-year fight for freedom and independence,[16] showcasing on the government website (GIO) the figure of Zheng Chenggong (or Koxinga), the Ming general who actually "sinicized" Taiwan in the seventeenth century to better resist the Qing conquest, as the forefather of this movement. He emphasized the Taiwanese character of many cultural customs or traditions that can also be found on the Chinese mainland, especially in southern Fujian, the place of origin of the Taiwanese language. And he presented Taiwan as a cultural melting pot in which each outside ingredient (Chinese, Taiwanese, aboriginal, Japanese, American) had the same level of influence.[17] Made in continuity with Lee's own changes, many of these initiatives were aimed at bolstering Taiwan's sense of community and national security.[18] But in retrospect, the most radical manifestations of this new Taiwanese nationalism appear to be convenient substitutes for the independence-leaning policies that Chen wanted but was unable to introduce, not only because of China's opposition and intimidation, but also because of the US government's, and particularly President George W. Bush's, growing irritation after 2003. These symbolic exaggerations triggered KMT and Blue camp accusations that Chen was "desinicizing" (qu Zhongguohua) Taiwan, precisely at the time (April 2005) of KMT chair Lien Chan's historic trip to China and resumption of party-to-party relations with the Chinese Communist Party (CCP). In a sense, it can be argued that in promoting a dark Green narrative, the Chen Shui-bian administration contributed to moving the KMT narrative to a darker Blue position. Political polarization in those years (2004–8) also played a role in the promotion of two radically opposite narratives and identities on the island. However, it is appropriate to explore the connection between the KMT's promotion of Taiwan's Chinese identity and its rapprochement policy with the PRC, and probably to look there for the main explanation of the Nationalist Party's attempt to return to its mainland roots and initial values. In any event, this short overview of Taiwan identity politics before 2008 constitutes the background of Ma Ying-jeou's attempt to restore what can be called a more traditional "ROC Chinese" identity as well as the negative reactions it has provoked in Taiwanese society, in spite of, or because of, increasing interaction between China and Taiwan.

THE KMT'S NEW CHINESE NATIONALISM

After Ma came to power in 2008, the KMT revived, to some extent, its traditional and somewhat old-fashioned Chinese nationalism, a nationalism that once again placed the unity and the future unification of the Chinese nation/race (zhonghua minzu) at the heart of its ideological discourse. This new/reborn narrative was aimed not only at denouncing and reining in what the KMT and Beijing described as Chen Shui-bian's "desinicization" policy but also at negating Lee Teng-hui's earlier attempted localization—Taiwanization or nativization—of the KMT and the ROC. In doing so, Ma reactivated a narrative and a discourse that had been dominant at the time of the martial law and could only revive bad memories, associated with the authoritarian period and the nondemocratic inclinations of the KMT, in the minds of older-generation Taiwanese. Although Ma did not endorse the dark Blue view, according to which Taipei, since 1949, has merely been the provisional capital of the ROC and unification should take place rapidly, he and the KMT tried to restore the centrality of Chinese culture and identity and contributed to creating tensions between their brand of Chinese nationalism and the need to cultivate local Taiwanese identity and voters.[19] In other words, instead of reuniting the Taiwanese, their official objective, Ma and the KMT's new discourse created new fault lines in society.

Before his first election in 2008, Ma had published a book titled *Native Spirit: The Model Story of Taiwan* that challenged the "four hundred years of tragedy" narrative and emphasized the contributions of Qing administrators such as Liu Minchuan and ROC leaders such as Chiang Ching-kuo to Taiwan's modernization.[20] In this book, he minimized the role of the Japanese and exaggerated the number of native Taiwanese who joined the Chinese resistance against Japan (the majority of the Taiwanese who fought in the war did it on the Japanese side). He also criticized the DPP's version of nativization as a chauvinistic and divisive attempt at desinicizing Taiwan. And after he came to power, Ma introduced a number of changes that highlighted his real intentions: in his inaugural address, he described the people on both sides of the Strait as parts of a *zhonghua minzu* (Chinese nation), where the concept of *minzu* referred to a common racial and cultural identity; he renamed Taiwan Post (Taiwan's mail service) China Post, its original name before the Chen Shui-bian presidency; while promoting democratic values, he also revived the traditional KMT discourse on the need to enhance Confucian ethics; he restored Chiang Kai-shek Memorial Hall's original name (Chen had renamed it National Taiwan Democracy Memorial Hall and hung large butterflies in it during the last year of his presidency), giving the impression of politically rehabilitating the old dictator, much to the pleasure of Chinese tourists. More importantly, he emphasized the continuity between today's Taiwan and the old ROC in terms of institutions and territories, insisting on the legal definition of the ROC as the mainland plus Taiwan. He also asserted the existence of solely "one China," according to the PRC and ROC's approved 1992 Consensus that the phrase "one China" could have differing interpretations as to which government was the legitimate representative of that China) and even, later in 2012, according to the formula "one country, two areas" (*yiguo liangqu*). Finally, he adopted a very assertive discourse on his country's territorial claims in both the East and the South China Sea (Diaoyutai, Spratlys), flirting with the idea of cooperating with the PRC against other claimants on these issues.[21] In other words, as Stéphane

Corcuff has indicated, Ma, a mainlander born in Hong Kong, embarked on a policy of de-Taiwanization and, as Chris Hughes has pointed out, tried in doing so to "resinicize" Taiwan in order to "justify his own legitimacy as a leader."[22]

The KMT's new or revived Chinese nationalism was also clearly aimed at anchoring Taiwan in the Chinese nation, bridging the gap with the PRC, opposing Taiwan independence, favoring reconciliation and eventually unification between the two sides of the Strait (with steep conditions), and legitimizing its own rapprochement policy toward Beijing. It is true that Ma Ying-jeou and his party declared in 2008 that they opposed reunification in the foreseeable future. And it is true that their strategy's objectives also included mainland China's gradual democratization, but they did not do much to that end, and they showed extreme prudence toward PRC dissidents: for instance, Ma refused to see the Dalai Lama or blind activist Chen Guangcheng when they visited the island or to issue a visa to Uighur World Congress president Rebiya Kadeer. In any event, for the Ma administration, what mattered was Taiwan's economic integration with the PRC, which they saw as the best way to boost the economy, avoid marginalization, and embrace regionalization and globalization. The coziness of KMT-CCP relations prompted increasing suspicion among Taiwanese about Ma's rapprochement policy, and not only among DPP voters.[23]

As we know, between 2008 and 2016, unprecedented developments took place across the Strait, including the establishment of direct air and sea links, the conclusion of twenty-three agreements, and an increasing number of Chinese tourist visits to the island (over 4.3 million in 2015). These developments clearly deepened interactions between not only both governments but also both societies. However, have they affected the Taiwanese's identity?

IMPACT AND BACKLASH OF MA'S CHINESE NATIONALISM

The answer is no, or to be more accurate yes, but not in the ways expected. If anything, as we alluded to at the beginning of this chapter, political rapprochement and growing economic integration between Taiwan and China under Ma have paradoxically strengthened the predominance of the Taiwanese identity. And this predominance is even stronger among youth. According to the Taiwan Brain Trust, a "Green" think tank that does produce balanced surveys and opinion polls, in August 2014, 78 percent of interviewees between ages twenty and twenty-nine see themselves as Taiwanese, as opposed to 52 percent for ages fifty to fifty-nine and 48 percent for those over seventy. Women tend feel more Taiwanese than men (67 percent compared to 54 percent for men). Educated people (with a bachelor's degree or above) also feel more Taiwanese (63 percent compared to 57–59 percent). Likewise, the support among young Taiwanese for independence in a three-option survey (independence, reunification, and status quo) is much higher: 44 percent for ages twenty to twenty-nine, as opposed to 18 percent for ages fifty to fifty-nine and 19 percent for over age seventy; the respective figures for status quo supporters are 45 percent, 64 percent, and 54 percent, and the figures for unification supporters are 2 percent, 8 percent, and 8 percent.[24]

It is easy to understand the reasons for this trend. Although most Taiwanese supported Ma's mainland policy after he was elected in 2008, gradually a large segment of them started to criticize it for going too far in accommodating Beijing without yielding the fruits that he had promised. In the public sphere and especially on the Internet, ethnic representations continued to be debated and promoted.[25] A first indicator of a backlash to the KMT's resinicization plan occurred in late 2011. Then Ma had to drop his idea of starting political negotiations with the PRC after his reelection in 2012 because of the strong opposition of a majority of Taiwanese. KMT leader Wu Bo-hsiung's announcement of the "one country, two areas" formula in March 2012 in China, perceived as too close to the now infamous "one country, two systems" concept, was supported by only 33 percent of Taiwanese (and opposed by 55 percent).[26] But it was in Ma's second term that tensions started to intensify, reaching their peak when some KMT legislators tried in March 2014 (without, in the view of the DPP, enough parliamentary discussion of its content) to ratify the Cross-Strait Service Trade Agreement (CSTA), which Taipei and Beijing negotiators had signed in June 2013. This calamitous decision precipitated one of the largest civil disobedience mobilizations in democratic Taiwan's history: the twenty-three-day Sunflower Movement protest. While its causes were both multiple and complex, political and socioeconomic, this movement was a clear manifestation of Taiwan's civic identity. Between March and June 2014, the proportion of Taiwanese claiming a Taiwanese identity climbed from 58.2 percent to 60.5 percent.[27] In other words, Ma's Chinese nationalism was clearly out of sync with the trends at play in Taiwanese society and contributed to weakening the KMT's discourse and policy toward the mainland as well as strengthening the island's Taiwaneseness.[28] More importantly, Ma's discourse and policies intensified the frustrations of the Taiwanese, who had already been badly affected by their stagnating standard of living as well as the island's economic slowdown and growing social inequalities. More generally, Ma's Chinese nationalism reduced the chances of the KMT to stay in power after 2016. Turning into a blatant defeat for the KMT and a landslide victory for the DPP, the November 2014 local elections confirmed, among other things, the unpopularity of Ma's Chinese nationalism. So did Tsai's clear victory (56 percent of the vote) against KMT candidate Eric Chu Li-luan (31 percent) and People's First Party's James Soong Chu-yu (13 percent) in the January 2016 presidential election, and the emergence from the Sunflower Movement of the New Power Party (*shidai liliang*) on the "Greener" and more proindependence side of the political spectrum (five legislators, 6 percent of the vote).

The consolidation of Taiwan's distinct identity can also be interpreted as part of a reaction against globalization that has taken place around the world, including in Europe. It that sense, it is much less paradoxical than it may appear. Nevertheless, in the case of Taiwan, it also demonstrates that national identity is not shaped by the state (the ROC) but by broader political and social trends such as "the practice of sovereignty through the ballot box and the evolution of multi-party politics in the context of a thriving, pluralistic civil society in which identities shift, interact and compete."[29] In the Taiwan case, the consolidation of a distinct identity is also a reaction to the PRC's increasing military threat and ability to influence Taiwan's society, business people, media, and elites: in other words, it is a response to as well as an attempt at compensating for and rebalancing the growing asymmetry of cross-Strait relations.[30]

The next question is of course whether Taiwan's assertion of a distinct identity is not due to eventually fail. The asymmetrical integration process between Taiwan and China may already be affecting identity politics and, perhaps more importantly, gradually delinking the existing close relationship between identity and mainland policies.

A DOMINANT BUT CHANGING TAIWANESE IDENTITY

It is clear that Taiwan is not Hong Kong and that, unlike the former British colony, which has agreed to reintegration in the PRC as long as this occurs within the "one country, two systems" framework, the ROC is a de facto sovereign state whose future cannot be decided without its consent. However, there are some similarities between the two civil societies with regard to their identity politics: both societies are asserting the local versus the global, the protection of their interests in the face of an overwhelming force—the rise of China.[31] Many young Hong Kong activists went to Taiwan in the summer of 2014 to study from the Taiwanese involved in the occupation of the Legislative Yuan, and some of the latter went to Hong Kong to support the Occupy Central movement. Since the Sunflower Movement in spring 2014 and the subsequent seventy-nine-day Umbrella Movement in Hong Kong in autumn 2014, these similarities between the two movements have become even more striking: both highlight a will to resist and a sense of crisis.[32] At the same time, another dimension of this crisis is that Taiwan's and Hong Kong's stronger local identities have become more and more disconnected from the options that political parties can offer to their citizens and that individuals, especially young people, can contemplate in terms of life and career.

As far as Taiwan is concerned, since she came into office in May 2016, Ms. Tsai Ing-wen has tried very hard to preserve the status quo in the Strait, and this despite Beijing's obvious lack of cooperation and insistence that she endorse the so-called 1992 Consensus. In the run-up to her electoral campaign and during her trip to the United States in June 2015, she had already made clear that, if elected, she would preserve the "status quo," preserve the "ROC constitutional order," and, contrary to Chen Shui-bian, not give any bad "surprises" to Washington or Beijing.[33] If the DPP has become much more cautious, it is also because Taiwan's society, mind-set, and elites have gradually changed. For instance, it is clear that today an increasing number of young Taiwanese are tempted to start or continue their professional development in China, a place that is much more attractive in terms of both salary and job opportunities than the island, even if a majority of them would prefer staying in Taiwan (40 percent versus 32 percent, according to a recent survey).[34] Moreover, before 2008, those Taiwanese keen to develop a closer political and functional relationship with the mainland were usually associated with big enterprises or KMT-leaning companies. This is no longer the case: today, a growing number of Taiwanese small businesses, including those in the "Green" South (Kaohsiung, Tainan, Chiayi), have a vested interest in maintaining stable relations with China. For example, their economic reliance on Chinese tourists has become more obvious, particularly since 2012, and the drop in Chinese tourists since early 2016 has led some of them to protest against the new ROC government and even ask it to endorse the 1992 Consensus. As a result, although since Tsai took office she has actively promoted a "New Southbound Policy" aimed at reducing Taiwan's dependence upon China's economy and developing closer links with ASEAN, South Asia, and Australia, Tsai has also clearly indicated that she will not scrap any of the agreements concluded by the Ma administration with Beijing or stop the flow of Chinese tourists visiting Taiwan. And in any event, despite this new policy priority, the level of Taiwan's economic dependency upon China is likely to remain high.

Consequently, Taiwan's identity, while getting stronger, is being increasingly constrained by these realities and gradually disconnected from Taiwan's quest for full statehood, let alone formal independence. While still contributing to protecting Taiwan's political autonomy, Taiwanese identity can no longer protect against the island's asymmetrical dependence upon China. While trying to reduce it, Taiwan must accept and manage this dependence: in other words, Taiwanese identity is becoming more and more "Hongkongized" or constrained by Beijing's "one-China" principle and request.

To be sure, there are still major differences in identity between Hong Kong and Taiwan, since the latter is a de facto state and a democracy and the former is neither a city-state (despite this new aspiration among a minority of young Hong Kong activists) nor a full democracy. However, it appears that more Taiwanese, particularly youth, have adopted a more relaxed and realistic approach to their own identity; it appears also that identity politics is losing steam and may become less of an electoral issue in the future.

Identities and Political Options

As Taiwanese society is getting more globalized, it is also becoming more diverse. And new forms of postmodern political and cultural expression have contributed to deemphasizing the importance of identity as a whole. For one thing, several studies have shown that young Taiwanese have a more flexible and pragmatic approach to the PRC[35]: as already mentioned, their professional careers often include at least a temporary relocation to the mainland, since the local employment market remains sluggish and offers less well-paid jobs. In case of war, most would rather flee than face conscription and fight for the survival of the ROC, and they are becoming increasingly open-minded about long-term solutions to the cross-Strait conflict, including the prospect of unification.[36]

There is another irony, more cultural, in the rise of Taiwanese identity: the slow erosion of the Minnan language in Taiwan, particularly in the north and the center of the island. While it is still widely used in the electoral campaigns, it tends to be less often spoken or even mastered by young citizens. For instance, Sunflower Movement activists mainly used Mandarin or *guoyu* among themselves or when negotiating with the authorities. And rather than fighting in the name of Taiwanese identity, this movement was fighting for Taiwan's interests as a whole, as a political community and more particularly for the social strata that have not taken advantage of or have been excluded from the benefits of the emerging cross-Strait economic integration. In other words, new social and economic cleavages have to some extent replaced identity differences and clashes.[37] While some of the social movements that have developed since 2008 have an identity component, they more and more focus on very specific issues, such as the environment (the anti–Fourth Nuclear Plant protest), farmers' protection, human rights (such as the abolition of the death penalty), and gender inequalities.[38]

In this context, it has become harder and less convincing to promote a fully Taiwanese cultural identity. Members of postmodern and globalized societies actually do not see themselves through a unique identity. Today, the features shared by Taiwanese and Chinese cultures are still well recognized and accepted by most Taiwanese as is the dominant influence of Chinese culture in Taiwan, if that culture is understood differently from the official and neoconservative Chinese culture propagated by the communist authorities of the PRC. As a result, only a few militants are still trying to Taiwanize all aspects of the local culture, and an even smaller minority recognize the existence of a Taiwanese race distinct from the Chinese race, on the basis of the large number of intermarriages between Hokkien or Hakka migrants and local aborigines in the past four centuries. In any event, the culture and linguistic diversity of the Native Taiwanese themselves (Hoklo,

Hakka, and the fourteen recognized aboriginal tribes), a diversity also fed by the presence on the island of around six hundred thousand Southeast Asian workers mainly from the Philippines, Thailand, and Vietnam, prevents the construction of a Taiwanese culture, let alone a Taiwanese nationalism around the still dominant Hoklo subethnic group and its language.

The growing numbers of PRC spouses and other residents in Taiwan and *taishang* (Taiwanese business people) on the mainland are also having an influence on the Taiwanese people's identity that is not always easy to assess, for there is still a dearth of thorough research on them.[39] While around 350,000 mainland Chinese spouses have married Taiwanese citizens in the last twenty years or so (roughly 320,000 of them reside in Taiwan, the others mainly in the PRC), it is by definition impossible to estimate the total number of PRC nationals living on the island.[40] The number of illegal PRC nationals is also increasing and difficult to track. Conversely, between one and two million Taiwanese people are living on the mainland, and some of them have married local spouses. In any event, these two distinct but growing communities and their offspring have already started to influence and alter Taiwan's view of the PRC (and China's view of Taiwan), much as mixed marriages and the growing number of mainlanders residing in Hong Kong (10 to 15 percent of the population) have been slowly changing the local social fabric there. The sheer magnitude of these interactions cannot be discounted as marginal, especially in a society whose fertility rate has continuously decreased during the last twenty years (1.12 births per woman in 2016, down from 1.76 in 2000).[41] While this phenomenon may not have immediate consequences yet—Taiwan's and Hong Kong's local civic identity has so far continued to consolidate—it is likely to facilitate Beijing's promotion of unification under the formula "one country, two systems" and eventually to modify both places' sense of identity vis-à-vis China.

Studies on the *taishang* tend to conclude that most Taiwanese people working in China have kept a strong Taiwanese identity. One simple reason is that the bulk of them are native Taiwanese, as opposed to mainlanders, and have tended to stay together, live in the same areas, and speak Hokkien rather than Mandarin among themselves. It can also be argued that the PRC administrative category in which they have been put from the very beginning of the reform era (1979)—"Taiwanese compatriots" equipped with a special identification and travel document, the *taibaozheng*—has not made them more Chinese but has instead kept them outside local Chinese society, much in the way that Hong Kong business people (who have been equipped since the beginning of the reform era with a "hometown return permit," *huixiangzheng*) have remained outsiders. While according to estimates around two-thirds of them are inclined to vote for the KMT or Blue camp candidates, the majority still claim a Taiwanese identity (50 percent, compared to 62 percent of those who do not work in China). Though a higher proportion of them claim a dual identity (40 percent compared to 32 percent for those who do not work in China), few see themselves as only Chinese (6 percent compared to 4 percent). Moreover, most *taishang* continue to identify with the ROC, not the PRC; they believe nearly as much as the rest of the Taiwanese population that Taiwan is a "sovereign, independent country" (59 percent vs. 65 percent for those who do not work in China); they remain massively in favor of the status quo in the Taiwan Strait (56 percent vs. 59 percent); and they even continue to prefer independence (25 percent against 26 percent) to reunification (11 percent vs. 6 percent).[42] All in all, although the *taishang* have become what I would call "agents of accommodation," they are not yet, and probably will not become, "agents of unification."[43]

The Decline of Identity Politics

It is somewhat paradoxical to propose that while a Taiwanese identity has consolidated on the island, identity politics is declining. But there is some logic in this paradox. As most ROC voters were born and have been socialized in Taiwan, the distinction between mainlanders and natives has been gradually losing its pertinence. For a large majority of islanders, Taiwanese identity is now a given.

It is true that in promoting to government and various state agencies a large number of mainlanders Ma, himself a mainlander, was partly responsible for reactivating the debate. But in so doing he also contributed to dividing his own party and alienating Taiwanese KMT leaders. The rift between Ma and Legislative Yuan speaker Wang Jin-pyng, a local Taiwanese and a key mediator in the peaceful end of the Sunflower Movement and the occupation of the Legislative Yuan by some activists, can be seen through that lens. But in the latest elections identity politics has been less of an issue, being sidelined in favor of bread-and-butter, public policy, and social issues. For instance, in the campaign preceding the January 2016 election, while promoting Taiwan's aboriginal roots and multiculturalism, Tsai Ing-wen and the DPP have been keen to avoid reviving identity politics, knowing full well that it is both a risky weapon and an argument that may not appeal to most of the electorate, particularly young voters.

The Ko Wen-je phenomenon also illustrates the receding importance of identity politics in Taiwan. Elected Taipei mayor in November 2014 against KMT candidate Sean Lien Sheng-wen, Lien Chan's son, this surgeon is new to politics and ran as an independent. Although supported by the DPP, he embodies the emergence of a new political force that many Taiwanese, including in the Sunflower Movement, have been hoping for, in order to break the debilitating KMT-DPP and mainlander-native polarization.[44]

This development has forced both the DPP and the KMT to adjust and also if not sideline at least downgrade identity politics. On the DPP side, Tsai Ing-wen has been keener to reassure the electorate about her party's ability to revive the economy and adopt a workable China policy than to emphasize its Taiwaneseness.

And even independence-leaning politicians and think tanks now recognize the special nature of Taiwan's relation to China. For instance, although critical of Tsai's moderation, dark Green leader Ku Kuan-min proposed in 2013 that both sides of the Strait become "brotherly states" (*xiongdi zhi bang*), or, more accurately, brotherly entities within the same confederation.[45]

On the KMT side, we perceive a gradual deemphasizing of Chinese identity as a new generation of leaders has taken over, even if Hung Hsiu-chu, the daughter of a mainlander from Zhejiang and a dark Blue leader, became party chair in March 2016. The fact that the KMT replaced Hung as its presidential candidate in October 2015 because of her pro-PRC leanings, just three months after having handpicked her, with New Taipei City mayor Eric Chu, a more popular figure (and KMT chair from January 2015 to January 2016), highlights a willingness to better connect with the electorate and re-Taiwanize the party. Eric Chu has a mixed family background, and the strong Taiwanese identity that he acquired through his father-in-law, his wife, and his mother has helped him: he speaks excellent Hokkien, and Kao Yu-jen, his father-in-law, a local Taiwanese who was promoted in the 1970s and 1980s by Chiang Ching-kuo (he was the speaker of Taiwan's Provincial Assembly from 1981 to 1989) has close connections both with local KMT and DPP elites. But more importantly, distancing himself from the KMT "unificationists" like Wu Poh-hsiung and "Chinese nationalists" like Ma Ying-jeou or Ms. Hung, Eric Chu has been aware of the need for his party to refocus on social and economic rather than identity issues. For these reasons, it is unlikely that Hung will be able to reunite the Nationalist Party around a credible policy platform and allow it to come back to power.

This decline of identity politics reflects a diversification of the ways to be Taiwanese, the strengthening of local identities in different parts of the island, and to some extent the resilience of multiple identities, an attribute of most postmodern and free societies. As noted above, it also indicates that Taiwanese identity is now taken for granted. In other words, the decline of identity politics is a sign of the maturation and perhaps consolidation of Taiwanese democracy.

CONCLUSION

Closely linked to the island's democratization and democratic life, Taiwanese identity will probably continue to consolidate while Chinese and even dual identities weaken on this island. The spring 2014 Sunflower Movement and KMT's landslide defeats in both the November 2014 local elections and the January 2016 national elections have to a certain extent illustrated this trend. But at the same time, we are witnessing a diversification of the ways to be Taiwanese. It has led some to associate their identity with the local culture and language and with the building of a new Taiwanese nation de facto if not de jure and forever independent from

China, while it has led others to accommodate their identity to a democratized, sovereign, and de facto independent ROC on Taiwan, and still others, though a small minority, to envisage a future in which Taiwan is eventually reunified with the mainland (probably after the PRC democratizes) but keeping their Taiwanese cultural identity.[46] The disconnect between identities and political options for the future of Taiwan will probably continue to widen, as most Taiwanese, while attached to their distinct identity, are very much aware that the only viable solution for their country is the ROC institutional envelope, the status quo in the Strait, US informal but reliable protection, and growing communication and cooperation with the PRC. With that said, most Taiwanese now, contrary to the 1990s or the early 2000s, identify the ROC with Taiwan and do not countenance any legal inclusion of the mainland in their own polity:[47] even if they feel partly Chinese, in their eyes, the PRC is another country. In other words, the distinction between state and national identity has clearly disappeared. The Taiwanese civic identity that has emerged today identifies only with the ROC or Taiwan, or with what Lee Teng-hui liked to call in the late 1990s the Republic of China on Taiwan: it is therefore, for most Taiwanese, a form of national identity.

For some Taiwanese, their identity will remain holistic, both political and cultural, and will influence all aspects of their life. But this group will probably get smaller as Taiwan is more and more integrated with China but also globalized and divided by deepening social and economic inequalities. As a result, identities and identity politics will lose some of their importance in Taiwan. However, as Taiwan continues to be militarily threatened by the PRC, a power that denies its existence even under its official name, the ROC, and wants to annex it, Taiwanese identity, understood as a political or civic identity, is likely to survive and remain, with democracy, one of the most natural ramparts against Beijing's imperial dream of reunification.

NOTES

1. Election Study Center, National Chengchi University, "Taiwanese/Chinese Identification Trend Distribution in Taiwan (1992/6–2016/6)," August 24, 2016, http://esc.nccu.edu.tw/course/news.php?Sn=166.

2. Some more recent studies have tried to establish a distinction between the two, arguing that "Taiwanese culture is not a significant factor in influencing Taiwanese people's national identity." See Yang Zhong, "Explaining National Identity Shift in Taiwan," *Journal of Contemporary China* 25, no. 99 (2016): 350.

3. Transcribed here in the Taiwanese language's accepted but not unique romanization.

4. Wang Fu-chang, "Zuqun yishi, minzuzhuyi, yu zhengdang zhichi: Yijiujiuling niandai Taiwan de zuqun zhengzhi" [Ethnic consciousness, nationalism, and party support: Taiwan ethnic politics in the 1990s], *Taiwan shehuixue jikan* 2 (1998): 1–45. *Shandiren* means "mountain people," excludes the "plain" (*pingpu*) aborigines, supposedly more "assimilated," and is derogatory; *yuanzhumin* is the correct translation of "aborigines," and this concept was included in the ROC Constitution in 1992. There

are fourteen recognized groups of *yuanzhumin* today. In the PRC, the Taiwan aborigines are still called *gaoshanzu* or "ethnic group of the high mountains" and are considered as a single minority.

5. Shelley Rigger, *Politics in Taiwan: Voting for Democracy* (London: Routledge, 1999), 19.

6. Christopher Hughes, *Taiwan and Chinese Nationalism: National Identity and Status in International Society* (New York: Routledge, 1997), 70–94; Yi-huah Jiang, "Is Taiwan a Nation? On the Current Debate over Taiwanese National Identity and National Recognition," in *The Dignity of Nations: Equality, Competition and Honor in East Asian Nationalism,* ed. Sechin Y. S. Chien and John Fitzgerald (Hong Kong: Hong Kong University Press, 2006), 141–64.

7. Shiau-chi Shen and Nai-teh Wu, "Ethnic and Civic Nationalisms: Two Roads to the Formation of a Taiwanese Nation," in *The "One China" Dilemma,* ed. Peter Chow (New York: Palgrave Macmillan, 2008), 117–46; Frank Muyard, "The Formation of Taiwan's New National Identity since the End of the 1980s," in *Taiwan since Martial Law: Society, Culture, Politics, Economy,* ed. David Blundell (Berkeley: University of California, Berkeley; Taipei: National Taiwan University Press, 2012), 297–366.

8. A civic identity can emerge in any kind of political community, be it national or subnational; it does not necessarily coincide with a national identity. For instance, Hongkongers have a strong civic identity, but the large majority of them still identify with China.

9. Jean-Pierre Cabestan, "Specificities and Limits of Taiwanese Nationalism," *China Perspectives,* no. 62 (November-December 2005): 32–43.

10. Rou-lan Chen, "Beyond National Identity in Taiwan: A Multidimensional and Evolutionary Conceptualization," *Asian Survey* 52, no. 5 (2012): 845–71.

11. The "Huangpu spirit" still strongly influences the ROC armed forces; the KMT based it on the ethos of the Huangpu (or Whampoa) Military Academy, created by Sun Yat-sen in 1924 in one of Guangzhou (Canton)'s districts. This army academy (*lujun guanxiao*) trained the officers that would lead in 1926–27 the "Northern Expedition" and unify China under the KMT regime, based in Nanking. After 1949, the ROC military academy was relocated in Fengshan, near Kaohsiung.

12. Stéphane Corcuff, ed., *Memories of the Future: National Identity Issues in the Search for a New Taiwan* (Armonk, NY: M. E. Sharpe, 2002); Christopher R. Hughes, "Negotiating National Identity in Taiwan: Between Nativisation and Desinicisation," in *Taiwan's Democracy: Economic and Political Challenges,* ed. Robert Ash, John W. Garver, and Penelope Prime (London: Routledge, 2011), 51–74.

13. J. Bruce Jacobs and I-hao Ben Liu, "Lee Teng-hui and the Idea of 'Taiwan,'" *China Quarterly* 190 (June 2007): 375–93.

14. Election Study Center, "Taiwanese/Chinese Identification Trend."

15. Shen and Wu, "Ethnic and Civic Nationalisms."

16. Shi Ming, *Taiwanren sibai nian shi* [Four hundred years of history of the Taiwanese] (1962; repr., Taipei: Huacao wenhua, 1998).

17. Cabestan, "Specificities and Limits."

18. Hughes, "Negotiating National Identity," 69–71.

19. Christopher R. Hughes, "Revising Identity Politics under Ma Ying-jeou," in *Political Changes in Taiwan under Ma Ying-jeou: Partisan Conflict, Policy Choices, External Constraints and Security Challenges,* ed. Jean-Pierre Cabestan and Jacques deLisle (London: Routledge, 2014), 120–36.

20. Ma Ying-jeou, *Yuanxiang jinshen: Taiwan de dianfan gushi* [Native spirit: The model story of Taiwan] (Taipei: Tianxia yuanjian chuban, 2007). A Chinese official close to Li Hongzhang, Liu Mingchuan was appointed in 1885 as governor of the newly created Taiwan Province (before it was a prefecture of Fujian Province). He played an important role in the modernization and the defense of the island. He resigned in 1891 for health reasons.

21. In 2010, Liu Fu-kuo (a National Cheng Chi University Institute of International Relations research fellow) and Wu Shicun (president of the Chinese National Institute for South China Sea Studies) cohosted a project that produced policy proposals recommending that Taiwan and China join forces to protect the territory of "one China" and that cross-Strait military and political cooperation

be implemented in the South China Sea; DPP legislator Chen Chi-mai claimed that the Taiwanese Foreign Ministry had endorsed Liu's project, but the ministry denied this. *Taipei Times*, June 8, 2015. See also on this issue J. Michael Cole's "Taiwanese Academics Are Playing with Fire," *Thinking Taiwan*, May 29, 2014, http://thinking-taiwan.com/taiwanese-academics-are-playing-with-fire/; Liu Fu-kuo and Wu Shicun, eds., *2010 Nian nanhai diqu xinshi pinggu baogao* [Report on the assessment of the status of the South China Sea area in 2010] (Taipei: Institute of International Relations, Chengchi University, 2010).

22. Stéphane Corcuff, "Ma Ying-jeou's China Leaning Policy and the 1683 Fall of the Zheng in Taiwan: A Cross-centuries Geopolitical Comparison," in *National Identity and Economic Interest: Taiwan's Competing Choices and Their Implications for Regional Stability*, ed. Peter Chow (New York: Palgrave Macmillan, 2011), 93–134; Hughes, "Revising Identity Politics," 123.

23. André Beckershoff, "The KMT-CCP Forum: Securing Consent for Cross-Strait Rapprochement," *Journal of Current Chinese Studies* 43, no. 1 (2014): 213–41.

24. Taiwan Brain Trust, *2014 Taiwan Brain Trust Trend Survey* (Taipei: New Taiwan Peace Foundation and Taiwan Brain Trust, 2014), en.braintrust.tw/userfiles/images/Trend/201412TBTsurvey.pdf.

25. Jens Damm, "Taiwan's Ethnicities and Their Representation on the Internet," *Journal of Current Chinese Affairs* 40, no. 1 (2011): 99–131.

26. Hughes, "Revising Identity Politics," 130.

27. Taiwan Brain Trust, *2014 Taiwan Brain Trust Trend Survey*. This result was confirmed by Election Study Center, "Taiwanese/Chinese Identification Trend."

28. Syaru Shirley Lin, *Taiwan's China Dilemma: Contested Identities and Mutliple Interests in Taiwan's Cross-Strait Economic Policy* (Stanford, CA: Stanford University Press, 2016).

29. Hughes, "Revising Identity Politics," 131.

30. Chien-jung Hsu, *The Construction of National Identity in Taiwan's Media, 1986–2012* (Leiden: Brill, 2014).

31. Malte Phillip Keating, "Identity Formation in Taiwan and Hong Kong: How Much Difference, How Many Similarities?," in *Taiwanese Identity in the Twenty-First Century: Domestic, Regional and Global Perspectives*, ed. Gunter Schubert and Jens Damm (Abingdon: Routledge, 2011), 258–80.

32. Syaru Shirley Lin, "Bridging the Chinese National Identity Gap: Alternative Identities in Hong Kong and Taiwan," in the "National Identity Approaches to East and South Asia" section of *Joint US-Korea Academic Studies*, vol. 25, ed. Gilbert Rozman (Washington, DC: Korea Economic Institute of America, 2014), 113–32, www.keia.org/sites/default/files/publications/syaru_shirley_lin.pdf.

33. Tsai Ing-wen, "Taiwan Meeting the Challenges, Crafting a Model of New Asian Value," speech to the Center for Strategic and International Studies (CSIS), Washington DC, June 3, 2015, http://english.dpp.org.tw/dr-tsai-ing-wen-speaks-at-center-for-strategic-and-international-studies/.

34. China Youth Corps Survey, quoted in *Taipei Times*, March 25, 2015, 3.

35. Shelley Rigger, *Taiwan's Rising Rationalism: Generations, Politics, and « Taiwanese Nationalism»* (Washington, DC: East-West Center, 2006), 44.

36. Tanguy Le Pesant, "Generational Change and Ethnicity among 1980s-Born Taiwanese," *Journal of Current Chinese Affairs* 40, no. 1 (2011): 133–57; Tanguy Le Pesant, "A New Generation of Taiwanese at the Ballot Box," *China Perspectives* 2 (2012): 71–79.

37. Jonathan Sullivan, "Taiwan's Identity Crisis: The Conundrum for the DPP Is That the Taiwanese Identity That Has Been Trampled On and Discarded under Ma Is Both a Trump Card and a Liability," *National Interest*, August 18, 2014, http://nationalinterest.org/feature/taiwans-identity-crisis-11093.

38. Min-sho Ho, "The Resurgence of Social Movements under the Ma Ying-jeou Government: A Political Opportunity Structure Perspective," in Cabestan and deLisle, *Political Changes in Taiwan*, 100–119.

39. A useful exception is Gunter Schubert, "The Political Thinking of the Mainland Taishang: Some Preliminary Observations from the Field," *Journal of Current Chinese Affairs* 39, no. 1 (2010): 73–110.

40. "320,000 Chinese Married to Taiwanese: Agency," *China Post*, April 29, 2013, www.chinapost. com.tw/taiwan/national/national-news/2013/04/29/377256/320000-chinese.htm; "Most High Income Chinese Couples Want a Second Child," *Women of China*, February 17, 2014, www.womenofchina.com. cn/html/report/6834–1.htm.

41. Index Mundi, "Total Fertility Rate: Children Born/Woman," Taiwan, www.indexmundi.com/ g/g.aspx?c=tw&v=31 (accessed November 1, 2016).

42. Taiwan Brain Trust, *2014 Taiwan Brain Trust Trend Survey*.

43. Chun-Yi Lee, *Taiwanese Business or Chinese Security Asset: A Changing Pattern of Interaction between Taiwanese Businesses and Chinese Governments* (London: Routledge, 2011); Shu Keng and Gunter Schubert, "Agents of Unification? The Political Role of Taiwanese Businessmen in the Process of Cross-Strait Integration," *Asian Survey* 50, no. 2 (2010): 287–310. Lee is more pessimistic than Schubert or Keng about the *taishang*'s chances of not being influenced by the political and ideological environment in which they live.

44. Frank Muyard, "Voting Shift in the November 2014 Local Elections in Taiwan," *China Perspectives* 1 (2015): 60.

45. Ku Kuan-min, *Xiongdi zhi bang: Taiwan yu zhongguo guoji zouyi* [Brotherly states: A brief discussion on relations between Taiwan and China] (Taipei: Taiwan Brain Trust, 2013).

46. Zhong, "Explaining National Identity Shift."

47. On their attitudes in the 1990s and 2000s, see Jiang, "Is Taiwan a Nation?"

4

Mingling but Not Merging

Changes and Continuities in the Identity of
Taiwanese in Mainland China

Shu Keng and Emmy Ruihua Lin

WHY IS THE IDENTITY OF THE TAIWANESE ON THE MAINLAND AN ISSUE?

In the past two decades, identity has been the key issue in Taiwanese politics.[1] Internally, identity issues are central to social cleavages and political competition. Some have used Taiwan's political transition as a way to refute its Chinese origins. Externally, almost everything Taiwan has been doing is related to efforts to defend its national identity. Identity politics has also been at the heart of Taiwan's efforts to determine its foreign policy with China, the United States, and other countries. But "the Taiwanese identity project" may have an Achilles' heel: the identity of the Taiwanese living on the mainland. Since the post-Mao reforms in China, the rapprochement of the Kuomintang (KMT) and the Chinese Communist Party, and the rise of global production/outsourcing networks, the mainland has become the number one destination for Taiwanese foreign investments (and Taiwan is definitely one of the primary sources of China's FDI). Close economic ties triggered several waves of migration from Taiwan to the mainland. According to some estimates, there are between three hundred and four hundred thousand Taiwanese residing in China.[2]

This is a relatively large portion of the small island's population. They and their immediate/direct families amount to about two million people, which is about one-tenth of Taiwan's population. An important question arises as to how these Taiwanese identify themselves. Are they adapting to a Chinese identity or do they still uphold their Taiwanese identity? If the former is the case, they may be a strong and expanding "fifth column" in Taiwanese politics[3]— but most *taishang* would be heartbroken to feel that their compatriots viewed them in such a light. Therefore, the identity of Taiwanese in mainland China has always been a controversial issue in Taiwan. Some scholars consider these Taiwanese as immigrants and look for signs of assimilation, while others consider them as expatriates and stress their mobility (their travels back and forth between the mainland and Taiwan) and their psychological steadfastness. But the empirical research, after rejecting the earlier "melting-pot" expectations of assimilation (such as Fong Xiaoqian's), has also not fully supported expectations of assimilation that draw on theories of migration (such as Shu Keng's), stressing migrants' difficulties in maintaining ties to their original culture and in withstanding pressures to adopt a new identity.[4] More than a decade of research has been conducted on this particular subject, but scholars have not reached any agreement on it.

Our own research on this topic started in 2002 and has since been extended via both interview and survey data. In this chapter, we would like to provide a concluding statement on the subject to clarify the current status of Taiwanese identity in China and then to provide some explanation for it. The chapter is divided into five sections. The next one describes the identity of the Taiwanese and raises a puzzle: Why do Taiwanese settle down and blend in, yet refuse to identify themselves as Chinese? The third section tries to explain why Taiwanese maintain their identity. We argue that this has to do with the mobility factor. Being able to travel allows Taiwanese to maintain their strong ties with Taiwan and therefore reduces the impact of living in mainland China. The fourth section deals with the question of why Taiwanese have been reluctant to assume a less "exclusive Taiwanese identity." In this section, we explore the differences and conflicts between Taiwanese and Chinese political and social cultures. In the last part we conclude that the identity of Taiwanese residing on the mainland is typical of identity in the globalizing era. Globalization brought Taiwanese to the mainland, and the resulting changes and continuities illustrate phenomena of transnationalism, cultural conflicts, and the mosaic of national identity.

TAIWANESE ON THE MAINLAND: SETTLING AND ASSIMILATION BUT NO IDENTITY CHANGE

As mentioned earlier, scholars have made different assertions about the identity of Taiwanese residing on the mainland. This could be explained by looking at the political background of the scholars, but it may have more to do with the different dimensions these scholars are focusing upon. In other words, different foci lead to different conclusions. The problem arises as a result of the concept "identity." *Identity* in this chapter refers to "social identity" or "identity of the related person," especially his or her identification with a social category or group and the degree to which the person considers him- or herself a member of the social category or group. In the context of cross-Strait relations, the identity of Taiwanese people could be represented as a choice between Chinese and Taiwanese. But the distinction of "Chinese" versus "Taiwanese" may be confusing in the differing contexts where the concept might apply. *Chinese identity* could mean "Chinese in a cultural sense" or "Chinese in a nationalistic sense." The survey question commonly used in Taiwan specifies a three-option answer: being Chinese, being Taiwanese, or being both. This could help clarify the issue. On the basis of these types of questions, we can distinguish two types of identities among Taiwanese: an "inclusive Taiwanese identity" (i.e., identifying oneself as "Chinese" or "both") or an "exclusive Taiwanese identity" (i.e., identifying oneself as Taiwanese only).

There are some preliminary qualifications to the issue of identity among Taiwanese residing in mainland China. First, in terms of career planning, only those who would like to settle down and stay on will face the question of identity. Second, regarding social life, only those who would like to reach out and make friends outside their ethnic boundaries confront the question of identity. We can, then, distinguish three aspects of the identity issue: (1) psychological settling, captured by questions about "bringing over the whole family" and "having a long-term plan to stay on"; (2) social assimilation, captured by questions about "who are your close friends" and "who can you and your children marry"; and (3) attitudinal identity: imagined membership in a social group and especially the claiming of an inclusive or exclusive Taiwanese identity.

The study uses data from a collaborative project between the University of Hong Kong and National Chengchi University named "Lives and Attitudes of the Taiwanese in Mainland China," carried out between the summer of 2009 and the winter of 2012. In that survey, the twelve researchers or six research teams spent a total of six weeks interviewing Taiwanese who were settling in both the greater Shanghai area and cities surrounding Dongguan. During the interview, we first asked the interviewees the questions on our semi-structured questionnaire. We then asked further questions regarding previous questions and started more casual talks on related issues. The dialogues were recorded and turned into transcripts for the researcher to keep track of the attitudes and thoughts of the Taiwanese sojourners being interviewed.

Since we have little information about Taiwanese communities in China, the population of our sample, it was difficult for us to design any forms of random sampling on the basis of preexisting information. Instead, we applied the method of snowballing for interviewees and followed the rule of "maximum variation" to diversify our sources of information. As a result, our interviewees include both Taiwanese businessmen and their families and Taiwanese students; both first- and second-generation Taiwanese; employees from both labor-intensive and high-tech manufacturers; employees of Taiwanese firms, joint ventures, foreign firms, and Chinese firms; Taiwanese sojourners of different educational statuses, ranging from primary school to PhD; Taiwanese affiliated with different political factions;

and Taiwanese of different ethnic origins. In the end, a total of 452 Taiwanese in China were interviewed and their attitudes were documented in a project that proved to be the largest systematic survey of the Taiwanese in China. This allows us to better understand the identity of the Taiwanese in China.

On the basis of the findings summarized in table 3, we can easily see a trend in the identity of the Taiwanese in mainland China: Taiwanese are for the most part settled and can easily blend in, but they refuse to identify themselves as "Chinese."

We find that, first, in terms of physical settling, more than half of the Taiwanese surveyed (52.3 percent) had already brought over their family and settled down in the mainland or had plans to do so. This often is related to long-term career planning, family planning, and a sense of "home" in the locality. As one Taiwanese settled in Shanghai stated, "I have no problem referring to myself as a new Shang-hainese." This lays the foundation for the next step, assimilation.

The social assimilation of the Taiwanese can be gauged in two different ways. The first is behavioral and is measured by a question about close friends: even constrained by factors such as arrival time and contacting opportunities, about one-fourth of the Taiwanese (26.3 percent) already considered mainland Chinese as their best friends. The second is attitudinal and is measured by a question about the person they would marry: only about 5 percent (5.2 percent) exclude mar-riage with mainlander Chinese, while most (58.9 percent) feel very agreeable to marrying them. In other words, Taiwanese have no problem at all with crossing the ethnic border to make friendships and establish trust. According to one local Shanghainese, "Compared with the migrants from Jiangsu and Anhui, Taiwanese are nothing special for me, and I would never keep away from them."

Even though Taiwanese plan to settle down and have no problem blending in, they do not want to give up their original identity or adapt to a more lenient and less inclusive identity. As table 3 shows, at least 62 percent of the Taiwanese uphold the "exclusive Taiwan identity." As one young Taiwanese said, "I do come from Shanghai, but if I am mistakenly identified as a Chinese, of course I will correct them immediately. I would never accept the identity of local Chinese." This trend can be better observed by comparing the identity of the Taiwanese in Taiwan to that of the Taiwanese in mainland China, summarized in table 4.

From table 4, we can see that with regard to political positions, especially those related to party identification, there are huge difference between the Taiwanese in Taiwan and those who have moved to China. The percentage of those in the pan-Blue camp (KMT, People First Party [PFP], New Party [CNP], or Minkuotang [MKT]) is almost doubled (26.4 percent vs. 45.1 percent), while the percentage of those in the pan-Green camp (Democratic Progressive Party [DPP], Taiwan Solidarity Union [TSU], Taiwan Independence Party [TAIP], or Taiwan Constitution Asso-ciation [TCA]) significantly decreases (dropping from 28.6 percent to 15.7 percent). In addition, with respect to a deeper independence-unification position, there are

TABLE 3 Aspects of Taiwanese identity

	Settling and staying			Close friends			Someone to marry			Personal identity	
	Counts (#)	Ratios (%)		Counts (#)	Ratios (%)		Counts (#)	Ratios (%)		Counts (#)	Ratios (%)
Very unwilling	31	5.7	Largely as Taiwanese	247	45.6	Taiwanese only	27	5.2	Inclusive Taiwan ID	200	38
Unwilling	136	25.1	More as Taiwanese	152	28	Preferably Taiwanese	187	36	Exclusive Taiwan ID	327	62
No opinion	91	16.8	Roughly equal	101	18.6	Both are acceptable	300	57.7			
Willing	203	37.5	More as Chinese	31	5.7	Preferably Chinese	6	1.2			
Very willing	80	14.8	Largely as Chinese	11	2						
Total	541	100	Total	542	100	Total	520	100	Total	527	100

SOURCE: Joint Research Project on the Lives and Attitudes of the Taiwanese in Mainland China (National Chengchi University and Hong Kong University, 2009–12).

TABLE 4 Political attitudes of Taiwanese in Taiwan compared to Taiwanese on the mainland (%)

Party identification	Taiwanese in Taiwan	Taiwanese in China	Unification-independence position	Taiwanese in Taiwan	Taiwanese in China	Personal identity	Taiwanese in Taiwan	Taiwanese in China
Pan-Blue	26.4	45.1	Pro-independence	25.8	5.5	Taiwanese	62.7	60.2
Neutral	45	39.2	Pro-status quo	64.3	73.1	Chinese	3.6	6
Pan-Green	28.6	15.7	Pro-unification	9.9	21.4	Both	33.7	30.8
Total	100	100	Total	100	100	Total	100	100

SOURCE: Information about Taiwanese in Taiwan draws from Taiwan's Election and Democratization Study (TEDS; 2012). Information about Taiwanese on the mainland draws from the Joint Research Project on the Lives and Attitudes of the Taiwanese in Mainland China (National Chengchi University and Hong Kong University, 2009–12).

even larger gaps between the Taiwanese in Taiwan and China. The proportion who support independence drops from 25.8 percent to 5.5 percent while the proportion who support pro-unification rises from 9.9 percent to 21.4 percent. If this is the case, then how have attitudes regarding personal identity changed, given that these are often tied to the two above-mentioned positions? As we can see in table 4, there is almost no difference between the Taiwanese in Taiwan and in China: in terms of the "exclusive Taiwan identity," the former proportion is 62.7 percent while the latter is 60.2 percent. In other words, partly because of self-selection and partly because of environmental influences, with respect to party identification and position on the unification/independence issue, the Taiwanese in China are very different from those staying in Taiwan. But the two groups do not significantly differ on the dimension of identity. What explains this puzzling fact? Why are Taiwanese willing to live in China and blend in but at the same time unwilling to change their attitudes toward their identity?

MOBILITY, ASSIMILATION, AND IDENTITY: WHY TAIWANESE HOLD ON TO THEIR IDENTITY

What is wrong with earlier propositions, which expect a gradual fading away of the Taiwanese identity? And how do Taiwanese uphold their exclusive Taiwanese identity while residing in a new environment? The key here is a tug-of-war between "environmental pressures" and "personal will." In the scenario of conventional immigration, migration is strongly impelled and one-way, and it is difficult for migrants to maintain ties with the sending country/hometown. Therefore, the "environmental pressures" are formidable and most migrants are unable to resist, especially those who are not protected by ethnic communities. In the end, they have to gradually give up their old identity and assume the new identity in a process similar to that envisioned by the "melting pot" model of social assimilation.

This scenario applies to some extent to earlier waves of immigration, such as those of migrants who arrived in New York in the earlier twentieth century. But even historically it has not always applied, and it applies even less in the global era. Often borders can be frequently crossed and recrossed, and, because of innovations in transportation and communication, migrants can easily maintain their ties with their motherland. As a result, we assume that it is easier for them to resist environmental pressures and adhere to their desired identity.

Changing global production networks have brought Taiwanese to an economically and socially less favorable environment in mainland China. Their choice to travel or stay there is to some extent voluntary. Taiwanese are free to come and go. In addition, because of revolutions in transportation and communication technology, cross-border travel and communication are easier and more convenient. Therefore, the pressure to assimilate is not so formidable and irresistible. In addition, it is not difficult for Taiwanese to maintain their social and psychological ties with their hometowns. Most Taiwanese that we surveyed had traveled four to six times a year (not for business purposes) back and forth across the Taiwan Strait. As one Taiwanese entrepreneur from Dongguan described, "Many of us still have business in Taiwan. . . . At least, we have parents, brothers and sisters, and friends in Taiwan. Of course we have to go and visit them from time to time." And another Taiwanese settled in Shanghai says, "Most of the Taiwanese here subscribe to satellite TV so that they can watch Taiwanese programs, especially Taiwanese news. Of course, some others do not subscribe. But this is because they do not watch TV. I have never heard that any Taiwanese watch Chinese programs all day."

Moreover, in order to promote economic and cultural exchanges internationally, most nation-states manage to facilitate and expedite the process of transferring personnel across national borders. This is also true for travel across the Taiwan Strait, given the unique political situation between China and Taiwan. Both governments accept some replacements for passports and allow some degree of "flexible citizenship" with respect to permanent residence, property ownership, and welfare programs.[5] This is an arrangement that Tomas Hammar has called denizenship: a status of permanent residency without citizenship, allowing migrants to work and reside permanently in a country but not to have political rights.[6] Therefore, as one Taiwanese entrepreneur from Kunshan observes, "I have never heard of any Taiwanese giving up their medical insurance program [*jianbao*], let alone their Taiwanese identity card [*shenfenzheng*]. No matter how long you stay in China, you would never give up those things."

In other words, all these factors—convenient travel, everyday communications, and the residency arrangements—make it possible for the Taiwanese to easily resist assimilation pressures on the mainland. But mobility does not just "enable" them to hold onto their Taiwanese identity; it also "constrains" them from not doing so. Many of these Taiwanese are uncertain about whether they will settle in China, Taiwan, or perhaps even other places. In this regard, China is just a place to stay. One Taiwanese uses jet lag as a metaphor to describe the mentality: "If you know that you are going to leave in a week, you probably have little incentive to adjust your biological clock." In a sense, the lifestyle of mobility that has developed in an era of globalization has greatly decreased the pressures and incentives to localize, let alone to revise one's personal identity.

From this perspective, the resistance of the Taiwanese to revising their identity has a lot to do with globalization. Therefore this trend does not just apply to the case of Taiwanese in mainland China. It is applicable to most skilled workers and business entrepreneurs traveling across the world. The case of the Taiwanese is unique in the sense that they have traveled to a place with which they share cultural origins. In sum, the ability of the Taiwanese to resist assimilation into local

Chinese society fully illustrates the significant impact of globalization on the state and its citizens.

CONTACTS, IMAGES, AND IDENTITY: WHY TAIWANESE NEVER GIVE UP THEIR IDENTITY

Even though Taiwanese *can* stick to their old identity, they do not necessarily have to. Since most Taiwanese will settle down on the mainland and since few of them have problems blending in there, why do they still refuse to revise their Taiwanese identity to make it more open and inclusive?

Identity refers to a confirmation of one's distinctiveness from others (the contrast of "us" against "them"). The sense of distinctiveness normally comes from the experience of intergroup contacts. If the experiences are negative, so that people create a negative (hostile or derogatory) image of the other, the group boundary will be strengthened and it will be more difficult to relax or break the boundary. This is probably the case with Taiwanese in mainland China. It is very common to find that Taiwanese who hold a positive attitude about China (*da zhongguo zhuyi*) while living in Taiwan become cynical and negative about China once they when they actually visit or move there. But if so, another thesis (the "contact hypothesis") suggests that frequent and constant contacts may still revise their identity and gradually adjust their relation to Chinese society. And if this is the case, is it be possible that the Taiwanese currently living on the mainland are halfway through a process that will culminate in the replacement of the old Taiwan identity with a new Chinese identity? In other words, is it possible that the assimilation process is just not finished yet and that our conclusion is too hasty?

We believe, on the basis of our fieldwork, that this hypothesis is not true. Intergroup contact does influence migrants and can in the end change one's identity, but it also has its limitations. Migrants do not need to meet everyone; they just deal with those they want to deal with. So identity based on past experiences also directs who one makes contact with and screens some people out. Once people develop a prejudice or stereotype, they avoid some contacts, with the result that they never have experiences that would enable them to revise that prejudice/stereotype and, ultimately, their identity. As one member of our research team concludes, "Once these Taiwanese believe in the stereotype, they keep minimal contacts with local Chinese. And those superficial contacts cannot challenge the stereotype. More often than not, the stereotypes are confirmed and reconfirmed by their 'selected' contacts. The stereotypes thus reproduce themselves and perpetuate themselves."[7] This generalization especially holds for migrants in a higher or superior position: they can choose to meet with whomever they want. And ordinarily Taiwanese on the mainland hold such higher positions. As a result, unless there are some unusual events, it is likely that most Taiwanese will not revise their identity no matter how long they stay. Settling down, even permanently, thus has little impact on identity change.

What kinds of experiences, then, play a key role in shaping the image of the Chinese and Chinese society among Taiwanese residing on the mainland? According to our field research, the most influential experiences are those that highlight the differences between Taiwanese and Chinese cultures, which in turn are deeply rooted in economic and political differences between the two countries. Such experiences strengthened respondents' sense of a group boundary between the Chinese and the Taiwanese. In the private sphere, such differences concern how Chinese people show "class" or "civilization" in everyday life (*shenghuo shuizhun*). If you ask Taiwanese about their impressions of local Chinese, they normally give you examples of spitting, littering, talking loudly, and never observing traffic rules. All these constitute the basis of the belief that Chinese people "have no class" (*mei shuizhun*) and cause most Taiwanese on the mainland to "feel ashamed if they are misidentified as Chinese." As one young man coming to China for a couple of months commented, "I did not know about this before coming to China. Once I am here, I have a strong feeling: Why should I be a Chinese?" In the public sphere, such differences concern how civilized the Chinese government is perceived to be; respondents describe it as "so backward, so uncivilized, falling behind the government of Taiwan almost a century." In a nutshell, Taiwanese residents' experiences of encountering local Chinese and the local government create a "ladder of class between ethnic groups," and most Taiwanese feel that "we" are superior and "they" are inferior. Therefore, even though they have already physically settled in China and had few problems mixing with Chinese, these Taiwanese simply do not want to "become Chinese." And when they get together with Taiwanese, they often make fun of local Chinese (*a-lar-a*).

There is variation: for example, Taiwanese settling in metropolitan areas like Shanghai or Beijing tend not to mock local Chinese, whereas those residing in isolated rural factory locales, who encounter local Chinese that are mostly peasants or migrant workers, tend to have negative impressions of local Chinese and to hold an "exclusive Taiwanese identity." Younger Taiwanese are in general more sensitive to the despotism and corruption of local Chinese governments and thus more likely to hold an "exclusive Taiwanese identity." In contrast, those who have had the experience of running a business under the authoritarian government of Taiwan are much less likely to disparage the Chinese government. From these observations we can confirm our field findings that experiences matter: perceived "class" or "civilization" of the Chinese people and government is an important factor that contributes to the variation in negative impressions Taiwanese hold about "China" and explains why they wish to distinguish themselves from the Chinese. We used the data to test the hypotheses drawn from our field research. The results are summarized in table 5.

TABLE 5 Explaining the settling, assimilation, and identification of Taiwanese in mainland China

	Settling and staying		Close friends		Someone to marry		Personal identity		
	Coeff.	S.D.	Coeff.	S.D.	Coeff.	S.D.	Coeff.	S.D.	Exp(B)
Education ("above college" as base group)									
Below college	-0.166	0.115	-0.19	0.097	-0.034	0.058	0.081	0.22	1.084
Gender (female as base group)									
Male	0.054	0.129	0.288**	0.109	0.226**	0.066	-0.879**	0.264	0.415
Ethnic origin (Hakka as base group)									
Mainlanders	0.274	0.204	-0.063	0.17	0.135	0.103	-0.704	0.381	0.494
Minnan	0.057	0.173	-0.113	0.145	0.099	0.089	0.278	0.326	1.321
Generation ("born between 1970 and 1978" as base group)									
Before 1969	0.021	0.134	0.161	0.113	0.04	0.068	-0.621	0.259*	0.537
After 1979	-0.094	0.156	0.094	0.131	-0.309***	0.08	0.072	0.313	1.075
Arriving time	-0.012	0.011	-0.012	0.009	-0.003	0.006	-0.004	0.021	0.996
Living environment	0.122	0.058*	0.001	0.048	0.003	0.029	0.105	0.112	1.111
Location ("settling at Zhu River Delta" as base group)									
Yangtze Riv. Delta	0.281	0.111*	-0.089	0.093	0.024	0.057	-0.091	0.214	0.913
Sector (manufacturing sector as base group)									
Service	0.016	0.115	0.226*	0.097	0.073	0.059	-0.156	0.224	0.855

Hometown in Taiwan ("coming from Central Taiwan" as base group)

Northern TW	−0.045	0.142	−0.052	0.119	0.02	0.072	−0.133	0.275	0.875
Southern TW	0.131	0.196	0.013	0.165	−0.011	0.1	−0.317	0.378	0.728

Political positions (neutral as base group)

Pan-Blue	0.039	0.119	0.094	0.1	−0.064	0.06	−0.416	0.221	0.66
Pan-Green	−0.305	0.158	−0.125	0.133	**−0.285*****	**0.081**	**1.123****	**0.371**	**3.074**
Constant	27.373	22.488	25.794	18.842	7.732	11.403	9.79	41.974	17858
N	541		542		520		527		
Adj. R²	0.029		0.027		0.078		Nagelkerke R²	0.182	
S.E.E.	1.163		0.979		0.579		G²	35.155	
d.f.	14		14		14		d.f.	14	
p	< .05		< .05		< .001		p	< .001	

SOURCE: Joint Research Project on the Lives and Attitudes of the Taiwanese in Mainland China (National Chengchi University and Hong Kong University, 2009–12).

Let us first focus on the background of the interviewees. As we can see in table 5, education does not have a significant effect on identity status—a finding quite different from findings of surveys conducted in Taiwan. Also, gender is significant in shaping the sociability and identity of the mainland-dwelling Taiwanese: men (most businesspeople are male) more easily become close friends with mainlanders and are more conscious and outspoken about their identity. But our research found no evidence of a difference in identity between men and women. As for whether Taiwanese are "natives" (*benshengren*) or originally migrants to Taiwan from the mainland after the Chinese Civil War (*waishengren*) does not seem to have any significant effect on their identity. This suggests that the distinction between Taiwanese who came from the mainland and native Taiwanese loses its function as a demarcation line of social cleavage once Taiwanese come to China. Finally, the "generation" factor also fails to demonstrate significant effects on shaping the identity of the Taiwanese, although we found differences between different generations. The general pattern was that younger respondents were more likely to assume an exclusively Taiwanese identity.

In the "contacts and experiences" category, the only category that exerted a significant effect on the identity of the Taiwanese was employment in the service sector, which contributed to cultivation of friendships with local Chinese). None of the factors such as (1) time of arrival, (2) residential area, (2) geographical location, and (4) past life experiences exerted a significant effect. This suggests that earlier expectations about Taiwanese assimilation to Chinese society—based on immigration theories predicting that longer stays in the host country, residence in locations with greater likelihood of intergroup contacts, and more positive experiences of contacts will result in migrants' rapid assimilation—are not supported by empirical evidence.

Finally, one other factor demonstrated significant influence and led to a more open and inclusive position on Taiwanese identity: the person's political position. This may have to do with the above-mentioned factor of the person's impressions of the Chinese government.

IMMIGRATION AND IDENTITY IN THE GLOBAL ERA: WILLINGNESS, RESISTANCE, AND A MOSAIC LANDSCAPE OF NATIONAL IDENTITY

The purpose of the study is to explore the puzzle of why Taiwanese who have settled on the mainland and could easily blend in persistently refuse to concede on the aspect of identity. In our opinion, a study like this can help enrich and illuminate the theory of migration. Of course, the first controversy we have to face is whether Taiwanese on the mainland can be considered as migrants or whether they are just expatriates. Many, if not most, of the Taiwanese in our study who settled down in China would never go back to Taiwan. From this point of view, they are not expatriates. Even though they moved to China without any intention of migration, they finally settled anyway and have had few problems mixing with local Chinese.

But there is another reason that many Taiwanese scholars do not consider these people to be migrants: they still cling to their Taiwanese identity. And that contradicts conventional theories of migrants' assimilation. But in our view, this may have to do with the limitations of the conventional theories. In the common scenarios of those theories, most migrants move in order to migrate and are traveling from worse to better places. In the era of globalization, however, migrants are also traveling around the world and may not plan to permanently reside; also, a significant proportion settle in places with a lower living standard. As a result, many migrants have little incentive to assimilate into the local society, and at the same time they have the ability to keep traveling or to maintain close ties with their motherland. These migrants are thus not migrants in the traditional sense. Some scholars refer to them as "transnational communities."

Our study shows that the Taiwanese in mainland China do not fit the classical definition of "immigrants" and actually exemplify "immigration in the global era." Because Taiwanese share many cultural traits with mainland Chinese, have the ability to blend in with them, yet are reluctant to revise their identity, they perfectly illustrate the new migration process triggered by globalization. Consequently they can give us a better understanding of such concepts as borderlessness, transnationalism, and mosaic-like national identity. They can also help us better understand how cultural gaps and the ability to travel produce changes and continuities in identities in the era of globalization.

Another finding from the research is that the issue of identity for Taiwanese in mainland China is significantly affected by cultural differences across the Taiwan Strait. These have gradually developed over the past six decades of separation, to the point that people on the two sides of the Strait lack many common experiences, thoughts, and feelings. It will take time to narrow this cultural gap. Before China and Taiwan do so, Chinese unification will never occur from the bottom up. These findings help explain why Taiwanese prefer the cross-Strait status quo to either unification or independence. From this perspective, given similar attitudes among the public in Taiwan, it doesn't matter that much whether the KMT's president Ma or the DPP's president Tsai is in power: their China policy would be much the same.

NOTES

We would like to thank Prof. Richard Weixing Hu, of the University of Hong Kong, for the financial support for data collection and Professor Liping Wang, the Director of the Institute of the Fujian Pilot

Free Trade Zone at the Party School of Fujian, for administrative support. Also, without the financial support that Shu Keng received from the General Grants for Humanities and Social Sciences Research, Ministry of Education, PRC (Project Code: 14YJAGAT001), this collaborative research would not have been possible.

1. Alan Wachman, *Taiwan: National Identity and Democratization* (New York: M. E. Sharpe, 1994); Lowell Dittmer, "Taiwan and the Issue of National Identity," *Asian Survey* 44, no. 4 (1994): 475–83.

2. Shu Keng, Gunter Schubert, and Emmy Ruihua Lin, eds., *Taishang yanjiu* [The study of Taiwanese businesspeople in China] (Taipei: Wunan, 2012).

3. Shu Keng and Gunter Schubert, "Agents of Taiwan-China Unification? The Political Roles of Taiwanese Business People in the Process of Cross-Strait Integration," *Asian Survey* 50, no. 2 (2010): 287–310.

4. Fong Xiaoqian, "Quanqiuhua chongji xia dalu taishang de rengtong wenti" [The identity of mainland China's Taiwanese businesspeople under globalization], in *Shimao zuzhi yu liang'an fazhan* [The World Trade Organization and cross-Strait development], ed. Xu Guangtai (Taipei: Institute of International Relations, 2003), 489–504; Shu Keng, "Zixunren yihuo Taiwanren? Dashanghai diqu gaokeji taishang de guojia renting" [Merely professionals or still Taiwanese? The national identity of the Taiwanese in the high-tech sector in Greater Shanghai], paper presented at the Second Annual Conference on Politics and Information (Yilan: Foguang University, 2002).

5. Aihwa Ong, *Flexible Citizenship: The Cultural Logics of Transnationality* (Durham, NC: Duke University Press, 1999).

6. Tomas Hammar, "State, Nation, and Dual Citizenship," in *Immigration and the Politics of Citizenship in Europe and North America*, ed. W. R. Brubaker (Lanham, MD: University Press of America, 1989), cited in Yen-fen Tseng and Jieh-min Wu, "Reconfiguring Citizenship and Nationality: Dual Citizenship of Taiwanese Migrants in China," *Citizenship Studies* 15, no. 2 (2011): 265–82.

7. Jiang Yiqing, "Qunji jiechu dui denglu taiwanren dangdihua zhi yingxiang: Yi Dongguan ji Shanghai weili" [The impacts of inter-group contacts on the assimilation of the Taiwanese in mainland China: The study of Dongguan and Shanghai] (MA thesis, Graduate Institute of East Asian Studies, National Chengchi University, 2006).

5

Chinese National Identity under Reconstruction

Gang Lin and Weixu Wu

Soon after Mao Zedong declared on the stage of Tiananmen that the Chinese people had stood up, it seemed that the People's Republic of China (PRC) had almost finished the process of nation building, which had been stimulated by one hundred years of national humiliation and periodic foreign invasions; the only exception then was Taiwan, which had been under the control of Chinese Nationalists (Kuomintang, KMT) since 1945. Over the past seven decades, there have been two Chinese societies governed by different political regimes across the Taiwan Strait. From the perspective of the Chinese mainland, people living in Taiwan, or the so-called Taiwanese, are of course part of "the Chinese," including the overwhelming majority of Han Chinese and the tiny percentage of Taiwanese aboriginals, who are regarded as one of the fifty-five minority ethnicities within the Chinese nation.

The growing sense of Taiwanese identity on the island despite peaceful development of cross-Strait relations over the past eight years, however, has highlighted the marginal existence of Chinese national identity (*guojia rentong*) on the island. As more people on Taiwan nowadays identify themselves as Taiwanese, rather than as Chinese or both, people on the mainland have worked hard to reconstruct the concept of one China through political communication, economic integration, social exchange, and cultural assimilation across the Taiwan Strait. New slogans such as "two shores, one close family" (*liangan yijiaqin*) and "both sides [of the Strait] realizing the Chinese Dream" (*gongyuan zhongguomeng*) have been created and added into the existing political phraseology of "a community of cross-Strait shared destiny" (*liangan mingyun gongtongti*) and "the great rejuvenation of the Chinese nation" (*zhonghua minzu de weida fuxing*).

This chapter discusses Beijing's efforts to reconstruct Chinese national identity in relation to Taiwan. Theoretically, Chinese national identity is both indigenous and reconstructive. The ancient concept of the Middle Kingdom has been enriched continuously, thanks to political expansion and cultural assimilation throughout history. From 1949 to 1979, amid political confrontation and military tension, the Chinese people on the mainland were educated to liberate miserable people on Taiwan and bring the island back to its motherland. From 1979 on, Taiwan's developmental experience and increasing cross-Strait civic exchanges have expanded mainlanders' imagination of modernization and increased their understanding of national identity. Past experience suggests that reconstruction of a Chinese national identity that spans the Taiwan Strait is contingent not only on economic modernization and integration, mutual cultural exchange and assimilation, and reinterpretation of contemporary Chinese history and political relations between the two entities prior to China's reunification, but also on improvement of public governance and political engineering on the mainland.

THE FACTOR OF TAIWAN IN CHINA'S RECONSTRUCTION OF NATIONAL IDENTITY

The mainland Chinese government is obviously worried that if most people in Taiwan identify as Taiwanese and prefer independence this could seriously undermine the prospect of unification in the future. Since the return of Hong Kong and Macau to the motherland, Taiwan's final unification with the mainland has become even more important for China's rejuvenation. This does not mean Taiwan is the last lost territory to be recovered by the motherland, thus ending China's century-old national humiliation by foreign powers. Rather, from Beijing's perspective, the issue of territory recovery has been resolved since the end of World War II. As the Chinese leader Hu Jintao once claimed:

> Although the mainland and Taiwan have not been reunited since 1949, the circumstances per se do not denote a state of partition of Chinese territory and sovereignty. Rather, it is merely a state of political antagonism that is a legacy—albeit a lingering one—of the Chinese civil war waged in the mid- to late-1940s. Nevertheless, this does not alter the fact that both the mainland and Taiwan belong to one China. For the two sides of the Strait, to return to unity is not a recreation of sovereignty or territory but an end to political antagonism.[1]

From this perspective, separatists in Taiwan are similar to those in Tibet and Xinjiang, even though Tibet and Xinjiang are already under the PRC's control and Taiwan is yet to be unified. To maintain national sovereignty and territorial integrity, Beijing has pragmatically combined these three regions together in its agenda of enhancing national identity. In recent years, Chinese academics have proposed to reshape their country's national identity in the new era by strengthening of institutions, good governance, and democratic progress. He Donghang and Xie Weimin point out the problem in the process of China's national identity building: the development of civic identity has fallen behind that of ethnic identity.[2] According to Yao Dali, it is important to speed up political democratization in order to cultivate and consolidate national identity in a multiethnic country like China. For Yao, the ideas of sovereignty and equality among people of different strata are the spirit of the modern nation-state and also the basic principle of democracy.[3] Jin Taijun and Mi Jing argue that political ideas such as democracy, freedom, and human rights, as well as institutions based on them, are most important to national identity, particularly to a country where individuals have diverse identities and multiple affiliations, a result of globalization.[4] Lin Shangli agrees that the most fundamental dimension of national identity is identification with state institutions, which have decisive significance for building modern countries. Democracy is the political foundation of national identity in modern society.[5]

In the case of Taiwan, however, political discourse on the mainland has focused more on cultural similarities, ethnic equivalence, and common economic interests of people between the two sides of the Taiwan Strait, and less on so-called institutional identity (*zhidu rentong*)—accepting the identity of the economic and political system on the other side of the Taiwan Strait. Obviously, this is because the Taiwanese population is predominantly Han Chinese (except for a tiny portion of aboriginals), and Beijing's unification formula of "one country, two systems" excludes the likelihood of institutional convergence of the two sides of the Strait. It is also because, as Jean-Pierre Cabestan says in chapter 4, many people in Taiwan would easily admit that they are politically Taiwanese but culturally Chinese. Assuming that "blood is thinker than water" (*xue nong yu shui*), the Chinese mainland government proposed people-to-people exchanges with Taiwan as early as 1979, when the political and symbolically military confrontation with Taiwan was ended by Beijing's unilateral announcement. Since then, rather than voicing a goal of "liberating miserable Taiwanese *compatriots*" from the despotic rule of the KMT, Beijing appealed to the island for peaceful unification, pinning its hope not only on the Taiwanese people but also on KMT authorities under the leadership of Chiang Ching-kuo. Blood ties, hometown connections, and ethnic attachment were all employed to reconstruct a linkage between the two long-separated societies. The most dramatic example was a July 1982 open letter to Chiang Ching-kuo written by Liao Chengzhi, minister of the United Front of the Chinese Communist Party (CCP) Central Committee. In the letter, Liao appealed to Chiang Ching-kuo that "brothers are still brothers even after painful fighting experience between them, and they can easily forget their mutual hatred with a smile when they meet again" (*dujin jiebo xiongdi zai, xiangfeng yixiao min enchou*). The story behind this sentimental letter was that Liao's father, Liao Zhongkai, had been a senior leader of the KMT back in the 1920s, supporting the KMT-CCP United Front to fight against the Northern Warlords government. Following this open letter, some correspondence by mail continued under the table between leaders of the two sides, and former PRC president Yang Shangkun openly proclaimed in 1987 that the Taiwanese authorities should respect the Chinese "overall national interest" (*minzu dayi*) and have peace talks with Beijing on unification. On the other side of the Strait, Chiang Ching-kuo even considered sending his formal representative to Beijing for a preliminary political dialogue just before he passed away in January 1988.[6] Although peace talks on China's reunification between the two ruling parties on each side of the Taiwan Strait did not occur in the 1980s, Chiang Ching-kuo did make a decision in November 1987 to allow cross-Strait family reunions for old soldiers who had followed Chiang to Taiwan in the late 1940s. Beijing's open-door policy and peaceful unification appeal to the island, plus Taipei's 1987 decision, have encouraged more people-to-people exchanges between the two sides based on their family ties, hometown connections, and ethnic feelings, as well as for business reasons. From the mainland perspective, in the absence of meaningful political dialogue between the two sides, cultural and economic factors can serve as antidotes against separatist tendencies on the island that have been beyond PRC control since 1949. Both Jiang Zemin's "Eight Points" (1995) and Hu Jintao's "Six Points" (December 2008) have highlighted the functions of Chinese culture and economic cooperation in linking the two sides of the Taiwan Strait, despite the ups and downs of cross-Strait relations over the past three decades.

"TWO SHORES, ONE CLOSE FAMILY"

To narrow the gap between the two sides on the issue of national identity and to reconstruct an inclusive Chinese identity across the Taiwan Strait, the Chinese leader Xi Jinping most recently promoted the idea that "compatriots from the two shores of the Taiwan Strait are one close family" when he met the honorary chair of the KMT, Lien Chan, on February 18, 2014. According to Xi Jinping, the blood ties between people on the Chinese mainland and in Taiwan would never be severed. This idea is rooted in the two countries' common ancestry, history, and culture.[7] Cross-Strait ties are not relations between neighbors or friends (let alone enemies) but relations between family members.[8] By using sentimentally appealing phraseology, such as "both sides fulfilling the Chinese Dream," Xi Jinping attempts to convey the similar ideas that both the mainland and Taiwan belong to one China and that both can "strive for China's reunification." He has emphasized that the unification is a common project of people on both sides of the Taiwan Strait and that unification can be achieved only through China's rejuvenation. Thus peaceful unification is contingent upon peaceful development of the two sides, as well as the "great rejuvenation of the Chinese nation."

While the appeal to a common culture has long been employed by Chinese mainland leaders in dealing with Taiwan, it has been increasingly used since the mainland's economic takeoff and cultural reconstruction in the 1990s. When former Taiwanese leader Lee Teng-hui recognized Chinese culture as the foundation of cross-Strait exchanges in 1995, he was more confident about Taiwan's role in preserving and reconstructing Chinese culture than mainland China's role. Indeed, cultural sinicization (*wenhua zhongguo hua*) was one of the four preconditions for national unification according to Taipei's guidelines for it in 1991—with the other three preconditions being economic liberalization, political democratization, and social pluralism. Many people in Taiwan, including some supporters of the pro-independence Democratic Progressive Party (DPP), have claimed that Chinese culture is better preserved on the island than on the mainland, since Taiwan has been free of the iconoclastic May Fourth movement and the Cultural Revolution on the other side of the Strait. Cultural reconstruction on the mainland, however, has achieved great progress since the 1990s. Some Confucian ethics and manners have been well adapted to the modernizing Chinese society, and cultural industries have developed quickly. A good example is the architecture of the China Art Museum at Shanghai Expo 2010, which mixed a traditional outlook with modern design. Taipei's desinicization activities under the DPP administration only reminded the mainland of the importance of Chinese culture as the spiritual tie between the two sides.

Cultural exchanges have made great progress since the KMT came back to power in 2008, thanks to Ma Ying-jeou's strong affection for traditional Chinese culture and the Chinese nation. The Cross-Strait Cultural Industries Fair started in 2008 and continued in the following years. The fifth CCP-KMT forum convened in Changsha, Hunan, in 2009 and selected culture and education as the main theme, focusing on (1) preserving the continuity of Chinese culture and fostering innovation; (2) promoting cross-Strait cooperation in cultural industries; and (3) expanding cross-Strait exchange and cooperation on education. In the same year, Fujian initiated the first Strait Forum (*haixia luntan*) and has convened it every year, focusing on civil and cultural exchanges between the two sides. For example, the 2010 Strait Forum hosted a cultural week focused on Mazu (a sea goddess worshipped by ancient people living in southern Fujian and Taiwan); a cultural festival for Zhu Xi, a famous Confucian scholar in the Song dynasty who was born and spent his life in Fujian; and a forum on Hakka culture. All these activities were aimed at highlighting aspects of Chinese culture that have been shared by people on both sides of the Strait. Meanwhile, other cultural activities with Taiwanese participation, including ancestor worship of the Yellow Emperor in Shanxi and Henan Provinces and an arts festival for Chinese calligraphy in Beijing, occurred on the mainland.[9] Although the two sides of the Taiwan Strait were unable to sign an agreement on cultural exchanges in Ma Ying-jeou's first term as expected, cultural exchanges continued in his second term. The topics of cultural exchanges have ranged over education, publishing, libraries, exhibitions, media communications, religions, music, dance, drama, secular customs and arts, and local culture. The year 2012 witnessed the Cross-Strait Intangible Cultural Heritage Month and the Cross-Strait City Arts Festival in Taiwan, as well as Cross-Strait Cultural Friendship Weeks and the Cultural Exhibition on the mainland. To make books published on the mainland readable by Taiwanese youth, they were converted from simplified Chinese into traditional Chinese and reprinted on the island. In the same year, 1,858 young Taiwanese came to the mainland to study, while 951 mainlanders went to Taiwan as full-time students. According to the statistics of the Department of Culture under the PRC State Council, 324 cross-Strait cultural exchange programs were held in 2013, with 10,802 participants from the two sides. The figures for 2014 were 500 programs and 12,593 participants.[10] As Liu Xiangping observes, cultural identity is one of the basic elements in national identity, followed by ethnic identity (minzhu rentong) and state identity (guojia rentong). In terms of cultural identity, the two sides are more alike than different, but in terms of national identity, the gap between the two sides has widened.[11]

As Lowell Dittmer points out, one of several objects of national identification is the historical legacy, including consensual interpretations of certain problematic phases in a nation's development when the basic issues of national purpose were raised and decisively resolved in some way.[12] The mainland government understands very well that differing historical memories may affect national identity negatively. As Xi Jinping said to Lien Chan on February 18, 2014, Chinese mainlanders share the painful feelings that Taiwanese people hold on account of political events in the past, and this is a tragedy for the whole Chinese nation. According to Xi, a strong nation can ensure good fortune for all Chinese compatriots, and a weak and chaotic nation simply means disaster for them.[13] Because common historical memory is an important factor in shaping civic national identity, mainland media and academic discourse have in recent years highlighted how the CCP and the KMT joined forces to fight the Japanese invasion back in the 1930s and 1940s, as recapped in various movies, newspapers, and journals. In particular, Tengchong, a frontier city in southwestern China and a famous battleground between Japanese troops and the KMT military with US aid, has become a popular location for holding academic conferences that involve scholars from Taiwan, including some from the Green (pro-independence) camp. The mainland's intention is clearly to build up common historical memories with Taiwan, even though young Taiwanese without connection to the old KMT regime may feel that historical events in Tengchong are irrelevant to them. For the same reason, the mainland has retold the story of the famous aboriginal Wushe uprising (also referred as the Wushe incident) against Japanese colonial rule during the 1930s to highlight the common fate of the two sides during a miserable period of Chinese history. Indeed, Japan's brutal crackdown on the Wushe uprising and its massacre of the inhabitants of Nanjing occurred in the same decade across the Taiwan Strait. The uprising occurred in October 27, 1930, in a place called Wushe, located in Nantou County, and its participants were the inhabitants described as Seediq, who at that time were considered a subgroup of the Atayal tribe but in April 2008 were recognized as the fourteenth tribe of aboriginals in Taiwan.[14] The trigger for the uprising was colonial officials' mistreatment of the Seediqs. Under the leadership of Mona Rudao, the Seediqs rose up against the Japanese occupiers in an armed rebellion lasting fifty days and killing well over one hundred Japanese before they themselves were slaughtered in retaliation—about one thousand Seediqs died during the uprising. About eighty years later the Taiwanese film director Wei Te-sheng planned to make a film titled *Warriors of the Rainbow: Seediq Bale* in September 2008 and finished the film three years later.[15] The film awoke historical memories of the incident, raising differing views of the incident on the two sides of the Taiwan Strait as well as abroad, particularly on the Internet. The mainstream opinion on the mainland, however, was to link this incident to Chinese resistance against Japanese rule or invasion on both sides of the Strait.[16]

As 2015 was the seventieth anniversary of the Chinese victory in the Chinese People's War of Resistance against Japanese Aggression as well as the Second World War, many activities occurred on the mainland in memory of this victory, aimed at enhancing national identity across the Taiwan Strait. On September 2, the eve of Victory Day in China, Chinese president Xi Jinping awarded medals to veterans who fought in the resistance, including representatives for "eight hundred brave soldiers" (*babai zhuangshi*) of a KMT troop. In his speech, Xi emphasized that both frontline (*zhengmian zhanchang*) soldiers led by the KMT and rearguard (*dihou zhanchang*) soldiers led by the CCP contributed to the final victory and that people fighting on different battlefields were all national heroes.[17] On September 3, a series of commemorative events—including a rally, a military parade, a reception, and an evening gala—were held in Beijing as planned. Thirty country leaders, as well as representatives from nineteen countries and ten organizations, took part in the events.[18] Some retired soldiers originally from the KMT troops took part in the military parade, and former KMT chair Lien Chan, New Party chair Yu Mu-min, People First Party general secretary Chin Chin-sheng, and some other dignitaries from Taiwan also attended the commemorative events. In his speech on the rally, Xi said that the Chinese people had fought tenaciously for fourteen years before winning a great victory in their War of Resistance against Japanese Aggression without mentioning specifically who led that war, the KMT or the CCP, though he did mention, in the reception following the parade, that the war had proceeded under the banner of the "United Front of Resistance against Japanese Aggression Initiated by the CCP."[19] When Xi met Lien Chan and other Taiwanese representatives on September 1, he highlighted the role of the United

Front established cooperatively by the CCP and the KMT and expressed appreciation for the cooperation between frontline and rearguard soldiers during the war.
Further, Xi intentionally included Taiwanese people's struggle against the Japanese
occupation over fifty years as an important part of the whole Chinese nation's war
of resistance.[20] Yu Zhengsheng, chair of the Chinese People's Political Consultative
Conference, mentioned one day earlier when he met Lien Chan that during the
1930s and 1940s more than fifty thousand Taiwanese came to the mainland and
joined the War of Resistance against Japanese Aggression.[21] Lien Chan made similar statements during his meetings with Xi and Yu, respectively.

However, few people in Taiwan, including KMT leaders, endorsed Lien's activities in Beijing. Both Ma Ying-jeou and Hau Pai-tsun, a senior general and the
father of former Taipei mayor Hao Lung-pin, criticized Lien for participating in
Beijing's commemorative event. For them, the War of Resistance against Japanese
Aggression had been conducted under the leadership of the Republic of China
(ROC), which deserved the honor. From the KMT's perspective, the war was part
of ROC history. From the perspective of the DPP, however, Taiwan had had nothing to do with the War of Resistance. In fact, during the war more Taiwanese had
been recruited by Japanese troops, and toward the end of the war native Taiwanese
had suffered from US aircraft bombing.[22] The typical example of such views is Lee
Teng-hui, who openly declared himself as a Japanese before 1945 and who claimed
that Diaoyu Island belonged to Japan. It is interesting to note that Lee and Lien
were running mates in the 1996 presidential elections and were elected president
and vice-president. Lee's remarks reflect a certain nostalgia for Japanese colonial
rule, particularly in its late period, among some native Taiwanese. Such feelings,
through political socialization, were passed on to some youths, who were uneasy
about calling that period between 1895 and 1945 the Japanese "occupation" (ri ju),
as the new teaching outline (kegang) endorsed by the Ma administration did. This
resulted in anti-kegang demonstrations in August 2015. Retrospectively, the migration of mainlanders to Taiwan after the war ended in 1945 have has created different "ascriptive categories" in national identification in Taiwan,[23] an important
social feature to be taken into account in political construction and reconstruction
of historical memories of the War of Resistance against Japanese Aggression on
the island. For the mainland, reconstructing a common memory of the war among
people on the two sides of the Taiwan Strait is crucial for building national inclusion. Therefore, Beijing has employed historical memories, in addition to cultural
similarities and ethnic equivalence, to retrospectively consolidate the ideational
framework of "a community of cross-Strait shared destinies."

Another typical example of historical reconstruction has been the raising of
a public memorial in December 2014 for both soldiers of the People's Liberation
Army (PLA) and Nationalist troops who died in battle with each other on Jinmen
Island in October 1949. The PLA troops, numbered at nine thousand or so, attacked

Jinmen and held the island for three days but were finally defeated by the Nationalist military with troop reinforcements and an advanced air force. The casualties for each side were several thousand. The political purpose of the memorial is to assuage the lingering historical grievances of people on both sides of the Chinese Civil War and to cherish cross-Strait peace from the perspective of "two shores, one close family." As one retired soldier from Shanghai said during the event, he came to Jinmen in memory of his old colleagues who died on the battleground but ended up with a feeling of respect for all who had died there, regardless of which army—the PLA or the KMT—they had belonged to. Interestingly, at the end of the event, all participants made a military salute to PLA and Nationalist soldiers who had died during the anti-Japanese war.[24] By doing so, they converted the memory of the tragic civil war into another memory, the glorious cause of all Chinese soldiers fighting against the brutal Japanese invasion prior to 1945. Retrospectively, as a military frontier between Taiwan and the mainland in the 1950s, Jinmen served as a symbolic link between the two sides under the "one-China" framework, simply because both the Nationalist regime on the island and the PRC government on the mainland claimed sovereignty over it, suggesting that China's civil war was not yet over. In recent years, however, Jinmen has served as a peace frontier, starting with the three minilinkages (*xiao santong*) between it and the PRC-administered island of Xiamen during the Chen Shui-bian administration and followed by an increasing number of visits by mainland tourists. The story of kitchen knives made in Jinmen, using artillery shells left over from the history of bombing Jinmen between the late 1950s and 1970s, when more than one million shells were fired on the small island, is well framed by the public media to encourage the peaceful development of cross-Strait relations. Both Jinmen kitchen knives and Jinmen Gaoliang (a strong liquor) are big sellers for mainlanders traveling there. The role of Jinmen in narrowing the gap between the two sides of the Taiwan Strait has been highlighted by an official meeting there in May 2015 between Zhang Zhijun, director of the Beijing-based Taiwan Affairs Office (TAO) of the State Council, and Xia Liyan, chair of the Taipei-based Mainland Affairs Council (MAC). Because Jinmen is much closer to the mainland than to Taiwan, the two parties have agreed to expedite a contract signed by relevant departments in Fujian and Jinmen to supply water to the island. Other cooperative projects between Jinmen and Xiamen have been discussed in recent years, including a proposed bridge and the supplying of an electrical grid that would cross the two islands.

A COMMUNITY FOR TWO SHORES' SHARED FORTUNE

Economic exchanges and integration are also considered important for forging community between the two sides of the Strait. According to neoliberal or neofunctional assumptions, economic integration will eventually lead to political accommodation and even political integration, as the experience of the European Union has suggested. At least, growing functional interdependency, according to Karl Wolfgang Deutsch's concept of a "security community," will make war too mutually costly to be feasible. Business exchanges between the two sides have evolved from an indirect format in the 1980s to a direct and comprehensive mode nowadays, particularly since 2008. For example, cross-Strait trade increased from $129 billion in 2008 to $188 billion in 2015, accounting for about 30 percent of Taiwan's total foreign trade. Taiwanese direct investment on the mainland that has been approved by the island's authorities increased from $1.9 billion in 2008 to $2.8 billion in 2012, though it decreased to $1.5 billion in 2015. Tourists from Taiwan to the mainland increased from 4.37 million person-visits in 2008 to 5.5 million in 2015, while tourists from the mainland to Taiwan jumped from less than 0.28 million person-visits to 4.14 million during the same period.[25] This increasing economic interdependency has created "linkage communities" (*liansuo shequn*) between the two sides of the Taiwan Strait, as Yung Wei pointed out one decade ago.[26] During the 2012 elections in Taiwan, a number of big entrepreneurs publicly supported the KMT idea of "one China, differing interpretations," which is close to Beijing's principle that there is only one China and that only one government (the PRC's) can legitimately represent it but significantly different from the DPP's position that the PRC and the ROC should have "state-to-state" relations. On the other hand, most Taiwanese people have arguably not received direct benefits from increasing economic integration. Despite Beijing's "benefit-offering" (*rangli*) policy in Strait negotiations on economic affairs, including the signing of the Economic Cooperation Framework Agreement and the Cross-Strait Service Trade Agreement, ordinary people in Taiwan have not experienced much economic revival, for the island in general or their daily life, as a result of cross-Strait exchange. Social cleavages in Taiwan between the rich and poor and between upper strata and lower strata have partly contributed to the strong reaction against the progress of cross-Strait economic and social exchanges, as was vividly revealed by students' Sunflower Movement protesting the Cross-Strait Service Trade Agreement in March 2014. In view of social cleavages in Taiwan, Beijing has paid more attention to the voice of Taiwan's grassroots and youth, who have felt frustrated and relatively exploited amid the process of regional economic integration.

To rebuild a shared Chinese national identity across the Taiwan Strait, Beijing's Taiwan policy makers, in the spirit of neofunctionalism, propose to resolve "economic and easier issues first, and political and difficult issues later." The CCP-KMT forums on cross-Strait economic and cultural exchanges after 2006 largely focused on the issue of economic cooperation, except for the 2009 forum, which took cross-Strait cultural and educational exchanges and cooperation as the main theme. Beijing's immediate political goal during the Ma administration was to sign a peace agreement with Taipei and reach a common understanding on the nature of political relations between the two sides prior to China's reunification. The years 2013 and 2014 witnessed Beijing's increasing efforts to push political dialogue with Taipei on these issues within a "one China" framework. From Beijing's perspective, if the two sides can have political talks within the framework and can appropriately resolve the issue of Taiwan's participation in the international arena, political relations between the two sides will improve and Taiwanese political identification with the mainland will increase. When Xi Jinping met with KMT chair Chu Li-lun in May 2015, he proposed that the two sides of the Taiwan Strait work together to construct a community with a shared destiny. Xi made five suggestions about how to do this. First, the political foundation of peaceful development of cross-Strait relations would be insistence on the 1992 Consensus (the idea that Taiwan and the mainland constitute one China, though the two sides disagree regarding which of them is its legitimate representative) and opposition to Taiwanese independence. Second, the purpose of promoting peaceful development of cross-Strait relations would be to encourage a convergence of interests of the mainland and Taiwan, reach creatively mutual benefits and win-win outcomes, and increase happiness of compatriots on both sides of the Taiwan Strait. Third, fundamentally speaking, cross-Strait exchanges would be people-to-people exchanges, and heart-to-heart exchanges would be the most important. The two sides would need to enhance ethnic identity, cultural identity, and national identity. Fourth, the CCP and KMT as well as both sides of the Taiwan Strait would need to grasp the general situation and have respect for each other. They would need not only to seek convergence while keeping different views but also to work hard to reduce divergence while increasing common views and political mutual trust. Fifth, the great rejuvenation of the Chinese nation would presuppose the cooperation of both sides. Responding to Xi Jinping's call, the PRC's TAO made it clear that Taiwan was welcome to join the infrastructure development of the so-called "One Belt and One Road" (a network of railways, roads, pipelines, and utility grids linking China to West Asia, Central Asia, parts of South Asia, and Europe) and to participate in the Beijing-initiated Asian Infrastructure Investment Bank in an appropriate capacity.

Beijing's efforts to build a cross-Strait community with a shared destiny have been interrupted by political changes in Taiwan. As the Sunflower Movement protests on March 18 and the outcome of Taiwan's local elections in November 2014 suggested, the January 2016 presidential elections led to another power turnover from the pro-status quo KMT back to the proindependence DPP. Because the ruling DPP does not want to accept the 1992 Consensus, the official and semiofficial relations between the two sides have been broken off, and new agreements for economic and cultural exchanges between the Association for Relations across the Taiwan Strait on the mainland and the Straits Exchange Foundation in Taiwan cannot be reached. Just as Xi Jinping predicted one year earlier, if the foundation of 1992 Consensus was damaged, cross-Strait relations would return to the earlier situation of chaos and instability.[27]

This does not mean that Beijing will necessarily employ military means against Taiwan. Reflecting a fundamental change in China's international standing, Beijing's grand strategy of "peaceful development through reform and opening" has led to the mainland's interdependence with the outside world, especially the Asia-Pacific region.[28] The mainland's growing national capacity has increased its leverage to use either hard or soft tactics, making hard tactics harder and soft tactics softer. Without political consensus between Beijing and the new leadership in post-Ma Taiwan, it is possible that small diplomatic allies of Taiwan will switch their diplomatic ties to the mainland. From the mainland perspective, the issue of Taiwan's international participation can be resolved only within the "one-China" framework. As long as Taipei does not attempt to change the status quo of cross-Strait relations in general and to increase its diplomatic allies in particular, Beijing does not need to cut off all of Taiwan's external ties during the transitory period prior to China's reunification. While the maintenance of twenty or so diplomatic allies has only symbolic meaning for Taiwan's foreign relations, their reduction would become a hot issue on an island torn by acute confrontation between the two main parties. Should this happen, Taipei might react strongly against Beijing in one way or another, thus bringing previous tensions back to the Taiwan Strait.

In this situation, Beijing is maintaining its strategy of asymmetric engagement with the two main parties in Taiwan, preferring the KMT to the DPP. The main engines for cross-Strait relations, therefore, are city-to-city and people-to-people exchanges, in addition to the present CCP-KMT platform. However, the September 2016 mainland trip of local executives from one city and seven counties that are under the control of the "Blue" camp (parties more amenable to rapprochement or eventual unification with China, such as the KMT), suggests Beijing's reluctance to have city-to-city exchanges with Green (more proindependence parties such as the DPP) mayors and magistrates unless they accept the "one-China" framework. At a lower level, city districts and neighborhoods, towns and townships, and social groups may become important units for exchange and cooperation. By fostering such connections, the mainland government hopes that its beneficial measures of economic exchange with Taiwan will be felt as much by ordinary Taiwanese people, particularly youth, as by big businesspeople. As TAO director Zhang Zhijun remarked in September 19, 2016, Beijing will insist on the 1992 Consensus, oppose Taiwanese independence, promote peaceful development of cross-Strait relations, and encourage common feelings and benefits of people on both sides of the Taiwan Strait.[29]

RESPECTING EACH OTHER'S SOCIAL SYSTEM

Another issue regarding national political identity is the two sides' different political institutions. Beijing has tried to resolve this structural problem by increasing the attractiveness of the unification model to Taiwan. According to the formula of "one country, two systems," Taiwan could maintain its own economic, political, and social systems unchanged after unification. Although a postunification China would remain a unitary state, the executive, legislative, and judicial powers enjoyed by Taiwan would surely strain the institutional boundaries of a unitary government and make the relation between mainland and Taiwanese administrations more like that of a federal authority to a state authority. In Taiwan, unlike Hong Kong, political autonomy is rooted in the legal system, rather than being delegated by the central government in the form of basic laws. After unification, Taiwan would retain the right to exercise some sovereign-related powers while giving up other jurisdictions such as national defense and diplomacy, resulting in a quasi-federal relationship between Beijing and Taipei.[30]

The desirability and feasibility of "one country, two systems" are related to two issues facing a rising China: nation building and institution building. Most Chinese studies of "one country, two systems" have focused on the first issue while marginalizing the second. Will the two different economic, social, and political systems coexist forever? How can they work without any conflicts? Will the two systems reduce institutional gaps between them through long coexistence and mutual learning?

In the long process of China's modernization, the PRC has experienced several stages of institution building. In the first three decades from 1949 to 1978, the regime believed that the socialist system was vastly superior to the capitalist system and would inevitably replace it. Since reform and opening started in 1979, Beijing has relied more on the uniqueness of Chinese circumstances to justify socialism in general and socialist democracy in particular for the Chinese mainland. According to a white paper, entitled *Building Political Democracy in China*, that was issued by the Chinese government in 2005, there is no single, absolute, and universally applicable democratic model in the world.[31] In the revised party charter, eliminating class exploitation and social polarization is no longer considered a basic feature of socialism. Moreover, socialist and communist ideals are regarded as suitable to Chinese circumstances and not the only path for other peoples in the world. Although the party at its Eighteenth National Congress in 2012 called for people to retain their confidence in socialism and its theories and institutions, it still defined socialism as suitable to the Chinese situation, rather than as the universal truth for all human beings. Beijing's "one country, two systems" formula, a product of the reform era, seems to match nicely with its outlook on institutional development in the contemporary world, assuming different social systems can coexist and learn from each other, as Jiang Zemin recognized one decade ago.[32]

Whereas "one country, two systems" has been the standard model chosen by Deng Xiaoping and followed by successive Chinese leaders, Xi Jinping has attempted to make it acceptable to Taiwan by repeating that the Taiwanese model of "one country, two systems" is different from the Hong Kong model, which is particularly important in the wake of social protests in Hong Kong against the 2017 electoral formula approved by Beijing. When meeting with Lien Chan in February 2014, Xi expressed his understanding that the Taiwanese people *cherish* (*zhenshi*) the social system and living style they have chosen for themselves. While *social system* here obviously includes both economic and political systems, the word *cherish* suggested that these systems were good for Taiwan and therefore should be appreciated. According to Xi, the mainland not only respects the social system and living style in Taiwan but also wants to share the developmental opportunities on the mainland with the Taiwanese people.[33] When Yu Zhengsheng, chair of the Chinese People's Political Consultation Conference, made opening remarks at the Sixth Strait Forum, he reiterated Beijing's respect for the Taiwanese social system and lifestyle and added *values* and ideas to the list.[34] TAO director Zhang Zhijun repeated what Xi had told Lien Chan while meeting with Kaohsiung mayor Chen Chu in June 2014. Xi's September 2014 remarks on "one country, two systems" when he met with several prounification or prointegration delegations from Taiwan could be interpreted from the same perspective.

Many politicians in Taiwan have argued that the lack of collective identity between the two sides of the Taiwan Strait is primarily due to different social systems, a democratized Taiwan as opposed to an undemocratic mainland, and have insisted on the importance of Taiwanese democracy as a defense tactic against unification pressure from the mainland.[35] According to Lin Xinhua from Taiwan, however, the fact that about one million Taiwanese businesspeople live on the mainland with a social system different from that of Taiwan is quite unusual, suggesting that institutional disparity per se cannot prevent people of the two sides from coming together.[36] For Li Peng of Xiamen University, institutional differences between the two societies should not become problematic as long as each side can humbly and sincerely consider these differences.[37]

This does not mean that the issue of institutional difference, let alone conflict, can be totally neglected. As mentioned above, institutional identification is one of the important elements in national identity. Since the two sides have different political, economic, and social systems, they need to find more commonalities in their institutions, particular in terms of governance. As a matter of fact, the economic system on the mainland has changed dramatically from a planned economy to a market economy over the past thirty-five years, making theoretic differences between capitalism and socialism in the Chinese context increasingly insignificant and Taiwanese businesspeople on the mainland less and less uncomfortable. With the growth of civil society, social organizations, and human rights on the mainland, the institutional gap between the two sides of the Taiwan Strait has been greatly reduced. As the mainland has striven to enhance state governance capacities in recent years, Taiwan's experience in governance and public policies can provide useful guidance. While the spirit of "one country, two systems" suggests that different societies can have their respective institutions, accommodating two systems in one country requires overlapping institutional linkages to some degree. As a first step, Taiwanese neighborhood officials (*lizhang*) and mainland officials at the equivalent level in Shanghai have paid mutual visits and shared their worksite experience. This practice may help to reduce the institutional gap between the two sides at the local level. City-to-city exchanges have also helped to improve government performance and the quality of municipal services on the mainland through learning experience.

CONCLUSION

The growing sense of a national identity in Taiwan, both on cultural/ethnical dimensions and on political/civic dimensions, has presented a challenge to the mainland's efforts to reconstruct Chinese national identity in modern times. Most people in Taiwan identify themselves as Taiwanese from a civic and political perspective, and a significant portion, though less than one-quarter, would like Taiwan to be independent sooner or later. The gap between Taiwanese consciousness (*Taiwan yishi*) and the idea of Taiwanese independence is well perceived by Beijing, which has tried its best to accommodate Taiwanese culture under the big umbrella of Chinese culture. That the overwhelming majority of people in Taiwan also recognize they are part of the Chinese nation seems like a good message for a confident Beijing. However, more people in Taiwan prefer independence to unification, and the majority of them would not accept unification with the mainland even if the latter had democratic institutions as Taiwan does.

Despite Beijing's efforts to lay economic, cultural, social, and political foundations for peaceful development of cross-Strait relations as a step toward its final goal of unification, it has a long way to go. Taiwanese feelings toward economic benefits offered by the mainland are neutralized by social dislocation on the island; similar historical and cultural backgrounds of the two sides were interrupted by Japanese colonial rule and long-existing separate governments thereafter; and periods of political détente have been interrupted by crises. All these obstacles have suggested to the mainland that the reconstruction of a shared Chinese national identity across the Taiwan Strait requires not only economic modernization and integration, mutual cultural exchange and assimilation, and reinterpretation of contemporary Chinese history and political relations between the two entities prior to China's reunification but also improvement of public governance and political engineering on the mainland. In other words, the reconstruction of Chinese national identity is a long-term project involving all people on both sides of the Taiwan Strait.

NOTES

1. Hu Jintao, "Let Us Join Hands to Promote the Peaceful Development of Cross-Straits Relations and Strive with a United Resolve for the Great Rejuvenation of the Chinese Nation," speech presented at the Forum Marking the Thirtieth Anniversary of the Issuance of a Message to Compatriots in Taiwan, December 31, 2008, transcript, Taiwan Affairs Office of the State Council, PRC, www.gwytb.gov.cn/en/Special/Hu/201103/t20110322_1794707.htm.

2. He Donghang and Xie Weimin, "Zhongguo guojia rentong de licheng yu zhiyue yinsu" [Process of Chinese national identity formation and its constraining factors], *Makesi zhuyi yu xianshi*, no. 4 (2012): 16.

3. Yao Dali, "Bianhuazhong de guojia rentong" [National identity in transition], *Yuanda*, no. 1 (2010): 147.

4. Jin Taijun and Mi Jing, "Cong lingtu fenzhen kan quanqiuhua Beijingxia guojia rentong chonggou" [Reconstruction of national identity under the background of globalization: From the perspective of territory disputes], *Jianghai Xuekan*, no. 4 (2013): 113–14.

5. Lin Shangli, "Xiandai guojia rentong jiangou de zhengzhi luoji" [The political logic of identity construction in the modern state]," *Zhongguo shehui kexue*, no. 8 (2013): 27–28.

6. Wu Yuenong, "Qikai haixia liangan heping jiechu lianxi zhimen: Liao Chengzhi gei Chiang Ching-kuo gongkaixin de muhou gushi" [Open the door of peaceful contact between the two sides of the Taiwan Strait: Stories behind Liao Chengzhi's open letter to Chiang Ching-kuo], *Zhongshan Fengyu*, no. 3 (2004): 8–12.

7. Xi Jinping, "Gongyuan zhonghua minzu weida fuxing de zhongguo meng" [Work together to realize the Chinese dream of great rejuvenation of the Chinese nation], Xinhua Net, February 18, 2014, http://news.xinhuanet.com/politics/2014–02/19c_119394028.htm.

8. Zhang Nianchi, "Xi Jinping de yijiaqin lunshuo yu dangqian liangan guanxi" [Xi Jinping's 'one family' remarks and current cross-Strait relations], *China Review* (Hong Kong), no. 8 (August 2014): 18.

9. Peng Fuzhi, "Liangan wenhua jiaoliu zhong de zhonghua wenhua rentong yanjiu" [A study on Chinese cultural identity amid cross-Strait cultural exchanges], in *Liangan guanxi: Gongtong liyi yu hexie fazhan* [Cross-Strait relations: Common interests and harmonious development], ed. Zhou Zhihuai et al. (Beijing: Jiuzhou Press, 2010), 309.

10. Ministry of Culture of the People's Republic of China, *2013 nian wenhua fazhan tongji gongbao* [Statistical bulletin on cultural development in 2013], May 20, 2014, www.mcprc.gov.cn/whzx/whyw/201405/t20140520_433223.html, and *2014 nian wenhua fazhan tongji gongbao* [Statistical bulletin on cultural development in 2014], May 19, 2015, www.cssn.cn/zx/yw/201505/t20150519_1939724.shtml.

11. Liu Xiangping, "Laingan rentong zhi jiben yaosu jiqi dacheng lujing tanxi" [A study on basic elements of cross-Strait identification and approaches to reach the goal], *Taiwan yanjiu*, no. 1 (2011): 1–6.

12. Lowell Dittmer, "Taiwan as a Factor in China's Quest for National Identity," *Journal of Contemporary China* 15, no. 49 (November 2006): 675.

13. Xi Jinping, "Gongyuan zhonghua minzu weida fuxing de zhongguo meng."

14. "Sediq Recognized as 14th Tribe," *Taipei Times*, April 24, 2008, www.taipeitimes.com/News/taiwan/archives/2008/04/24/2003410107.

15. Roy Berman, "Wushe Then and Now," *Mutantfrog Travelogue*, September 13, 2008, www.mutantfrog.com/2008/09/13/wushe-then-and-now/; Bruce Foreman, "'Seediq Bale': Taiwan's Biggest Movie Sparks Indigenous Tourism," *CNN* News, November 23, 2011, http://travel.cnn.com/hong-kong/visit/seediq-bale-401232.

16. "Taiwan wushe shijian: Seediq beihou de gushi" [Wushe incident in Taiwan: The Story behind the *Seediq Bale*], November 29, 2012, www.360doc.com/content/12/1119/15/2068001_248784403.shtml; "Huanyuan zuren yanzhong de wushe shijian" [Recovering the Wushe incident in the eyes of people in

the tribe], *Zhongguo Xinwen Wang*, November 5, 2012, www.chinanews.com/tw/2012/11–05/4302994. shtml.

17. Xi Jinping, "Zai banfa zhongguo renmin kangri zhanzheng shengli 70 zhounian jinianzhang yishi shang de jianghua" [Address at the ceremony of issuing medals of commemoration of the seventieth anniversary of the victory of the Chinese People's War of Resistance against Japanese Aggression], *Zhongguo gongchandang xinwenwang* [Chinese Communist Party News Net], September 2, 2015, http://cpc.people.com.cn/n/2015/0902/c64094–27542514.html.

18. "China to Hold Commemorative Events on September 3," *Xinhua Net News*, August 26, 2015, http://news.xinhuanet.com/english/video/2015–08/26/c_134555451.htm.

19. See Xi Jinping, "Zai jinian zhongguo renmin kangri zhanzheng ji shiji fan fascist zhanzheng qishi zhounian zhaodaihui shang de jianghua" [Address at a reception commemorating the 70th anniversary of the victory of the Chinese People's War of Resistance Against Japanese Aggression and the World Anti-Fascist War], *Xinhua Daily Telegraph*, September 4, 2015, 1–2, 4.

20. "Xi Jinping huijian taiwan gejie renshi" [Xi Jinping meets with representatives of all walks of life in Taiwan], *Xinhua Daily Telegraph*, September 2, 2015, 1.

21. *United Daily*, September 1, 2015, A4.

22. Author's interviews, September 2, 2015, Taipei.

23. Dittmer, "Taiwan as a Factor," 675.

24. "Liangan minjian jin shouci gongji Jinmen zhanyi zhenwang jiangshi" [First public memorial of casualties of two fighting troops in Jinmen battle by people of the two sides of the Taiwan Strait], Xiamen Net, December 4, 2014, http://news.xmnn.cn/a/xmxw/201412/t20141204_4230944.htm.

25. Su Chi, "Ma zhengfu shiqi liangan guanxi de gaikuang he zhanwang" [The general situation and prospects of cross-Strait relations during the Ma administration, in *Liangan guanxi de jiyu yu tiaozhan* [Opportunities and challenges for cross-Strait relations], ed. Su Chi and Tung Chen-yuan (Taipei: Wunan Press, 2013), 8; Mainland Affairs Council (Taiwan), "Trade between Taiwan and Mainland China," www.mac.gov.tw/public/MMO/MAC/275_1.pdf, "Transit Trade between Taiwan and Mainland China," www.mac.gov.tw/public/MMO/MAC/275_2.pdf, "Taiwan Investment in Mainland China," www.mac.gov.tw/public/MMO/MAC/275_7.pdf, "Number of Taiwan Tourists to Mainland China," www.mac.gov.tw/public/MMO/MAC/275_14.pdf, and "Number of Mainland China Tourists to Taiwan," www.mac.gov.tw/public/MMO/MAC/275_15.pdf.

26. Yung Wei, "Toward 'Intra-national Union': Theoretical Models on Cross-Taiwan Strait Interactions," *Mainland China Studies* 45, no. 5 (September/October 2002): 23.

27. Xi Jinping's speech at meeting with Lien Chan, reported by New Chinese News Agency, February 18, 2014.

28. Jing Huang, "Hu Jintao's Pro-Status Quo Approach in Cross-Strait Relations: Building Up a One-China Framework for Eventual Reunification," in *The Changing Dynamics of the Relations among China, Taiwan, and the United States*, ed. Cal Clark (Newcastle upon Tyne: Cambridge Scholars, 2011), 149.

29. Zhang Zhijun, "Jiang caiqu cuoshi tuidong yu Taiwan ba xianshi jiaoliu" [Measures will be taken to promote exchanges with eight counties and cities in Taiwan], *People's Daily* (Overseas edition) September 19, 2016, 3.

30. Wang Yingjin, "Guanyu yiguo liangzhi Taiwan moshi de xin gouxiang" [New thinking on the Taiwan model of "one country, two systems"], *Taiwan yanjiu jikan*, no. 6 (2009): 4.

31. State Council Information Office, PRC, Building of Political Democracy in China, 2005, www.china.org.cn/english/2005/Oct/145718.htm.

32. Jiang Zemin, speech at the Central Party School, May 31, 2002, New Chinese News Agency, www.xinhuanet.com.

33. Xi Jinping, speech at meeting with Lien Chan, reported by New Chinese News Agency, February 18, 2014.

34. Yu Zhengsheng, Opening remarks at the Sixth Strait Forum, Zhongguo Taiwan wang [China Taiwan Web], June 15, 2014.

35. Zhang Yachung, *Liangan tonghe lun* [On integrating the two sides of the Taiwan Strait] (Taipei: Shengzhi Cultural Publishing, 2000), 130.

36. Lin Xinhua, *Chaoguojia shehuixue: Liangan guanxi zhong de xin Taiwan shehui* [Transnational sociology: A new Taiwanese society in cross-Strait relations] (Taipei: Weber Culture International Publishing, 2003), 199.

37. Li Peng, "Liangan yijiaqin linian xia de jiangxinbixin siwei qianxi" [An analysis on the thinking of 'put oneself in somebody else's position' under the idea that compatriots from both sides of the Taiwan Straits are of one family], *Taiwan yanjiu jikan*, no. 1 (2015): 7.

6

Chinese Youth Nationalism in a Pressure Cooker

Rou-lan Chen

The first decade of the twenty-first century witnessed an explosion of anger among Chinese youth.[1] In contrast to the peasants and workers who erupted in anger over their marginalization from China's economic boom, the flame of the raging youth (*fenqing*) burned in the name of patriotism. In the wake of the 1999 bombing of the Chinese embassy in Belgrade, the 2001 China-US aircraft collision, the 2008 Beijing Olympics, and the 2012 disputes over the Diaoyu Islands (referred to as the Senkaku Islands by Japan), the power of spontaneous mass protest spread like a raging fire to include an enormous number of students, particularly in September 2012, when the Japanese government purchased the Diaoyu Islands, triggering indignant protests in as many as one hundred cities in China. Hundreds of thousands of young people participated in massive rallies and took to the streets with violence, vandalism, and arson. In fact, the dispute over the Diaoyu Islands was not new. It had been recurring over the previous three decades. In 1972, at the end of the American occupation of Okinawa, the Japanese government resumed its administration of the Diaoyu Islands, sparking the dispute, which never burnt out. For the first time, the Republic of China (ROC) officially claimed the Diaoyu Islands as a part of Taiwan, which presumably should have been returned to Chinese jurisdiction in 1972. To dispute the original Japanese claim of sovereignty over the Diaoyu Islands, massive student national movements erupted in Taiwan through the 1970s. In 1996, when Japanese right-wingers erected a lighthouse on the main island, protesters in Taiwan and Hong Kong again marched through the streets and attempted to land on the Diaoyu Islands.

It was the first time as well that the Kuomintang (KMT) government allowed a large-scale student movement in Taiwan. The dilemma was that nationalism inevitably triggered social mobilization, which, if uncontrolled, could easily be turned against the authoritarian KMT regime. In a sense, the youth nationalism of the 1970s was revived by the KMT as a displacement of affect over the diminishing legitimacy of Chinese identity in Taiwan. The 1970s saw a switch in diplomatic recognitions from the ROC to the People's Republic of China (PRC). At the same time, Taiwan's economic growth was accompanied by rising pressure for far-reaching changes in governance. However, with the KMT government tightly restricting political participation, young people had nowhere to voice their anxieties and to reassert their identity. To reclaim the legitimacy of the KMT and maintain political stability, the KMT instigated nationalism with a clear enemy (Japan) as an efficient strategy to divert youth's attention from the legitimacy problem and to elicit political support. Hence, the Diaoyu Islands functioned as a condensation symbol for irredentist nationalism, on the basis of a discourse of Chinese territory being taken away from the self by Japan. Through new editions of geographic maps and historical textbooks in 1972, the Diaoyu Islands were constructed as China's lost land. In short, the 1972 Diaoyu Islands movement arose from Taiwan's international isolation coupled with its fast-growing economy, which led to a state of anomie in which young people suffered from identity crisis and powerlessness in the market economy.[2] Therefore, it is reasonable to infer that in the 2000s the weakening hold of Chinese identity in Taiwan and the Taiwan-centered pedagogy found in school curricula tended to deflate enthusiasm for the movement to protect the Diaoyu Islands (Baodiao), which the younger generation in Taiwan associated with support for cross-Strait reunification.[3] We hardly see online anti-Japan protests among Taiwan's youth before Japan's 2012 nationalization of the Diaoyu Islands.

Before 2012, the Chinese Communist Party (CCP) remained at a distance from the dispute. When the first two waves of protests over the Diaoyu Islands flared in 1972 and 1996, major anti-Japanese demonstrations were held in Taiwan and Hong Kong but not in Beijing. The authorities in China suppressed xenophobia and decided to "shelve the dispute" to be resolved in the future.[4] Why was Chinese youth nationalism regarding the Diaoyu Islands disputes revived in 2012? Some observers attributed the rise of Chinese nationalism to the state's construction. They regarded the new nationalism of the post-1980 generation as "official nationalism" or "pragmatic nationalism," anchored in a patriotic ethos that looked to the CCP as a guardian of the national interest.[5] Specifically, they saw it as the creation of the CCP's "Patriotic Education Campaign" of the 1990s and 2000s, which attempted to shore up the party's declining legitimacy by focusing on China's historic glory and the subsequent "hundred years of humiliation," through repeated submission to foreign powers, that began with the First Opium War in the nineteenth century.[6] They also noted that, by using the United States as a reference group, the authorities aroused xenophobia to consolidate the communist regime.[7] Other scholars believed that the 1990s witnessed as well the emergence of a popular nationalism that should not be conflated with official nationalism. Unable to suppress the protesters, the CPP was losing control over nationalist discourse and was forced to plead with protesters.[8] Increasingly scholars also related grassroots nationalism to the rise of the Internet, which unified the Chinese cyber community against foreign pressure. Chinese cyber nationalists have been utilizing the Internet as a communication center, organizational platform, and implementation channel for their cause.[9]

However, without knowing the mind-set of Chinese youth, we cannot explain why in 2012 the once unimportant Diaoyu Islands became an indivisible part of China for the younger generation. Why did protests over the Diaoyu Islands spread so rapidly and then turn violent? To explore these questions, this chapter is divided into two parts. The first part aims at investigating the process by which the Diaoyu Islands made their way into the imagination of the younger generation. In the process of identity construction, Taiwan and Japan served as important reference groups for Chinese youths. The second part hinges on why Chinese youth movements took a nationalist turn and galvanized millions in the disputes over the Diaoyu Islands in 2012. In many ways China's situation was analogous to the crisis over the Diaoyu Islands in Taiwan in 1972. Specifically, I posit that the "raging youth" phenomenon derives from ambivalence between national pride and disappointment in the CCP. What made the post-1980 generation proud yet ashamed? This chapter brings to light the structural factors that facilitated the youth movements in 2012. After three decades of economic reform, the CCP still has a tight grip on the political system and legitimates itself by maintaining high economic growth. I will show how China's youth, given a limited organizational life, sanctioned or monitored by the state, found in the Internet a public space in which to vent their anger, circulate ideas, and engage in civil actions, all of which aided their collective pursuit of national identity. Finally, we show how interactions between the Internet and globalization precipitated the resurgence of an outraged nationalism in contemporary China. Globalization unavoidably brings people together, and this paper investigates why, in an age boasting an upsurge in Internet access, Chinese identity is always affirmed against a foreign enemy.

WHY THE DIAOYU ISLANDS?

Before we begin the analysis of the "raging youth" phenomenon in 2012, it is crucial to know when and how Chinese youth expanded their imagination of China's boundaries to the Diaoyu Islands. As in Taiwan in the 1970s, the authorities made the Diaoyu Islands a part of the imagined community for Chinese youth to ensure their own legitimacy and adjust to the changing international and domestic conditions.

Shelving the Dispute

In 1968, the discovery of massive oil deposits near the East China Sea for the first time put the Diaoyu Islands in the spotlight. Before then, neither China nor Taiwan had shown any interest in these uninhabited and barren islands. The dispute over the Diaoyu Islands was sparked in 1972, when the United States turned over administrative rights of the islands to Japan, as stipulated by the Okinawa Reversion Treaty. The core of the controversy lay in whether the Diaoyu Islands had belonged to Taiwan in April 1895, at which time, under the Shimonoseki Treaty, the Chinese (Qing) government had ceded Taiwan and "all islands pertaining to it" to Japan. With the end of the Second World War, all Chinese-ceded territory had to be returned to China, according to the provisions of the Cairo Declaration of 1943, the Potsdam Proclamation of 1945, and the Treaty of Peace with Japan of 1952. Both the PRC and the ROC claimed the Diaoyu Islands as a part of Taiwan, which presumably should have been returned to Chinese jurisdiction in 1972.

Japan originally claimed sovereignty over the Diaoyu Islands in 1884 on the basis of the principle of *terra nullius* and incorporated them into Japan in January 1895. In protest, massive student national movements erupted in Taiwan and Hong Kong through the 1970s but, surprisingly, not in Beijing. Between 1966 and 1976, Chinese young people were embroiled in the Cultural Revolution, with a large number of urban youth being transferred to rural regions through the Down to the Countryside Movement. Even though schools resumed regular schedules in 1978, the curriculum in the 1980s was dominated by revolutionary views with the purpose of restoring the CCP's legitimacy.[10] Hence, the Chinese Cultural Revolution and Reform generations were not concerned with the Diaoyu Islands. More importantly, in the 1970s, both Japan and the United States were in the midst of approaching China to normalize diplomatic relations. Given his keen interest in having the PRC replace the ROC as the only legitimate representative of China in the international arena, Deng Xiaoping decided to downplay the sovereignty dispute with Japan and leave the issue to future generations in 1972 and 1978.

The Shadow of Taiwan and Japanese Actions

After three decades of silence, the CCP started to voice its concern over the Diaoyu Islands. From the 1970s until the mid-1990s, what had kept the territorial dispute between Tokyo and Beijing under control was a tacit agreement to "shelve the dispute."[11] Nevertheless, since the mid-1990s Japanese politics has grown increasingly nationalistic and has resulted in flaring tensions in Asia. In 1996, soon after the Japanese government announced the two hundred nautical miles centering on the Senkaku Islands as the Japanese Exclusive Economic Zone (EEZ), a Japanese nationalist group rebuilt a lighthouse on one of the disputed islands, outraging Chinese nationalists in Taiwan and Hong Kong. The rise of Japanese right-wing nationalism became obvious when Shintaro Ishihara, who wrote a patriotic book entitled *A Japan That Can Say No* in 1989 and announced a plan by the Tokyo Metropolitan Government to purchase the Senkaku Islands in April 2012 and fortify them, was elected mayor of Tokyo in 1999. Since 2000, the Japanese government has increased police patrols of the disputed Senkaku Islands to give evidence of Japan's effective control. As a result of Japan's 2005 textbook screening, the number of references to the Senkaku Islands increased in the textbooks of primary and secondary schools to support an official statement about there being "no territorial problem" over the Senkaku Islands with Taiwan and China.[12] For the CCP leadership, losing the tug-of-war over sovereignty of the Diaoyu Islands to Japan not only would undermine its legitimacy but also could jeopardize its economic interest in the massive oil deposits near the islands.

Meanwhile, the trajectory of Taiwan's future shifted closer toward independence following the victories of Lee Teng-hui in the 1996 presidential election and of the Democratic Progressive Party (DPP) in the two subsequent ones. During this period, the Taiwan government made only lukewarm statements to claim the ROC's sovereignty over the disputed islands. As Taiwanese nationalism became the top issue of the political platform, the enthusiasm for the movement to protect the Diaoyu Islands ran low. The issue of the Diaoyu Islands, which the younger generation in Taiwan associated with support for cross-Strait reunification, was labeled "politically incorrect." In 1996, the Japanese claim on the EEZ around the Diaoyu Islands led Lee Teng-hui to reiterate the ROC's sovereignty over the disputed islands, but he also set aside sovereignty disputes to enable fisheries negotiations with Japan. During the DPP period (2000–2008) as well, the Taiwanese government was more concerned to negotiate the historic fishing rights of Taiwanese fishermen around the disputed waters with Japan. In February 2005, a lighthouse that had been erected on the largest of the Diaoyu Islands by Japanese activists in 1978 came under Japanese government control. In June, Japan Coast Guard vessels chased away Taiwanese fishing boats, arousing protests among Taiwanese fishermen and Diaoyu Islands activists. In response to the anger of the fishermen, Chen Shui-bian sent out patrol ships to protect Taiwanese fishing boats and even set foot on the Pengjia Islet to claim Taiwan's sovereignty over the Diaoyu Islands. At the same time, he stated that the Taiwan government should handle the fishing rights issue separately from the sovereignty issue to avoid complicating the situation and escalating tensions. KMT legislators criticized Chen Shui-bian's response as merely "making a show," and Taipei's mayor, Ma Ying-jeou, said it showed a lack of courage.

After years of playing down the sovereignty issue, Taiwan and Japan finally made a diplomatic breakthrough in late August 2005. The Japanese Diet passed legislation to give Taiwanese a visa waiver but made no conciliatory offer to China. Hence, this move was seen as a break from Japan's balancing act on the cross-Strait issue. The sovereignty issue in Taiwan touched a raw nerve in China, particularly after

Lee Teng-hui declared "special state-to-state relations" to define the relationship between Taiwan and China in 1999 and then declared—in a 2002 interview carried in a local daily in Okinawa Prefecture—that the Diaoyu Islands actually belonged to Japan.[13] For China, reassertion of its sovereignty over the Diaoyu Islands became essential, as the islands were directly related to China's claim to Taiwan, and vice versa. National unity was essential to reinforce the CCP's legitimacy, which was in decline after the collapse of the Soviet Union. In short, various political changes in Japan and in Taiwan had eroded China's longtime policy of "shelving the dispute."

The Construction of an Imagined Community through Linkages with Taiwan

At the beginning of the twenty-first century, the CCP embarked on a deliberate publicity campaign to instill in Chinese youth the vision of the Diaoyu Islands as an inseparable Chinese territory. As in Japan, textbooks are in the front line of China's propaganda to stir up patriotism. In 2001, the PRC's Ministry of Education issued the *Basic Education Curriculum Reform Outline (Trial)*, which put a central focus on the two dominant themes of Chinese patriotic education: Chinese tradition and history, and national unity and territorial integrity.[14] Moreover, new teaching manuals published by the People's Education Press were changed to reflect the CCP's new stance on its territorial claims. For example, on the topic "Taiwan: Part of the Sacred Territory of China" in year 8's *Geography I*, teachers are encouraged to guide students through maps to identify places in Taiwan and islands affiliated with it, including the Diaoyu Islands. In "Geography of the Ocean" in the high school curriculum, the learning goal is to foster sovereignty consciousness by outlining China's natural ocean resources. To achieve that goal, the suggested teaching instruction is to discuss the illegal seizure of islands in the East and South China Seas and show how that poses a threat to China's interest and to its freedom of navigation.[15] China is also embroiled in a map battle with Japan to support its historical claims and legal right over the Diaoyu Islands. Like all scholars on the subject, CCP officials cite a collection of historical maps dating back to the sixteenth century, which include the map *Coastal Defense Stretching Thousands of Miles*, showing that the Diaoyu Islands were incorporated into China's maritime defense in 1561.[16] Several other maps show the Diaoyu Islands serving as navigational aids for tributary missions between China and the Ryukyu Kingdom. The *Great Universal Geographic Map* drawn in 1767 shows that the Diaoyu Islands, as part of Taiwan's fishing grounds, were included in the territory of the Qing Empire. The *Map of East China Sea Littoral States* created by the French cartographer Pierre M. Lapie in 1809 colored Diaoyu Dao, Huangwei Yu, and Chiwei Yu the same color as Taiwan. Those maps are considered to have been created on the premise that the Diaoyu Islands were part of Chinese territory prior to the sixteenth century and were not *terra nullius* before 1885, as claimed by Japan.

Through discourses of mapping, the Diaoyu Islands as part of Chinese national community have made their way into the imagination of the young generation.

China also reinforced the concept of the Diaoyu Islands as an inherent part of the territory of the PRC through several practical actions designed to strengthen the PRC's claims over the disputed islands. In 2008, soon after Ma Ying-jeou took the oath of office as the president of the ROC, a Taiwanese fishing ship, the *Lien Ho*, sank following a collision with a Japan Coast Guard vessel near the Diaoyu Islands. The Ma administration immediately demanded a public apology and compensation for the *Lien Ho*, suspended fisheries negotiations, and recalled Hsu Shih-kai, Taiwan's envoy to Japan, who had handled bilateral ties between Taiwan and Japan in absence of an official diplomatic relationship, for a decade. The KMT legislators went further to organize a voyage to the disputed waters aboard a navy La Fayette frigate. DPP legislators saw these moves as paving the way to forging closer ties with Beijing because the first Chen-Chiang summit of cross-Strait meetings, after a decade-long stalemate between Taiwan and China, was to take place in a week in Beijing. For China, it was the beginning of an attempt to create a community of interest on the issue with Taipei. Four days after the cross-Strait summit, China sent two patrol boats to the East China Sea to challenge Japan's effective control for the first time. This act, covered to the saturation point by China's state-controlled media, marked a new phase in the troubled relationship between China and Japan, signifying the end of "shelving the dispute." Since 2010, when a Chinese fishing trawler collided with Japanese Coast Guard boats, China began to dispatch patrol ships to the disputed waters on a regular basis.

China has since gained more momentum on disputes over the Diaoyu Islands and has marginalized Taiwan's response on this issue. In August 2012, to affirm Taiwan's position on disputed waters, the Ma administration proposed the East China Sea Peace Initiative—a plan that aims at shelving disputes and peacefully resolving disputes in the East China Sea by reciprocal negotiation and cooperative development. The DPP regarded this initiative as supporting the one-China principle because it allowed the PRC to form a community of interest with Taiwan on the sovereignty claims over the Diaoyu Islands. However, the response from Beijing was less than enthusiastic. The director of China's Taiwan Affairs Office, Wang Yi, commented—in a underwhelming way—that China was aware of the initiative but that China's standpoint on the East China Sea had always been crystal clear. To underline China's dominance on the issue of the Diaoyu Islands, Chinese state media and online censors downplayed coverage of the initiative.

RESEARCH METHODS

On September 11, 2012, a week before the eighty-first anniversary of the Manchurian incident, the Japanese government purchased three of the five Diaoyu Islands, causing uproar in as many as one hundred cities in China and sparking street protests of one million young people. Why did a piece of land on a map emerge as a powerful and attractive vision of Chinese youth nationalism in 2012? Why did national sentiments turn into a "rage" among Chinese youth?

Conceptualization

Answering these questions first requires defining *Chinese nationalism*, *youth*, and *outrage*. Consideration of the full range of scholarship on Chinese nationalism, which takes on different meanings at different junctures in Chinese history and for various scholars, is beyond this chapter's scope. In this study *Chinese nationalism* denotes patriotism, love, loyalty, and devotion to China. *Youth* refers to the post-1980 generation, or "millennials" who grew up witnessing China's reform and opening and who experienced the Tiananmen incident and the Patriotic Education Campaign. In theory, a group that shares "common historical memories due to the fact that they were born in the same period and lived through the same political and economic development" during adolescence is regarded as a "political generation."[17] On the basis of this definition, the people in China can be divided into five political generations: the war generation (before 1943), the Cultural Revolution generation (1944–61), the Reform generation (1962–80), the post-1980 generation (1981–90), and the post-1990 generation (1991 to the present). *Outrage* in this study is defined as a feeling of righteous anger in defense of China's survival and prosperity.

Data

To explore its research questions, this chapter relies on three complementary forms of data. First, the Strong Nation Forum plays an integral part in this chapter's primary research. It is a Chinese bulletin board on the website of the *People's Daily* and was created in 1999 to serve as an outlet for Chinese anger over the US bombing of the Chinese Embassy in Belgrade. Soon after the Strong Nation Forum appeared online, it became the most important online forum for nationalist sentiments. As shown in the online survey conducted by the *Liao wang dong fang zhou kan* (Oriental outlook) in 2008, 68 percent of Internet users on the Strong Nation Forum belonged to the youth cohort aged twenty to forty.[18] In this regard, the Strong Nation Forum can serve as a valid unit of observation on Chinese youth nationalism. This study reviews and analyzes comments and discussions on the Strong Nation Forum during the 2008–15 period to understand Chinese youth nationalism, its emergence, and its evolution into anti-Japan nationalism in 2012. The data for the analysis were collected via a keyword search on the Strong Nation Forum for posts containing the term *Diaoyu Islands*. Repeated postings and similar posts by the same Internet users were deleted to limit the amount of spamming on the site or to avoid the attempt of prominent users to multiply their own opinions. In total, 1,355 valid posts regarding the Diaoyu Islands were collected for analysis. Content analysis was further used to analyze this text-based data set. To avoid the disadvantages of automated (fully computerized) content analysis that tends to make arbitrary associations between words and phrases and to overlook the context of each post, posts in this study were read and coded manually.[19] We pulled as much information out of each post in a way that linked each of them to major themes and categorized them into cause, resolution, attitudes toward the CCP, Japan, the United States, and Taiwan, and so on (see table 6). Since content analysis is prone to coder bias, two coders coded and cross-checked the same data to ascertain the results' reliability. This study was complemented by two other data sources. First, it explored the online survey on patriotic and nationalistic attitudes that was conducted by the *People's Daily* in 2012 and 2013. Several characteristics of this data type were well suited for this research. Most obviously, the survey asked questions concerning individual autonomy and independent thinking for the post-1980 generation. The final data source consisted of face-to-face interviews in China, conducted in 2012 by the World Values Survey, which tracks values and cultural change over time. The target population consisted of Chinese citizens over eighteen years old. Analyzing these three data sets enabled us to investigate the nature of Chinese nationalism and why Chinese youth nationalism erupted in 2012.

Limitations of the Data

Using the Strong Nation Forum as our unit of observation met with some skepticism regarding selection bias. Two factors contribute to possible bias. The first is that rural Internet penetration in China remained roughly 27.5 percent compared to 62 percent in urban areas in 2013. This led to the underrepresentation of rural youth in our sample. Although just over half of the rural population uses the Internet, a relatively larger percentage (55.3 percent) of them belong to the 20–40 age bracket, almost two-thirds of the people in rural areas in 2013, similar to the ratio in the cities.[20] In this regard, we can rule out the first concern about selection bias. The second selection bias involves the Strong Nation Forum's management by the *People's Daily*, an organ of the CCP's Central Committee. The general guidelines of the Strong Nation Forum involve prohibitions and censorship of inciting subversion of state power, separatist movements, and illegal activities.[21] Messages on sensitive topics such as Tiananmen and Falun Gong certainly cannot appear. If discussions are beyond the CCP's tolerance limits, webmasters will delete all postings and block the IP addresses and registered names. To some extent, freedom of speech on the Web is constrained, leading to a bias in public opinion. However, the government has been relatively tolerant toward online discussions that are critical of its policies but appeal to nationalist sentiments. The estimated deletion rate is about 1 to 1.5 percent.[22] Furthermore, as online political forums hosted by SINA, Tianya, and many other privately operated media have multiplied, is the CCP has become less likely to turn against Internet users with a zealous crackdown on the Strong Nation Forum. In general, the Strong Nation Forum is probably a good venue for observing Chinese youth nationalism because that is where it appears in great profusion. Using the online survey as research data might also encounter a self-selection bias. The problem is that since respondents are allowed to decide whether they want to participate in a survey, specific groups turn out to be overrepresented, such as youth cohorts, the middle class, and people with higher education. As a result, the respondents participating in online surveys will not represent the entire population. However, we can mitigate this concern about self-selection bias, since this study aims to study youth, not the general population.

THE 2012 DIAOYU ISLANDS INCIDENT: A "RAGING YOUTH" PHENOMENON

Why did Chinese youth nationalism revive and escalate in 2012? Despite the Chinese government's prohibition, Chinese Internet users launched a widespread campaign on the Web to boycott Japanese products, leading to a plunge in the sales of Japanese automobiles and consequently forcing Toyota and Honda to temporarily halt production in China. Did the movement simply reflect an imagined community or historical hatred revived in textbooks, or did it reflect national pride in China's exceptional economic growth, eager to transcend conditions of oppression?

Driven by Ambivalence toward the CCP

The empirical analysis shows the "raging youth" phenomenon to derive from ambivalence between national pride and disappointment in the CCP. As evident in the Strong Nation Forum (table 6), about 8.5 of the Internet posts mentioned that since ancient times China had had indisputable sovereignty over the Diaoyu Islands, now illegally occupied by Japan. As seen in the World Values Survey in 2012 (table 7), 91.4 percent of the post-1980 generation were proud of China, and 84.1 percent were willing to fight for China in the event of a war, with an average 15 percent higher than the previous two generations. However, regarding the 2012 Diaoyu Islands incident, the Strong Nation Forum (table 6) was flooded with messages expressing shame and disappointment in the CCP. Approximately 16.6 percent of the posts criticized the CCP for being "too soft" on Japan, specifically accusing the government officials and experts of failing to reassert sovereignty over the islands. Around 3.8 percent of the posts recognized the government's efforts of dispatching patrol ships to a disputed area but were concerned that the intention was to shift people's attention away from the economic slowdown. One user stated, "Sending patrol ships is just tiptoeing around the issue." What made the post-1980 generation proud yet ashamed?

In the early 1990s, the weakening hold of Chinese socialism due to China's market transition and the sudden collapse of the Soviet Union gave rise to the search

TABLE 6 Opinions and attitudes on the Diaoyu Islands dispute

Theme	Percentage	Subcategory	Percentage
Sarcastic messages	19.2	Controversial figures	4.1
		Mockery of the CCP	5.0
		Boasting, bragging of plans to seize islands	3.5
		Others	6.6
Disappointment with CCP	16.6		
Awareness of patrol vessels	3.8		
Diaoyu Islands as inseparable from China	8.5		
Resolution by force	12.3	Declaration of war	6.9
		Retrieve at any cost	2.8
		Inevitable war	2.6
Resolution by talk	4.3		
Taiwan factor		Unification as crucial	4.3
		Taiwan must act to signal control over Diaoyu Islands	4.2
Japan's responsibility	6.5	Japan's provocation	1.9
		Japan's ambition	4.7
US's responsibility	12.3	Obama's foreign policy pivot toward Asia	6.1
		Occupation of Okinawa	6.2
Ethnic slurs	5.8	Against Japan	3.7
		Against US	2.1
Criticizing attitudes of Chinese netizens toward Japan and US	5.9	Calling pro-Japan and pro-US attitudes unpatriotic	2.1
		Calling anti-Japan and anti-US attitudes irrational	3.8
Others	11.3		

SOURCE: Strong Nation Forum, bbs1.people.com.cn/.

for a new ideology. Announced in 1991 and fully functioning by 1994, patriotic education was initiated by Jiang Zemin in the hope of filling the ideological vacuum. The content of Chinese patriotic education, reviving patriotism as a replacement for diminishing socialism, had two dominant themes: Chinese tradition and history, and national unity and territorial integrity. Through patriotic education and educational reforms since 2001, the post-1980 Chinese have grown up embracing a commitment to safeguarding Chinese sovereignty and to defending territorial integrity. National identity for the Chinese youth was not simply evoked by a "nationalism of despair" that evoked memories of a former glory dashed by a

TABLE 7 National pride and patriotism in China in 2012

			Generation			
			War generation (before 1943)	Cultural Revolution generation (1944–61)	Reform generation (1962–80)	Post-1980 generation (1981–90)	Total
How proud of nationality	Very proud	N	41	124	212	123	500
		%	33.9	24.2	24.9	23.2	24.8
	Quite proud	N	68	313	557	362	1300
		%	56.2	61.1	65.3	68.2	64.5
	Not very proud	N	11	72	75	41	199
		%	9.1	14.1	8.8	7.7	9.9
	Not at all proud	N	1	3	9	5	18
		%	0.8	0.6	1.1	0.9	0.9
	Total	N	121	512	853	531	2017
		%	100.0	100.0	100.0	100.0	100.0
Willingness to fight for your country	Yes	N	88	392	740	470	1690
		%	70.4	70.8	81.6	84.1	78.8
	No	N	37	162	167	89	455
		%	29.6	29.2	18.4	15.9	21.2
	Total	N	125	554	907	559	2145
		%	100.0	100.0	100.0	100.0	100.0

SOURCE: World Values Survey in China (2012). WVS [World Values Survey], Wave 6 (2010–2014), China 2012, conducted by the Research Center for Contemporary China (RCCC) at Peking University in 2012. Data can be retrieved from www.worldvaluessurvey.org/WVSDocumentationWV6.jsp.

NOTE: % in the parentheses is the row percentage.

subsequent "century of humiliation."[23] Built on thirty years of economic reforms and opening to the world, China's remarkable economic growth boosted national confidence to an unprecedented level to underpin a new era of Chinese nationalism. Michel Oksenberg described it as a "confident nationalism," patient and moderate, rooted in the assurance that China could eventually regain its greatness through economic growth.[24] By and large, post-1980 Chinese have believed in a strong China and the idea that "China can say no" to US hegemony and assert itself against other countries attempting to dominate it. Hence, seeing the Diaoyu Islands as a vital part of the motherland, many of the Internet users demanded tougher actions to defend them. Although 4.3 percent of the posts on the Strong Nation Forum voiced concern for a peaceful resolution through negotiations or economic sanctions, approximately 6.9 percent urged a declaration of war against Japan (table 6). "It is a piece of cake because we have nuclear weapons." Around 2.8 percent of the posts claimed that China should retrieve the islands at any cost, and 2.6 percent believed that war was inevitable. Some posts (4.3 percent) pointed out that the fundamental cause of the territorial dispute between China and Japan was Taiwan's status as an inalienable part of China. "To facilitate cross-Strait unification would make things easier." Taken together, 12.3 percent of the messages approved of using force to resolve the issue. In conclusion, as a consequence of patriotic education and China's exceptional growth, Chinese youth increasingly took pride in China's growing status and felt a strong obligation to defend China from hostile external forces.

Nevertheless, with China's integration into the world economy, it is not easy for China to say no. It is widely acknowledged that China's rapid integration into the global economy has heightened interstate conflicts. Simultaneously maintaining patriotism and prioritizing economic development has become especially difficult for the authorities in Beijing.[25] In December 2003, Chinese premier Wen Jiabo used the term *peaceful rise* in his speech at Harvard University.[26] Since then, a peaceful rise to power, backed up by economic development, has been the main priority of CCP leaders. The party has demonstrated its peaceful attitude by actively participating in international organizations, hosting the Olympic Games, and being involved in multilateral trade negotiations with as many as twelve countries. In 2012, at the eighteenth conference of the CCP, market pressures simultaneous with mainstream public demand for tough responses to Japan created a dilemma for Xi Jinping, the new general secretary of the CCP. As ongoing territorial disputes over the Diaoyu Islands have hampered the progress of the China-Japan-South Korea Free Trade Agreement (FTA) negotiations, the return of the United States to the Asia-Pacific region has posed a critical challenge to China's political and economic clout. Specifically, negotiations have been under way since 2010 to create the US-led Trans-Pacific Partnership (TPP), which will be the world's largest free trade zone, in an attempt to contain China's rise. These efforts make more urgent the need for China to aggressively seek barrier-lowering FTAs with Japan and South Korea to harness the huge trade potential within ASEAN and across the Pacific Rim. China knows very well the cost of pushing Japan toward a military response. Although Chinese authorities have dispatched a marine surveillance plane and patrol vessels to enter the disputed waters to prove that Japan had no exclusive control over the islands, the CCP has since then made no attempt to land on the islands or to impose any economic sanctions against Japan. Many Chinese youth perceive the CCP's patrols and diplomatic gestures as "making shows of defiance," in Christopher Hughes's words.[27] As a result, ambivalence toward the CCP has galvanized the post-1980 generation into action.

Facilitated by the Rise of Network Society

How can this proud generation minimize the anxieties associated with emotional conflicts between national pride and disappointment in the CPP's failure to live up to its nationalist rhetoric? As psychoanalysts point out, ontological uncertainties and existential anxiety have intensified the search for stable identities. Aggression and radical movements often develop as a consequence of anxieties and uncertainties.[28] China's youth protest movements also show these dynamics. After three decades of economic reforms, the CCP still keeps a tight grip on political control. With a limited organizational life, sanctioned or monitored by the state, young people have been deprived of channels to vent their anger. While direct elections and party turnover are not allowed in the foreseeable future, young people also lack a public arena to express their dissatisfaction. To reach a stable state of coherent attitudes on the issue of the Diaoyu Islands, Chinese youth can shift from virtual reality to collective action.

To overcome the barriers to collective action in a large group, such as a nation, two kinds of tools are required—effective institutions to mobilize people toward collective ends and unifying ideas to convince people that they share a common fate.[29] For the first tool, the advent of the Internet in China exerts a mobilizing influence by opening channels for civic engagement and the circulation of ideas. In the twenty-first century, Chinese modernization has led to a communications revolution. The rise of Internet-based communication heralds the emergence of a new form of communication: mass self-communication, which is "self-generated in content, self-directed in emission, and self-selected in reception by many that communicate with many."[30] Individuals construct their own system of mass communication and asynchronous discussion through BBS, blogs, Weibo, Tencent QQ, and other social media—a development that has facilitated civic engagement and opened new channels for the circulation of ideas. The past decade has seen a tremendous increase in Internet use in China, with over six hundred million users in 2014. The Internet has become a virtual community for China's post-1980 generation, who account for nearly two-thirds of Internet users.[31] Thus the Internet serves as a vehicle for Chinese youth to express and discuss national sentiments, as a means of fusing atomized individuals into a collectivity, and as a promoter pushing them toward protest activities.

With regard to the second tool, unifying ideas, the fast-growing educational system in China goes further to create unified fields of communication by using standardized languages and homogenized contexts with which to promote a common discourse of nationalism. As the statistics in 2014 show, higher education in China is continuously growing, with over two thousand universities and more than 7.27 million college graduates.[32] Education does more than cultivate loyalty to the state and the ruling party, or construct an imagined community to incorporate the Diaoyu Islands: it also produces a better-informed and more open-minded generation, increasing their ability to scrutinize the authenticity of information, engage in skepticism, and question authorities. Empirical evidence from the *People's Daily* online survey confirmed that 70 percent of the post-1980 generation perceived themselves as more independent thinking than older generations.

In terms of action, in an online opinion poll on populism, also conducted by the *People's Daily* from October 21 to 31 in 2012, 42.8 percent of the post-1980 generation approved of radical movements for the sake of patriotism compared to 32.4 percent from earlier generations.[33] These findings explain why vehement protests were sparked by Japan's purchase of the Diaoyu Islands in 2012, even though the government asked for calm and restraint.[34] In other words, the effects of education are Janus-faced, for education does not simply stimulated patriotism in young people, it also creates mechanisms for them to correct the state when they feel that the government has strayed onto the wrong path. On the streets, young protesters shouted, "Never forget national humiliation" and "Protect China's inseparable territory," even venting their anger at the Chinese government, blaming it for being "shamefully weak," and urging it to "take Japan down."

Reinforced by a Sense of Crisis

Finally, why did protests over Diaoyu Islands turn violent? The resurgence of an outraged Chinese nationalism in 2012 can be explained by a strong sense of crisis. Many Strong Nation Forum posters believed that the United States was an even larger threat than Japan ("Of first importance now is the necessity to check the United States") and that it had been behind Japan's national resurgence. On the forum (table 6), 6.5 percent of posts expressed the belief that Japan should be held responsible for the dispute, whereas 12.3 percent held the United States responsible. About half of the posts that held the United States responsible (6.1 percent of the total sample) expressed the belief that Japan's nationalization of the Diaoyu Islands was a conspiracy of the United States to escalate tensions between Japan and China so as to advance itself across the Asia-Pacific. They pointed to the Treaty of Mutual Cooperation and Security between the United States and Japan, as well as US-Japan joint military drills, to validate the posters' worries. They stated that Japan would not dare go to war without US endorsement. The other half (6.2 percent of total posts) looked to historical reasons for why the United States was to blame. For these Internet users, China's claims to the disputed Diaoyu Islands rested primarily on international contracts dating back to the 1943 Cairo Declaration, the 1945 Potsdam Proclamation, and the 1951 Treaty of San Francisco. However, the islands had never been returned to China because the Ryukyu Islands were under US administration at the end of the Second World War. "The Diaoyu Islands were used for US bombing practice to fulfill US greed," posted many Internet users. Many also believed that in the 1971 Okinawa Reversion Treaty the United States deliberately left the question of sovereignty over the Diaoyu Islands unresolved and ambiguous to this day, thereby opening a window for the United States to plant itself in Asia.

China's immediate concerns about the US threat may have been partly driven by new US foreign policies toward Asia. In 2011, the Obama administration declared that the United States would pivot back to Asia, a move that posed a critical challenge to China's political and economic clout. In economic terms, Obama came to the 2011 Asia-Pacific Economic Cooperation (APEC) summit to promote the TPP, which would forge a pathway to free trade across the Asia-Pacific and encompass 40 percent of the global GDP. The standards to join the TPP conformed to American conceptions of labor rights, intellectual property rights, and environmental protections that would strategically exclude China from the world's largest free trade zone. Not surprisingly, among hundreds of comments on the Strong Nation Forum, online posters unanimously regarded the TPP as an instrument for containing China's rise. Many Internet users perceived it as a "revival of US imperialism" and "US hegemony over the world." Power rivalry between the United States and China was further complicated in 2012, when the United States persuaded Japan to join TPP negotiations amid rising tensions with China over the Diaoyu Islands. At the same time, the United States clarified in a statement that the bilateral Treaty of Mutual Cooperation and Security covered the Diaoyu Islands and obliged the United States to defend them in the event of an armed attack. Later that same year, the United States and Japan began joint military exercises. The US expansion of its military involvement in Japan's conflict against China escalated concerns about an unstated US aim to block China, especially after Japan's Liberal Democratic Party won the House of Representatives elections by a landslide in December 2012, encouraging the new Japanese prime minister Shinzo Abe to more stridently push issues concerning the Diaoyu Islands. In 2013, the Abe government declared that joining the TPP would strengthen Japan's security. He continued to push ahead in reinterpreting Japan's constitution to authorize the right to collective self-defense.

China's youth perceive an immediate threat to China's existence in policies of economic and military containment by Japan and the United States, and their sense of crisis is grounded in the shared memory of China's century of humiliation and its isolation during the Cold War. From this sense of threat and crisis arise two mechanisms that reinforce their national identity and radicalize their actions. The first one is a clear enemy to target. Identity is about belonging, what you have in common with your own group, and what differentiates you from others.[35] Hence, in forming identity, the first and foremost need is to define "others." It requires the establishment of a boundary between "us" and "them," and across this boundary differences between the groups are signaled.[36] However, for young Chinese, it is difficult to form a clear sense of "us." During the Cultural Revolution an enormous number of cultural treasures and traditional values were eradicated. As stated by Lucian Pye, the building blocks for a coherent identity in China are missing because the symbols and ideals of the culture have been so severely damaged. The content of Chinese contemporary nationalism appears to be exceedingly thin, without shared ideas and worthy principles that can inspire people.[37] Moreover, China's transition from communism to capitalism has led to a state of anomie in which young people suffer from a disbelief in socialism and a sense of powerlessness in the market economy. Accordingly, the new generation holds an insular attitude and loses meaningful connections to others. Hence, Chinese identity for the post-1980 generation had been unstable in and of itself, inasmuch as it was a result of state construction through patriotic education and state propaganda. Nevertheless, as international conflicts increase, Chinese youth become more aware of their membership in the Chinese nation in a sense of perceiving it as threatened and uniting against enemies. They begin to strengthen their Chinese identities in contrast to clear rivals—Japan and the United States.

The second mechanism that a sense of threat and crisis provides is the motivation for collective resistance. The Chinese have been fighting against deep-seated doubts about their ethnic dignity for a century. In spite of China's economic successes, the narrative of the "century of humiliation" has been reiterated in historical textbooks and official documents to remind people of the agonies and shame of foreign aggression. The Japan-US alliance, which young Chinese see as intended to contain the rise of China, threatens not only China's rise but its national dignity. In Gordon Allport's analysis, an enemy who threatens people's positive values stiffens their resistance and makes them exaggerate the merits of their cause.[38] In the same vein, Chinese youth nationalism is found in unity against shared enemies—Japan and the United States—especially in a time of rapidly increasing Internet access. Verbal aggression on the Internet is the most convenient way to boost self-esteem by stigmatizing others. On the Strong Nation Forum (table 6), a handful of posts (5.8 percent) attacked the United States and Japan with derogatory words. They called Americans *yang gui-zi* (foreign devils) and added the new term *mi-guo,* insinuating a "rotten country." They also called the Japanese "dogs," "little Japan," *gui-zi,* and mostly *wo kou* (dwarf bandits), all of which are extremely pejorative ethnic slurs. Although the movement started with peaceful demonstrations, nationalist movements on a large scale aim at venting xenophobic sentiments easily go out of control. Despite the calls for peaceful protests and a prohibition of the boycott, Chinese Internet users launched a widespread campaign on the Web to boycott Japanese products, leading to a plunge in the sales of Japanese automobiles and consequently forcing Toyota and Honda to temporarily halt production in China. Why did Chinese youth nationalism turn into a hazard? From many transitional states, it is observed that the motivations behind ethnic violence are fear and insecurity, not hatred.[39] The more insecure a person feels, the more violently he or she reacts. As a consequence of the immediate threat and the need to contain the US-Japan alliance advancing across the Pacific, China's xenophobic nationalism in 2012 spread more swiftly and epidemically than ever, and youth movements have shockingly caused near riots in large Chinese cities.

CONCLUSION

In 2012, before the eighty-first anniversary of the Manchurian incident, tensions between China and Japan escalated sharply amid fiercely anti-Japan protests against Japan's nationalization of the Diaoyu Islands. This phenomenon attracted worldwide attention and rekindled the debate on the causes of Chinese nationalism. This study has gone beyond the hotly debated issue of whether Chinese nationalism has been instigated from the top down or has developed from the bottom up. It has investigated the psychological mechanisms that encourage Chinese youth nationalism. Through content analysis of the data gathered from the Strong Nation Forum, it has found three major reasons why Chinese youth nationalism in 2012 had taken on a violent character.

In 1972, the US transfer of administrative rights to Japan spawned disputes over the Diaoyu Islands. Both China and Taiwan held tenacious views about ownership of the Diaoyu Islands, considering them part of Taiwan. Hence, with the end of the Second World War, the Diaoyu Islands along with Taiwan should have been returned to Chinese jurisdiction. In the meantime, after the PRC replaced the ROC as China's representative in the United Nations, the weakening hold of Chinese identity gave rise to a search for a set of new policies to maintain the KMT's legitimacy. During periods of low public mobilization, one strategy of the KMT government was to use the Diaoyu Islands disputes to galvanize young Taiwanese into participating in nationalist movements. Meanwhile, Japan and China were in the midst of normalizing diplomatic relations. Although disputes ignited anger and indignant protests in Taiwan and Hong Kong, the CCP leadership avoided controversy over the issue throughout the 1970s, 1980s, and the 1990s. However, since the mid-1990s, the resurgence of Japanese nationalism and Taiwanese nationalism has changed China's longtime policy of "shelving the dispute." In the face of new threats in international relations, Chinese youth nationalism was revived by the CCP as a replacement for diminishing socialism. At the dawn of the twenty-first century, the CCP initiated a program of patriotic education to assert its claim over Taiwan and the Diaoyu Islands. Through geography and history lessons at schools, Chinese young generations have been infused with the ideal of safeguarding territory unity. Through a propaganda war against Japan, Chinese young generations are visualizing Taiwan and its annexed islands—the Diaoyu Islands—as an inalienable part of China.

We then ask why protests to dispute Japanese claim to the Diaoyu Islands in 2012 turned violent. The first reason is rooted in ambivalence between national pride and disappointment in the CCP. Through patriotic education and on the basis of China's remarkable economic growth, the post-1980 generation has grown up believing in a strong China and in a mission of defending national unity. As evident in the World Values Survey in 2012, the post-1980 generation is more proud of being Chinese than other generations and is more willing to be dedicated to the country. However, in 2012, as the imbroglio of the Diaoyu Islands was ongoing, negotiations over a China-Japan-South Korea FTA were about to begin. In the meantime, the CCP was torn in different directions in the battles between economic interests and national sentiments. Many Chinese youth regarded the CCP's rhetorical protests as merely for show and believed that the CCP was actually putting economic interests ahead of national dignity. The Strong Nation Forum was overwhelmed with posts expressing disappointment in the CCP and demanding tough responses to Japan. Without elections to vent their anger, Chinese youth went out in the streets to express themselves and to mitigate their anxieties associated with emotions in conflict. With the advent of the Internet and enlightenment by education, rampant protests were widespread, despite the pressure of government suppression. Finally, Chinese "raging youth" nationalism is reinforced by its resistance to shared enemies. In 2012, youth protests were a reaction to Japan's nationalization of the Diaoyu Islands, whereas on the Strong Nation Forum many people believed that the United States had triggered Japan's aggressive nationalism and should be responsible for the 2012 Diaoyu Islands incident. China's concern about the US threat is highly related to US policies of containing China through the TPP and a military alliance with Japan. The conflict between China and the United States peaked in 2012, as the United States persuaded Japan to join the TPP amid simmering tensions over the disputed islands. A shared memory of China's century of humiliation and isolation during the Cold War has enhanced the sense of crisis with the sense of an immediate threat to China's existence. Chinese youth tend to strengthen their Chinese identities in contrast to clear enemies—Japan and the United States. The crisis of threat is the motivation for collective resistance as well. A shared enemy provides common cause for national unity. As a consequence of the immediate threat and the need to contain the US-Japan alliance advancing across the Pacific, China's xenophobic nationalism in 2012 spread swiftly. In the end, Chinese youth's identity was affirmed against the alien.

NOTES

1. *Fenqing*, as Wu defines it, refers to a large group of online Chinese users who detest anything conformist or foreign. They call for aggressive action against foreign pressure. See also Xu Wu, "Chinese Cyber Nationalism: How China's Online Public Sphere Affected Its Social and Political Transition" (PhD diss., University of Florida, 2005), 122.

2. Anomie, as defined by Durkheim, is a condition of societal instability that creates a sense of normlessness and purposelessness. See Émile Durkheim, *Division of Labour in Society*, trans. G. Simpson (Glencoe, IL: Free Press, 1947).

3. Xiancai Chen, "Why Is the Democratic Progressive Party Anxious about Cross-Strait Cooperation on the Baodiao Movement," *Formosa*, September 24, 2012, www.my-formosa.com/article.aspx?cid=5,6&id=32406.

4. H. Peter Gries, "Popular Nationalism and State Legitimation in China," in *State and Society in 21st-Century China: Crisis, Contention, and Legitimation,* ed. Peter H. Gries and Stanley Rosen (New York: Routledge, 2004), 188–91.

5. Suisheng Zhao, *Nation-State by Construction: Dynamics of Modern Chinese Nationalism* (Stanford, CA: Stanford University Press, 2004), 209–47.

6. Susan Shirk, *China: Fragile Superpower: How China's Internal Politics Could Derail Its Peaceful Rise* (New York: Oxford University Press, 2007), 164–65; Christopher R. Hughes, "Nationalism in Chinese Cyberspace," *Cambridge Review of International Affairs* 13, no. 2 (2000): 195–209.

7. Lowell Dittmer and Samuel S. Kim, "In Search of a Theory of National Identity," in *China's Quest for National Identity,* ed. Lowell Dittmer and Samuel S. Kim (Ithaca, NY: Cornell University Press, 1993), 1–31.

8. Gries, "Popular Nationalism," 183, 191.

9. Wu, "Chinese Cyber Nationalism," 150.

10. Shubo Li, "Configuring a Threatening Other: Historical Narratives in Chinese School Textbooks," in *The Dispute over the Diaoyu/Senkaku Islands: How Media Narratives Shape Public Opinion and Challenge the Global Order,* ed. Thomas A. Hollihan (New York: Palgrave Macmillan, 2014), 27–28.

11. Reinhard Drifte, "The Japan-China Confrontation over the Senkaku/Diaoyu Islands: Between 'Shelving' and 'Dispute Escalation,'" *Asia-Pacific Journal* 12, no. 30 (2014), www.japanfocus.org/-Reinhard-Drifte/4154/article.html.

12. Hiroko Okuda, "Historical Narratives in Japanese School Textbooks," in Hollihan, *Dispute,* 63.

13. On July 23, 2015, during his trip to Japan, Lee Teng-hui sparked a firestorm in Taiwan by restating that the Senkaku Islands belonged to Japan. President Ma Ying-jeou published an article in the *Washington Times* harshly rebutting Lee's statement. See Ma Ying-jeou, "The Diaoyutai Islands: ROC Territory," *Washington Times,* August 23, 2015, www.washingtontimes.com/news/2015/aug/23/ma-ying-jeou-diaoyutai-islands-are-republic-china/.

14. The objective of *Basic Education Curriculum Reform Outline (Trial)* is outlined in the government document "Basic Education No. 17," issued by the Ministry of Education of People's Republic of China in 2001. See also Suisheng Zhao, "A State-Led Nationalism: The Patriotic Education Campaign in Post-Tiananmen China," *Communist and Post-Communist Studies* 31, no. 3 (1998): 296; Christopher R. Hughes, "Interpreting Nationalist Texts: A Post-structuralist Approach," *Journal of Contemporary China* 14, no. 43 (2005): 254.

15. The People's Education Press is under the direct leadership of the Ministry of Education. It has become the national center for school textbooks, which are used in most of the provinces in China. For teaching guidelines for geography, see Cheng Cai, "Bian xie yi liu jiao cai tui jin su zhi jiao yu" [Producing first-class teaching materials and promoting teaching excellence], *Kecheng Jiaocai Jiaofa / Curriculum, Teaching Material and Method* 6 (June 2000): 1–5, www.pep.com.cn/gzdl/jszx/tbjxzy/pg/jxsj/xxe/.

16. For scholarship, see Kiyoshi Inoue, *Senkaku Islands: A Historical Explanation of the Diaoyu Islands* (Tokyo: Daisan shokan, 1996); Tianying Wu, *Chia-wu chan-chein Tiao-yu-t'ai lieh-yu kuki-shu k'ao—Chien chih Jih-pen Ao-yuan Min-hsiung Chu Chiao-shu* [A textual study on the ownership of the Diaoyu Islands prior to the Sino-Japanese War of 1894–95—Also a query to Professor Toshio Okuhara and others] (Beijing: Shehuei kexue wenxian chubanshe, 1994); Deyuan Ju, *Rename Diaoyu Islands: Historical Sovereignty and International Law* (Beijing: Kunlun chu ban she, 2006). In 2014, the State Oceanic Administration of the PRC set up an official website regarding the Diaoyu Islands, which provides the historical maps, legal documentation, and videos to support China's assertion that the Diaoyu Islands were Chinese territory before 1884; see www.diaoyudao.org.cn.

17. Karl Mannheim, "The Problem of Generations," in *The New Pilgrims: Youth Protest in Transition,* ed. Philip G. Altbach and Robert S. Laufer (New York: David Mckay, 1972), 276–332.

18. For the result, see "Wang luo gong min bu wan quan bao gao" [Incomplete report on netizens], *Liao wang dong fang zhou kan,* July 2008, http://bbs1.people.com.cn/post/2/1/2/87405005.html.

19. William Lawrence Neuman, *Social Research Methods: Qualitative and Quantitative Approaches* (Boston: Allyn and Bacon, 1997), 275.

20. China Internet Network Information Center (CNNIC), *Statistical Report on Internet Development in Rural China* (Beijing: CNNIC, 2013), 6.

21. For the guidelines of the Strong Nation Forum, see *People's Daily,* http://bbs1.people.com.cn/gltl.html.

22. Wenzhao Tao, "The Regulation of BBS in China People Daily," *First Monday* 6, no. 1 (January 8, 2001), http://journals.uic.edu/ojs/index.php/fm/article/view/826/735.

23. Lucien Bianco, *Origins of the Chinese Revolution: 1915–1949* (Stanford, CA: Stanford University Press, 1971), 154.

24. Michel Oksenberg, "China's Confident Nationalism," *Foreign Affairs* 65, no. 3 (December 1986): 501–23, 507.

25. Chih-yu Shih, *Navigating Sovereignty: World Politics Lost in China* (London: Palgrave/Macmillan, 2003), 112–13; Shirk, *China,* 108–9.

26. Wen Jaibo, "Turning Your Eyes to China," speech at Harvard University, December 2003, transcript, www.people.com.cn/GB/shehui/1061/2241298.html.

27. Christopher R. Hughes, *Chinese Nationalism in the Global Era* (Abingdon: Routledge, 2006), 140.

28. K. Lewin, *Resolving Social Conflicts* (New York: Harper, 1948); Catarina Kinnvall, "Globalization, Identity, and the Search for Chosen Traumas," in *The Future of Identity: Centennial Reflections on the Legacy of Erik Erikson,* ed. Kenneth Hoover (Lanham, MD: Lexington Books, 2004), 111–36.

29. Jack Snyder, *From Voting to Violence* (New York: Norton, 2000).

30. Manuel Castells, "Communication, Power and Counter-power in the Network Society," *International Journal of Communication* 1 (2007): 238–66.

31. For more details on Chinese Internet users, see CNNIC [China Internet Network Information Center], "Ji chu shu ju" [Basic statistics], June 30, 2014, www.cnnic.cn/hlwfzyj/jcsj/.

32. National Bureau of Statistics in China, "Gao deng xue xiao pu tong ben zhuan ke xue xiao he xue sheng qing kuang" [The distribution of schools and students in the higher education system], 2014, http://data.stats.gov.cn/easyquery.htm?cn=C01.

33. For the survey report, see "Zhong guo gong zhong de min cui hua qing xiang diao cha bao gao" [A report on the populist orientation of Chinese people," *People's Daily,* December 6, 2012, http://theory.people.com.cn/n/2012/1206/c49152–19807772–1.html.

34. See "Ren min wang ping: Wo men zen yang bao wei Diaoyu Dao" [People's online comments: How can we protect the Diaoyu Islands," *People's Daily,* September 17, 2012, http://edu.people.com.cn/n/2012/0917/c1053–19026485.html.

35. J. Weeks, "The Value of Difference," in *Identity: Community, Culture, Difference,* ed. Jonathan Rutherford (London: Lawrence and Wishart, 1990), 88.

36. Fredrik Barth, *Ethnic Groups and Boundaries* (Boston: Little, Brown, 1969); Henri Tajfel, *The Social Psychology of Minorities,* Report No. 38 (London: Minority Rights Group, 1978), 9.

37. Lucian W. Pye, "How China's Nationalism Was Shanghaied," *Australian Journal of Chinese Affairs* 29 (January 1993): 107–33.

38. Gordon Allport, *The Nature of Prejudice* (Cambridge, MA: Addison-Wesley, 1954).

39. Anthony Oberschall, "The Manipulation of Ethnicity: From Ethnic Cooperation to Violence and War in Yugoslavia," *Ethnic and Racial Studies* 23, no. 6 (2000): 982–1001.

PART II

Political Economy

7

Varieties of State Capitalism across the Taiwan Strait

A Comparison and Its Implications

Chih-shian Liou

The past few years have seen an upsurge in interest, both practically and academically, in state capitalism.[1] While state capitalism is not a new phenomenon, the 2008 global financial crisis sweeping through a large part of liberal capitalist system made it a viable alternative approach to economic development. A number of developing economies with a relatively large state sector, such as Brazil, China, India, and Russia, outperformed their liberal developed counterparts.[2] These economies had the state's heavy hand involved and relied on their state-owned enterprises (SOEs) to stand against and buffer the impact of the crisis. Yet if we take a closer look at these economies, the SOE sector is not the only player in the game. Different from the old model of state capitalism in the 1970s, new varieties of state capitalist economies sprouted in the late 1990s and flourished in the late 2000s. These new varieties have witnessed more strategic cooperation between their SOE and non-SOE sectors.[3]

Most scholars, policy makers, and journalists pay attention only to how such strategic cooperation associated with the new species of state capitalism effectively challenges Western capitalist systems. There has been little investigation of the variations in domestic market structures within the group of state capitalist regimes—as if they were all the same. However, as the cases of China's state capitalism in the post-1990s period and Taiwan's state capitalism from the 1960s to the 2000s show, there is obvious heterogeneity in their ownership structures. Under China's state capitalist regime there is a political pecking order where SOEs occupy the top of the hierarchy and private firms are relatively small, numerous, and weak.[4] On the other hand, Taiwan's state capitalist regime is characterized by small and medium-size private firms holding equal footing in the governmental industrial policy.[5] What explains this variation? In particular, given that state capitalism is a political-economic regime for the sake of national development, it is reasonable to expect that the economies under state capitalism will share similarities in their domestic ownership structure, specifically an emphasis on the SOE sector. While China's state capitalism conforms to such an expectation, Taiwan's state capitalism does not. These variations in domestic ownership structures are puzzling. This chapter aims to analyze the rationale behind the variations in domestic market structure across the Taiwan Strait and its implications for understanding cross-Strait economic interaction.

This chapter uses Aldo Musacchio and Sergio G. Lazzarini's work to define state capitalism. Musacchio and Lazzarini define state capitalism as "the widespread influence of the government in the economy, either by owning majority or minority equity positions in companies or by providing subsidized credit and/or other privileges to private companies." On the basis of this definition, there are three subtypes of state capitalism: "leviathan as an entrepreneur"; "leviathan as a majority investor"; and "leviathan as a minority investor."[6] The first model refers to the old model of state capitalism existing primarily in the 1970s, and the second and third models refer to the latest wave of state capitalism that we observe today. According to their definition, Musacchio and Lazzarini put China's state capitalism in the category of "leviathan as a majority investor" and Taiwan's state capitalism in the category of "leviathan as a minority investor." To be specific, Taiwan's state capitalism has experienced a transformation from "leviathan as an entrepreneur" in the pre-1989 period to "leviathan as a minority investor" with the agenda of democratization in the late 1980s.[7]

One justification makes China's and Taiwan's state capitalism models a comparable fit. That is, both China's and Taiwan's industries have experienced a Leninist model of control.[8] Compared to the prereform era, when Chinese Communist Party (CCP) control penetrated every work unit in China, the Chinese party-state of the reform period has loosened its grip over industry through various SOE reform agendas.[9] Industrial policy still favors the SOE sector over other types of ownership, however, and China is a "commanding-heights economy," in which the CCP's Leninist model of control still has its place in the Chinese political economic system.[10] Leninism was also once an essential part of the Kuomintang's (KMT)'s governance of Taiwan's political-economic system during its nearly four decades of authoritarian rule.[11] A decade after Taiwan made its democratic transition, the KMT's Leninist control model has yet to fade from the decision-making process.[12] In short, both China's and Taiwan's state capitalism have their roots in the Leninist legacy.

My central argument regarding the rationale behind the variations in domestic market structure between China's and Taiwan's state capitalist regimes and its implications has three parts. First, the similar institutional foundations of the

Leninist legacy do not necessarily determine the evolution of state capitalism in authoritarian China and Taiwan. Second, the evolution of state capitalism in both authoritarian regimes hinges on the resources that the leaders have at their disposal in the pursuit of national development. During the time when leaders in Taiwan cultivated the state capitalist system, the authoritarian KMT regime had just been defeated in the civil war and could rely only on assistance from the United States to build its economy. The ideology of market liberalism associated with US assistance supported private ownership rather than public ownership. Private ownership was thus not discriminated against under Taiwan's state capitalism in the first place. In contrast, during the time when leaders in China cultivated their state capitalist system in the post-1990s period, China had tense relations with other major powers in the global community. Backed by a gigantic state-owned banking system, various state actors, including state firms, a diverse array of bureaucratic agencies, and state research institutes, provided reliable and efficient assistance to develop the state capitalist system. Public ownership functioned as the bedrock of China's state capitalism. Third, China's preference for state ownership over private ownership has caused concerns about unfair competition and security issues in Taiwan, making economic interaction in the region more complicated and unstable.

This chapter is structured as follows. I begin by examining how state capitalism evolved in Taiwan from the 1960s to the 2000s. I then look in detail at the development of China's state capitalism since 2003. I end by discussing implications of variations in domestic market structure across state capitalist systems in Taiwan and China for understanding cross-Strait relations.

STATE CAPITALISM IN TAIWAN

Before studying the case of Taiwan, I need to clarify that the state capitalist regime in Taiwan lasted nearly four decades, from the 1960s to the beginning of the 2000s. Before the privatization agenda was initiated in 1989, Taiwan's state capitalism fell into the category of "leviathan as an entrepreneur," the primitive type of state capitalism under Musacchio and Lazzarini's definition.[13] As the agendas of democratization and its consolidation proceeded throughout the second half of the 1980s and the 1990s, the Taiwanese government revamped its own role in the marketplace and started to privatize state firms, resulting in what Musacchio and Lazzarini label "leviathan as a minority investor."[14]

The democratic impetus continued to grow, and the state's penetration into society and intervention into the marketplace finally ended with the first party turnover from the KMT to the Democratic Progressive Party (DPP) in 2000,[15] signifying the breakdown of the state capitalist regime in Taiwan. The continuous efforts put forth by the Taiwanese government on the privatization agenda finally marginalized the importance of state ownership in Taiwan's domestic market. Although the Taiwanese state capitalist regime experienced a transformation from "leviathan as an entrepreneur" to "leviathan as a minority investor" during four decades, it is worth pointing out that the private sector had always been significant throughout this time (see table 8). Below I tackle the reason why the private sector was the dominant component under Taiwan's state capitalism by looking at the international and domestic environments in which the authoritarian KMT leaders operated and from which they could extract resources to engage in economic buildup.

Once Chiang Kai-shek and his KMT regime retreated to Taiwan in 1949, the United States became the most important ally of the Taiwanese government. For the KMT authoritarian regime in Taiwan, China's potential invasion has always been the biggest threat to its survival, especially because China has never abandoned its ambition to liberate the island. Nonetheless, ties with the United States have lessened such pressures. Keeping Taiwan from being taken over by the communist camp was one of the most important agendas in American grand strategy during the first half of the Cold War period.[16] Even when the American domestic political atmosphere played down the strategic importance of Taiwan after the Sino-US rapprochement in the 1970s, the United States continued to provide Taiwan security assurance on an unofficial basis.[17] American development assistance, security assurance, and access to the US market gave the authoritarian Taiwanese government more leverage at its disposal to build up its economy during the 1950s and 1960s, when the Taiwanese state capitalist regime began to take root. Putting it differently, during Taiwan's early stage of state capitalism the authoritarian Taiwanese government was brought into the American security orbit and was under no pressure to rely on its own security. Thus, constructing a team of national champions to play catch-up was desirable but not imperative.

Influence from the United States was also translated into Taiwan's domestic economic agenda. As discussed, Taiwan's authoritarian regime relied heavily on assistance from the United States, both economically and militarily. This gave the United States leverage to influence Taiwan's political-economic system by imposing its liberal market ideology. During most of the aid period from 1950 to 1965, the SOE sector as part of the KMT regime was under constant pressure from the United States to reduce state shares in public firms.[18] In the meantime, the US government also pushed the KMT government to carry out land reform, which transformed a large number of landowners into private entrepreneurs who were later sponsored by the KMT government to engage in export-led development.[19] Specifically, because the KMT authoritarian government was a non-native regime, it needed to cultivate local networks to consolidate its rule. In this respect, private entrepreneurs, mostly native Taiwanese, were good candidates for becoming part of KMT's patron-client system. Advised by the United States, the KMT authoritarian government gave private entrepreneurs numerous privileges in doing businesses in exchange for their political support.

TABLE 8 The privatization agenda in Taiwan

Firm	Time of privatization	Revenue (NT$100 million)
China Petrochemical Development Corporation	6/20/1994	170.95
BES Engineering Corporation	6/22/1994	113.69
China Steel Corporation	4/12/1995	1195.08
Taiwan Machinery Manufacturing Corporation (Steel Production Plant)	5/20/1996	48.24
Taiwan Machinery Manufacturing Corporation (Shipbuilding Plant)	1/10/1997	22.75
Taiwan Machinery Manufacturing Corporation (Alloy Steel Production Plant)	6/30/1997	3.54
Taiwan Fertilizer Co., Ltd.	9/1/1999	170.29
Taiwan Hsing Chung Paper Co., Ltd.	10/16/2001	0.05
Taiwan Machinery Manufacturing Corporation (Head Office & Manufacturing Plant)	11/19/2001	35.09
Tang Eng Iron Works Co., Ltd. (Transportation division)	8/1/2002	0.2
Tang Eng Iron Works Co., Ltd. (Steel Plan, Machinery Plant)	9/1/2002	0.198
Taiwan Agricultural and Industrial Development Corporation (Chiayi Machinery Plant)	12/31/2002	0.078
Taiwan Salt Industrial Corporation	11/14/2003	28.36

SOURCE: State-Owned Enterprise Commission, Ministry of Economic Affairs, ROC, *Jingjibu suoshu shiye minyinghua* [Privatization of state-owned enterprises in Taiwan] (Taipei: Ministry of Economic Affairs, ROC, 1996), 179.

Moreover, their failure during the civil war shaped KMT leaders' perception of the market. Before retreating to Taiwan, the KMT regime had suffered from hyperinflation during the second half of 1940s. Learning from the financial disaster, decision makers in the KMT government in Taiwan respected market mechanisms in managing its economy.[20] Hence, while adopting Leninist control over its economy, Taiwan's authoritarian regime had no ideological commitment to state ownership and never used bureaucratic coordination to replace market mechanisms as communist regimes did. As a result, the KMT regime did not discriminate against private ownership, one of the core elements of a liberal market economy, in its development programs.

Admittedly, compared to other newly industrialized economies in East Asia such as South Korea, bonding between the KMT regime and private capitalists was relatively loose because of mistrust between the former, a non-native regime dominated by mainlanders, and the latter, composed of local Taiwanese.[21] The distrust, however, was mediated by two factors: the above-mentioned US pressure and the fragmentation of local elites following the February 28 incident of 1947 (an uprising in Taiwan that was violently suppressed by the KMT-led ROC government).[22]

Within this context the private sector was picked by the KMT authoritarian government to play an essential role in the transformation of Taiwan's development pattern from an import substitution strategy to a strategy of export-led economic growth.[23]

Finally, it is important to keep in mind that the activism of the private sector would not be possible without a meritocratic and Weberian bureaucracy in Taiwan. As Peter Evans has demonstrated, bureaucracy in Taiwan enjoyed "embedded autonomy" that enabled it to formulate and implement policy goals independent of any special interests while remaining connected to those interests by various social ties.[24] Such bureaucratic capability kept the authoritarian KMT regime from overprotecting its SOEs at the expense of the private sector in its industrial policy. The high-tech industry is a good example. With a variety of policy preferences such as tax breaks and financial and infrastructure support, the Taiwanese government started to engage in industrial upgrading in the 1970s. It then established the Hsinchu Science Park in 1980 to assist high-tech firms, mostly composed of private capital, to operate businesses. Numerous economic technocrats such as Kwoh-ting Li played an essential role during the whole process. It is not an exaggeration to say that private firms have an equal footing in Taiwan's industrial policy, as is not the case of China.

STATE CAPITALISM IN CHINA

State capitalism in China is a different story. Given that China is a transitional economy, it is useful to specify when state capitalism became the major feature of China's political-economic system. While Chinese reformers have repeatedly initiated policies to separate SOEs from the state since the early stage of economic reform, it was not until the second half of the 1990s that the reform program of "grasping the large, releasing the small" paved the way for corporatization of the remaining state firms. Instead of managing the corporatized SOEs by itself, the Chinese state delegated the authority to managers of the corporatized firms, who were ministerial-level cadres selected by the central organization department of the CCP. At the same time Chinese reformers further diversified these firms' ownerships through public listing and transformed them into shareholding entities. Parallel to the corporatization agenda in the SOE sector, in 2003 the Chinese state created the State-Owned Assets Supervision and Administration Commission (SASAC) to supervise the operations of the SOEs. It is fair to claim that the engineering of China's state capitalist regime was initiated in the late 1990s and completed in 2003 upon the creation of the SASAC (see table 9). Since 2003 the Chinese political economy has been a good example of state capitalism with the feature of "leviathan as a majority investor."[25]

Like Taiwan, the Chinese state created the state capitalist regime in its pursuit of national development. Yet rather than relying on a large number of private

TABLE 9 Distribution of industrial production by ownership in China (%)

Year	State-owned and state-holding enterprises	Collective enterprises	Private enterprises	Others
1957	53.77	19.03	0.83	26.37
1963	89.33	10.67		
1964	89.54	10.46		
1965	90.07	9.93		
1966	90.18	9.82		
1967	88.46	11.54		
1968	88.42	11.58		
1969	88.71	11.29		
1970	87.61	12.39		
1971	85.91	14.09		
1972	84.88	15.12		
1973	84.02	15.98		
1974	82.41	17.59		
1975	81.09	18.91		
1976	78.33	21.67		
1977	77.03	22.97		
1978	77.63	22.37		
1979	78.47	21.53		
1980	75.97	23.54	0.02	0.47
1981	74.76	24.62	0.04	0.58
1982	74.44	24.82	0.06	0.68
1983	73.36	25.47	0.12	0.78
1984	69.09	29.71	0.19	1.01
1985	64.86	32.08	1.85	1.21
1986	62.27	33.51	2.76	1.46
1987	59.73	34.62	3.64	2.02
1988	56.80	36.15	4.34	2.72
1989	54.06	35.69	4.80	3.44
1990	54.60	35.62	5.39	4.38
1991	56.16	33.00	4.83	6.01
1992	51.52	35.07	5.80	7.61
1993	46.95	34.02	7.98	11.05
1994	37.34	37.72	10.09	14.85
1995	33.97	36.59	12.86	16.58
1996	36.32	39.39	15.48	16.65
1997	31.62	38.11	17.92	18.45
1998	28.24	38.41	17.11	22.91
1999	28.21	35.37	18.18	26.14
2000	47.33	13.90		64.07
2001	44.41	10.53		71.46
2002	40.78	8.68		75.73
2003	37.54	6.65		80.36
2004	34.81	3.90		84.49
2005	33.28	3.42		85.67

Continued

TABLE 9 *Continued*

Year	State-owned and state-holding enterprises	Collective enterprises	Private enterprises	Others
2006	31.24	2.90		87.40
2007	29.54	2.51		88.51
2008	28.34	1.77		89.03
2009	26.74	1.75		89.93
2010	26.61	1.49		90.35
2011	26.81	1.31		90.79

SOURCE: National Bureau of Statistics of China, *China Industry Economy Statistical Yearbook* (Beijing: China Statistics Press, 2012), 19.

NOTE: The total percentage figures for several years exceeded 100 percent, which challenges the accuracy of the data. Yet the data provided by the National Bureau of Statistics of China can still convey useful information on the general trend of changes in the SOE sector.

firms, China chose to restructure its ailing state firms into national champions. This choice reflected Chinese decision makers' calculations of resources available from both international and domestic environments. In terms of international resources, during the reform era China received development assistance from international organizations such as the World Bank, yet the Chinese leadership had no confidence in the aid regimes that were dominated by major Western powers, mainly the United States and other major powers that had tense relations with China. For example, the Tiananmen incident in 1989 and the corresponding sanctions from the West made the creation of a strong SOE sector high on Chinese leaders' agenda.[26] In the decade following the incident, China's relationship with the United States, the only superpower by that time, was entangled with American domestic issues such as the bipartisan debate over extending most-favored-nation trade status to China.[27]

At the turn of the new century, China's entrance into the World Trade Organization put Chinese firms in direct competition with firms that had been cultivated in developed economies. Making all these pressures more severe was a persisting distrust regarding China's economic rise in the international community, manifested by the debate over whether the PRC was a revisionist or a status quo state.[28] Compared to Taiwan's state capitalism, which was fostered when the United States provided a stable alliance, China's state capitalism was engineered in the midst of a security dilemma in which only SOEs at the Chinese state's disposal provided reliable and effective support for national development.

Given that only state ownership provides the CCP regime with a source of legitimacy, its distrust of the growing class of private entrepreneurs also influences leaders' decisions about building the state capitalist system. In the early years of China's economic reform, the continued influence of ideological battles against the exploitation of the class of workers made Chinese leaders limit the actors in the nonstate sector to individually owned enterprises with a maximum of only eight employees.[29] In the meantime, insecure property rights led to the widespread phenomenon of "wearing a red hat," whereby private capitalists registered their enterprises as collective ones as a cover for their trade.[30] Although Deng's 1992 Southern Tour of China to stress the importance of his agenda of economic reforms reinvigorated private capitalists' confidence in running businesses, it was not until 2002, when Jiang Zemin asserted the "three represents" that the PRC stood for (advanced economic production, cultural development, and political consensus), that they were entitled to legal protection.

Official discrimination against the private sector in China still exists even as private entrepreneurs and their property rights have gained legal status. As a regime that resorts to socialist ideology for its legitimacy, China's party-state continues to privilege state ownership at the expense of other types of property rights. A good example is China's stimulus package of US $586 billion in response to the global financial crisis in 2008. The investment plan mostly went to infrastructure projects in which state firms were the main operators. Private firms, in contrast, had difficulty securing stable funding sources such as bank loans and government subsidies. As a result, the saying that "the state advances, the private sector retreats" (*guo jin min tui*) became a reality.[31] Even today several industries that are critical for national development still shut the door to private firms and remain monopolized by the state.[32] Given that the class of private capitalists is the main agent of democratization in a number of countries, it is not surprising that the CCP's leaders keep a vigilant eye on the private sector and adopt the preceding ownership discrimination strategy. On the basis of the above elaboration of China's international and domestic concerns, it is obvious that leaders in Beijing, wary of the political implications of the private sector, can rely only on SOEs to play economic catch-up.

In sum, both Taiwan's and China's state capitalist regimes are characterized by strong states and have similar industrial policies; however, the effect of state intervention in the two political-economic systems is far from the same. Industrial policies under Taiwan's state capitalism have emphasized social performance indicators such as social equality, whereas industrial policies under China's state capitalism have focused on the resilience of the authoritarian political system.[33] These different concerns have led to divergent ownership structures in the domestic markets under the two varieties of state capitalism.

CONCLUSION: RETHINKING ECONOMIC INTEGRATION ACROSS THE TAIWAN STRAIT

An increasing body of research focuses on the development of state capitalism across different parts of the globe as a response to the new economic environment brought about by the 2008 financial crisis. The scholarship has done an excellent job of presenting how states adopting the state capitalist system employ flexible strategies to interfere in markets and succeed in achieving growth. Although the literature has identified various forms of state capitalist regimes, it has yet to offer an explanation of why the variations exist. Using state capitalism in Taiwan and China, this chapter finds that resources available to leaders when they engage in the cultivation of state capitalist regimes condition the main agent of economic development and thus the ownership structures in the domestic markets. Assistance from the United States and the commitment to a liberal market explain the prevalence of small and medium-sized private firms under Taiwan's model of state capitalism, while tensions with major powers and the CCP's reliance on state ownership as one of its sources of legitimacy account for the dominance of the SOE sector under China's state capitalism.

This finding corresponds to the latest development of historical institutionalism, in which researchers are paying renewed attention to human agency in an effort to avoid determinism brought about by the analytical concept of path dependence.[34] In other words, even though both Taiwan and China had a history of using Leninist control models in their markets, their similar starting points did not mean they followed the same evolutionary path for domestic market structures. Their differences, however, cannot be explained away by the positive effects of increasing returns associated with the process of path dependence. Rather, as the cases of Taiwan and China demonstrate, the evolution of state capitalist regimes hinges on the choices of political leaders.

It is useful to close my argument by discussing how my research findings would affect the development of cross-Strait relations. As of this writing in the second half of 2016, relations between the two sides of the Taiwan Strait have been facing a downturn since Tsai Ing-wen of DPP was sworn in as the new president of Taiwan in May 2016. Tsai's rejection of the so-called 1992 Consensus (the previous agreement that there is only one Chinese nation but that the PRC and the ROC can differ as to which of them is its legitimate representative), which served as the foundation for détente between the two sides from 2008 to early 2016, was interpreted as a defiant assertion of Taiwanese separateness and independence. While it remains to be seen how both sides adapt to this new situation, it is fair to say that Tsai's stance toward China has generated distrust in China-Taiwan interactions. Below I focus only on the implications of these research findings for cross-Strait relations during the 2008–16 period.

Ma Ying-jeou of the KMT, Tsai's predecessor, adopted a policy of engagement with China and cultivated extensive economic ties with the Chinese market. Ma's approach totally reversed the hostile policy stance toward China under DPP president Chen Shui-bian from 2000 to 2008. Despite being charged with selling Taiwan out to China, Ma's effort has been fruitful. China and Taiwan signed the

Economic Cooperation Framework Agreement in 2010, and cross-Strait trade has risen by more than 50 percent, reaching US$198 billion in 2014. At the same time, the Ma administration gradually relaxed restrictions on foreign direct investment from China.[35] This growing economic integration developed in tandem with more social exchanges between Taiwan and China. Ma's first term was the first time that Chinese students could register for and get degrees from Taiwanese universities. In the meantime, the opening of Taiwan to Chinese tourists, with a daily quota of five thousand visitor groups and four thousand individual travelers, is said to be an economic boon for Taiwan's domestic market. All of the preceding exchanges created the foundation for peaceful development across the Taiwan Strait and thus the prospect of détente between Taiwan and China.[36]

Without a doubt the argument for cross-Strait détente has its theoretical underpinnings, namely the commercial peace research agenda. Revised from the democratic peace research program, which emphasizes that democratic countries have the ability to promote peace among themselves, the commercial peace literature argues that economic institutions associated with these democracies and frequent commercial exchanges among them create the space for political stabilization among these countries.[37] If we apply the logic of commercial peace studies to cross-Strait relations under Ma's presidency, there are reasons for optimism. As noted above, cross-Strait exchanges with regard to trade, capital, and personnel have been boosted to an unprecedented level. At the same time, the economic system in China has been transformed into a capitalist economy and the market mechanism has been the major institution to coordinate domestic economic activities.[38] Together, these two trends have further integrated economic activities across the Taiwan Strait to the degree that neither side would escalate political tension in cross-Strait relations. Yet the findings of this chapter suggest that caution is warranted in interpreting the effect of economic integration on cross-Strait peaceful development during Ma's presidency.

While international trade is said to promote the welfare of the country as a whole, individuals within the country experience different impacts, depending on whether they work for sectors with comparative advantages. In other words, international trade generates a distributional issue that creates winners and losers within a country. As a result, political rivalry associated with the trade issue is heightened when both groups try to lobby and influence decision makers.[39] In this respect trade politics in Taiwan is no exception, especially when the Chinese political-economic system is dominated by a strong SOE sector, as mentioned in the previous section. As deepening economic ties with China were the hallmark of Ma's presidency, his party, the KMT, experienced a difficult situation during the Sunflower Movement protests and suffered an overwhelming election defeat in 2014 and again in January 2016.[40] Three key aspects derived from this study help us understand the public backlash against Ma's economic engagement with China.

First, the visible hand of the Chinese state causes concerns about fair market competition in Taiwan. As noted earlier, China's state capitalist regime favors the SOE sector at the expense of the private sector. State interference and state subsidies have facilitated the expansion of Chinese state firms not only in the domestic market but also in the global market.[41] The two trends in China's domestic market described by the saying "The state advances and the private sector retreats" and China's "going out policy" in the global market where SOEs have played the dominant role manifest such a discriminatory industrial policy. Certainly the Taiwanese government has also wielded power in the market and adopted industrial policy to pursue national development under state capitalism. Yet as noted above, the Taiwanese government interfered in the market without incurring ownership discrimination against private property rights. Rather, private ownership played an essential role in the course of economic development in Taiwan. As a result, whenever the Ma administration took actions to further open Taiwan's domestic market to Chinese capital, there were concerns that Chinese firms supported by state subsidies would drive out Taiwanese local private businesses.

Second, and relatedly, the distributional issue in Taiwan brought about by trade with China has worsened with the progress of economic integration across the Taiwan Strait. Although Ma's engagement policy is said to boost Taiwan's economy, the benefits of economic exchanges are not shared evenly within Taiwanese society. Income and wealth inequality has been one of the top issues in public discussions since Ma's second term started in 2012. While there is no evidence showing that widening domestic income inequality is a result of increasing cross-Strait economic integration, public sentiment toward the lack of transparency in China's political economic system is becoming even more complicated. This is largely because the new pattern of economic growth is different from what Taiwanese people ever experienced under Taiwan's state capitalism, which emphasized both high economic growth and low income inequality.

That is, the seemingly similar state capitalist regimes on both sides of the Taiwan Strait actually have divergent experiences in development. As the illustration of "the domestic version of commercial liberalism" argued by Patrick McDonald, international trade per se does not necessarily lead to peace between countries; only international trade among economies in which private ownership plays the predominant role can pacify potential military conflicts.[42] Seen in this light, although the Chinese government has engaged in economic liberalization for decades and although internationalist economic interests in China's domestic politics have had pacific effects on its foreign policy agenda, a preponderance of state ownership in its economy still makes economic actors in Taiwan skeptical about China's political goals in promoting cross-Strait economic exchanges. This leads us to the next point.

Last but not the least, extensive economic integration with China stimulates popular awareness of Taiwan's sovereign status. International trade leads to interdependence between/among economies and entails the issue of security externality.[43] Numerous studies show that in general trade among allies generates a positive security externality while trade among nonallies generates a negative security externality.[44] Given that China has the claim of sovereignty over Taiwan, according to a new national security law that China passed in July 2015, political rivalries between the two parties remain as intense as ever. Consequently, security concerns about growing economic dependence on China have never disappeared from Taiwan's trade politics, even under the presidencies of Lee Teng-hui and Chen Shui-bian.[45] Ma's engagement policy and China's increasingly active and aggressive stance on the world stage have deepened Taiwanese people's concerns about further integration. In particular, a certain percentage of Chinese investment in Taiwan comes from the state sector,[46] making the public in Taiwan suspect that their operations may have goals other than economic profits.

NOTES

I thank Kevin O'Brien, Lowell Dittmer, and other conference participants for their constructive comments, and Chia-Chi Cheng for her research assistance. Research for this article was partly funded by the Ministry of Science and Technology, Republic of China, Taiwan (MOST 103-2410-H-004-060-MY3).

1. For works on the recent wave of state capitalism in policy-making circles, see Ian Bremmer, "The Return of State Capitalism," *Survival: Global Politics and Strategy* 50, no. 3 (2008): 55–64. See also Ian Bremmer, "State Capitalism Comes of Age: The End of the Free Market?" *Foreign Affairs* 88, no. 3 (2009): 40–55. For works on the recent wave of state capitalism in academia, see Usha C. V. Haley and George T. Haley, *Subsidies to Chinese Industry: State Capitalism, Business Strategy, and Trade Policy* (New York: Oxford University Press, 2013). See also Aldo Musacchio and Sergio G. Lazzarini, *Reinventing State Capitalism: Leviathan in Business, Brazil and Beyond* (Cambridge, MA: Harvard University Press, 2014); Kellee S. Tsai, "The Political Economy of State Capitalism and Shadow Banking in China," *Issues and Studies* 51, no. 1 (March 2015): 12–19; Barry Naughton and Kellee S. Tsai, eds., *State Capitalism, Institutional Adaptation, and the Chinese Miracle* (New York: Cambridge University Press, 2015); Benjamin L. Liebman and Curtis J. Milhaupt, eds., *Regulating the Visible Hand: The Institutional Implications of Chinese State Capitalism* (New York: Oxford University Press, 2016).

2. These four countries are known as BRIC, a term coined by the British economist Jim O'Neill.

3. Musacchio and Lazzarini, *Reinventing State Capitalism*, 1–20.

4. Yasheng Huang, *Capitalism with Chinese Characteristics: Entrepreneurship and the State* (New York: Cambridge University Press, 2008).

5. Alice H. Amsden, "Big Business and Urban Congestion in Taiwan: The Origins of Small and Regionally Decentralized Industry," *World Development* 19, no. 9 (1991): 1121–35; Wan-wen Chu, "Industrial Growth and Small and Medium-Sized Enterprises: The Case of Taiwan," paper presented at "Transitional Societies in Comparison: East Central Europe versus Taiwan," conference jointly held by the National Science Council, Republic of China, and the Academy of Sciences of the Czech Republic, in Prague, May 27–29, 1999.

6. Musacchio and Lazzarini, *Reinventing State Capitalism*, 2.

7. It is worth noting that while it is popular to label Taiwan's political economy as a developmental state, for two reasons I have adopted the label of "state capitalism" instead. The first is methodological: the core characteristic of both state capitalism and the developmental state is the prominent role of the state in the marketplace. Compared to the concept of state capitalism, the developmental state is a much narrower concept to capture the feature of state interference in economic activities, under which only a few East Asian economies are included. Using Collier and Mahon's words, both concepts have "family resemblances" and occupy different positions along the "ladder of generality." See David Collier and James E. Mahon Jr., "Conceptual 'Stretching' Revisited: Adapting Categories in Comparative Analysis," *American Political Science Review* 87, no. 4 (1993): 845–55. Second, and practically, whether or not China's political economy is development oriented, one of the main features of developmental state is still a matter of debate. Some scholars, such as Pei, argue that the Chinese state is predatory rather than developmental toward its economy. See Minxin Pei, *China's Trapped Transition: The Limits of Developmental Autocracy* (Cambridge, MA: Harvard University Press, 2006); Minxin Pei, *China's Crony Capitalism: The Dynamics of Regime Decay* (Cambridge, MA: Harvard University Press, 2016). In addition, there are academic precedents that place the developmental state in the broader category of state capitalism, as in Frieden's analysis of South Korea in the 1980s. See Jeffry Frieden, "Third World Indebted Industrialization: International Finance and State Capitalism in Mexico, Brazil, Algeria, and South Korea," *International Organization* 35, no. 3 (1981): 407–31.

8. Edward S. Steinfeld, *Playing Our Game: Why China's Economic Rise Doesn't Threaten the West* (New York: Oxford University Press, 2010), 224–26.

9. For Leninist control in the working place in China, see Andrew G. Walder, *Communist Neo-traditionalism: Work and Authority in Chinese Industry* (Berkeley: University of California Press, 1986).

10. Huang, *Capitalism with Chinese Characteristics*, 276; Sebastian Heilmann, "Regulatory Innovation by Leninist Means: Communist Party Supervision in China's Financial Industry," *China Quarterly* 181 (2005): 1–21.

11. For the details of Kuomintang's (KMT) Leninist control over Taiwan's industry during the authoritarian period, see Ming-sho Ho, "The Rise and Fall of Leninist Control in Taiwan's Industry," *China Quarterly* 189 (2007): 162–79.

12. Shelley Rigger, *Politics in Taiwan: Voting for Democracy* (London: Routledge, 1999), 64–65.

13. Musacchio and Lazzarini, *Reinventing State Capitalism*.

14. Ibid.

15. Yu-Shan Wu, "Taiwan's Developmental State: After the Economic and Political Turmoil," *Asian Survey* 47, no. 6 (2007): 977–1001.

16. On the domestic debate over the Taiwan issue, see Thomas J. Christensen, *Useful Adversaries: Grand Strategy, Domestic Mobilization, and Sino-American Conflict, 1947–1958* (Princeton, NJ: Princeton University Press, 1996).

17. On Sino-US rapprochement, see Warren I. Cohen, *America's Response to China: A History of Sino-American Relations*, 4th ed. (New York: Columbia University Press, 2000), 195–210.

18. Alice H. Amsden, "The State and Taiwan's Economic Development," in *Bringing the State Back In*, ed. Peter B. Evans, Dietrich Rueschemeyer, and Theda Skocpol (New York: Cambridge University Press, 1985), 90–94.

19. Cohen, *America's Response to China*, 183.

20. Stephan Haggard, *Pathways from the Periphery: The Politics of Growth in the Newly Industrializing Countries* (Ithaca, NY: Cornell University Press, 1990), 84.

21. Ibid., 97. Peter Evans, *Embedded Autonomy: States and Industrial Transformation* (Princeton, NJ: Princeton University Press, 1995), 56–57.

22. Yun-han Chu, "Gua zhan jing ji yu wei quan ti zhi" [Oligopoly economy and authoritarian system], in *Long duan yu bo xiao: Wei quan ti zhi de zheng zhi jing ji fen xi* [Monopoly and exploitation:

The political economic analysis of authoritarian systems], ed. Zhon Gji Wu (Taipei: Taiwan Research Fund, 1989).

23. Haggard, *Pathways from the Periphery*.

24. Evans, *Embedded Autonomy*, 12–13.

25. According to Musacchio and Lazzarini, the type of "leviathan as a majority investor," differing from the type of "leviathan as an entrepreneur" in that the state has full control over and ownership of the state sector, exemplifies a transformation in the relationship between the state and its firms. That is, "The government corporatizes or lists firms on stock exchanges . . . in which the state retains control while attracting minority private investors." This is what the Chinese central government has done in the reform program of corporatization. See Musacchio and Lazzarini, *Reinventing State Capitalism*, 8.

26. Zhijun Ling, *Chen fu: Zhongguo jingji gaige beiwanglu (1989–1997)* [Ups and downs: The memorandum of China's economic reform (1989–1997)] (Beijing: People Daily Press, 2011).

27. For the impact of the Tiananmen incident on the interactions between China and the West, especially Sino-US relations, see Cohen, *America's Response to China*, 211–42.

28. On how this debate evolved, see John J. Mearsheimer, *The Tragedy of Great Power Politics* (New York: Norton, 2001). See also Aaron L. Friedberg, *A Contest for Supremacy: China, America, and the Struggle for Mastery in Asia* (New York: Norton, 2012); Adam P. Liff and G. John Ikenberry, "Racing toward Tragedy: China's Rise, Military Competition in the Asia Pacific, and the Security Dilemma," *International Security* 39, no. 2 (2014): 52–91.

29. Bruce J. Dickson, *Wealth into Power: The Communist Party's Embrace of China's Private Sector* (New York: Cambridge University Press, 2008), 34.

30. For various strategies of wearing a red hat, see Kellee S. Tsai, *Capitalism without Democracy: The Private Sector in Contemporary China* (Ithaca, NY: Cornell University Press, 2007).

31. For an in-depth analysis of "The state advances, the private sector retreats," see Sheng Hong and Zhao Nong, *China's State-Owned Enterprises: Nature Performance and Reform* (Singapore: World Scientific Press, 2013), 125–56.

32. Sarah Eaton, "Political Economy of the Advancing State: The Case of China's Airlines Reform," *China Journal* 69 (2013): 64–86.

33. Huang, *Capitalism with Chinese Characteristics*, 278–85.

34. See Kathleen Thelen, *Varieties of Liberalization and the New Politics of Social Solidarity* (New York: Cambridge University Press, 2014).

35. On the positive results of Ma's cross-Strait policies, see Office of the President, ROC, *Policy Standpoints*, January 21, 2016, http://english.president.gov.tw/Default.aspx?tabid=491&itemid=36626&rmid=2355.

36. See Richard Weixing Hu, "Taiwan Strait Détente and the Changing Role of the United States in Cross-Strait Relations," *China Information* 27, no. 1 (2012): 31–50.

37. For a literature review on commercial peace in the international relations field, see Scott L. Kastner, *Political Conflict and Economic Interdependence across the Taiwan Strait and Beyond* (Stanford, CA: Stanford University Press, 2009). See also Patrick J. McDonald, *The Invisible Hand of Peace: Capitalism, The War Machine, and International Relations Theory* (New York: Cambridge University Press, 2009).

38. János Kornai, "What the Change of System from Socialism to Capitalism Does and Does Not Mean," *Journal of Economic Perspectives* 14, no. 1 (2000): 27–42. See also Edward S. Steinfeld, "Moving beyond Transition in China: Financial Reform and the Political Economy of Declining Growth," *Comparative Politics* 34, no. 4 (2002): 379–98.

39. For a detailed study of trade politics, see Michael J. Hiscox, *International Trade and Political Conflict: Commerce, Coalitions, and Mobility* (Princeton, NJ: Princeton University Press, 2002).

40. The Sunflower Movement was a student-led protest against the Cross-Strait Service Trade Agreement.

41. Haley and Haley, *Subsidies to Chinese Industry*.

42. McDonald, *Invisible Hand of Peace*, 263. However, McDonald argues that "economic liberalization has promoted peace in the Straits and helped to limit some of the conflict-heightening pressures unleashed by democratization."

43. For security externality of free trade, see Joanne Gowa and Edward D. Mansfield, "Power Politics and International Trade," *American Political Science Review* 87, no. 2 (1993): 408–20.

44. See Edward D. Mansfield and Jon C. Pevehouse, "Trade Blocs, Trade Flows, and International Conflict," *International Organization* 54, no. 4 (2000): 775–808. See also Joanne Gowa and Edward D. Mansfield, "Alliances, Imperfect Markets, and Major-Power Trade," *International Organization* 58, no. 4 (2004): 775–805.

45. For details on Taiwan's security concerns for economic integration with China and its changing policy toward China, see Kastner, *Political Conflict*, 42–75.

46. There are no official statistical data on the ownership types of Chinese capital in Taiwan.

8

The Nature and Trend of Taiwanese Investment in China (1991–2014)

Business Orientation, Profit Seeking, and Depoliticization

Chung-min Tsai

In January 1990, the Taiwanese government announced the "Measures on Indirect Investment and Technical Cooperation with the Mainland" (*Dui dalu diqu jianjie touzi huo jishu hezuo guanli banfa*) and officially lifted the ban on investing in China. Simultaneously in this era of change, Deng Xiaoping's Southern Tour promoting economic reforms, and the adoption of a socialist market economic system in the Fourteenth National Party Congress, both in 1992, ensured a more business-friendly investment climate in China. Regardless, cross-Strait relations would continue to stumble over the next few years along with industrial restructuring in Taiwan and changing economic development in China respectively. In 1994, former president Lee Teng-hui (hereafter Lee) promoted a "southward policy" to redirect Taiwanese investment from China to Southeast Asia, and in 1996 he issued his motto, "Don't rush, be patient" (*jieji yongren*), advocating a more gradual and careful approach to Taiwanese investment in China (TIC), accompanied by new regulations on such investment. In 2000, Lee's successor Chen Shui-bian (hereafter Chen) won the election and the Democratic Progressive Party (DPP) became the ruling party. Chen's hostile attitude toward China and the DPP's proindependence stance made cross-Strait relations very difficult, and political exchanges were suspended. But after incumbent president Ma Ying-jeou (hereafter Ma) took power in 2008 the Taiwanese government reinitiated interaction with China and cross-Strait relations made great progress.

Against this background, this chapter aims to explore the following questions: Has the change of political authority affected the patterns and amount of Taiwanese investment in China (TIC)? How have Taiwanese businesspeople (*taishang*) responded to the changing political landscape? What has changed and what has not about TIC since the 1990s? In general, what is the trend of TIC in the past two de-cades? Concerning data availability and the shifts of political power in Taiwan, this chapter focuses on TIC between 1991 and 2014 (under three Taiwanese presidents). Drawing on data from both Taiwan and China, this chapter argues that TIC has been driven mainly by economic motivations and is barely affected by tumultuous political situations. The depoliticization of business characterizes TIC. *Taishang* have continued to prosper despite political turbulence but have been excluded from the domestic policy-making process. In recent years, TIC has been gradually declining because of a deteriorating investment environment on the mainland.

This chapter demonstrates that while the amount of TIC has been generally increasing over the past twenty-five years, its composition has radically changed because of both endogenous constraints and exogenous factors. In terms of en-dogenous constraints, rising labor costs and shifting local preferential policies have degraded the benefits and forced *taishang* either to look for new sites with lower production costs or to devote themselves to technological and industrial upgrades. Regarding exogenous factors, volatile global markets and growing com-petitiveness from domestic enterprises have prompted Taiwanese companies to integrate themselves into China's local markets. These trends show that TIC has been heavily influenced by the macroeconomic environment in China and that political struggles between Taiwan and China have not led to changes in TIC.

The next section of this chapter begins by elaborating on Taiwanese investment in China over the past two decades and demonstrates how little impact unstable poli-cies and power fluctuation across the Strait have had on it. The third section describes the role of Taiwanese entrepreneurs across the Strait. *Taishang* are neither political agents nor economic hostages. They are businesspeople who look for greater oppor-tunities and higher returns and are no different from their counterparts conducting business in other countries. The fourth section examines the "go south" strategy as an alternative for *taishang* and TIC to diversify the risk of relying too heavily on China. The evidence shows that after having been implemented for twenty years, the policies are still struggling to encourage *taishang* to shift their investment to South-east Asian countries. The chapter concludes with a discussion of the broader impli-cations for TIC and its future. While China is now implementing its grand economic strategy, incorporating TIC as part of that strategy is a clear political tactic. Nonethe-less, *taishang's* decisions on whether to invest in China have been driven primarily by economic motives, and this is especially the case now, since China has gradually withdrawn most of its policies that once favored Taiwanese investors.

GO WEST: TAIWANESE INVESTMENT IN CHINA

In Taiwan, it is commonly believed that in general the Kuomintang (the Nation-alist Party, KMT) is pro-China and the DPP is anti-China and that the former is

more willing to facilitate economic interaction while the latter is reluctant to foster economic ties with China. Taiwanese society and media have focused on how
the DPP's anti-China sentiment has had a spillover effect that has greatly influenced TIC, especially during the Chen administration. However, there is neither
clear evidence nor statistical data to support this argument. The trend of TIC has
not necessarily been closely linked to political administrations' orientation and
fluctuation and is instead more related to business considerations and economic
motivations. Statistical data released by the Taiwanese government show little
clear impact of the turnovers of political power in 2000 and 2008 on the levels of
TIC approved by the Taiwanese authorities. Contrary to the parties' orientations
toward China as these are generally perceived, TIC increased in 2001, one year
after the DPP took power in 2000, and declined in 2009, one year after the KMT
took power in 2008. That is to say, the DPP government did not strictly regulate
Taiwanese investment as it was expected or said to do. In fact, ongoing cross-Strait
economic integration has thrived under both parties.[1]

The Taiwanese government lifted the ban on foreign exchange and facilitated capital outflow in July 1987; it removed restrictions on visiting China that
November. These policy shifts initiated TIC. In January 1990, the Taiwanese
government promulgated "Measures on Indirect Investment and Technical
Cooperation with the Mainland" to promote TIC conditionally. At this early
stage, most TIC was from Taiwanese entrepreneurs who owned small and medium-sized enterprises and moved their factories to China to seek competitive
advantages and low wage costs. *Taishang* established joint venture enterprises
and cooperative companies with their Chinese counterparts because wholly
foreign-owned enterprises were not yet permitted. They used the productive
pattern of taking orders in Taiwan, producing in China, and then exporting to
the Western countries. This explains why Taiwanese investors sought to invest in
sectors where the profit ratio was high instead of in resource-rich areas as their
Japanese and Korean counterparts did. The initial TIC was small and cautious
because of restrictions on the Taiwanese side. Figure 3, based on calculations by
the Republic of China (ROC), shows that the amount of TIC approved by the
Taiwanese government increased in 1992–93 and 1996–97.[2] The former was the
positive response to Deng Xiaoping's Southern Tour and the establishment of a
socialist market economy system in the Fourteenth National Party Congress in
1992. The latter trend demonstrates Taiwanese government's self-contradiction:
the amount of TIC it approved in 1997 was 30% more than in the previous year,
when Lee promoted the policy of "No haste, be patient" and imposed many
new regulations on TIC. Ever since his visit to the United States in 1995, pre-
cipitating a missile crisis and freezing cross-Strait talks, Lee had shown a tough
attitude toward China, but the Taiwanese authorities remained generous with
approved TIC. The amount of approved TIC significantly declined in 1998 and

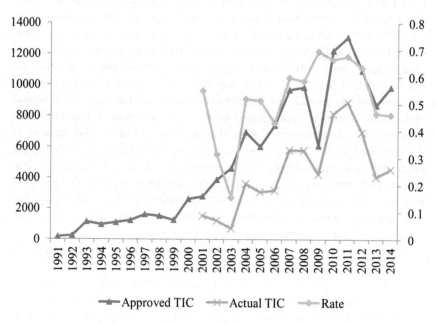

FIGURE 3. Approved TIC, actual TIC, and the rate (million US$).

SOURCE: Investment Commission, Ministry of Economic Affairs, ROC, https://www.moeaic.gov.tw.

1999 because of the Asian financial crisis, and, despite some later, larger fluctuations, its overall tendency has been to rise since 2000. Surprisingly, the trend did not reflect the political turbulence evoked by Lee's assertion, in July 1999, of the so-called "two-state theory" (*liangguo lun*) that Taiwan and China should engage in special state-to-state relationships—a controversial move to which China soon responded by canceling the third Koo-Wang talk, which had originally been scheduled in Taipei in the fall. In 2000, Chen won the presidential election and the DPP became the ruling party. The DPP government promoted an "invest in Taiwan" policy and provided a low-interest loan fund, tax breaks, and subsidies to incentivize Taiwanese companies to do so. Nonetheless, during Chen's administration the approved amount of TIC only slightly decreased in 2004 and 2005. That is to say, the DPP government did not adopt effective policies to prevent *taishang* from investing in China or convince them to stay in Taiwan. Ironically, the amount of TIC dropped radically in 2009, one year after Ma took power, and then abruptly rose in 2010. Affected by shrinking demand resulting from the global financial crisis and rising labor costs in China, the approved amount has lessened since 2011.[3] Obviously the trend of the approved amount of TIC has not generally reflected power shifts in Taiwan.

On the China side, in 1979 the Chinese government released a "Message to Compatriots in Taiwan" (gao Taiwan tongbao shu) proposing an opening up of trade and economic exchanges; this was followed up by the Ministry of Foreign Trade's promulgation of "Interim Provisions Concerning Trade with Taiwan" (Guanyu kaizhan dui Taiwan maiyi de zhanshi guiding). Later, China's State Council passed the "Special Preferential Regulations on Taiwanese Patriots' Investment in the Special Economic Zones" (Guanyu Taiwan tongbao dao jingjitequ touzi de tebie youhui banfa) to make it easier for Taiwanese entrepreneurs to invest in the special economic zones (Shenzhen, Zhuhai, Shantou, Xiamen) that had been established in 1979. The first wholly owned Taiwanese enterprise (TE) was established in Fuzhou in 1984 with the acquiescence of the local government and later received its first approval by the central state's Ministry of Foreign Economic Relations and Trade (formerly the Ministry of Foreign Trade) in 1986. Two years later, the number of TEs grew to eighty with an investment of US$100 million in 1986. By the end of 1989, there were two thousand TEs and the amount of TIC was over US$1 billion. In general, TIC in the 1980s was initially limited because of China's unclear investment environment and the Taiwanese government's restrictions. It followed the development model of "two ends out" (liangtou zaiwai), referring to a pattern in which both the sources of raw materials and the ultimate products were nondomestic. The demand in the foreign market had been rocketing up but that in local market remained quite low. Obviously, for taishang in the 1980s and early 1990s political concerns were more important than economic considerations in their investment decisions. Once the macroeconomic climate had become stable and beneficial to TIC, TIC was less sensitive to political turbulence, and in the 1990s Taiwan's investment rapidly became the second highest in China, second only to Hong Kong's.

Figure 4 shows actual TIC as calculated by China's National Statistical Bureau. The amount increased between 1989 and 1996, only slightly decreasing in 1995. This trend reflects the friendly investment environment that the Chinese government created in order to develop TIC. Actual TIC radically declined between 1997 and 2000 (figure 4), but the approved amount declined only slightly from 1997 to 1999 and increased from 1999 to 2000 (figure 3). We find that the deteriorating macroeconomic environment, namely the Asian financial crisis, has had greater impact on TIC than political fluctuations. Although Lee promoted his ideas about jieji yongren, the approved TIC remained relatively stable between 1996 and 1999. In 2001, China, by entering the World Trade Organization (WTO), greatly improved the institutional environment for investment, which strengthened taishang confidence in investing in China. This was reflected in the radically increased amount invested in 2001 and 2002, even though Chen had

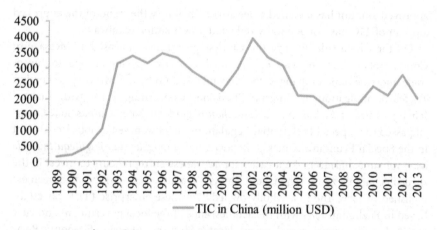

FIGURE 4. Taiwan's actual direct investment in China (million US$).

SOURCE: China's National Statistical Bureau, "National Data," multiple years, http://data.stats.gov.cn/.

won the presidential election and had not yet presented clear mainland policies. Nonetheless, the amount of actual TIC declined between 2002 and 2007 while the approved amount rose in the same period. This suggests that what restricted TIC was neither the Taiwanese authorities nor the Chinese state but *taishang* themselves, who were suspicious of Chen's mainland policy and became more conservative about investing in China even though the door remained open. In August 2002, Chen asserted his "one country on each side of the strait" (*yibian yiguo*) stance (that the PRC and the ROC were two different countries rather than two political entities within the country of China) and declared that the Taiwanese people would consider holding a referendum to decide Taiwan's future. China rapidly responded with tough comments and suspended interaction with the Taiwanese government. In 2005 China passed the Anti-Secession Law, demonstrating its commitment to unification and adding tension to cross-Strait relations. The law proclaims that Taiwan is part of China and that China may take nonpeaceful action if Taiwanese proindependence forces push Taiwan to secede from China.[4] Surprisingly, Hsu Wen-long, an important Taiwanese entrepreneur and founder of the Chi Mei Group, whose support for Chen had been crucial in the 2000 presidential election, published an open letter to support the law and mentioned that the law made him feel confident about investing in China.[5] Although China could retaliate against Taiwan by imposing clear economic sanctions or issuing tougher regulations over TIC, there was no clear evidence of China taking substantial actions during Chen's tenure. Ironically, Chen's provocative political statement did not inspire China's revenge but instead raised the alarm of *taishang*.

Nonetheless, China's entry into the WTO brought some challenges to TIC. More and more multinational companies started to invest in China. Meanwhile, China's own domestic enterprises gradually developed and became competitive after experiencing economic reform for two decades. With greater institutionalization and openness, the Chinese government has been pressured to create a level playing field in the marketplace. TIC originally benefited from many preferential policies exclusively provided to *taishang*, but these advantages lessened or even disappeared because of both WTO regulations and competition from local enterprises. Hence, the fluctuation of actual TIC in the 2000s can be attributed more to the shifting economic environment than to the changing political landscape.

In general, figures 3 and 4 present very different pictures of TIC in China. The amount of TIC approved by the Taiwanese government increased between 1999 and 2008, but the data of actual TIC gathered from Chinese authorities demonstrate a continuing decline between 2002 and 2008 and an increase afterwards. One may argue that the Chinese government obstructed TIC in order to pressure the DPP administration and promoted it during the KMT administration. But we found no clear evidence of this from either China's policies or interviews with *taishang*.[6]

As Taiwan has enhanced its involvement in China's economy, it has been said that Taiwan has been losing its economic autonomy and ceding leverage over its continued prosperity to China. With its rapid economic growth in the past two decades, China has surpassed Japan in 2010 to become the second-largest economy in the world.[7] While China thus has increasing leverage over Taiwan's economy, and more than 50 percent of Taiwanese overseas investment is located in China, *taishang* and TIC have confronted more challenges from both inside and outside China, and we cannot simply attribute the fluctuation of TIC to shifting political power. In addition, the statistical data have exhibited a generally rising amount of TIC, and neither Taiwanese and Chinese governments have issued clear economic bans and sanctions on TIC. Economic factors play a key role in influencing TIC trends.

TRENDS CHARACTERIZING THE DEVELOPMENT OF TIC

At the earliest stage, TIC was concentrated in traditional labor-intensive industries, such as shoemaking, textiles, and plastic products. Later, it expanded to different industries in the manufacturing sector, such as consumer electronics, chemicals, and food and beverages. Over the years TIC evolved from small factories to large capital-intensive companies with advanced technology, such as electrical appliances, precision instruments, and computer hardware. Since 2008 TIC has increasingly gone into all economic fields, including real estate, finance, tourism, media, and various service industries.[8] Accordingly, the major Taiwanese investors have shifted from small and middle-scale enterprises to large exchange-listed and OTC-listed enterprises with investment projects involving amounts over US$10 million. Unlike their predecessors who exported their products abroad, *taishang* are now targeting China's huge developing domestic market because they are encountering a shrinking global market. Moreover, Taiwanese enterprises have gradually increased their usage of raw materials and semifinished products purchased from local companies while reducing imports from Taiwan. Taiwanese companies have occupied a position in China's industrial chain and have closely linked themselves to China's economic development.

In general, TIC has demonstrated a gradual spread from south to north, from east to west, and from coastal regions to interior areas. Since the early 1990s, the Pearl River Delta area in Guangdong and the Yangtze River Delta area in Jiangsu have attracted the most TIC because of their proximity to Hong Kong and to Shanghai respectively.[9] In recent years, in order to respond to global financial crisis and promote industrial upgrading, Guangdong first promulgated the strategies of "clearing the cage and replacing the bird" (*tenglong huanniao*) and "transferring industries and labor" (*shuang zhuanyi*) in 2008. The local government plans to move low-margin, low-tech, labor-intensive industries out of the Pearl River Delta region and to introduce capital-intensive industry in its place. This desire to change the type of economic activities within the province has great impact on TIC because many Taiwanese factories were regarded as the "birds" that needed to be replaced. Similar policies were adopted in Zhejiang and Shanghai. Some Taiwanese entrepreneurs were encouraged to move their labor-intensive factories to Anhui Province, where the local government promised them more land.[10] Some Taiwanese investors bargained to keep one building or a small piece of land in the original location so that they could retain a base there even while moving a majority of their assets out.

In figure 5 we see how the approved amount of TIC has increased from the early 1990s in Central and South China and especially in East China.[11] While Jiangsu and Guangdong have radically lost TIC since 2010, Shanghai and Fujian have attracted more TIC since 2009. North China and Southwest China have welcomed more TIC since 2005. Northwest China and Northeast China have long been left behind in periods of economic transition because of a lack of infrastructure, and the amount of TIC reflects this situation as well.

BENEFICIAL POLICIES AT CENTRAL AND LOCAL LEVELS

The central Chinese government has promulgated several preferential policies to promote TIC. As early as 1988 the State Council first issued the "Regulations on

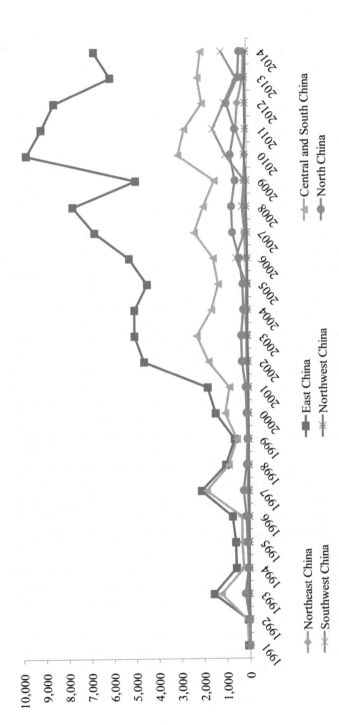

FIGURE 5. Taiwan's approved investment in mainland China by region (US$).

SOURCE: Investment Commission, Ministry of Economic Affairs, ROC, https://www.moeaic.gov.tw. The demarcation of China's regions is different in Taiwan's statistical data. North China includes Beijing, Tianjin, Hebei, Shanxi, and Inner Mongolia. Northeast China refers to Jilin, Liaoning, and Heilongjiang. East China covers Shanghai, Jiangsu, Zhejiang, Anhui, Fujian, Shandong, and Jiangxi. Central and South China includes Henan, Hubei, Hunan, Guangdong, Guangxi, and Hainan. Southeast China includes Chongqing, Sichuan, Guizhou, Yunnan, and Tibet. Northwest China covers Xinjiang, Gansu, Ningxia, and Shaanxi.

Encouraging the Investments of Taiwan Compatriots" (*Guanyu guli Taiwan tong-bao touzi de guiding*).[12] This document provided very comprehensive and detailed regulations on how Taiwanese entrepreneurs could invest in China. It had been less than a decade since China embarked on its economic transition, and the idea of regime change remained fraught with uncertainty and ambiguity. As a means to promote investment stability, China's Taiwan investment regulations attempted to enhance investor confidence by specifying that "the state will not nationalize the investment of Taiwanese investors and other assets" and "the legal benefits the Taiwanese investors obtain can be remitted abroad according to relevant law."[13] In 1994 the Chinese government passed the "Law Regarding the Protection of Investment by Taiwan Compatriots" (*Taiwan tongbao touzi baohu fa*) and made it very clear that its purpose was to protect and encourage Taiwanese investment in China and to promote cross-Strait economic development.[14] The law also permitted Taiwanese entrepreneurs to organize business associations. In the same year, the State Council announced the "Decision Concerning Further Development of Economic Issues across the Strait" (*Guowuyuan guanyu jinyibu fazhan haxialiang'an jingjiguanxi ruogan wenti de jueding*) and promoted the principles of "priority and relaxation" (*tongdeng youxian, shidang fangkuan*).[15] After this law had been implemented for five years, the Chinese government approved the "Rules for Implementation of the Law on the Protection of Investment of Taiwan Compatriots" (*Taiwan tongbao touzi baohufa shishi xize*) to provide more detailed regulations in 1999. In 2012, the Jiangsu provincial government passed the "Regulation on the Protection and Promotion of Investment of Taiwan Compatriots" (*Baohu he cujin Taiwan tongbao touzi tiaoli*), which is the first and only legal document at the local level.[16] These statutes have never been revised, so some of the articles are outdated. In 2009 China announced the launch of an amendment process for "Rules for Implementation of the Law on the Protection of Investment of Taiwan Compatriots," but it has not made any substantial progress as yet.[17]

The major functions of Taiwanese business associations (TBAs) include protecting the legal rights of *taishang*, managing public relations with and taking care of Taiwanese people in China, and improving the local investment environment.[18] The first TBA was registered in Shenzhen in 1990, and there are now 142 TBAs across China.[19] To better manage TBAs, the Chinese government issued a notice entitled "Interim Measures on Administrating Taiwanese Business Associations" (*Taiwan tongbao touzi qiye xiehui guanli zhanxing banfa*) in 2003. Nonetheless, TBAs are not official institutions and are not allowed to have national headquarters. Some TBAs worked together to establish a nonprofit organization, the Association of Taiwan Investment Enterprises on the Mainland (ATIEM, *quanguo Taiwan tongbao touzi qiye lianyihui*), in 2007. The ATIEM is supervised by both the Taiwan Affairs Office and the Ministry of Civil Affairs and is able to communicate with the central government directly. That is, it acts as a two-way channel between TBAs and the Chinese government. It transmits *taishang*'s voices to the authorities and delivers central directives to the entrepreneurs.[20]

At the local level, provincial and city governments have offered various forms of preferential treatment to attract Taiwanese investment, such as providing a wide range of tax incentives and reinvesting profits, facilitating cheap land acquisition, and reducing bureaucratic hurdles. For example, one of the most popular programs is called the Two Free, Three Half (*liangmian, sanjianban*), meaning that a Taiwanese firm scheduled to operate longer than ten years is qualified to enjoy a five-year concessionary tax term with two years of exemption and three years of paying only half the corporate income tax after its profit-making year.[21] Nonetheless, in December 2014 the central government announced Notice No. 62, which requires ministries and local governments to clean up and regulate preferential policies that violate laws.[22] Because Taiwanese investing firms have long enjoyed more incentives than other foreign companies from local governments in China, *taishang* will bear the brunt of the new requirements. In the press conference after the National People's Congress concluded in March 2015, Premier Li Keqiang stressed that China will continue to safeguard the legitimate rights and interests of Taiwanese-invested enterprises and will sustain appropriate preferential policies for them.[23]

Contrary to this trend, in Taiwanese society the major debate is whether TIC is hollowing out Taiwan's economy. Those who disagree argue that the problem is a lack of investment opportunities instead of capital, so that industrial upgrading is key to reviving the economy. Those who agree contend that the rise of the unemployment rate and loss in domestic investment and the proportionate size of manufacturing gross domestic product (GDP) are attributable to increasing TIC. But there is no consensus yet.

THE ROLE OF *TAISHANG*: POLITICAL AGENTS OR ECONOMIC HOSTAGES

While cross-Strait political relations were suspended under the Chen administration, it was predicted that TIC would be affected and even prohibited by China. Theories of economic statecraft proposed that China might implement economic sanctions as a coercive political tactic to pressure Taiwan.[24] The possibility of economic warfare across the Strait is much greater than that of military warfare because China could not achieve its desired goals through military tactics.[25] Hence *taishang* are potential hostages or vulnerable victims if the Chinese government decides to launch economic sanctions as political retaliation.[26]

But such a viewpoint does not take into account the complicated interaction between both governments and the commercial interests that Taiwanese businesspeople have pursued. Instead of wielding a big stick, the Hu administration implemented a "carrots" policy of "counting on the Taiwanese people" to pressure the DPP administration. Nonetheless, this attempt to use *taishang* as political leverage over Taiwan was ineffective and showed that *taishang*'s political significance is rather limited.[27] During Chen's tenure, while official interaction between the PRC and the ROC was generally suspended, Taiwanese businesspeople became implicitly a channel of information that helped the Chinese government understand Taiwan. *Taishang* had had no impact on the DPP's mainland polices, nor were they able to communicate with the Taiwanese government. When President Ma took power in 2008 and cross-Strait relations dramatically improved, the role of *taishang* changed both politically and economically. The KMT administration would regularly host gatherings with *taishang* where President Ma would participate, listening to their advice. *Taishang* have more and more frequently taken part in cross-Strait interactions organized by both the Taiwanese government and the KMT. But the key officials of TBAs and the ATIEM see these activities as the KMT's lip service and believe there has been no substantial progress in improving the *taishang*'s situation.[28] In general, *taishang* are vulnerable to volatile political situations but unable to participate in the policy-making process. In other words, they are influenced but not influencing in cross-Strait political interactions.

Voting for the KMT may be regarded as a passive reaction to Taiwanese politics: *taishang* rely on this party for a stable and predictable mainland policy. We should not interpret it to mean that *taishang* support China or further political progress toward unification. Ironically, they are the people who know how untrustworthy China is. The rising competitiveness of domestic enterprises and a lack of official support from the Taiwanese have left *taishang* struggling to do business in China. Quite often the Taiwan Affairs Offices in Beijing are too weak to help when dealing with other government bodies such as local governments, the Ministry of Commerce, and the State Administration for Industry and Commerce in China.[29] *Taishang* have played a less important role in cross-Strait relations than the public has generally believed. In short, *taishang* are neither political agents nor economic hostages. They are unable to make a positive contribution to policy, but they have not seriously suffered from political turbulence. They are businesspeople who look for commercial opportunities in China and hope for a stable political environment, as their counterparts would when investing in any other part of the world.

GO SOUTH: TAIWANESE INVESTMENT IN SOUTHEAST ASIAN COUNTRIES AS AN ALTERNATIVE

The "go south" strategy was initiated in 1993 by former president Lee Teng-hui in order to diversify risks faced by Taiwanese investors and lessen their reliance on China.[30] The Taiwanese government issued its "Guidelines for Strengthening Economic and Trade Ties with Southeast Asia," which are now in their seventh edition.

During the Asian financial crisis, the Taiwanese government further promulgated the "Measures on Strengthening the Promotion of Economic and Trade Relations with Southeast Asia" to help Taiwanese businesspeople with financing problems. Unfortunately these policies were not particularly effective, and most Taiwanese capital ended up leaving Thailand and Indonesia.[31] In 2002 then-president Chen reannounced the "go south" strategy, declaring that China was just one part of the global market and that Taiwan should not depend on it too heavily. When incumbent president Ma took power in 2008, he reconfirmed the necessity for Taiwan to participate in regional economic integration in Southeast Asia.

Unlike his predecessors, Ma has considered "go south" (invest in Southeast Asia) and "go west" (invest in China) to be not zero-sum games but win-win games, and he has encouraged Taiwanese investment flow in both directions. Nonetheless, these initiatives have carried no new ideas and concrete plans to benefit Taiwanese investment.[32] The amount of Taiwanese investment in Southeast Asia skyrocketed in 1994 when the policy was first initiated. But after the Asian financial crisis it decreased to the same levels as 1993 and remained there for the following eight years until 2006 (see figure 6). There was huge fluctuation between 2007 and 2009. In general, no matter what reasoning the government adopted to promote Taiwanese investment moving to Southeast Asian countries, we do not find a clear trend in capital flows. Additionally, many Southeast Asian countries set many constraints on FDI policies and typically sought out large-scale investments only, preventing many Taiwanese from investing in the region.[33] Because of the unstable political and economic environment, anti-Chinese movements, and fluctuating local policies, the future of investment in Southeast Asia remains unclear.[34] According to the Secretariat of ASEAN, Taiwan was not among top ten investor countries in ASEAN between 2008 and 2010.[35]

In recent years, however, confronting rising labor costs, Taiwanese entrepreneurs started to move their factories from Shenzhen and Dongguan to Southeast Asian countries, especially Vietnam and Cambodia. Obviously, *taishang*'s profit-driven considerations do more than government policies to motivate them to "go south." Moreover, in 2012 the Taiwanese government issued the "Measures on Promoting Taiwanese Entrepreneurs to Invest in Taiwan," the so-called "salmon returns" policy, which includes a higher quota of foreign laborers and low interest rates for bank loans. It has been ineffective, however, because of high land costs and a lack of skilled laborers.[36] The amount of *taishang* investment returning to Taiwan decreased by 55 percent in 2014.[37]

CONCLUSION

The Taiwanese government has been worrying about becoming increasingly irrelevant to the international market. Efforts by former presidents Lee and Chen

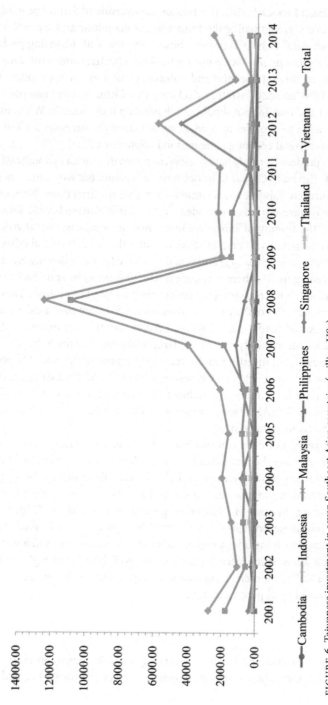

FIGURE 6. Taiwanese investment in seven Southeast Asian countries (million US$).

SOURCE: Investment Commission, Ministry of Economic Affairs, ROC, https://www.moeaic.gov.tw.

to divert trade away from China have largely failed. Lower production costs in the competitive global economy and similarities in culture and languages have pulled Taiwanese entrepreneurs unavoidably into China's economic orbit. Such cross-Strait interactions have not demonstrated the capacity of economic liberalization to promote peace, and the potential for political conflict remains. Taiwanese have accused Beijing of manipulating economic incentives to facilitate unification, but we have not found clear evidence of this from either statistical data or China's policies. Interestingly, discontent has broken out domestically within Taiwan rather than in blunt confrontation between Taiwan and the mainland. Examination of cross-Strait interactions over the past two decades shows that economic integration has promoted peace and helped to constrain certain conflict-heightening pressures created by democratization in Taiwan.[38]

Undoubtedly, TIC is a critical factor in cross-Strait interactions, if not the most important one, and is characterized by three prominent trends. First, in terms of targeted industry, TIC has shifted from labor-intensive manufacturing of items such as consumer goods to high-technology electronics and precision products. Second, the scale of TIC has changed from small and medium-sized factories to large business conglomerates. Third, geographically speaking, TIC has moved from south to north and from east to west within China, and investors who have decided to leave China have moved to Southeast Asia.

Economic considerations have played a more important role than political concerns in determining approved and actual levels of TIC. Changes in political administrations have not resulted in bans on the further advance of TIC, and the Chinese government has not announced any concrete policy to prohibit TIC. *Taishang's* economic motivation and investor confidence, rather than politics, are the factors stopping them from pouring more money into China. Southeast Asian countries and Taiwan may not be the best investment locations for *taishang* at the moment, but the question of how to fully integrate them into the Chinese economy is becoming urgent.

The comparable phenomenon in China is Chinese investment in Taiwan (CIT). The Taiwanese government has lifted its ban on CIT and allowed Chinese entrepreneurs to invest in Taiwan since June 2009. As of 2016, 729 approved projects have been recorded and the total amount has been US$1.3 billion.[39] Relatively speaking, the numbers and investment amounts are small when compared to TIC. Moreover, to some companies, especially state-owned enterprises, the scale of the Taiwanese market is too small to benefit their business. Unlike their Taiwanese counterparts, Chinese businesspeople are investing in order to carry out political tasks, such as promoting cross-Strait relations.[40]

While China has been proposing the grand strategy of "One Belt, One Road" (*yi dai, yi lu;* also known as the Silk Road Economic Belt, the Twenty-First-Century Maritime Silk Road, a plan to build economic corridors linking China to

Europe—both overland via West Asia and maritime via the South China Sea, the Indian Ocean and the Red Sea), the Chinese government seems to be incorporating TIC as part of the plan in order to prevent it from pulling out of China. The Taiwanese government is also trying to lure *taishang* back.[41] It might be a good chance for TIC to move inland and reap the benefits of cheap land and low labor costs. On the other hand, while the Economic Cooperation Framework Agreement (ECFA) between Taiwan and China may make a positive contribution to TIC, Taiwan's domestic politics make the issue very controversial for the Taiwanese themselves. We still need time to watch how the issue develops before clarifying its impact on TIC.

NOTES

1. Douglas B. Fuller, "The Cross-Strait Economic Relationship's Impact on Development in Taiwan and China: Adversaries and Partners," *Asian Survey* 48, no. 2 (2008): 239–64; Kerry Brown, Justin Hempson-Jones, and Jessica Pennisi, *Investment across the Taiwan Strait: How Taiwan's Relationship with China Affects Its Position in the Global Economy* (London: Chatham House, 2010), www.kerry-brown.co.uk/files/website-8.pdf.

2. Surges were reported for TIC in 1993, 1997, 2002, and 2003 because these years were deadlines for *taishang* to complete the procedure for their unregistered investment. The amounts are not included in figure 3 because they did not get permission in advance.

3. The minimum-wage system was implemented in China in 2004. From then to 2015 the amount was been tripled. For example, in Beijing, Shanghai, and Shenzhen, the minimum wage was ¥580, 690, and 690 in 2005 but ¥1,720, 2,020, and 2,030 in 2015.

4. See Articles 2 and 9.

5. "Hsu Wen-long of Chi Mei Supports Anti-secession Law," Huaxia Net, March 27, 2005, http://big5.huaxia.com/zt/pl/05-015/600455.html.

6. I made two field trips to Beijing and Shanghai respectively in 2013 and interviewed more than fifteen Taiwanese entrepreneurs, including officials in the Beijing TBA, the Shanghai TBA, and ATIEM. None of them felt substantial political pressure from the central or local governments in China during the DPP administration.

7. China overtook Germany in 2007 to become the third-largest economy in the world.

8. For example, Eslite is a famous bookstore in Taiwan and has not only opened branches in Suzhou and Shanghai but also invested in the real estate market; see "Eslite Eyes Home Sales in Suzhou," *Taipei Times*, May 16, 2014, http://money.udn.com/storypage.php?sub_id=5641&art_id 777297.

9. The Yangtze River Delta area is regarded as the best-targeted region for TIC. Seven of the best locations for TIC are all in this area, including Suzhou, Yuyao, Xiaoshan, Hangzhou, Fenghua, Yangzhou, and Jiading. See "Pearl River Delta Area and Yangtze River Delta Area Compete for Taiwanese Investment," Sina Net, June 5, 2012, http://finance.sina.com.cn/g/20020605/217245.html.

10. Taiwanese entrepreneurs in Taiwan, interviews by author, March 2013.

11. Dongguan in Guangdong and Suzhou in Jiangsu are two cities that have attracted the most TIC.

12. In the 1980s China passed a few laws to attract foreign investment, but these did not specifically target TIC. Examples are the Law on Economic Contracts Involving Foreign Interest (Shewai Jingji Hetong Fa; 1985), the Law on Foreign-Funded Enterprise (Waizi Qiye Fa; 1986), and the Law on Sino-Foreign Contractual Joint Ventures (Zhongwai Hezuo Jingying Qiye Fa; 1988).

13. See Articles 8 and 10.

14. See Article 1.

15. "Decision of the State Council on Several Issues Concerning the Further Development of Economic Relations across the Taiwan Straits," August 1, 1994, www.people.com.cn/zixun/flfgk/item/dwjjf/falv/1/1–4–3.html.

16. "Jiangsu wanshan dui Taiwan tongbao touzi wushi youxiao baozhang cuoshi" [Jiangsu improved the regulations on Taiwanese investment], Sina Net, December 27, 2012, http://finance.sina.com.cn/china/dfjj/20121227/185614136902.shtml.

17. "'Law Regarding the Protection of Investment by Taiwan Compatriots' Is Outdated and Planned to Be Amended," UDN Net, March 10, 2015, http://udn.com/news/story/7334/754798.

18. Shiuh-shen Chien and Litao Zhao, "Local Economic Transition in China: A Perspective on Taiwan Investment," in *China's Reform in Global Perspective*, ed. John Wong and Zhiyue Bo (Singapore: World Scientific, 2010), 254–55.

19. The complete list is published by the Straits Exchange Foundation; see "Taishang xiehui lianxi yilanbiao" [Contact information of Taiwanese business associations], Straits Exchange Foundation, November 1, 2016, www.seftb.org/mhypage.exe?HYPAGE=/01/01_1_2.asp. There are 116 TBAs listed on the Taiwan Affairs Office's website; see "Gedi taizi qiye xiehui huizongbiao" [Collections of Taiwanese business associations], Taiwan Affairs Office, January 11, 2011, www.gwytb.gov.cn/lajm/tsstzz/201101/t20110111_1690852.htm.

20. AEITM official in Beijing, interview by author, February 2013.

21. The program is based on the former Income Tax Law for Foreign Invested Enterprises and Foreign Enterprises, enacted in 1991.

22. "Guowuyuan guanyu qingli guifan shuishou deng youhui zhengce de tongzhi" [Notice on reviewing and regulating preferential policies for taxation and other aspects], No. 62 (2014), State Council. The notice seeks to eliminate preferential terms, especially those issued by local governments that violate laws and central directives.

23. "Chinese Mainland to Maintain Appropriate Preferential Policies to Taiwan," Xinhua Net, March 15, 2015, http://news.xinhuanet.com/english/2015–03/15/c_134067977.htm.

24. See David Baldwin, *Economic Statecraft* (Princeton, NJ: Princeton University Press, 1985); James M. Lindsay, "Trade Sanction as Policy Instruments: A Re-examination," *International Studies Quarterly* 30, no. 2 (1986): 153–73; Tse-kang Leng, "A Political Analysis of Taiwan's Economic Dependence on Mainland China," *Issues and Studies* 34, no. 8 (1998): 132–54.

25. Quansheng Zhao, "Beijing's Dilemma with Taiwan: War or Peace?" *Pacific Review* 18, no. 2 (2005): 217–42.

26. See Murray Tanner, *Chinese Economic Coercion against Taiwan: A Tricky Weapon to Use* (Santa Monica, CA: RAND Corporation, 2007); Paul J. Bolt, "Economic Ties across the Taiwan Strait: Buying Time for Compromise," *Issues and Studies* 37, no. 2 (2001): 80–105; Chen-Yuan Tung, "Cross-Strait Economic Relations: China's Leverage and Taiwan's Vulnerability," *Issues and Studies* 39, no. 3 (2003): 137–75; Seanon S. Wong, "Economic Statecraft across the Strait: Business Influence in Taiwan's Mainland Policy," *Asian Perspective* 29, no. 2 (2005): 41–72; and Scott L. Kastner, *Political Conflict and Economic Interdependence across the Taiwan Strait and Beyond* (Stanford, CA: Stanford University Press, 2009).

27. Shu Keng and Gunter Schubert, "Agents of Taiwan-China Unification? The Political Roles of Taiwanese Business People in the Process of Cross-Strait Integration," *Asian Survey* 50, no. 2 (2010): 287–310.

28. TBA official in Tianjin, interview by author, February 2013.

29. TBA official in Beijing, interview by author, February 2013.

30. Xiangming Chen, "Taiwan Investments in China and Southeast Asia: 'Go West, but Also Go South,'" *Asian Survey* 36, no. 5 (May 1996): 447–67.

31. Taiwanese investment in Singapore and Vietnam has been quite stable in the past two decades.

32. Chao-jen Huang and Haw Ju, "An Analysis of Economic Interactions between Taiwan and the ASEAN-6," *Taiwan International Studies Quarterly* 8, no. 3 (Fall 2012): 185–204.

33. Taiwan Institute of Economic Research, *Analysis of Investment Location Choice and Strategy under New Go South Policy* (Taipei: Council for Economic Planning and Development, Executive Yuan, 2003), 62–68, http://ebooks.lib.ntu.edu.tw/1_file/CEPD/152/south@664854.7334842238@.pdf.

34. In May 2014 there was a large-scale anti-Chinese movement in central and southern Vietnam that involved Taiwanese factories.

35. Zunci Hsu, "Our Economic and Trade Relationship with ASEAN," Special Report, World Trade Organization and Regional Trade Agreements Center, January 11, 2013, www.aseancenter.org.tw/CenStudyDetail.aspx?studyid=13&natstudyid=2.

36. Official of Straits Exchange Foundation in Taipei, interview by author, June 2014.

37. "Taiwanese Investment Returning to Taiwan Decreased by Half," *Now News*, April 23, 2014, http://legacy.nownews.com/2014/04/23/320-3021684.htm.

38. Patrick McDonald, *The Invisible Hand of Peace: Capitalism, the War Machine, and International Relations Theory* (New York: Cambridge University Press, 2009), 233–63.

39. Investment Commission, Ministry of Economic Affairs, ROC, "Monthly Press Release," October 20, 2015, www.moeaic.gov.tw/system_external/ctlr?PRO=NewsLoad&id=1072.

40. Official of State-Owned Assets Supervision and Administration Commission, interview by author, Beijing, July 2014.

41. "The Ministry of Economic Affairs Urges Taiwanese Entrepreneurs to Return to Taiwan," *China Times*, September 30, 2015, www.chinatimes.com/newspapers/20150930000086–260203.

9

Cross-Strait Economic Relations and China's Rise

The Case of the IT Sector

Tse-Kang Leng

Cross–Taiwan Strait economic relations have experienced tremendous shocks since 2008. High expectations in the early stage of Ma Ying-jeou's administration were eroded by domestic difficulties and skepticism. Taiwan's attempts to embrace economic globalization through China were weakened within the complex domestic environment. The student-led Sunflower Movement in 2014, protesting the Cross-Strait Service Trade Agreement, put that and other cross-Strait economic pacts on ice. At the same time, China has adjusted its grand strategies by broadening economic engagements around the globe. China's paramount leader Xi Jinping has also demonstrated his strong will by consolidating political control and concentrating his power. The rise of China's comprehensive power and Taiwan's hesitation to institutionalize the cross-Strait economic relationship provide unique cases for academic exploration.

This chapter will discuss whether Taiwan can still maintain its existing position in cross-Strait economic relations within the new context of the rise of China's economic power. I will first introduce the current development models of Taiwan's information technology sectors in the context of the cross-Strait division of labor and then discuss the changes to China's position in the global political and economic arenas. The third section will analyze the strengths and weaknesses of Taiwan's IT sector in coping with state-driven pressure coming from the other side of the Taiwan Strait. Finally, I will provide some policy reflections on Taiwanese strategies to cope with the rise of China.

DYNAMICS OF CROSS-STRAIT ECONOMIC
RELATIONS: TAIWAN'S GLOBALIZED IT INDUSTRY

Taiwan's IT Industry as the Foundation of Economic Globalization

Taiwan's economic globalization is based on its ability to be flexible and adjust in managing the global supply chain. In the post–developmental state era, Taiwanese firms are characterized by their reputation among global brand holders for punctual and precise manufacturing. This original equipment manufacturing/original design manufacturing (OEM/ODM) model of development was founded on mutual trust with upstream designers, close interaction with major high-tech hubs, and access to the major manufacturing bases of mainland China. In other words, Taiwanese firms are the major platforms linking American technologies, Taiwanese know-how, and Chinese processing capabilities.[1]

Taiwan's industrial structure has increasingly become dominated by the IT and electronics sector. As a result, IT and electronics products now account for an excessively large share of Taiwan's overall exports. On the basis of export data compiled by Taiwan's Directorate General of Budget, Accounting, and Statistics, information and communications technology (ICT) products consistently account for over 30 percent of Taiwan's total exports. As IT and electronics products are characterized by a high level of income elasticity, consumers will often delay purchase of these items. However, fluctuations in the global economic climate can therefore have a significant negative impact on Taiwan's exports and its economic growth rate. Taiwan's ability to implement adjustments in response to global economic fluctuations is also affected.[2]

Traditional wisdom indicates that, thanks to the outsourcing policies of the main IT design centers like Silicon Valley, Taiwan is a major beneficiary within the global division of labor. Overseas returnees serve as major mediators of cross-Pacific talent circulation. However, recent studies provide different views of this unique pattern of IT globalization. For instance, Martin Kenney, Dan Breznitz, and Michael Murphree are skeptical about the importance of overseas returnees for Taiwan's IT development and globalization. They argue that overseas returnees established only three of the top ten firms for integrated circuit (IC) design in Taiwan; only one of the firms' founders has a direct connection to Silicon Valley, having worked there, while the other two have founders with Silicon Valley educations. Kenney and his colleagues claim that the returnee-centric version of Taiwan's development does not recognize the important role of multinational corporations, indigenous entrepreneurship, and the spin-off policy of the Industrial Technology Research Institute (ITRI) in creating an environment that would be attractive to returnees. In other words, scholars have underestimated the significance of the ecosystem that was built before the appearance of the returnee entrepreneurs, mostly in the 1990s. Such an ecosystem created the conditions within which returnees could utilize the education and skills learned abroad to provide the Taiwanese node of the structural niche they would fill and later expand.[3]

The overseas connection may not have had a substantial impact in terms of quantity, but it did improve the quality of Taiwanese IT production capabilities. Overseas returnees spread the seeds of cultural change in the IT sector. Instead of focusing on the impact of overseas returnees on the globalization of Taiwan's IT industry, Taiwanese companies have been increasing the learning curve to accumulate technological know-how in the IT and electronics sectors. The progress of such a learning model is reflected in the economic links between Taiwan and Japan. Expansion of the transnational division of labor and the long-term economic downturn in Japan sparked by global capitalism created a crucial strategic opportunity for dependency management within the Taiwanese thin-film-transistor liquid-crystal-display (TFT-LCD) industry. The Taiwanese effectively imported Japanese human resources, learning their manufacturing technologies directly from Japanese engineers. Taiwanese TFT-LCD manufacturers subsequently innovated their own next-generation technology without relying on Japanese engineers or continuously purchasing Japanese technologies.[4]

After May 20, 2016, the new government under the Democratic Progressive Party (DPP) launched new policy packages to promote innovation and IT development. The "Asian Silicon Valley" initiative is one of President Tsai's five major industrial development objectives. This project aims to increase Taiwan's share of the global IT market by creating a robust environment for entrepreneurs and start-ups. It also intends to upgrade Taiwan's IT research and design capacities by fostering innovative talent, facilitating the development of capital markets, and revising related laws. Furthermore, the Taiwanese government is going to establish a one-stop center to promote the integration of its R&D capabilities with California's Silicon Valley and other innovation hubs around the world.[5]

Unlike previous policies of IT development over the past two decades, the Asian Silicon Valley plan intends to promote Taiwan's participation in international standard formulation and certification of IT-related technologies. The policy goals include integrating Taiwan's hardware advantages into software applications and commercializing research findings of universities and research institutes. This plan also focuses on the consolidation of IT and other high-tech infrastructure. For instance, it plans to establish a quality Internet environment, build diversified smart test beds, and develop applications based on smart logistics, smart transport, and smart medicine.[6]

Embracing the Chinese Market in the Global Supply Chain: The Hon Hai Model

It has long been argued that the most effective protection against Taiwan's economic dependence on China is to diversify Taiwan's economic engagements around the world. In addition to establishing technological linkages with the United States, Taiwan has depended on Japan economically in terms of industrial know-how, upstream technological innovation, and enhancement of the service sector. For Taiwan, the main driving force of economic interaction has remained OEM and ODM types of investments in China. Major Taiwanese IT manufacturers like the Taiwan Semiconductor Manufacturing Company (TSMC) concentrate on perfecting the manufacturing process rather than the initial design. Because of their orientation, Taiwanese firms do not aspire to control the upstream core technologies. Even though these OEM/ODM firms link US and Japanese technologies, Taiwanese know-how, and mainland Chinese manufacturing capacities, the profit margin has been shrinking. Companies like Foxconn have had to squeeze their manufacturing costs, which results in problems like sweatshop-style factories and labor disputes. In response, Foxconn and other OEM manufacturers have tried to globalize their operations and make new breakthroughs in international markets. But well-known Taiwanese brand names like Acer, Asus, and HTC are still rarities in the global marketplace.

Despite all the setbacks surrounding labor disputes and controversies over sweatshop factories in China, Hon Hai/Foxconn remains one of the most successful Taiwanese OEM/ODM companies in the world. The major reason for Foxconn's ascendance in the world IT manufacturing arena is its close integration with Apple's global supply chain. Through Apple's comprehensive supply chain, Foxconn is also able to form partnerships with other manufacturers and establish extensive networks of mutual cooperation. For instance, Apple's iconic iPhone brings together several increasingly global production networks, one of which comprises one of the world's leading brand-name firms (Apple) and its manufacturing partner and the world's largest provider of electronics manufacturing services (Taiwan's Hon Hai). Another combines three specialized suppliers: the world's leading integrated semiconductor manufacturer (South Korea's Samsung), a leading fabless smartphone chip design firm (Qualcomm from the United States), and a top semiconductor foundry (Taiwan's TSMC). In these intersections of multiple production networks across several segments of the ICT sector, the interfirm partnerships creating the market success of one major consumer product are realized.[7]

The Foxconn/Hon Hai model of globalization is noteworthy in that it does not reflect strong state intervention and support. Instead, it demonstrates the dynamics of self-reinforcement and innovative forces at the enterprise level. According to Henry Yeung, Hon Hai was not a direct recipient of state support. Its success cannot be attributed to the state's industrial policy. Hon Hai is not a "national champion" according to the standards of the developmental state. Instead, its emergence is largely due to its strategic coupling with leading global firms in the electronics industry. Hon Hai's competitive advantages are predicated on its ability to combine discretion with a solid record of quality control and competitive pricing. Yeung argues that Hon Hai's emergence as Taiwan's largest industrial firm owes neither to state-led industrialization efforts nor to indigenous industrial capabilities derived from the "brain circulation" of transnational technologist elites.

Instead, its success as the world's leading electronics manufacturing service provider can be explained by the changing industrial dynamics of global production networks, which offer critical windows of opportunity for it to serve as a strategic manufacturing partner of leading global firms.[8]

In addition to strengthening its status as a key manufacturer in the Apple supply chain, Hon Hai has extended its reach to high-tech service sectors and has formed various strategic alliances with other ICT vendors and service providers. Hon Hai released a plan for the establishment of a intelligent society that incorporates devices with services, integrating hardware and software. The company is set to transform itself into a technology services company to meet consumer demand and has no intentions of launching own-branded products.

In the future 5G era, the company will focus on the development of automation and artificial intelligence, combining hardware/software capabilities, using technology to improve human life, and creating greater value for its shareholders.[9] For this reason, Hon Hai/Foxconn is working with Google on robots for use in the manufacturing process. It needs Google's help to step up automation at its factories, as the company has the lowest sales per employee among the contract makers, given its large workforce.[10] Furthermore, the company is looking to trim labor costs and diversify its operations, seeking new avenues of growth as revenue from contract manufacturing slows. Hon Hai has established multiple relationships with its customers, including a cloud server cooperation agreement signed in late April 2013 with the American PC vendor Hewlett Packard.[11]

Hon Hai has taken steps to reduce its dependence on Apple. In 2014, Apple accounted for 25 to 30 percent of Hong Hai's overall revenue. Since then, Hon Hai has acquired controlling shares in Taiwan's Asia Pacific Telecom and has made plans to expand into the automotive industry. In late December 2014 it publicly announced that it had taken a 10.5 percent stake in China Harmony, a major luxury car dealer in China. Recently, it announced that it has begun partnering with Tencent, which operates the Chinese social network WeChat, to build electric vehicles that will be connected to the Internet. It says it can build electric vehicles for under US$15,000—significantly cheaper than the current models of major manufacturers.[12]

Foxconn's acquisition of the Japanese IT giant Sharp in 2016 demonstrates Gou's ambition to expand in the global arena. According to Gou, Sharp has lots of technology but isn't able to market it; Foxconn plans to accelerate commercialization of Sharp's patents, turning them to technology and then turning technology to products that will help turn the business profitable. Because Foxconn is now facing challenging market conditions, including a trend of growing protectionism in many countries, new strategic moves are necessary for survival and development.[13]

The $ 3.5 billion deal, for a 66 percent stake in Sharp, is intended to make Foxconn a more attractive partner for Apple. The American technology company uses

Sharp screens, which could give Foxconn added leverage in dealings between the two. In recent years, Apple has been diversifying its supply chain, giving some production contracts to other assemblers and component makers, and Foxconn is grappling with China's rising labor costs and a slowdown in the global smartphone market. While Foxconn's revenue has been padded by a boom in orders for less expensive Chinese-branded smartphones, analysts have highlighted the concern of increased competition from China-based suppliers. Also, Apple, as part of its efforts to diversify its supply chain, has given orders for iPhone assembly to Pegatron, another Taiwan-based contract manufacturer, which operates a huge factory near Shanghai.[14]

Attempts to Establish the IT Brand: The Challenges of the HTC Model

Another issue to consider with regard to Taiwan's global links in the IT industry is the transition from an OEM to an own-brand manufacturing (OBM) model of production. As profit margins are increasingly squeezed, some Taiwanese OEM manufacturers have begun to shift their direction and take on more risks. The established smartphone manufacturer HTC provides an example. HTC was founded in 1997 and initially produced notebook computers. For years, it was a contract manufacturer of hand-held devices for other companies, pioneering phones with touch-screen interfaces. In 2006, it started making products under its own name, and a year later Google introduced Android, which became the operating system of choice for HTC products. By 2011, the company's market capitalization exceeded that of Nokia, once the Goliath of the industry. In 2011, HTC sold more smartphones in the United States than any other maker. Since then, shares of HTC have plunged almost 90 percent, shrinking its market cap from $33 billion to $4 billion.

However, the HTC case also demonstrates the competitive weakness of Taiwanese IT firms with regard to their own brands. World-class experience in the manufacturing process does not easily translate into a capacity for survival in the global marketplace. For instance, the HTC One, released in 2013, was named "Smartphone of the Year" at the Mobile World Congress held in Barcelona in February and became only the third phone to earn a five-star review. However, HTC's biggest problem is not a lack of sophistication in its design. Rather, it is HTC's biggest rival, Samsung, which last year spent $14 billion on advertising—about the same as the GDP of Iceland. HTC posted its first-ever operating loss in the third quarter of 2013, after which ABI Research, a consulting firm, said that once such handset companies become unprofitable, only 10 percent can be expected to survive the next two years.[15]

In China, the world's biggest market of consumer electronics, HTC is being squeezed further by global brands and cheap local producers. As a brand-name manufacturer, HTC has difficulties in identifying its brand position in the Chinese market. Mainland consumers know relatively little about the Taiwanese brand whose initials once stood for "High Tech Computer." They navigate toward Apple and Samsung plus their own smartphone brands, such as Coolpad, Huawei, Lenovo, Xiaomi, and ZTE. Local brands sell for no more than HTC-equivalent handsets and in some cases have better specifications, while HTC is set back by higher production costs.[16]

HTC's downturn and losses indicate how second-tier smartphone makers are struggling in a maturing market. HTC's shares in Taipei sank to a record low of NT$71 on June 30, 2015, compared with an all-time high of NT$1,300 in April 2011. The shares ended flat at NT$73.80, ahead of the company's announcement. According to HTC chair Cher Wang, the company has recently launched a fitness band and a virtual reality device.[17]

In August 2015, HTC's market value fell below its cash on hand, leading to headlines stating that the brand no longer had any value. This company with a proud tradition of design seemed to have lost a piece of its soul. If the company is going to avoid declining any further, it will need killer hardware, a revamped software experience, and a more coherent (and less defensive and negative) marketing message.[18] In 2016, HTC shifted its strategies to serve as Google Android mobile phone Pixel's OEM manufacturer. Responses from the market are mixed. Experts indicate that since Google emphasizes that the new mobile phone is "made by Google," HTC has been relegated to the role of OEM manufacturer rather than coengineering the device with Google. This approach is no different from Apple's partnership with IPhone builder Foxconn.[19] For HTC, it is a retreat from an OBM to an OEM model of development. On the other hand, critics also argue that since the market performance of HTC's own products is sluggish, using safer ways to accumulate revenues for the adjustments of the next stage is a rational choice for HTC. The potential target for HTC's niche could be virtual reality devices.[20]

The Hon Hai and HTC models provide mixed examples of the strengths and weaknesses of Taiwanese IT firms in cross-Strait economic relations. Taiwan has put cross-Strait economic relations in the global arena. However, China is no longer an underdeveloped market with low wages and technological know-how. "The rise of China" has become a key phrase in academic as well as political debates around the world. In other words, China is not just a processing zone for cheap, labor-intensive products. China has demonstrated strong ambitions to be the new global economic powerhouse on the basis of its newfound power and status in the international arena.

The following section will discuss China's new political and economic grand strategies for reorienting itself given its new global position. In terms of cross-Strait economic relations, Taiwan is coping with a partner that is markedly different from the one circa pre-2000. These political and economic strategies help explain whether China will be a competitor, a dominant player, or a partner in economic interactions.

CHALLENGES OF CROSS-STRAIT ECONOMIC RELATIONS: THE RISE OF CHINA'S MACRO POLITICAL AND ECONOMIC INITIATIVES

The Emergence of China's New Global Political Initiatives

The term *grand strategy* is heavily influenced by international as well as domestic political calculations. The Chinese leadership has put special emphases on the linkages of domestic and external politics. The recent proactive actions of Chinese foreign policy are attempts to handle domestic and international situations—the "two major situations"—at the same time. In the Third Politburo Studying Meeting in January 2013, Xi elaborated upon a theory for integrating the two major situations. Such integration has become a focus of Chinese foreign policy under Xi's leadership. This policy directive can be seen in the context of integrating domestic development with external relations, Chinese development with global development, and the interests of the Chinese people with the interests of other countries. Guided by the principle of integration, according to Xi, the Chinese government should take a more positive and proactive attitude in international affairs and search for ways to contribute to global development.[21]

The policy of "handling the two major situations" reflects increasing Chinese confidence in managing foreign affairs. Moreover, maintaining domestic as well as international stability will contribute to the continuous development of China over the next few decades.

However, the policy still runs up against contradictions in international affairs. Wu Xinbo argues that contradiction is a normal situation in international affairs. As Chinese society progresses, the Chinese tend to use peaceful solutions instead of military solutions for contradictions in international affairs. They are searching for "natural ways" to cope with the contradictions. If the timing is not right, the best way is to put aside controversies and search for a balancing point where both sides' interests converge.[22] Wu Xinbo also argues that the current relations between political entities in the Asia Pacific region are driven by a mixture of concerns to maintain hegemonic stability, balance of power, and collective security. The Sino-American relationship is characterized as one of controlled competition and limited cooperation. The bottom line is the avoidance of direct conflicts.[23] From Wu's point of view, China is facing an "unharmonious world" in the Asia Pacific region, a situation that is full of conflicts, contradictions, and opportunities. The classic balance of power and great-power politics will prevail in high politics. But in the sphere of human security, countries in the region tend to cooperate on mutually beneficial goals.

Chinese scholars have also studied the shift in China's attitudes toward international order and governance. For instance, Wang Jisi notes that since 2005 the State Council white paper has not mentioned a policy of "establishing international political and economic order." Instead, the 2011 white paper emphasized the efforts to participate in international affairs and shoulder responsibilities. For Wang, such adjustments imply that China recognizes the existing international political and economic order and is working to promote further reform. In other words, China has shifted its identity into that of a "central nation," serving as a bridge between the North and the South.

The new identity of a central nation is facing new challenges. First, the greatest security challenges are from countries that have the closest economic interdependence, such as the United States and Japan. China's economic linkages with the United States and Japan reflect the global division of labor, which extends far beyond bilateral relations. Second, in order to guarantee the security of neighboring regions, China has to broaden its horizons and play a more positive role in the Middle East, Africa, and Indian Ocean region. Involvement in comprehensive security issues will have a major impact on China's domestic security. The only way to enhance the national security of surrounding areas is to develop a security policy that extends globally and integrates Chinese interests with global interests. Third, with such a new global strategy, China must stabilize relationships with major countries including Russia, India, Japan, and United States. It must shoulder more global responsibilities but be modest and prudent at the same time.[24]

The Chinese acknowledge that China's recent rise is due to its accumulation of wealth, not culture. The Chinese need to make their views heard in the international arena and upgrade their existing culture into "Chinese culture 2.0," which will handle more complicated domestic challenges such as ethnic autonomy and "one country, two systems" arrangements in which distinct Chinese regions retain their own economic, political, and legal systems. This upgraded culture will accommodate different religious, cultural, political, and even local subsystems within the whole of the Chinese territory. However, as a report by the Institute of National Development of Peking University indicates, cultural pluralism must operate within the context of the socialist system of the Chinese party state. It is the historical precondition for China's future development.[25]

As the preceding analysis demonstrates, Chinese leaders and academics are searching for a new "grand strategy" to guide the external behavior of their country. According to Barry Buzan, the functions of a grand strategy might be thought of as follows:

(1) To establish criteria for foreign and security policy formulation and evaluation.

(2) To create coherence in foreign and security policy by providing a stable overarching framework for policy choices.

(3) To embed and legitimize foreign and security policy politically by explaining it to the citizenry in broad terms, and especially to explain difficult choices.

(4) To project an image of the country to the rest of the world.[26]

On these four criteria, as Buzan argues, the Chinese policy of "peaceful devel-opment" qualifies as a grand strategy. It contains a theory about how the world works and how China should relate to that world in light of its overriding priority of development. It takes military, political, and economic elements into account and is sensitive to the kind of image China should project to the world. It thus sets a framework for defining China's national interests and offers a basic principle about how to relate means to ends.[27]

Under the general principle of peaceful development, Chinese leaders and aca-demics are searching for new ways to balance a traditional low-profile foreign pol-icy with more proactive diplomatic initiatives. For instance, Wang Jisi argues that a more sophisticated grand strategy is needed to serve China's domestic priorities. He introduces four ongoing changes in China's strategic thinking: (1) China's new comprehensive concept of security that extends beyond power politics to include such issues as disaster mitigation and environmental security; (2) a shift from country-oriented to more multilateral and issue-oriented policy; (3) more atten-tion given to economic efficiency, product quality, environmental protection, the creation of a social safety net, and technological innovation; (4) enhancement of Chinese cultural soft power and promotion of good governance.[28]

In contrast to a more prudent and low-profile external strategy, recent Chinese foreign policy directives demonstrate China's desire to adjust to its status as a major power in the international arena. Yan Xuetong uses the term *striving for achievement* to describe Xi's more proactive grand strategy. Yan argues that for the sake of a favorable international environment conducive to its national rein-vigoration, China has to actively shape the external situation instead of adapting itself to changes in external conditions. In addition to economic engagements, this approach targets regional cooperation in areas including politics, security, and culture. It also encourages China to take up international responsibilities consistent with China's interests, capabilities, and status as the second-largest power in the world.[29]

As Yan Xuetong argues, the most remarkable part of Xi's grand strategy is the greater emphasis on China's relationship with its neighbors. For many years, Chi-na has regarded Sino-American relations as the top priority. After Xi's adjustment, greater significance is now attached to diplomacy with neighboring countries, and particularly to the establishment of cross-regional economic corridors—not only a Silk Road Economic Belt (connecting China to Europe via western and cen-tral Asia) and a Twenty-First Century Maritime Silk Road (connecting China to Southeast Asia, Africa, and Europe via the South China Sea, the Indian Ocean, and the Red Sea), but also a China-India-Myanmar-Bangladesh economic cor-ridor, the goal of which is to promote integration in all three subregions.[30]

Efforts to reposition China's standing in the Asia Pacific region and to attend to more than great-power politics are reflected in China's strategies to "regionalize" its power. In an important address on China's foreign policy principles, Foreign Minister Wang Yi reemphasized the "Asia-Pacific Dream" introduced by Xi Jinping at the 2014 Asia-Pacific Economic Cooperation (APEC) meeting. In his remarks, Wang indicated that China would work to build consensus on how to advance all-around cooperation in the Asia Pacific region. He also pointed out the importance of promoting common, comprehensive, cooperative, and sustainable security in Asia and building a community of shared interests and destiny.[31]

As the previous pages indicate, Chinese leaders are striving for a more positive international environment in which to consolidate domestic stability and growth. As their comprehensive national power grows, the Chinese are utilizing their economic influence to reorient China's position in international affairs. This new policy must serve domestic interests and help allay suspicions of a "China threat." Moreover, the Chinese are searching for new strategies to reshape an international economic, political, and security arrangements in ways that will enhance China's leading role in the international arena.

The "One Belt, One Road" (OBOR) policy was announced by Chinese president Xi Jinping in 2013. According to the plan, China would set up a "Silk Road" infrastructure aid fund of US$40 billion to assist nations along the Silk Road Economic Belt. It would resemble the fabled trade network during the Han dynasty that connected China with Europe and ran through central and western Asia. The Twenty-First-century Maritime Silk Road was also announced as part of OBOR.[32]

Chinese foreign minister Wang Yi has elaborated that OBOR consists of projects designed to boost mutually beneficial cooperation between China and Eurasian countries in the spirit of mutual learning and harmonious coexistence reminiscent of the ancient Silk Road. China's leadership hopes that OBOR will serve as an overarching framework for China's endeavors in external cooperation in the modern era. Moreover, it will serve internal as well as external functions for national interests. As Wang indicates:

> Internally, this initiative dovetails with China's development strategy of developing our central and western regions while addressing regional imbalances and fits well with our "go global" strategy aimed at building all-directional cooperation with the outside world.
>
> Internationally, this initiative aims to secure common development and shared prosperity in all countries along the routes, as it upholds the vision for a community of shared destiny and highlights a win-win approach featuring consultation, joint development and sharing. The initiative is bound to bring new life and vigor to the ancient land of Eurasia and give this vast continent two strong wings on its journey toward prosperity.[33]

OBOR reflects China's intention to depart from the previous low-profile, or *taoguan yanghui*, model of foreign policy. Some have viewed OBOR as China's

Marshall Plan, with a long-term goal of gaining geopolitical preeminence on the Eurasian continent. In this context, OBOR is also deemed an economic counter-measure to American rebalancing in Asia Pacific. The baseline is that China will tap the opportunity of OBOR to expand investment in its extensive western region and attempt to sustain its growth rate, which is declining. China could use this strategy to hedge against potential contingencies if its sea routes become threat-ened. In addition, China could wield more political influence when the region's economy becomes further dependent upon Beijing. Promoting the intercon-nectedness of Eurasian countries would entail resources beyond those of any one country's own treasury, so it has to be a copaying and cosharing arrangement.[34]

OBOR also serves domestic interests by providing avenues for Chinese capital to "step out." In 2014, China was the world's biggest trading country with foreign exchange reserves of US$39 trillion. Such reserves can lay the foundation for Chi-na's more proactive external strategies. At the same time, appropriate channels are needed to guide domestic capital into the international market. Since the launch of a stimulus plan in 2008 to cope with global economic stagnation, China's infra-structure industries have become economic champions under the state capitalist system. Large-scale infrastructure-related projects have helped create China's iron triangle of rail lines, roads, and airports (*tiegongji*). Equipped with China's experi-ences and technologies of infrastructure construction, the OBOR policy provides timely channels for these state-owned enterprises to develop new initiatives for international markets. Such moves will also be buttressed by new institutional ar-rangements like the Asian Infrastructure Investment Bank (AIIB).

Details of Taiwan's participation in OBOR and the AIIB are still coming to light. However, Taiwanese firms have formed various strategic alliances with this new investment initiative. For instance, in 2011, Taiwan's Asia Vital Components Co., a thermal solution provider, acquired a 45 percent stake in a subsidiary company formed with China's China South Locomotive & Rolling Stock Corp. Local insti-tutional investors are expecting the company to benefit from expected growth in demand for high-margin railway heat dissipation and electrical products includ-ing power resisters, water-cooled transformers, and rackable connectors. Power Mate Technology Co., a power supply company, secured a role in China's railroad equipment supply chain in 2010 after its electronic equipment products received EN 50155 standard certification for railway applications. Since its founding, Power Mate's products have been used in a number of demanding industrial applica-tions including medicine, weaponry, solar power, and automobiles. The company is an original design manufacturer and markets products under the brand name P-Duke.[35]

China International Capital Corp., the largest investment banking and re-search firm in China, said it anticipates that Beijing will pour more than US$1.65 trillion into its OBOR strategy over the next decade, much of which will flow to neighboring nations in Asia. Meanwhile, the prospects of Taiwanese companies such as Asia Vital Components Co. and Power Mate Technology Co. have improved in the eyes of investors as they are deemed to be companies well positioned to reap rewards as the Beijing-led initiatives take shape.[36]

China's New IT Policies: Challenging Taiwan's Role in Cross-Strait Economic Interaction

As is the case with its more proactive foreign policy initiatives, the Chinese government has demonstrated its strong ambition to rebuild the high-tech and IT industry by direct intervention of the state. Such actions reflect a typical developmental state style of using financial instruments and industrial policy to pick winners and support technological breakthroughs. The Chinese government is now putting significant funding and efforts into new policies related to the development of the semiconductor industry. Chinese officials have convened a unique task force charged with setting an aggressive growth strategy. This group helped develop a policy framework that is targeting a compound annual growth rate for the industry of 20 percent between now and 2020, with potential financial support from the government of up to RMB 1 trillion (US$170 billion) over the next five to ten years. Investments will be made by a national investment vehicle (the National Industry Investment Fund) and provincial-level entities. These entities will invest across multiple categories, including project finance and domestic and foreign acquisitions, as well as traditional research and development subsidies and tax credits.

To avoid the fragmentation issues of the past, the Chinese government is focusing on creating national champions—a small set of leaders in each critical segment of the semiconductor market (including design, manufacturing, tools, and assembly and testing) and a few provinces in which there is the potential to develop industry clusters. What's different this time, however, is that the task force includes the top ten to fifteen leaders in China's semiconductor industry (convening executives from fabless designers, foundries, and equipment manufacturers), and overarching leadership for the project comes from Vice-Premier Ma Kai, one of the government's highest-ranking officials. This committee had a direct influence on the State Council during its drafting of the Guidelines of the National IC Industry Development Promotion, the high-level policy framework that was shared publicly in June 2014.[37]

In June 2014, the State Council of China issued the "National Guidelines for the Development and Promotion of the IC Industry" to support the domestic semiconductor industry. The document addresses development targets, approaches, and measures. It has created waves throughout the semiconductor industry and attracted global attention because of its ambitious development targets and sizable support for a national IC industry investment fund.

Meanwhile, local IC industry investment funds have been established by the cities of Beijing, Shanghai, Wuhan, and Hefei. Of these, Beijing took the lead in establishing a fund in June 2014, totaling RMB 30 billion (US$4.8 billion). It is structured as a "fund of funds" and two subfunds. One subfund, supporting IC manufacturing and semiconductor equipment, is managed by CGP Investment (the "fund of funds" is also managed by CGP); the other subfund, supporting IC design and packaging, is managed by Hua Capital. In addition, Shanghai's IC industry fund, which is named the Shanghai Summitview Capital IC Information Industry Merger Fund and which totals RMB 10 billion (US$1.6 billion), was established in November 2014. The total of all government funds is estimated to reach to US$100 billion with the implementation of local industry funds.[38]

As the majority of Taiwanese IT firms have set up their manufacturing centers in the Yangtze River Delta region, the new policy initiatives from the central government down to the local governments bring challenges as well as opportunities for the Taiwanese. Among various locations in China, Shanghai emerged as the center of IT development in the late 1990s. As Wang Zhan, director of the Shanghai Academy of Social Sciences, argues, the service sector is just one of the key sectors of an economic center. Shanghai's economic development should not be totally reliant on the service sector. The main goal in building Shanghai into an economic center is still the establishment of a high-end, globalized, innovative manufacturing industry. The current problem in Shanghai is a lack of integration of scientific research, technological innovation, and industrial development. Private enterprises are mainly in the service sector, such as trading and real estate. Foreign enterprises concentrate on low-end technologies, focusing on China's market instead of R&D capacities. State-owned enterprises are facing multiple institutional constraints. According to Wang, the most suitable policy for Shanghai is to combine market mechanisms and state guidance. The energy of innovation will come from small and medium-sized enterprises in the private sector. The duty of the government is to create an innovation-friendly environment, and the private sector does not need extra guidance from the government. However, under such policy schemes, the private sector will face uncertainties and risks when it encounters global competition.[39]

Under the scheme of new policy initiatives led by the local state, Taiwanese firms are searching for new forms of partnership with local governments. Shanghai's city government announced a ¥50 billion (US$8 billion) funding program for new infrastructure in the IC industry, including two production lines of twelve-inch wafers. Prior to the funding program, the city had just set up an RMB 10 billion (US$1.6 billion) fund, Shanghai SummitView IC Information Industry Fund, in which Taiwan-based chip designer MediaTek is an investor. MediaTek Inc. (Lianfake), the nation's biggest handset chip maker, signed an agreement in November 2014 to invest RMB 300 million (US$48.9 million) in a Chinese government fund in an effort to benefit from China's fast-growing semiconductor industry. MediaTek is currently Taiwan's largest chip designer and has the largest market share for smartphone processors in China. According to MediaTek chair Ming-kai Tsai, through investing in the fund MediaTek expects to benefit from a closer relationship between high-tech industries in China and Taiwan and to gain a better position in the global semiconductor industry. The fund, initiated by the Shanghai city government and Chinese venture capital firm SummitView Capital, will have ¥3 billion in funding during the initial phase, and that amount will gradually increase to ¥10 billion. Besides MediaTek, Shanghai Jiading Venture Capital Fund, Semiconductor Manufacturing International Corp. (SMIC), Tsinghua University's Tsinghua Holdings Co., and Knight Capital of the United States have joined as investors in the fund.[40]

The preceding pages demonstrate the new political and economic initiatives to consolidate China's economic autonomy and strength. The rise of China's comprehensive power creates direct challenges to the cross-Strait economic division of labor. The next section will analyze the impacts of the combination of state-driven efforts and firm-specific incentives on Taiwan's attempts to maintain its primacy in cross-Strait economic interactions.

THE EMERGENCE OF A "RED SUPPLY CHAIN" AND ITS IMPLICATIONS FOR CROSS-STRAIT ECONOMIC RELATIONS

New Policies of the Chinese Developmental State That Support the Emergence of a Red Supply Chain

The potential emergence of a mainland Chinese supply chain to supplant Taiwanese firms' role reflects strong state support of indigenous firms. In 2015 China's State Council unveiled a ten-year national plan, Made in China 2025, designed to transform China from a manufacturing giant into a world manufacturing power. Nine tasks have been identified as priorities: improving manufacturing innovation, integrating technology and industry, strengthening the industrial base, fostering Chinese brands, enforcing green manufacturing, promoting breakthroughs in ten key sectors, advancing restructuring of the manufacturing sector, promoting service-oriented manufacturing and manufacturing-related service industries, and internationalizing manufacturing.[41] The ten key sectors are information technology, numerical control tools and robotics, aerospace equipment, oceanic engineering equipment and high-tech ships, railway equipment, energy-saving and new energy vehicles, power equipment, new materials, medicine and medical devices, and agricultural machinery.[42]

In 2014, the Chinese government launched the "Outline to Promote National Integrated Circuit Development" program. The central government is going to establish an investment fund of US$20 billion to foster the development of the semiconductor industry. The Chinese government will become a direct player by establishing holding companies to boost the indigenous manufacturing of the semiconductor industry. Up until 2014, 80 percent of the domestic demand of China's semiconductor industry relied on imports.

In addition, the Chinese government is promoting the merger and acquisition of state-owned semiconductor firms. Increasingly, the Chinese government has encouraged firms to buy, rather than rent or steal, breakthrough innovation capabilities through acquisitions of both technology and talent.[43] For instance, in the past two years, the flagship Qinghua UNIS group acquired the Chinese IC company RDA for US$ 1 billion; UNIS also acquired another major IC designer, Spreadtrum, for US$1.78 billion. The obvious target, according to UNIS CEO Zhao Weiguo, is Taiwan's No. 2 semiconductor company, MediaTek. According to Zhao, his company will invest US$50 billion to surpass MediaTek within five years.[44]

In 2015, Apple added two more Taiwanese companies in consolidating its list of iPhone and iPad supply chain firms. Wistron Corporation was named as an iPhone assembler, and Compal Electronics was picked to build iPads. China's BYD was also added as a final assembler of Apple products. They join Hong Hai and Taiwan's Pegatron among the companies that piece together Apply products from China to Brazil. In other words, with Quanta making Macs and iPods, and Inventec supplying iPods, Taiwanese companies have maintained their dominance over Apple's assembly lines. BYD, which was previously on Apple's border supplier list, and Flextronics, which makes Macs in Austin, Texas, were the major non-Taiwanese players.[45]

However, the rise of China's domestic manufacturers also threatens the position of Taiwanese vendors in Apple's iPhone supply chain. According to the estimates of Taiwanese manufacturers, Apple's long-term strategy is to foster China's domestic manufactures and enlarge its domestic market share. For instance, Sunwonda, a Chinese Li-on battery producer, has become a new partner in the iPhone 6 supply chain. Chinese newcomers like the electro-acoustic producer GoerTek and AAC Technologies have replaced the Taiwanese vendor Merry in the iPhone supply chain.[46]

In a report released in 2014, Barclays Capital Inc. indicated that the rise of the Chinese supply chain could be a disruptive force for some second-tier players in the Taiwan supply chain that lack differentiating technology, scale, or relationships with Chinese domestic brands. Benefiting from the increase in scale and investment in R&D should also cause the Chinese supply chain companies to move up the chain and become internationally competitive component makers for top-tier brands. Among many factors leading to the decline of Taiwanese firms and ascendance of Chinese companies in the IT supply chain, the Barclay report indicates two key dimensions of the change. First, succession uncertainty and an aging corporate culture are negatively affecting the Taiwanese IT hardware indus-try. Only a portion of Taiwanese technology companies have seen control passed on by the founders to the second generation of leaders or new professional man-agement teams. A few Taiwanese companies, however, such as Acer, Asustek, and Compal, are currently being comanaged by both founders and professional man-agers during these firms' transition periods. Second, China's high-tech companies enjoy a competitive edge of government support that their peers outside China do not have. Government support comes in the form of favorable tax conditions, local government subsidies, and financial backing. Furthermore, the component subsectors where Chinese makers are gaining ground are traditional fiefdoms of Taiwanese suppliers, especially in the areas of batteries, casings, camera lenses and modules, handset antennas, and LEDs. The Barclays report argues that Chinese component makers are seizing market shares from their Taiwanese counterparts not only on the basis of price but also on the basis of service intensity and aggres-sive investment in R&D and capital expenditure, while the Chinese government is helping by offering subsidies and tax incentives.[47]

Shift in Marketing Strategies: The Rise of Localized Chinese IT Firms

As was argued above, the case of Taiwan's HTC reflects the limitations of a me-dium-sized Taiwanese firm with aspirations for the global market. As China has become a world market instead of a world factory, putting the Chinese market first is a natural choice for business leaders. This new situation gives indigenous mainland Chinese IT firms a competitive edge over foreign ones.

Five years ago, during the heyday of HTC, Xiaomi was a mere newcomer to the Chinese market, which at the time was dominated by famous brand holders such as Apple and Samsung. Xiaomi may not currently rank as one of the world's most innovative companies, but it does get points for its slick marketing campaigns, rapid growth, and online sales campaigns. It has been touted as an up-and-coming Chinese high-tech company that might follow in the footsteps of Alibaba. Xiaomi is also actively working to address one of its innovation weaknesses—a relatively thin patent portfolio—by working to double the number of patent applications that it files every year.[48]

One of Xiaomi's marketing strategies is to "gain strength at home first." The company has focused on China, with 97 percent of its shipments being local. It has been mentioned that Xiaomi's future targets will be in Southeast Asia and Brazil, Russia, and India. Hugo Barra, a former Google executive who himself hails from Brazil, has become new Xiaomi's international face. The company is not in a rush to enter more developed markets dominated by Apply and Samsung and prefers to stay focused on its own base, where the market is still booming.[49]

According to Xiaomi CEO Lei Jun, the company sells smartphones at cost, or close to it, and will make money through services. They are selling not so much smartphones as a lifestyle. The service Lei Jun is referring to—MiUI and Mi.com—sells the products and ties them all together, but they are all Xiaomi products in the end. The company does not just want to be a dominant player in smartphones; it wants the whole house.[50] This strategy is custom-made for the Chinese market and is geared especially to young professionals who want to furnish a new living space. It could also be applied to developing countries such as Brazil, Russia, and India. For the developed world, the house has already been furnished with brand-name products.

The Enhancement of China's R&D Capacities

Multinational high-tech firms, including Taiwanese IT companies, have enjoyed a technological advantage over Chinese firms for the past two decades. To move upstream in the supply chain and establish technological autonomy, the Chinese developmental state has endeavored to help consolidate firms' R&D capacities in various ways. In addition to governmental support of innovation, what China needs, according to foreign entrepreneurs, is "capable" companies far more than innovative companies. Having mastered the skills to assemble relatively simple products for foreign multinationals, Chinese companies next need to learn how to develop and manufacture more complex products themselves. They must become much more proficient at higher-order organizational capabilities, such as strategy formulation, multibrand management, relationship marketing, systems integration, and performance management.[51]

With foreign exchange reserves close to US$4 trillion, China has the money to buy the foreign industrial capacity it thinks it needs. Recent acquisitions support the view that a noticeable shift is under way. For example, Lenovo recently bought Motorola Mobility, Donfeng Motors made a bid for Peugeot-Citroen, and in the best-known case of all, Swedish carmaker Volvo was bought from Ford by Zhejiang Geely, an automobile company with enormous ambitions but lacking a strong brand and design expertise. In 2014, two-thirds of China's offshore investments were in services, where Chinese firms still have much to learn. Many Chinese firms have set up their corporate R&D centers in the United States and Europe through direct investment and acquisition. Their motive is to embed their companies in the innovation ecosystems of the developed world to acquire and develop foreign technologies, brands, and marketing know-how.[52]

Attracting Highly Talented Forces in the IT Sectors

The Chinese government fully understands that to achieve takeoff or leap-frogging in the IT sectors it must attract the top technological elite around the world. In 2010, China released an ambitious talent cultivation plan called the National Medium- and Long-Term Talent Development Plan. In addition to investing in hardware, the plan spells out how China can utilize international financial institutions' funds and foreign government loans to develop skilled labor programs. The plan stipulates that the overall talent pool will increase from its 2010 level of 114 million people to 180 million by 2020. The plan also lists six major categories of talent that the government will help cultivate: political leaders and officials; business entrepreneurs; technical professionals; highly skilled workers in various industries; those with practical skills for rural areas and agriculture; and professional social workers. Furthermore, to put more pressure on state-owned enterprises (SOEs) to change, the plan aims to cultivate around one hundred business leaders and CEOs who can lead Chinese firms to reach the ranks of the Fortune 500 companies by 2020. It also aims to have a total of forty thousand international business-savvy talented people working for SOEs by 2020, with 50 percent of them hired through market competition. This is actually quite an unusual move—in the past, almost all of the top managers of SOEs were promoted or hired from within the system.[53]

Moreover, Chinese companies are more than willing to take shortcuts by poaching top talent from Taiwanese competitors to enhance their technological capabilities and market presence. Epistar Corp, Taiwan's top LED chip maker, indicated in early 2015 that if Chinese LED epitaxy maker Sanan Optoelectronics Co. continued poaching its talent it would consider requesting that the government scrap an investment deal Sanan had proposed in 2013 to buy a 19 percent stake in local LED chip supplier Formosa Epitaxy Inc. for US$7.38 million.[54] In addition, Chinese local governments are copying the model of Taiwan's ITRI to establish public R&D facilities. China offers more than four times the salary of Taiwanese companies in recruiting ITRI's mid- and high-ranking managers. To cope with the brain drain to China, ITRI has enhanced its support for its talent to establish start-ups on domestic soil. What ITRI intends to do is to foster entrepreneurship instead of high salaries.

However, whether the Chinese system of authoritarian control can foster innovation and attract top elites is a highly debated issue. As the major agent of political socialization, the Chinese higher education system has experienced major upheavals in ideological indoctrination. In early 2015 China's Ministry of Education released a document of policy guidelines regarding propaganda work in colleges. According to the document, the government will promote the following four major tasks in colleges: (1) pushing materials of socialism with Chinese characteristics into the "classrooms and pupils' brains"; (2) improving the ideological purity of college teachers; (3) strengthening mainstream thought in colleges; and (4) enhancing the management of college ideological work.[55] Minister of Education Yuan Guiren, in elaborating these guidelines, indicated that China would consolidate the control of Western textbooks in colleges. China will never allow materials spreading Western values to penetrate college classrooms. Moreover, speeches attacking party leadership, socialism, the Chinese constitution, and legal systems will not be tolerated on college campuses.[56]

CONCLUSION

Cross–Taiwan Strait economic relations have entered a new era with the rise of China. In the earlier stages of interaction, Taiwan relied on its unique position in the global supply chain and benefited from the expansion of mainland China's manufacturing capacities. In most cases, Taiwan's close technological linkages with American and Japanese high-tech firms helped create an economic niche based on mutual trust and benefits with upstream brand holders. Such a cross-border division of labor was founded in part on the weakness of Chinese domestic vendors and the lack of technological know-how of Chinese manufacturers. China was regarded as a world factory, instead of a market, for global brand holders.

Today US high-tech firms still retain their technological superiority, but the general cross-Strait division of labor is changing. As the preceding pages demonstrate, Taiwan's OEM model of manufacturing is now facing a dual threat in the form of shrinking profit margins and the rise of Chinese domestic manufacturers. The OBM model of IT production is constrained by the lack of marketing and global logistics capabilities. Moreover, Taiwan's domestic politics impede the flows of advanced talent between Taiwan and China. The advantage of the "made in China, by Taiwan" model of IT manufacturing is gradually diminishing.

In addition to economic connections, Taiwan's cross-Pacific strategy of IT development is closely linked with its security and political dependency on the United States. The grand strategy initiated by the Xi administration demonstrates a more comprehensive ambition to explore the broader definition of "the West" beyond the Sino-American rivalry. By making the Asia Pacific region its priority, the Chinese have accumulated the confidence to reshape the rules of the international game by combining maritime and land-based economic plans into a grand strategy. From the Chinese perspective, the recent "assertiveness" in foreign policy is merely appropriate to China's new status as a major power. OBOR and AIIB also exemplify Chinese initiatives to escape from Sino-American entanglement and to grasp new opportunities presented by emerging types of geopolitics.

The formation of a new grand strategy in China does not necessarily imply an attempted delinking from US-dominated high-tech development. The United States still enjoys relative advantages in innovation and entrepreneurship. But the deepening engagements between China and the countries of continental Europe are making it possible for China to embrace a more comprehensive global cooperative mechanism. Taiwan needs to adjust its economic strategies to incorporate Southeast Asian and European regions into its global strategies of logistics. One of the policy options is to create strategic alliances with Chinese firms to explore these booming markets. Such a strategic partnership does not aim to replace the Chinese market. The real purpose is to ally with the new engines of global development and guarantee economic security at the same time.

However, political changes in Taiwan may impede such a "strategic move" to embrace the global market by cooperating with new Chinese initiatives. As indicated in a recent article in the *Economist*, Chinese producers of petrochemicals, steel, computers, and digital displays have moved into terrain once occupied by Taiwan. Taiwanese firms with operations in China are themselves buying more materials and machinery from Chinese suppliers. Chinese firms are now trying to break into semiconductors, Taiwan's last big industrial redoubt.[57] Enhancing integration with the Chinese domestic market in the manufacturing and service sectors could be a solution to the economic dilemma. But such a policy shift has turned out to be unacceptable in Taiwan's domestic political climate. The Sunflower Movement mobilized against the Cross-Strait Service Trade Agreement in the early spring of 2015 proved the political infeasibility of further economic integration with the other side of the Taiwan Strait.

Whether Taiwanese firms can transform themselves from pure hardware manufacturers into IT service providers is still in question. Such weakness will constrain these firms' ability to penetrate China's domestic market. Furthermore, whether the Taiwanese state has the capacity to redirect Taiwanese capital to the Southeast Asian market is uncertain. Past experiences of Taiwan's "Go South" policy in the 1990s proved that state-driven attempts did not have substantial impacts on business behaviors. Theories of economic statecraft may partially explain the enhanced competitiveness of Chinese IT firms. As the Taiwanese state meets with rising economic pressure from the other side of the Taiwan Strait, its bargaining power to boost its IT industry is limited.

All in all, China will be a key component in Taiwan's global strategies of development. Understanding the risks and opportunities of the rise of China in global instead of bilateral terms will help illuminate how Taiwan can grow and prosper in the future. The traditional wisdom of economic statecraft and interdependence thus needs further revision. Coping with the rise of China involves hard choices on the domestic front in Taiwan. Only by shouldering more risks and perceiving the changing world from a more realist perspective will Taiwan be able to reverse the inward-looking tendencies of national development.

NOTES

1. Douglas B. Fuller and Murray A. Rubinstein, eds., *Technology Transfer between the US, China and Taiwan* (London: Routledge, 2013).

2. Da-Nien Liu and Hui-Tzu Shih, "The Transformation of Taiwan's Status within the Production and Supply Chain in Asia," Brookings report, December 4, 2003, www.brookings.edu/research/opinions/2013/12/04-taiwan-production-supply-chain.

3. Martin Kenney, Dan Breznitz, and Michael Murphree, "Coming Back Home after the Sun Rises: Returnee Entrepreneurs and Growth of High Tech Industries," *Research Policy* 42, no. 2 (2012): 9, http://dx.doi.org/10.1016/j.respol.2012.08.001.

4. Mayumi Tabata, "The Absorption of Japanese Engineers into Taiwan's TFT-LCD Industry: Globalization and Transnational Talent Diffusion," *Asian Survey* 52, no. 3 (2012):593–94.

5. "The Executive Yuan Approves the Asian Silicon Valley Plan," *Taiwan Today*, September 9, 2016, http://taiwantoday.tw/ct.asp?xItem=247798&ctNode=2182.

6. National Development Council, "The Asian Silicon Valley Development Plan," n.d., accessed October 25, 2016, www.ndc.gov.tw/en/Content_List.aspx?n=90BEB862317E93FC&upn=7B70255F66F B9DF5.

7. Henry Wai-chung Yeung and Neil M. Coe, "Toward a Dynamic Theory of Global Production Networks," *Economic Geography* 91, no. 1 (2014): 22.

8. Henry Wai-chung Yeung, "Governing the Market in a Globalizing Era: Developmental States, Global Production Networks and Inter-firm Dynamics in East Asia," *Review of International Political Economy* 21, no. 1 (2014): 88–89; Henry Wai chung Yeung, "From Followers to Market Leaders: Asian Electronics Firms in the Global Economy," *Asian Pacific Viewpoint* 48, no. 1 (2006): 1–25.

9. Hon Hai Precision Industry, *Annual Report 2013*, www.foxconn.com.tw/Files/annual_rpt_e/2013_annual_rpt_e.pdf.

10. Lorraine Luk, "Foxconn Is Quietly Working with Google on Robotics," *Wall Street Journal*, February 11, 2014, http://blogs.wsj.com/digits/2014/02/11/foxconn-working-with-google-on-robotics/.

11. Central News Agency, "Hon Hai Will Transform into Technology Services Company," *China Post*, June 12, 2014.

12. Sam Reynolds, "How Can Taiwan Manufacturers Reduce Their Dependence on Apple," *VR World*, March 26, 2015, www.vrworld.com/2015/03/26/how-can-taiwan-manufacturers-reduce-their-dependence-on-apple/.

13. Eva Dou, "Foxconn to Close Inefficient Units of Sharpe," *Wall Street Journal*, June 22, 2016, www.wsj.com/articles/foxconn-to-close-inefficient-units-at-sharp-1466600005.

14. Paul Mozur, "To Woo Apple, Foxconn Bets 3.5 Billion on Sharpe," *New York Times*, March 30, 2016, www.nytimes.com/2016/03/31/business/dealbook/foxconn-sharp.html?_r=0.

15. David Segal, "Not the Best Way to Sell the Smartphone," *New York Times*, March 24, 2014, www.nytimes.com/2014/03/23/technology/marketing-missteps-at-htc.html?_r=0.

16. Ralph Jennings, "HTC Dials into China Market, but Who Will Answer the Call?," *South China Morning Post*, August 18, 2014, www.scmp.com/business/companies/article/1575660/htc-dials-china-market-who-will-answer-call.

17. Aries Poon, "HTC Returns to Loss," *Wall Street Journal*, July 6, 2015, www.wsj.com/articles/htc-returns-to-losses-1436171343.

18. Alex Dobie, "For HTC in 2016, the Problem Is Standing Out in a Very Big Crowd," Android Central, February 17, 2016, www.androidcentral.com/htc-2016-problem-standing-out-very-big-crowd.

19. "Google Silently Removed Mention of an HTC Cerberus from Pixel XL Source Code," *XDA-Developers*, October 22, 2016, www.xda-developers.com/google-silently-removed-mentions-of-an-htc-cerberus-from-pixel-xl-source-code/.

20. Wang Yixin, "Chonghui daigong zanqian hongdadian pinzhan VR langtoushang" [Back to the OEM, HTC struggles to earn money for VR], *Zhongguo Shibao*, October 5, 2016.

21. "Geng hao tong chou guo nei guo ji liang ge da ju ben shi zou he ping fa zhan dao lu de ji chu," *People's Daily*, January 30, 2013, http://politics.people.com.cn/n/2013/0130/c1001–20367778.html.

22. People's Republic of China, State Council Information Office, January 10, 2013, "Wúxīnbó lùn gòujiàn zhōngguó wàijiāo de 'héli'" [On the "consolidation" of China's diplomacy], www.scio.gov.cn/ztk/dtzt/2013/01/10/Document/1303021/1303021.htm.

23. Wu Xinbo, "Yatai diqu anquan zhixu xiankuang yu qianjing," *Dongfang Zaobao*, January 14, 2014, www.81.cn/big5/jmbl/2014–01/14/content_5735698.htm.

24. Wang Jisi, "Dongxi nanbei zhongguo juzhong," *Shijie Zhishi*, no. 21 (2013).

25. Institute of National Development, Peking University, "Weilai shinian de zhongguo," Report No. R201301, March 2013.

26. Barry Buzan, "The Logic and Contradictions of Peaceful Rise/Development as China's Grand Strategy," *Chinese Journal of International Politics* 7, no. 4 (2014): 385.

27. Ibid., 387–88.

28. Wang Jisi, "China's Search for a Grand Strategy: A Rising Great Power Finds Its Way," *Foreign Affairs* 90, no. 2 (March/April 2011): 68–80.

29. Yan Xuetong, "From Keeping a Low Profile to Striving for Achievement," *Chinese Journal of International Politics* 7, no. 2 (2014): 153–84.

30. Yan Xuetong, "Silk Road Economic Belt Shows China's New Strategic Directions: Promoting Integration with Its Neighbors," Carnegie-Tsinghua Center for Global Policy, February 27, 2014, http://carnegietsinghua.org/2014/02/27/silk-road-economic-belt-shows-china-s-new-strategic-direction-promoting-integration-with-its-neighbors.

31. Wang Yi, "Full Text of Foreign Minister Wang Yi's Speech on China's Diplomacy in 2014," *Xinhua News*, December 26, 2014, http://news.xinhuanet.com/english/china/2014-12/26/c_133879194_4.htm.

32. "China's 'One Belt' Tied in Knots," editorial, *Taipei Times*, February 3, 2015, www.taipeitimes.com/News/editorials/archives/2015/02/03/2003610687/1.

33. Wang Yi, "Full Text."

34. "China's 'One Belt, One Road' Strategy Is Not Another Marshall Plan," *CHINA US Focus*, March 16, 2015, www.chinausfocus.com/finance-economy/china-advances-its-one-belt-one-road-strategy/.

35. "Taiwanese Suppliers to Benefit from Beijing-Led Initiatives," *Asia Today*, April 13, 2015, www.asiatoday.com/pressrelease/taiwanese-suppliers-benefit-beijing-led-initiatives.

36. Ibid.

37. Gordon Orr and Christopher Thomas, "Semiconductors in China: Brave New World or Same Old Story?," McKinsey.com, August 2014, www.mckinsey.com/insights/high_tech_telecoms_internet/semiconductors_in_china_brave_new_world_or_same_old_story.

38. Adam He, "Will New Policy in China Trigger Big Changes?," SEMI, January 13, 2015, www.semi.org/node/53856.

39. "Yi 'keji zhanlyue tequ' tuidong shanghai chuangxin" [Using 'technology and creative special zone' to promote innovation in Shanghai," *Jiefang Ribao*, December 23, 2014, http://newspaper.jfdaily.com/jfrb/html/2014-12/23/content_49958.htm.

40. "MediaTek Participates in Government-Led Fund in Shanghai," *Digi Times*, April 17, 2015, http://digitimes.com/news/a20141125PD205.html?mod=0; "MediaTek Investing in Chinese Technology Fund," *Taipei Times*, November 11, 2015, www.taipeitimes.com/News/biz/archives/2014/11/25/2003605216; "Shanghai Government to Fund US\$8 Billion Program for IC Industry," *Want China Times*, February 14, 2015, www.wantchinatimes.com/news-subclass-cnt.aspx?id=20150214000015&cid=1102.

41. "'Made in China 2025' Plan Unveiled to Boost Manufacturing," *Xinhua News*, May 19, 2015, http://news.xinhuanet.com/english/2015-05/19/c_134252230.htm.

42. Shannon Tiezzi, "China's Master Plan to Become a World Manufacturing Power," *Diplomat*, May 20, 2015, http://thediplomat.com/2015/05/chinas-master-plan-to-become-a-world-manufacturing-power/.

43. Regina Abrami, William Kirby, and Warren McFarlan, "Why China Can't Innovate," *Harvard Business Review*, March 2014, https://hbr.org/2014/03/why-china-cant-innovate.

44. Wang Hsiao-wen, "Dazao zhongguo taijidian, lianfake zhongbing jingong bandaoti" [Building TSMC in China, Mediatek invests heavily in the semiconductor sector], *Tianxia*, August 19, 2014.

45. Tim Culpan, "Taiwan's Wistron, Compal New Winners in Apple Supply Race," *Bloomberg Business*, February 12, 2015, www.bloomberg.com/news/articles/2015-02-12/taiwan-s-wistron-compal-new-winners-in-apple-supply-race.

46. "Ping guo xin ji lian kuo da 'ran hong,'" [New supply chain of Apple i-Phone turns red], United Daily News, May 18, 2015, http://udn.com/news/story/7240/908960-%E8%98%8B%E6%9E%9C%E6% 96%B0%E6%A9%9F%E9%8F%88-%E6%93%B4%E5%A4%A7%E3%80%8C%E6%9F%93%E7%B4%85% E3%80%8D.

47. "Hello, China; Goodbye, Taiwan?," Barclays Equity Research, report, June 25, 2014, 14–33.

48. Dominic Basulto, "Can China's Xiaomi Challenge Apple as the Smartphone Innovation Leader?," *Washington Post,* January 2, 2015, www.washingtonpost.com/blogs/innovations/wp/2015/01/02/can-chinas-xiaomi-challenge-apple-as-the-smartphone-innovation-leader/.

49. Vladi Kaplan, "7 Lessons of XiaoMi's Marketing Success Story in China," SAMPi, August 13, 2014, http://chinamarketingtips.com/7-lessons-of-xiaomi-marketing-success-story-in-china/.

50. Ben Thompson, "Xiaomi's Ambition," *Stratechery,* January 7, 2015, https://stratechery.com/2015/xiaomis-ambition/.

51. John Julens, "Can China Innovate," *Strategy Business,* February 4, 2014, www.strategy-business.com/blog/Can-China-Innovate?gko=d49f3.

52. George Yip, "The Three Phases of Chinese Innovation," *Forbes Asia,* March 23, 2015.

53. Wang Huiyao, "China's National Talent Plan: Key Measures and Objectives," *Brookings Briefings,* November 23, 2010, www.brookings.edu/research/papers/2010/11/23-china-talent-wang.

54. "Recruiting, Retaining Talent Vital," editorial, *Taipei Times,* January 14, 2015.

55. "Jiao yu bu zhu yao fu ze tong zhi jiu 'guan yu jin yi bu jia qiang he gai jin xin xing shi xia gao xiao xuan chuan si xiang gong zuo de yi jian' da ji zhe wen" [The principal comrades of the Ministry of Education answered the reporters' questions on further strengthening and improving the propaganda and ideological work in institutions of higher learning in the new situation], *Xinhua News,* January 20, 2015, http://cpc.people.com.cn/BIG5/n/2015/0120/c64107-26419462.html.

56. "Yuan gui ren: Gao xiao jiao shi bi xu shou hao zheng zhi, fa lu, dao de san tiao di xian" [College teachers must insist on the three bottom lines of politics, law, and ethics], *Xinhua News,* January 29, 2015, http://news.xinhuanet.com/edu/2015-01/29/c_1114183715.htm.

57. "Straitened Circumstances," *Economist,* November 14, 2015, www.economist.com/news/finance-and-economics/21678276-weaker-growth-exposes-downside-ties-china-straitened-circumstances.

10

Social Entrepreneurialism and Social Media in Post–developmental state Taiwan

You-tien Hsing

In this chapter I use social entrepreneurialism as an analytical tool to understand the changing state-society relationship in Taiwan since the 1990s.[1] I adopt the usual definition of entrepreneurship, which includes the capacity to identify and exploit opportunities and resources, endure risks, innovate, and create new values. In the expanding literature on *social entrepreneurialism,* especially from the field of business management, much of the debate has focused on what social entrepreneurialism is and should be, framed by the role of commercial exchange (e.g., should social entrepreneurs worry about profitability?), the goals of entrepreneurial activities (e.g., can social entrepreneurs serve nonsocial purposes?), and the hybrid model exemplified by the Grameen Bank in Bangladesh and other microcredit agencies that are profit oriented but using profits to achieve social goals.

While these works are useful in establishing links between ideals and policy formulations, it is equally important to contextualize and politicize the formation and transformation of social entrepreneurialism and to examine its connections with other types of entrepreneurialism. By doing so, I hope to understand to what extent social entrepreneurialism is convergent with and divergent from the logic of the state and the market.

While this chapter focuses on Taiwan in the era of the post–martial law, post-developmental state, I will also discuss the role of the connection between Taiwan and mainland China in the development of social entrepreneurialism.

TAIWAN IN THE ERA OF THE POST-MARTIAL LAW, POSTDEVELOPMENTAL STATE

The developmental state is usually defined by the interventionist state's policies of industrial restructuring and export upgrading as well as investment in public education to produce an upgradable labor force. In Taiwan, the success of microelectronics and Hsinchu Science Park has been well recognized as the showcase achievement of the developmental state. The developmental state is also frequently typified by an authoritarian regime. The combination of single-party domination, legitimized by the threat of Chinese communist invasion from across the Taiwan Strait, and successful land reform that effectively removed the landed elite in rural areas in the 1950s helped to keep workers and farmers relatively quiet in the regime of accumulation, characterized by high investment, low wages, and large price scissors, from the 1950s through the 1980s.

These four pillars of the developmental state, namely, state-guided and export-oriented industrialization, public education, rural land reform, and authoritarianism, have been substantially transformed since the early 1990s. In the 1990s, Taiwan's political system evolved from single-party authoritarianism under the Nationalist Party (KMT) to multiparty democracy, accompanied by the rise of social activism after the lifting of martial law in 1987. Also in the 1990s, while Taiwan's microelectronics companies continued to occupy an important niche in the world market, they faced new challenges and began to shift standardized manufacturing to mainland China. Public education first took a neoclassical turn in the early 1990s, using a supply-side rationale to increase the number of universities, hence lowering the threshold to university entrance. It then made a neoliberal turn in the early 2000s, adopting quantitative measurements in performance evaluation in higher education and encouraging private investment in education at all levels. Traditional agriculture went through crises as a result of urban and industrial expansion, insufficient state protection, and the World Trade Organization. Some rural areas survived by shifting to high-value-added agriculture and leisure industries, while others deteriorated further. These transformations in the era of the postdevelopmental state intertwined with one another, generating dilemmas, contentions, and new dynamics among the state, society, and the market.

The transformation of microelectronics showcased the changing state-society relationship in Taiwan in the new era. Since the 1990s, microelectronics, along with many other export-oriented manufacturing sectors, began to move to mainland China. As the issue of Taiwan's growing connection with mainland China continued to dominate political debates in Taiwan, the Taiwanese government dealt with the challenge of industrial hollowing out by diversifying the high-tech sector and by expanding existing science parks and building new ones. New science parks were built in agricultural areas, such as Tainan in southern Taiwan,

Yilan on the northeast coast, and Houli in central Taiwan. Hsinchu Science Park triumphalism has lent much symbolic capital to the new parks. Some of the science parks were central government initiatives, but many more were local politicians' pet projects. This spatial strategy of decentralizing science parks reflects the changing political landscape in Taiwan in the postauthoritarian era. The two rival parties, the Democratic Progressive Party (DPP) and the Nationalist Party (Kuomintang, KMT), competed with each other to consolidate their political support by allocating public projects in their client counties and cities.

To ensure profitability in projects that involved both public and private interests, plans of science parks were usually accompanied by real estate development projects. A science park that could accommodate both industrial and residential/commercial development required the conversion of large areas of farmland.

In 2004, a plan to build a science park and develop the surrounding areas for real estate projects was prepared by the county government of Miaoli in central Taiwan. Given its location to the south of Hsin-chu, the planned park tried to borrow the fame of Hsinchu Science Park and was called Chu-nan (South of Hsin-chu) Science Park. One of the subsidiaries of Foxconn, the iconic Taiwanese firm that manufactures 80 percent of the world's iBooks and iPads and Nokia and Motorola cell phones, was a prospective tenant of the planned park. According to the plan, the farmland of a village called Dapu, among others, was earmarked for land use conversion. The proposal did not meet much resistance in the beginning, as the county governor promised Dapu villagers high compensation rates for their farmland, and the villagers' homes were to be left intact so there was no need for relocation.

By 2008, the Foxconn subsidiary requested a much larger area of land in the park for its future expansion. To accommodate the request, the Miaoli county government decided to expropriate more farmland from Dapu village; further, the new expansion plan would involve demolition of villagers' homes and hence villagers' relocation. Even more controversial, the compensation rates turned out to be much lower than the "premium rates" that the governor had originally promised. Villagers responded by organizing rallies and protests in front of the Executive Yuan and the Control Yuan, the national-level government branches in Taipei. On June 9, 2010, before any agreement was reached between farmers and the county government, and as the rice crop was almost ready for harvest, the county government unexpectedly sent more than twenty excavators into the rice fields in the wee hours of the morning. The excavators were accompanied by two hundred police officers and an ambulance. In the name of preparing the land for construction, the fleet of excavators began a rampage of destruction of the rice fields of Dapu village.

As the extractors destroyed richly laden crops, and as anguished old farmers and women with young children pleaded with the operators to stop the monster machines and were held back brutally by the police, a local resident videotaped the entire incident. A citizen journalist, pen-named Great Tyrannosaurus, edited the footage and posted the video on a popular Web platform of citizen journalism called PeoPo (or People's Post). The video, entitled *When the Excavators Came to the Rice Fields*, immediately went viral. It subsequently activated a massive mobilization of local farmers, social activists, media workers, students, public intellectuals, professionals, and artists across Taiwan to protest against the government's brutality in land appropriation. The Dapu incident triggered one of the most important social movements in Taiwan's recent memory. At the end, the chief of the Executive Yuan apologized to Dapu villagers, and President Ma Ying-jeou of the KMT vetoed the expansion plan.

The societal challenge to the expansion of microelectronics and science parks in Taiwan also came from other sources. Pollution created by the microelectronics firms in Hsinchu Science Park had been an important target of environmental activists and community groups since the mid-1990s. Yet because the park was embedded in the state bureaucracy and the sewer and drainage systems were centralized in the science park, the administration of the science park, rather than individual polluting firms, became the target of the environmental protesters. Also, complaints were lodged mainly by residents in the neighborhoods adjacent to the park, where many middle-class employees of the science park lived. The split interests and loyalties between employees of Hsinchu Science Park and nonemployees in the same community made it difficult for the movement to strengthen its solidarity and attract a greater following.

The movement against high-tech pollution started to gather momentum in the 2000s. The political strategy of building patronage by dispensing high-profiled science park projects in greenfield sites began to provoke waves of activism against high-tech pollution. As areas affected by high-tech pollution expanded from the neighboring middle-class communities to farmers' croplands, the environmentalists' voice became louder.

Meanwhile, the significance of the legendary Industrial Technology Research Institute (ITRI) and the Electronics Research and Service Organization (ERSO), the star state actors and the base of high-tech research and development in Taiwan in the 1980s and 1990s, has been diminishing. Since the late 1990s, most high-tech firms have developed worldwide technology sourcing and strategic partnerships; many have established in-house research centers as the war over intellectual property rights in the microelectronics industry has escalated.[2] Taiwan's anti-high-tech pollution activists linked up with activist groups in the United States, especially those based in the Silicon Valley. They learned from their Silicon Valley counterparts to target individual polluting firms, like Acer and Foxconn, that were located outside of park jurisdiction and were not under the protective umbrella of the science park administration.[3]

Targeting these well-known firms individually was also a way to get media attention and impose greater pressure on the firms. Similar protests against industrial pollution were found in other sectors, including another foundational industry of the developmental state: the petrochemical industry.[4] In April 2011, a persistent and well-networked campaign by farmers, students, public intellectuals, professionals, and environmentalist groups successfully forced the government to halt a plan to build a major petrochemical complex in a wetland area in Zhanghua County on Taiwan's southwestern coast, making another headline and benchmarking the progress of Taiwan's environmental movement.

Yet not all social mobilizations in Taiwan have brought victorious results. What is important about mobilization is the way people are mobilized. The mobilization that I briefly sketched above, among many other similar cases, marked a profound transformation of Taiwan's state-society relationship in the era of the postdevelopmental state. What had once been the showcase of the developmental state, the microelectronics and petrochemical industries, was now as much a political liability as an economic driver. Growth-based legitimacy projects were subjected to societal scrutiny on environmental and distributional fronts and became the platform of social contestations.

Another related issue in the post–developmental state era is a changing perception of development that has challenged the idea and ideal of development defined by economic growth. Along with expanding social activism over distributional issues with regard to labor, the environment, land rights, women, education, and aborigines' rights, the politics of recognition and representation are also on the rise. The developmental state that once prioritized quantitative growth is now challenged by a new socioculture that asks questions about development for whom, and for what.

The question of "development for whom" has driven distributional and representational social movements since the 1990s; the question of "development for what" has formed the basis of religious and spiritual movements. Both types of movements are tightly connected with social actions, social values, and social entrepreneurialism.

Before I go into case studies to elaborate on these two types of social entrepreneurialism, I will first sketch briefly the transformation of Taiwan's social movements from political entrepreneurialism in the 1990s, characterized by its dependence on political parties, to the social entrepreneurialism in the 2000s, characterized by more diverse and autonomous forms of social mobilization.

FROM POLITICAL TO SOCIAL ENTREPRENEURIALISM

In 2000, the opposition party that grew out of Taiwan's democracy movement, the DPP, won the presidential election. Its victory marked the shift of Taiwan's polity from single-party domination to competitive multiparty democracy. The

DPP started out opposing the monopoly of the KMT and came to encompass a wide spectrum of political opposition, including agendas for legislature reform, labor, ethnic minority rights, aborigines' rights, and women's rights. Consolidating a very diverse array of progressive political movements in the 1990s, Chen Shui-bian of the DPP won the presidency in 2000 and stayed in power for two four-year terms.

Through the election the DPP developed a symbiotic relationship with grassroots activists turned political entrepreneurs. The grassroots organizations gave the DPP candidates political credibility and a campaign agenda; the DPP, in return, endorsed and sponsored movement leaders' election campaigns or recruited them into the government and party bureaucracy at various levels. While the DPP enjoyed both political resources and social legitimacy, social movements were made highly dependent on the DPP regime throughout the 1990s and a good part of the 2000s.

But the story of political entrepreneurialism is not just one of co-opted radicalism or political opportunism. Since the 2000s, the repertoire of social contestation and mobilization started to expand from distributional politics, as in the case of labor protection and women's rights, to the politics of recognition, as in the case of the rights of aboriginals, religious groups, and gay men and lesbians. However, as the repertoire of social activisms expanded and diversified, not all of them were endorsed by the DPP establishment, which had shifted from being an opposition party to occupying the center of power.

Along with the diversification and expansion of social movements and agendas, there was another wave of cultural change in the 2000s: voicing opinions in public forums and protesting and mobilizing were normalized, and networking in real and cyber space became a way of life. The various forms of civil organizations and social movements as well as the culture of protest through new and old media created varied real and virtual spaces jointly occupied by different classes, including workers and farmers; community organizers; liberal media workers; student groups, teachers, public intellectuals, academics; white-collar workers and professionals in medicine, law, design, and engineering; spiritual and religious activists; parents, housewives, and even woman marriage migrants from Southeast Asia.

The organizational capacity of these groups varied greatly, and not all of them were "political" according to narrowly defined party and electoral politics. Some specifically labeled themselves as "apolitical." Nevertheless, all of them engaged in social networking, coordinated by active members of the networks, which expanded and overlapped with other networks. The culture of networking has always been deeply rooted in Taiwanese society. It was now much expanded and reinforced, thanks to the widely available IT infrastructure in the age of information.

These loosely or not-so-loosely organized networkers were socially engaged but were not necessarily "political" in the immediate sense. Members were highly aware of the public agenda and possessed a mobilizational capacity that could be readily put into action when the need arose.

Several commentators in Taiwan have pointed out that by the end of the 2000s Taiwan's social activism was moving toward a more autonomous arena. The new generation of social activists and organizers had looser connections, if any, with either the DPP or the KMT party machines. They were politically shrewd and were highly aware of the cost of dependency on dominant political parties. They were less constrained by the state's political and policy agendas and were more internationally connected. While these activists claimed to be more community oriented than "political," their networks had a strong political implication in that they marked the emergence of a nonstate space and remained mobilizable for political aims. Activists had well-coordinated social networks that they could mobilize politically, even if not for specific political projects like election campaigns. In the instance already noted of a recent environmental protest against a plan to build a mega petrochemical complex and a new science park in central Taiwan, student groups, environmentalists, writers, and artists organized, fought, and won the battle.

Growing out of a political mobilization confined by party politics of the 1980s and 1990s, social movements in Taiwan have gone through important transformations and have become increasingly conscious of the need to preserve their own autonomy in the volatile environment of party politics. I call this phenomenon social entrepreneurialism in the sense that resourceful and creative social activists have been able to mobilize for social causes, creating social meanings and defining social values.

CITIZEN JOURNALISM AND PEOPLE'S POST

Social entrepreneurialism in the new millennium has a lot to do with informational technology. With this in mind, I have identified a citizen journalist network called People's Post ("PeoPo" for short), established in Taiwan in 2007, to examine Taiwan's social entrepreneurialism and its relationship with social media.

In Taiwan in the 1990s and 2000s, as the relatively new democracy encountered the global trend of deregulation, the number of media outlets increased dramatically. Shifting from highly controlled and censored, state-dominant public media, by 2011 Taiwan had five terrestrial TV networks, nine twenty-four-hour news channels, nineteen national evening newscasts, 120 cable channels, and an over 85 percent cable TV penetration rate. There are four thousand magazines, 2,500 newspapers, and two hundred radio stations—all for a population of 23 million. While Taiwan ranked fourth of countries in Asia for freedom of the press, it ranked last in media credibility, at only 1 percent.[5] In 2007, a survey conducted by Taiwan Normal University found that two-thirds of the citizens thought the media was the most important cause of Taiwan's social disorder.[6] Under intense competition for advertising, news programs grew increasingly sensational, and political parties and politicians bought up slots in news programs in the form of product placement. As commodified news programs in the commercial media generated widespread public distrust, in 2007 Public Television in Taiwan—a public broadcaster much like the BBC in the United Kingdom–launched the multimedia citizen journalism website People's Post or PeoPo, based on the open-source operating system Linux.[7] The English pronunciation of *PeoPo* is close to that for the word "tips" in Taiwanese slang.

PeoPo is different from personal blogs in the sense that the reports are more public affairs oriented, focusing more on local community events; and the stories are firsthand reporting instead of commentaries at second hand on news reports.[8] Compared to one of the best-known citizen journalism projects in East Asia, OhMyNews of South Korea, Taiwan's PeoPo emphasizes grassroots autonomy and does not interfere with or moderate the materials sent by citizen journalists, as long as those journalists are registered with the public TV station by their real name to prevent frauds and hoaxes. If someone objects to a report, the objection is forwarded to the contributor, who is invited to reconsider and amend it if he or she wants to. The TV station reserves the right to remove material, but it has not found any case that made the removal necessary. Also, whereas contributors to OhMyNews in South Korea are known to have close affiliations with traditionally strong political groups like teachers' associations and labor unions, most PeoPo citizen journalists are independent news producers. Of the 5,313 citizen journalists in PeoPo as of September 2011, 45 percent were male and 55 percent female. They tended to be young (70 percent between ages twenty and forty), and well educated (90 percent with college or higher degrees, as compared to the 36 percent of Taiwan's population over age fifteen with college or higher degrees). Compared to the BBC, which "welcomes viewers' contribution of photos and videos" but nevertheless treats these contributors as "sources," and other social news organizations like ProPublica of the United States, which is mainly an outlet for elite grant-sponsored professional journalists, citizen journalists of PeoPo primarily come from a nonmedia background and have great control over their reporting. Between April 2007 and March 2012, citizen journalists contributed seventy thousand reports, and the number of visitors grew from less than two hundred thousand per month in 2007 to a million by 2012.[9]

When Typhoon Morakot hit southern Taiwan in August 2009, killing more than seven hundred people and causing widespread devastation, it was a local citizen journalist who uploaded the first video report from the disaster zone that alerted the political center of Taipei in the north, which was basking in the sun that day. With its widespread and persistent team of video reporters, the PeoPo project shamed the government into getting much-needed aid to the stricken areas, and

Taiwan's president Ma Ying-jeou came under fire for his slow response to the disaster and his belated appeal for international help.

As PeoPo was getting more participating citizen journalists and visitors, the Public Television channel began to integrate PeoPo's output into its news programs. There was a daily five-minute program on the best stories filed that day. On weekends the main news bulletins carried at least four PeoPo reports. And it was not just public television that used citizen journalists' reports. Commercial TV stations also covered stories that were first broken by citizen journalists and that became too widely circulated for the commercial media to ignore. PeoPo citizen journalists did not just report from the grassroots. They began to set the social agenda. By covering what the mainstream media shied away from, citizen journalists gained credibility that most of the commercial media had long lost. And as citizen journalists established their social credibility, their political legitimacy was also strengthened. During the 2008 presidential election, PeoPo initiated a program that selected twelve citizen-produced videos from three hundred submissions, in which each citizen raised a thirty-second question for the presidential candidates. These twelve participants were invited to appear at the live broadcast of presidential debates, and each had the chance to ask the candidates a follow-up question face to face.

The connection between Taiwan's social entrepreneurialism and PeoPo is about intensification and expansion of social networks, and the capability of creating richly interwoven and mutually reinforcing relationships among various types of networks: social and virtual networks, personal and institutional networks, existing and expanded networks. In a society that has had a long and rich tradition of networking among extended families, friends, businesses, neighbors, and colleagues, the newly opened political environment, high computer literacy rates, and the availability of information technologies have provided the foundation for existing personal and business networks to flourish with effective coordination and organization.

A good example of the accumulative and expansive nature of networking that integrates social and virtual networks is the frequent and regular meetings of citizen journalists. As a way to maintain the quality of reporting, with a strong focus on visual stories, the public television station organized an extensive training program for member citizen journalists. In addition to producing fifty online training videos and courses, the station has run more than four hundred face-to-face workshops, organized citizen journalist gatherings, field visits, and symposiums, given citizen journalist awards, and held summer camps in different regions in Taiwan. Also, Taiwan's nonprofit, non-degree-granting community colleges in Taiwan, which have proliferated since the early 2000s and now total seventy-five throughout the island, offer journalism courses for aspiring citizen journalists. In the training programs, newcomers and experienced citizen journalists meet, and community workers and social activists share their experiences and interact directly with like-minded citizens. The meetings, workshops, and courses are informative and fun. They are for professional training in camerawork, interview skills, writing, and editing, as well as for socializing and network expansion.

Networking also extends from information production and circulation to action. The networks between citizen journalists and social activists constitute another important dimension of social entrepreneurialism.

Generally speaking, about 80 percent of the agenda covered by the sixty-thousand-plus citizen journalist reports between 2007 and 2011 were directly related to public affairs. Within that 80 percent, 23 percent concerned social welfare, 17 percent education, 12 percent the environment, 8 percent politics and the economy, 7 percent the media, 6 percent community reform, 6 percent historic preservation, 4 percent agriculture, 15 percent daily life and leisure, and 2 percent sports and technology.[10]

Although citizen journalists are mostly independent producers, their concerns regarding public affairs bring them close to social movements and organizations. Social protests or mobilizational activities are rarely covered by commercial media, as the most media are entangled with political and corporate interests. Social activists consequently count on citizen journalists to spread the word and mobilize support. The connection between PeoPo and social movements has helped strengthened both. The mobilization around the Dapu incident in 2010, as presented earlier in this chapter, was triggered by a citizen journalist's video report. Active social groups in Taiwan, like the Taiwan Agriculture United Front, among others, decided to join the Dapu-triggered farmers' land rights movement after activists saw the posting. Activists provided much-needed organizational resources and mobilization skills to sustain the movement. The sustained mobilization in turn provided more materials for citizen journalists, brought them more visitors, and encouraged them to follow the movement in greater depth.[11] PeoPo itself is affiliated with fifteen college news centers (which are usually affiliated with schools of journalism) and more than two hundred nongovernmental and nonprofit organizations, holding training workshops for them. These training programs have turned socially concerned citizens not only into more effective visual and auditory communicators but also into regular visitors and active participants of PeoPo. A news platform with the idea of sharing and voicing from the bottom up has become an unparalleled example of networking for the production of social meanings and values.

Another example of the synergy created across different types of networks is the linkage between interpersonal and mobilizational networks. In the movement against the plan to build a petrochemical complex in southern coastal Taiwan, the turning point happened when a mainstream news magazine, *Business Weekly* in Taiwan, decided to cover the story, which all other mainstream media had shied away from. According to Zhuang Feng-jia, one of the reasons for *Business Weekly* to cover the story was that a leading activist of the movement, a university professor, was a close college friend of the executive editor of the magazine.[12] The latter was convinced by the college friend to do what other mainstream media intentionally neglected. The coverage was critical because it was only after reading the story in *Business Weekly* that President Ma decided to veto the project. What is also interesting is the cross-fertilizing between citizen journalism and liberal journalism. The report was filed by a woman journalist who had left a mainstream media outlet and had become a freelancer and a registered citizen journalist of PeoPo. She eventually won the prestigious national journalism award for her persistent reporting on the explosive environmental issue.

To sum up, the significance of PeoPo as a critical case of social entrepreneurialism in Taiwan in the era of the postdevelopmental state is as follows.

First, *PeoPo has an unusual relationship with the state and market.* Like citizen journalism in other parts of the world, PeoPo enjoys the social credibility that mainstream commercial media does not. What makes PeoPo particularly interesting is its relationship with the state in the era of the postdevelopmental state. From its birth, PeoPo was a part of the Taiwan Public Television Service (TPTS) and has enjoyed the privilege of not having to worry about its commercial viability. It could also tap into the infrastructure and platform of the public TV station, as one of the fruits of Taiwan's political opening. Unlike some of the North America–based public journalist platforms like NowPublic (Vancouver, established in 2005), Newsvine (Seattle, 2005), and Reddit (Medford, MA, 2005), which ran like business start-ups and were subsequently acquired by mainstream media and/or venture capital, PeoPo managed to maintain its autonomy from the market.

There is a price to pay for financial autonomy. The leadership of the TPTS has been a political appointment. In 2007, when PeoPo was first established at the TPTS, the general manager of the TPTS was a student leader turned senior professional journalist who was well respected in Taiwan's media circles. His vision and support helped PeoPo stay away from political entanglements during his tenure. After the general manager left the TPTS, PeoPo went through several ups and downs, during which its budgetary and personnel resources were much limited. According to the director of the PeoPo platform, PeoPo's saving grace came from its claim to be a form of "new media," the magic words at a time when traditional print media continued to decline and when, as mentioned before, conventional TV news had lost much of its credibility. Moreover, PeoPo has become so successful that it is frequently presented at various international conferences on media, democracy, or new media. Whenever Taiwan needs to show the world what democracy has done for the Taiwanese people, especially when compared to mainland China, PeoPo makes a good showcase for Taiwan and for the TPTS. Consequently, as the director of PeoPo told me, even though the new TPTS leadership does not always support what PeoPo does, it cannot afford to seriously trim its already humble budget (less than 1 percent of the total TPTS budget). The highly resourceful and low-paid staff at PeoPo has therefore found its small, yet relatively autonomous space within the TPTS and has kept partisan politics at bay.

Second, *PeoPo goes beyond elite professionalism*. It has maintained the nonelitist nature of reporting, while remaining devoted to the provision of technical training to grassroots journalists through regular workshops and joint training programs with community colleges and social activist groups.[13] These training workshops have proved to be very effective in both technical training and social networking.

Many active citizen journalists are teachers who took early retirement under Taiwan's generous pension plans in the 1990s. These primary and secondary school teachers, with their broad knowledge base, communication skills, and experiences in visual presentation, were able to get a handle on news production quickly. With the support of state-sponsored pension plans, these middle-aged retirees can afford to devote their time and energy to volunteer work, including citizen journalism. This is yet another link between the state and social entrepreneurialism.

Third, *PeoPo and network society reinforce one another*. Supported by a well-developed IT infrastructure in a highly urbanized island of high population density, and embedded in a society of high computer literacy and dense social networks, PeoPo exemplifies how different types of networks can overlap, connect, and expand into more extensive networks. These multilayered networks are simultaneously interpersonal, institutional, and communicational-informational. They reinforce one another, creating new synergy in a society that turned into a multiparty democracy only twenty years ago (or eleven years ago, if we use the successful presidential campaign of the oppositional DPP as the benchmark). The extensiveness of social-informational networks and a functioning democracy seem to have created a positive feedback loop in this case.

Last but not the least, PeoPo features *crucial links between its expansive and extensive communication networks and mobilizational actions*. PeoPo's nonpartisan and noncommercial stance in a highly commercialized and politicized Taiwan gave it the rarest commodity of all: public trust and social credibility that turned out to be an effective tool for mobilization for the public good.

THE INTERNET AND PUBLIC TRUST IN CHINA

The public trust that PeoPo enjoyed makes an intriguing contrast with the Internet culture that James Leibold and Rongbin Han have reported on.[14]

Leibold used Manuel Castells's concept of "networked individualism" to elaborate on the fraudulent culture of the Internet generally. In an article entitled "Blogging Alone" he argued that "while the internet has dramatically increased people's access to information, it also threatens to undermine the accuracy and meaning of much of this knowledge."[15] Examples of Internet rumors, misinformation, and deception abound in the China of the 2000s. In the wake of the 2003 SARS epidemic, online rumors suggested that the virus was a biological weapon invented by Taiwan and the United States to destroy China, while stores ran out of vinegar once it was suggested as the only antidote to the infection.[16]

One of the best-known examples of deception and forgery on China's Internet concerns a tiger. The South China tiger, *Panthera tigris amoyensis*, had not been seen in the wild since 1980. But in October 2007, when a farmer and amateur photographer in the northwestern Chinese province of Shaanxi claimed he had risked his life to shoot thirty-plus digital photographs of a South China tiger in the wild, the Provincial Forestry Bureau immediately threw their weight behind the authenticity of the farmer's snapshots. They rushed to hold a press conference to announce the "rediscovery" of the extinct tiger under their jurisdiction, in the hope that it would boost the fame of the place, get state recognition and funding to establish a protection zone for the tiger like the giant panda conservancy in Sichuan, and increase tourism. However, the photographs were soon questioned. Netizens doubted the pictures and claimed they were fake. Urged by the public and wildlife experts, the national Forestry Ministry formed an investigative team on October 24, but their report has remained unpublicized. By early 2008, the Shaanxi provincial government reprimanded the Forestry Bureau for violating official regulations by holding the press conference to support Zhou's "discovery" without further evidence. The Forestry Bureau subsequently issued a public letter apologizing for publicizing the photos, though it refrained from commenting about their authenticity.

What's interesting is that the embarrassing scandal did not stop others from trying their luck with the same hoax. Only one month after the farce of the "paper tiger" in Shaanxi subsided, another scandal involving a fake South China tiger was exposed. This time, the person who did the forgery was a journalist with a county TV station in Hunan Province, another poor and desperate region. The journalist announced that he had "unintentionally videotaped" a suspected South China tiger in a mountainous area of Hunan Province. Again, local officials immediately jumped to support the claims. High-level provincial and municipal officials paid an inspection tour to the site where the tiger had allegedly been videotaped. They concluded that the journalist's videotape was authentic. But just four days later, the provincial Forestry Bureau announced that the big cat in the film was in fact a Siberian tiger borrowed from a circus from another province that happened to be on a performance tour in Hunan. The journalist was subsequently blamed for making the forgery to enhance his own fame and commercial interests.[17] Neither the officials who supported the forgery nor the journalist was punished.

While the case of the South China tiger forgeries was eventually cleared up, many other forgeries have remained on the Internet. One immediate consequence of these scandals is that information on the Internet is increasingly considered unreliable. Online anonymity protects individuals while also creating space for frauds. Leibold cited one Chinese blogger's statement: "On the Internet, even [when] you provide facts about yourself, people won't believe it. They think that you make them up. So it doesn't matter whether you provide real or fake information because nobody trusts the information on the Internet."[18] In the same article Leibold cited a survey showing that those who thought the Internet was reliable decreased from 52 percent to 26 percent between 2003 and 2007, while those who thought it was unreliable more than doubled, from 9 percent to 22 percent.[19]

The culture of distrust is reinforced by and reflected in the regressive digital culture described by Leibold. The new technologies that enable fast-paced, widely spread flows of messages excite but also quickly exhaust and disillusion users. The culture of suspicion, in turn, comes back to haunt online activism. In Han's (2012) observation, Chinese netizens have been extremely anxious about each other's identity and intentions in their online communication. While netizens could be successful in discrediting the Chinese Communist Party regime by exposing the state's manipulation and distortion of public opinions online, they are equally, if not more, suspicious of alternative views to the party-state. As the regime challengers practice pop activism and mock official lines, they are also ready to question the intentions and competence of democratic activists. Take the two best-known leaders of the 1989 Tiananmen student movement, for example: according to Rongbin Han Chai Ling was accused of risking other students' lives for her personal ambition, and Wang Dan was accused of betraying China's national interests by receiving funds from the United States and Taiwan's proindependence DPP administration. Online platforms, therefore, could work to silence as much as to encourage public forums.[20] Han notes that such suspicion and anxiety over others' identity and intentions has led online communities to isolate themselves with highly guarded entrances instead of retaining more inclusive networks in cyberspace.

As a result, there has been a strong public outcry for more, rather than less, state control of the Internet to maintain social stability. Nearly 84 percent of respondents to a survey thought that content on the Internet should be controlled, with 83 percent identifying violence, 65 percent malicious speculation, and nearly 30 percent online chatting as in need of control, and 85 percent looked to the government to censor this content. Between 2003 and 2007, there was an over 50 percent decline in those who thought that the Internet empowered the people.[21]

THE POWER OF THE APOLITICAL: TZU CHI

A more systematic comparison of social media in Taiwan and China is beyond the scope of this chapter. But one of the possible directions for further investigation is the paradoxical and multidimensional connections between public trust and politics. While Taiwanese netizens have organized alternative forums with great potential for political mobilization, they have tended to shy away from outright partisan politics. In the Chinese case, as Leibold has pointed out, one consequence of the loss of public trust in social media has been increasing popular demand for more, not less, state intervention in regulating cyberspace.[22]

In this final section, I will bring in another case of social entrepreneurialism from Taiwan to further illustrate the paradoxical relationship between public trust and politics and to show how an allegedly apolitical group has built the most powerful social organization in Taiwan, an organization that has now established itself in China as well.

Post–martial law Taiwan has seen a rapid expansion of religious and spiritual institutions. Quite a few Buddhist temples have expanded into large-scale and well-financed modern organizations. Buddhist organizations have contributed to the proliferation of welfare institutions, the internationalization of the revival movement, and increasing religious links between Taiwan and mainland China.

One of the best-known and largest Buddhist organizations active in Taiwan and internationally is a religious philanthropy group called Buddhist Compassion Relief Tzu Chi Foundation (hereafter Tzu Chi). Tzu Chi started as a small Buddhist charity of fifty-plus members in the impoverished coastal region of eastern Taiwan in 1966. By 2009 it boasted five million followers in Taiwan and overseas. Tzu Chi is also markedly matriarchal. The leader is a woman, a small-framed yet highly charismatic Buddhist Dharma nun called Master Cheng Yan. Tzu Chi's thirty founding members were all women, and in 2009 about 80 percent of the most active followers and volunteer charity workers were women, particularly middle-class, middle-aged women.[23]

While the matriarchal nature of Tzu Chi distinguishes it from other religious institutions in Taiwan, Tzu Chi has also demonstrated impressive managerial capability. In three decades, Tzu Chi Foundation grew from a small charity to a large international organization with 63 branch operations in Taiwan and another 372 branches in forty-seven countries, eight hundred full-time staff, and five million followers. It is included in the case study bank of Harvard Business School. In addition to its religious activities and organizations, Tzu Chi operates charity and disaster relief agencies, which now run three state-of-the art, nine-hundred-bed hospitals, a television channel, a publishing house, and a secular university that includes a well-respected medical school, several middle schools, and one of the most important bone marrow donation centers in Taiwan. In addition to large investment projects like hospitals, universities, and schools, Tzu Chi runs five thousand volunteer-based recycling centers with two hundred thousand volunteers all over Taiwan, turning millions of recycled PET bottles into clothing and disaster relief blankets. By 2010 the company that was in charge of the recycle-reuse project had annual revenue over US$3 million.

An important feature of Tzu Chi is its principle of political neutrality. Master Cheng Yan has explicitly required Tzu Chi members to refrain from any kind of political activities. Unlike many celebrities in Taiwan, Master Cheng Yan herself has never openly supported any presidential candidates or politicians, and members of all ranks have to resign from Tzu Chi if they become involved in political campaigns, elections, or demonstrations. Master Cheng Yan's "ten precepts" include the five Buddhist ones of no killing, no stealing, no sex outside of marriage, no lying, and no drinking, as well as five more that she has added to the list: no smoking or using narcotics; no betel nuts; no gambling, no violation of traffic laws, and *no participation in political activities or demonstrations*. Tzu Chi's environmentalism, for instance, remained tied to recycling, for which the government also campaigns. Tzu Chi would not, however, protest against nuclear power plants or any specific polluting factories. In the name of universal love and harmony, and upholding the principle of not taking political sides, Tzu Chi systematically avoided any kind of confrontation.

This very explicit principle of political neutrality was not necessarily a "traditional" Buddhist value, however. Politically charged action has been characteristic of a long history of popularizing Buddhist movements in China. These sects often attempted to move Buddhism out of the monastery and into the streets, away from sophisticated philosophy and toward actions that anyone could perform, with a vision of this-worldly, collective salvation.

The case for the Buddhist tradition of political involvement is made even stronger if we look at Buddhist organizations and activities in other parts of Asia, including those in Thailand, Japan, Vietnam, Myanmar, Sri Lanka, and Tibet. In these societies we find that monks (mostly monks, not nuns) have not shunned either modest or aggressive political involvement and have engaged in protests against and resistance to secular states or have advocated alternative sources of authority. In contrast, Buddhist organizations in Taiwan general, and Tzu Chi in particular, have embraced no radical theology and have always adhered to the principle of political neutrality. Buddhist organizations were not part of the democracy movement in Taiwan in the 1980s, and they remained politically neutral after the lifting of martial law in 1987.[24]

Tzu Chi's political neutrality has been a form of moral capital in post–martial law Taiwan. As André Laliberté has suggested, the politics of post–martial law Taiwan was highly divided. The division was first drawn between those who were born in mainland China (mostly military and government personnel and those who moved to Taiwan in 1949 when the Nationalists were defeated by the communists), and those who identify themselves as genuine Taiwanese (whose ancestors, most of them peasants, had migrated to Taiwan from southern China three hundred years earlier). This line between "insiders" and "outsiders" was further reinforced by their presumed political stance over the issue of Taiwan-China relations. While "outsiders" were generally thought to be supportive of unification with mainland China, "insiders" were thought to lean toward Taiwan independence. Politicians of the DPP when it was an opposition party exploited this division to consolidate opposition energies and defeat the KMT, which had been dominating Taiwanese mainstream politics for half a century, in the 2000 presidential election. But this identity politics in Taiwan has not led to the type of violent conflicts found in many other parts of the world and history.

This is where the "apolitical" Tzu Chi and other Buddhist institutions come in. In a strongly politicized society with an active market of ideologies, and under increasing competition for resources with other religious and secular nongovern-mental and nonprofit organizations, Tzu Chi found itself a niche featuring no po-litical ideologies or claims. Positioned above and beyond secular politics, which was thought to be corrupted by money and power, Tzu Chi has attracted members from all ideological camps who were looking for a Pure Land in the mind. The more apolitical Tzu Chi insisted on being, the more its political influence over the state bureaucracy and politicians across different camps has increased. In a place where most people are sick and tired of politics and excessive commercialization, Tzu Chi and Master Cheng Yan stand on a moral plateau that few politician or CEOs can reach. In anthropologist Julia Huang's account, the secretariat office of the premier of the Executive Yuan told her that Tzu Chi's representative had en-joyed special treatment by the government.[25] Tzu Chi representatives did not have to make an appointment with the minister's secretariat in advance before they met. Often the former just called from a mobile phone while they were only minutes away from the Executive Yuan. And these representatives reiterated that they were "doing good things" when they negotiated with the minister's secretariat for the government's support. Even high-ranking government officials feel they cannot afford to offend Tzu Chi. Unlike other religious leaders in Taiwan, Master Zheng Yan has never made a public appearance in presidential election campaigns for any candidate. But President Ma Ying-jeou of the KMT attended one of Tzu Chi's recycling centers and worked as a volunteer sorting out plastic bottles for a couple of hours.

Tzu Chi, on account of its political neutrality, has also turned out to be very useful to the Taiwanese government in its attempts to expand its much-contracted position in international diplomacy. As the result of China's diplomatic campaign against Taiwan, Taiwan is recognized as an independent sovereignty by only twenty-three countries, many of which are island countries of the South Pacific. Tzu Chi has become one of the most important venues for the Taiwanese govern-ment to promote its "People to People" diplomacy, represented by the establishment of the Committee of Nongovernmental Organizations under Taiwan's Ministry of

Foreign Affairs. And given the political sensitivity of the issue of unification and independence, Tzu Chi, by declaring its political neutrality in humanitarian works, much like other international aid agencies, has paved the way for Taiwan's religious and social groups to cross the Taiwan Strait and expand their operations and networks in China. As mentioned earlier, Tzu Chi's relief workers have been able to enter mainland China despite the PRC's reputation for being highly cautious of accepting foreign aid and relief workers. During the Sichuan earthquake in China of 2008, Tzu Chi was the first non-PRC aid team approved by the PRC government to enter the quake zone. In 2010, after twenty years of working in various Chinese provinces, Tzu Chi became the first and the only international nonprofit organization to be approved by the State Department to establish a nationwide operation in China.

This chapter has explored Taiwan's changing state-societal relationship in the era of the postdevelopmental state, as well as the interplay of information technology, oppositional politics, and social activism. What I found most intriguing in this triangular dynamic is the paradox that in multiparty-democratic Taiwan, social mobilizers have claimed an apolitical stance in order to earn public trust, whereas in single-party-dominant China social media participants have turned to the state for restoration of public trust. The apolitical yet powerful charity organization of Tzu Chi further illuminates the power of the apolitical by pushing the limits of Taiwan's otherwise much-constrained diplomatic relationship internationally and with China. Changing state-society relationships in Taiwan and China are inevitably affected by the changing Taiwan-China relationship, and the reverse is also true.

NOTES

1. I ended this research in 2012, before the Sunflower Movement took place in 2014. Since I have not yet conducted enough research regarding the political and social implications of that movement and related events, I did not include them in this chapter.

2. Statistics regarding investment in Taiwan's Science Parks and the microelectronics industry in the last few years can be found in Hsinchu Science Park Bureau, Ministry of Science and Technology, Taiwan, ROC, "Hsinchu Science Park 2009 Annual Report," 2009, www.sipa.gov.tw/file/20100819093820.pdf.

3. An increasing number of firms, including Acer and Foxconn, among many others, are located right outside Hsinchu Science Park to avoid excessive government intervention, while taking advantage of the industrial cluster in the area.

4. In April 2011, as the result of persistent and well-networked campaigns by farmers, students, intellectuals, and environmentalist groups, the government was forced to halt a plan for a major petrochemical complex to be built on a wetland area in Zhanghua, southern Taiwan.

5. Leh-chyun Lin, keynote speech at the annual meeting of the International Press Institute, Taipei, September 2011.

6. Zhuang Feng-jia, "Impact of Citizen Journalism on Public Policies in Taiwan" (MA thesis, National Taiwan University, 2011), 24.

7. Philip Harding, "PeoPo Helps Taiwanese Public Broadcaster to Restore Trust," *Guardian*, February 15, 2010, www.guardian.co.uk/media/2010/feb/15/citizen-journalism-taiwan.

8. Zhuang Feng-jia, "Impact of Citizen Journalism," 25.

9. Lin, keynote speech.

10. Ibid.

11. Zhuang Feng-jia, "Impact of Citizen Journalism," 71.

12. Ibid.

13. Lin, keynote speech.

14. James Leibold, "Blogging Alone: China, the Internet, and the Democratic Illusion?," *Journal of Asian Studies* 70, no. 4 (2011): 1023–41; Rongbin Han, "Challenging the Regime, Defending the Regime: Contesting Cyberspace in China" (PhD diss., University of California, Berkeley, 2012).

15. Leibold, "Blogging Alone," 9.

16. Lisa Chiu, "Outbreak of Rumors Has China Reeling," SFGate.com, May 7, 2003, http://articles. sfgate.com/2003–05–07/news/17493093_1_sars-cases-beijing-mayor-meng-xuenong-sars-epidemic.

17. Wu Zhong "'Paper Tiger' Tales Shred Credibility," *Asia Times*, April 3, 2008, www.atimes.com/ atimes/China/JD03Ad01.html.

18. Liu Xun, "Online Posting Anxiety: Impacts of Blogging," *Chinese Journal of Communication* 3, no. 2 2 (2010): 202–22, cited in Leibold, "Blogging Alone."

19. Guo Liang, *Surveying Internet Usage and Its Impact in Seven Chinese Cities* (Shanghai: Center for Social Development, Chinese Academy of Social Sciences, 2007), 9–11, cited in Leibold, "Blogging Alone," 10.

20. Han, "Challenging the Regime."

21. Liang, *Surveying Internet Usage*, 86, cited in Leibold, "Blogging Alone," 11.

22. Leibold, "Blogging Alone." For details, see You-tien Hsing, "Development as Culture: Human Development and Information Development in China," in *Reconceptualizing Development in the Global Information Age*, ed. Manuel Castells and Pekka Himanen (Oxford: Oxford University Press, 2014), 116–39.

23. However, it has never organized as a women-only organization. In fact, in the last few years it has been getting an increasing number of male members and leaders at different levels.

24. André Laliberté, "'Buddhism for the Human Realm' and Taiwanese Democracy," in *Religious Organizations and Democracy in Contemporary Asia*, ed. Tung-ren Cheng and Deborah Brown (Armonk, NY: M. E. Sharpe, 2005), 55–82.

25. Julia Huang, *Charisma and Compassion: Cheng Yen and the Buddhist Tzu Chi Movement* (Cambridge, MA: Harvard University Press, 2009).

PART III

Political Strategy

11

Pivot, Hedger, or Partner

Strategies of Lesser Powers Caught between Hegemons

Yu-Shan Wu

Taiwan is strategically situated between the United States and the People's Republic of China (PRC). It is impossible to understand cross-Strait relations without looking into this global strategic context. Although one may not agree with the pessimistic prediction of the power transition theory, namely that the closing gap between the United States and China will result in a titanic clash between the world's hegemon and its challenger, it is nevertheless undeniable that the two strongest nations in today's world have been locked in tense strategic competition. China wants to reclaim its lost central place in the world, a wish that is naturally resisted by today's hegemon, the United States. This is not to deny that Washington and Beijing collaborate in many aspects of their relationship, such as the fight against international terrorism and their joint efforts to deal with climate change. However, as the capabilities of the two giants are getting closer and closer, the relation is strained, with China understandably striving for an equal say on international affairs and the United States hesitant to grant such status to its challenger. The refusal to give China a voting weight in the International Monetary Fund (IMF) that reflects its economic clout is one vivid example, and the competition between the two over the issue of Asian Infrastructure Investment Bank (AIIB) is another. The main geopolitical fault line for Sino-American competition is found in East Asia. Another great strategic conflict in today's world is between the West and Russia over Ukraine. The lesser powers in eastern Europe are in a situation similar to that of their counterparts in East Asia: both are caught in a competition between two great powers.

Given the strained relation between Beijing and Washington and between Moscow and the West, it is interesting to observe the behaviors of the lesser powers caught between the two giants on both geostrategic fault lines to see if there is a common pattern. Before we can do this, we need to consult the existing international relations (IR) literature. However, there is a theoretical paucity in this regard. Traditional IR theories focus on the behaviors of greater powers or treat actors as if they have equal capabilities. The international behaviors of small states are understudied, to say the least. Asymmetrical interactions between a great power and a lesser power seldom catch the attention of the theoreticians, let alone the behavioral pattern of a lesser power caught between two competing giants. In the following pages I first develop an analytical framework that specifically addresses this situation and then apply it to the East Asian and eastern European theaters. The core of the analysis is to identify the strategic roles that a lesser country can play between two competing great powers and then, through critical case analysis of Taiwan and Ukraine, to seek to identify the factors that can explain why a specific role is chosen by the lesser power and how that role may change over time. Although the main emphasis is on East Asia, a comparison with eastern Europe is made to add to the analytical depth. It is expected that through the development of this analytical framework we can better understand cross-Strait relations from a theoretical and comparative perspective.

THEORETICAL FORMULATION

The starting point is obviously the balance-of-power (BOP) paradigm. When facing a rising power, BOP theory predicts a balancing strategy that is either internal (building up military preparedness) or external (forming an alliance).[1] Traditional BOP theory is modified by Stephen Walt's "balance of threat" theory, in which perceived threat rather than capability is the criterion for the balancing behavior.[2] For weaker states, "bandwagoning" is added to the toolbox, which prescribes behaviors that conform or do not challenge the core values of the rising power.[3] However, as both balancing and bandwagoning entail great costs, in the form of either budgetary burden, alliance maintenance, or loss of strategic independence, yet another option presents itself: hedging. Hedging is a two-pronged strategy by which a country both engages and guards against the target country. The "hedger" does not simply adopt a balancing or engagement strategy but employs a mixture of the two. The engagement serves to enhance a friendly relationship with the target country, bring about commercial benefits, and hopefully transform the values and institutions of the target country so that it may stop posing a threat. The balancing serves to provide a security guarantee through either military buildup or an alliance with another great power. Typically engagement happens in the economic realm while balancing happens in the security realm.

Unfortunately, the above theoretical formulations are insufficient to capture the situation of a lesser power caught between two strong nations. First of all, not enough attention has been given to small countries and their international behaviors, as most IR theories are about great powers and their interactions. Second, for the literature on small states in world politics, the tendency is to explore their general strategies to survive in a realist world, not to focus on asymmetrical relations.[4] Third, for those studies that have power asymmetry in mind, the emphasis is typically on a dyad of nations, not a lesser power caught between two strong nations: that is, they focus on the relation between two actors, not three.[5] When a lesser country finds itself in the middle of great-power competition, it cannot seek advice from traditional IR theories that focus on bilateral relations. A trilateral theory is needed.

The inadequacies of bilateral IR theories can be demonstrated by the interconnectedness of the policies of the lesser power toward the two great powers. Assuming G_1 and G_2 are the two great powers, and L is the lesser power, we find that L's policy toward G_1 is not independent of its policy toward G_2. If L considers G_1 more powerful than G_2, or more of a threat, then it may do a balancing act against G_1. Since L is much weaker than G_1, L's balancing act cannot solely consist of military buildup: it needs to seek an external ally. G_2 as a competitor of G_1 is a natural choice. However, as L is also much weaker than G_2, the alliance between L and G_2 translates into L's bandwagoning with its ally. Hence L's bandwagoning with G_2 is concomitant with L's balancing against G_1. In this way, L is both balancing and bandwagoning at the same time, incurring the costs of both strategies. If L perceives G_2 as the main threat, then the opposite will happen, namely L will balance against G_2 by bandwagoning with G_1. This "coupling of strategies" is captured in figure 7 by L's rightmost and leftmost positions: "Balance against G_1 and Bandwagon with G_2" and "Balance against G_2 and Bandwagon with G_1" respectively.

Another strategy that L can adopt is hedging. Again, if we assume that G_1 is either more powerful or more threatening, then L may hedge against it. The engagement part of the strategy prescribes building economic ties between L and G_1. The balancing part consists of military buildup or external alliance. As L is much weaker than G_1, internal balancing is definitely insufficient, necessitating an alliance with G_2. This is the second from the rightmost position in figure 7. If G_2 is the main target, then L will take the second from the leftmost position. Now L does not need to choose between balancing and hedging toward G_1: it can bandwagon. However, since G_1 and G_2 are locked in fierce competition, bandwagoning with G_1 is tantamount to balancing against G_2. This leads L to the leftmost position in figure 7. If G_2 is the main threat, and L decides to bandwagon, then it will take the rightmost position and balance against G_1. In short, whichever policy taken by L toward G_1 (balancing, hedging, bandwagoning), there is a policy corollary for L toward G_2. The relations among the G_1, G_2 and L are thus intertwined. This shows there is a keen need to develop a trilateral analytical framework.

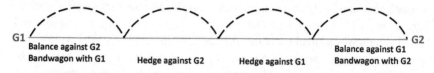

G1 ── G2

Balance against G2
Bandwagon with G1   **Hedge against G2**   **Hedge against G1**   **Balance against G1**
                                                                                            Bandwagon with G2

FIGURE 7. Choices of a lesser power placed between two great powers (G1 and G2).

The strategic triangle theory is geared toward analyzing trilateral relations. There are four ideal types of strategic triangle: ménage à trois (three amities), marriage (two enmities and one amity), romantic triangle (two amities and one enmity), and unit veto (three enmities).[6] In ménage à trois, all three players are "friends." In marriage, two "partners" act against an "outcast." In a romantic triangle, two "wings" court a "pivot." In a unit veto, the players are all "foes" to one another. With the four ideal types of strategic triangle (ménage à trois, marriage, romantic triangle, unit veto), and six roles (friend, partner, outcast, wing, pivot, foe), we can begin analyzing any triangular situation, using the strategic triangle types and roles to describe objectively the structure of the triangular game (see figure 8).

In a strategic triangle, a player considers its amity with other players to be always preferable to enmity. However, the player considers the other two players' mutual enmity to be preferable to their amity. Hence, the most preferable position is that of a pivot, in which the player has friendly relations with the other two players while they are at odds with each other. Interestingly, the pivot's role is not captured in figure 7.

Now we can integrate the perspectives from both figure 7 and figure 8, integrating the concepts of strategies and triangular roles.[7] Again we put L's choices on a continuum, as shown in figure 9. L can tilt toward G1 by bandwagoning with it and balancing against G2, which is the leftmost position on the continuum. This would make L a "partner" of G1 in a marriage triangle. Or L can tilt toward G2 by bandwagoning with it and balancing against G1, in the rightmost position on the continuum, which turns L into a partner of G2. L can also modify its stance by moving slightly toward its threat but keeping the principal connection with its ally. L would then "hedge against G1" or "hedge against G2." Either way, L becomes a "hedging partner."[8] If we push L's position to the middle of the continuum, but not so much as to tip it over to the other side, then L becomes the "pivot." A pivot is not principally committed to either of the two great powers but is tilting between them. Hence, we find three roles that a lesser power can play between two competing great powers: *partner, hedging partner,* and *pivot.* The three roles are shown in figure 9.

In strategic triangular analysis, pivot is the most desirable position, for it allows L to maintain amicable relations with the other two players while preventing them from collaborating against it. The pivot can tilt in different directions to

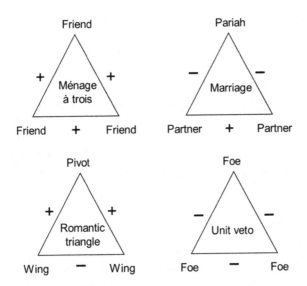

FIGURE 8. Types of strategic triangles.

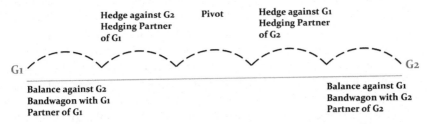

FIGURE 9. Choices and roles of a lesser power placed between two great powers (G1 and G2).

gain concessions from both "wings." However, to play pivot between two strategic giants is an unenviable task for a lesser power. Tilting by pivot naturally causes concern on the part of the wings, eliciting responses that are not necessarily positive. Thus, when L is tilting between G1 and G2, either or both of the giants may attempt to coerce L into their party line instead of courting it. A skillful L may be able to elicit positive concessions but always risks inviting the wrath of the giants and putting itself in a dangerous position.[9] The role of partner is theoretically less advantageous than pivot, especially for the junior partner, who may be double-crossed by its senior partner. It thus makes sense for a lesser power caught between two giants to opt for the role of a hedging partner, which entails reasonable security through alliance with one giant, while providing some flexibility of movement to elicit courting by the other giant, and possibly some countercourting by its ally, who cannot take the hedging partner for granted.

In the following analysis, I will apply the framework to analyze the relationship between the rising China and its East Asian neighbors, with the strategic competition between Beijing and Washington as the background. I will then use a similar analysis for the European theater. I will likewise put the different policy positions of East European countries toward Russia on a continuum and compare them with their Asian counterparts. The background there is the strategic competition between the US-led West and Russia. Then I will look into cross-Strait relations and the crisis in Ukraine as two critical cases, using the above framework and making comparisons.

RESURGENCE OF OPPOSING ALLIANCES AND
POSTURING ON THE FAULT LINE

During the Cold War, two hierarchically structured alliance systems opposed each other in East Asia. They were the continental system, composed of the Soviet Union, the PRC, North Korea, and North Vietnam (the communist league), and the US-centered, hub-and-spoke maritime system. The power shift in the continental system disrupted the Sino-Soviet pact, as the PRC rose to challenge Moscow's supremacy, while hegemonic stability in the maritime system buttressed the US-led alliance. The division in the continental system offered Washington opportunities to befriend Beijing, and Washington's allies were prompted to act likewise. The tension in competitive rapprochement was absorbed by the hegemonic structure of the maritime system. The result was collective hedging (balancing-with-engagement) against the PRC, with the exception of Taiwan, the Republic of China (ROC). Taiwan was the odd man out because it had a unique relation with mainland China: they claimed sovereignty over each other. The incompatibility of the fundamental goals of the two sides of the Taiwan Strait prevented cross-Strait relations from evolving toward the same direction that began to prevail in the region, namely collective hedging against the PRC. Taiwan's failure to join the chorus was not a sign of its being immune from the structural impetus but a reflection of domestic factors that acted to thwart systemic forces. Those factors, however, proved unable to prevail in the long run.[10]

In the post–Cold War era, the predominance of the United States caused the revival of the Beijing-Moscow nexus, now constructed as an equal partnership. Despite great structural changes, China and Russia are not considered full converts to Western values and institutions and thus are viewed suspiciously by the West. The two continental powers are seen as alien and threatening to the maritime alliance and thus must be guarded against. For Beijing and Moscow, the incessant eastward expansion of NATO and the EU threatens Russia, while the strengthening of security ties between Washington and its allies in East Asia puts great pressure on the PRC. Beijing and Moscow understand that the West expects nothing short of their complete conversion, in the form of regime change and peaceful evolution. With China's astronomical rise and Russia's recovery from its post-Soviet malaise, the two continental powers have clung together to form a semialliance, reviving a strategic tie that existed in the 1950s.[11] Again one finds the continental and the maritime systems confronting each other, just as they did during the Cold War, with the only difference being a shift of the United States' main target from the Soviet Union to the PRC.

Cross-system hedging is inevitable, as this increases the payoff for strategic players.[12] With China rising rapidly, both the tendency to balance against it and the need to engage it rise for US allies, such as Japan, South Korea, and Australia in the maritime system, causing tension in their domestic politics and their relation with the United States. The maritime system, however, remains robust, as it is sustained by US dominance.[13] Of particular interest is Taiwan's belated joining of the chorus, under the same systemic forces that disposed its former allies in the maritime system. Because of the issue of overlapping sovereignties, Taiwan was the last to adopt the hedging strategy and reach rapprochement with Beijing as late as 2008, when the Kuomintang (KMT) regained power and the domestic political condition was ready.

From the Cold War to the post–Cold War era, confrontation between the continental and maritime alliances has waxed and waned. Since the turn of the century, it has been on the rise. The first decade of the twenty-first century witnessed milder tension between the two systems than in the 1990s, as the threat of international terrorism rose to prominence and became a primary concern for both the maritime and continental alliances. The pledge of support for the United States in its war on terror by Jiang Zemin and Vladimir Putin in the aftermath of 911 was not merely an exploitation of that dramatic event to improve relations with Washington and to reduce pressure from the West but a reflection of shared interests.[14] However, the incessant expansion of NATO and the EU into former Soviet bloc coutries and even into the post-Soviet republics, the color revolutions (Georgia in 2003, Ukraine in 2004, Kyrgyzstan in 2005), the Russo-Georgian War (2008), the expediency of amassing political support by whipping up nationalism, and Russia's regained confidence with sustained economic growth led Putin toward greater assertiveness against the West.[15] For China, territorial disputes with East Asian neighbors allied with the United States, disgruntlement over rigidities in the decision-making process in major international organizations that fail to reflect China's astronomical rise, and a rapid shift of balance in favor of China since the eruption of the global financial crisis in 2008 add to Beijing's increasingly assertive foreign policy. The responses of the West as led by the United States (such as a turn of diplomatic attention "back to Asia," and sanctions against Russian aggression) further drove the continental powers together and strengthened the two alliances. Whenever the West was putting pressure on one continental power, the other would never join the chorus but would show "understanding" for the actions by its continental ally; thus there was no Russian criticism of China on Tibet or human rights when Beijing held the 2008 Olympics, a posture that China reciprocated when Russia held the 2014 Sochi Winter Olympics, which were severely criticized by the West. China also scratched Russia's back during and after the Russo-Georgian War by not joining Western criticism and declaring with other Shanghai Cooperation Organization members its support for "the active role of Russia in promoting peace and cooperation in the region" in the Dushanbe Declaration of August 2008. On Syria, neither would endorse sanctions on the Assad regime, and the Russian foreign minister Sergey Lavrov brokered a deal to stop an imminent Western invasion of the country. On Iran both countries advocated negotiations and opposed sanctions in response to Tehran's nuclear program. On Libya both Russia and China resented the West's military intervention against Qaddafi's forces that led to the killing of the dictator, a move legitimated by a liberal interpretation of Security Council Resolution 1973, which merely stated the need for protecting civilians. On Russia's annexation of Crimea, Putin gave special thanks to China for "taking into account the full historical and political context" there.[16] Under pressure from the West, Russia and China set aside their differences, solved border issues, conducted arms deals regarding state-of-the-art weapons, and intensified energy cooperation.[17] The two countries formed a Eurasian continental core to resist pressure from the US-led West.

Two geopolitical fault lines thus appeared. They were formed as a result of the pressure building up where "political plates" collide. The two fault lines cut across East Asia and eastern Europe. Lesser powers along these lines bear the pressure of the competing giants: United States plus Europe versus Russia in eastern Europe, and United States versus China in East Asia. The lesser powers have limited choices. They can choose among five options, from top to bottom: partner of the continental alliance (bandwagon with continental, balance against maritime), hedging partner of the continental alliance (bandwagon with continental, hedge against maritime), pivot (noncommittal and tilting in between), hedging partner of the maritime alliance (bandwagon with maritime, hedge against continental), and partner of the maritime alliance (bandwagon with maritime, balance against continental). A partner is fully allied with one great power and distanced from the other. A hedging partner is committed to one camp but engaged positively with the other camp. A pivot holds itself at equal distance from both camps, typically tilting between the two to gain benefits from them.

In figure 10 we present both the East Asian and eastern European fault lines and detail the choices for the lesser powers on those two lines. An East Asian lesser power can choose among the following positions: partner of the PRC, hedging

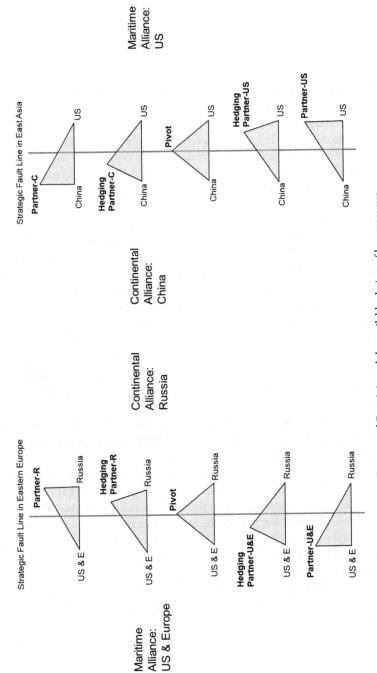

FIGURE 10. Strategic fault lines in eastern Europe and East Asia and the available choices of lesser powers.

partner of the PRC, pivot, hedging partner of the United States, and partner of the United States. An eastern European lesser power can choose among the following positions: partner of Russia, hedging partner of Russia, pivot, hedging partner of the United States and Europe, and partner of the United States and Europe.

We can also detect the two fault lines by locating the frontline US Air Force operating bases in Eurasia. The bases are located in Asia and Europe in a way to contain the PRC and Russia, or the Eurasian continental core. In East Asia the US operating locations range across Japan, South Korea, the Philippines, Singapore, Thailand, and Malaysia. In eastern Europe, they range across Germany, Poland, Hungary, Romania, Bulgaria, Turkey, and the Arab Peninsula.[18] Those countries on the border of the American military presence have to make a critical decision about their strategic relation with the United States and the maritime alliance versus their relation with the continental core, particularly when the relation between the two alliances is tense.

At times when there is little conflict between the Eurasian core and the US-led maritime alliance, as in the early 2000s, when international terrorism was the common enemy and the major concern for both alliances, the frontline countries find themselves in a ménage à trois triangle with the two camps, facing no pressure to take sides. The two fault lines thus look less obvious and relevant. When tensions flare up, as they have since the late 2000s, however, frontline countries are forced to take positions under the pressure of the two giants. Different factors in action tilt a particular frontline country to opt for a promaritime, procontinental, or noncommittal position. On the East Asian fault line, Myanmar has been basically a partner of the PRC, although its recent reform and opening to the West tilt it a bit toward being a hedging partner. Cambodia is pro-Beijing in its basic stance. However, Phnom Penh appeals to the international community (i.e., the West) for subsidies and support to overcome the country's tragic experience under the Pol Pot regime. It is a hedging partner of Beijing. South Korea has moved into a pivot position gradually in the East Asian strategic game.[19] Although it maintains security ties with the United States, its political link with Beijing has been greatly strengthened. China's displeasure with North Korea reduces Pyongyang's drag on PRC–South Korea relations. Beijing and Seoul share historical memories of their victimization by Japan before and during World War II. Furthermore, South Korea is a significant power to reckon with for Beijing in its strategic competition with the United States. Gradually Seoul has become aware of its pivot position and how that position may benefit it. Japan's relation with China has worsened considerably since 2010, primarily because of the territorial dispute over the Diaoyu Islands. However, the very close economic ties benefit both sides and act to mitigate tension in the relationship. Japan remains a hedging partner of the United States, although the balancing part of its strategy has become much more prominent. The Philippines also got into a territorial dispute with Beijing over the islands in the South China Sea. That provided enough impetus for Manila to welcome back American military presence in the country. The Philippines is a partner of the United States.[20]

On the East European fault line, frontline countries take different roles in the strategic triangles in which they find themselves. Belarus is a firm partner of Russia, partly because its regime type is unacceptable to the West. Bulgaria has been traditionally close to Moscow and has treasured the special friendship. For Sophia, unlike some of its neighbors, the relation with Moscow is its core and EU/NATO status its hedge. This makes Bulgaria a hedging partner of Russia. The most famous case of pivoting on the East European front is Ukraine prior to the Maidan Revolution, as the country tilted between the EU and the Russia-led Eurasian Economic Union for a better accession deal. After 2014, of course, Kyiv's pivoting led to virtual partition of the country. On the maritime side, Romania is a staunch NATO/EU member that also wishes to keep manageable relations with Russia. Bucharest has been playing the role of a hedging partner of the United States and the EU. The Baltic countries are the firmest allies of the West. Estonia, for example, worries about possible Russian incursion, especially after Moscow's annexation of Crimea, and clings tightly to NATO and the EU. Tallinn is an outright partner of the West.

In the following discussion, two critical cases are examined: Taiwan and Ukraine. They are chosen because they are frontline countries under great pressure that stems from their geopolitical positions on the strategic fault lines in East Asia and eastern Europe. They made different strategic decisions between the competing great powers (the United States and the PRC, the United States/Europe and Russia) over time, with different outcomes. The involvement of ethnic factors complicates the situation, making the lesser power's decision that much more difficult. The continental powers, China and Russia, are more willing to bear costs in order to safeguard their core interests in these cases than when ethnic factors are absent. Finally, dramatic and simultaneous developments on the ground in both cases in the spring of 2014, namely the eruption of the Sunflower Movement in Taiwan and the outbreak of a separatist civil war in Ukraine, make them highly comparable, as these events happened in the same international context.

TAIWAN: FROM SEMIPARTNER TO HEDGING PARTNER

A major change of Taiwan's frontline position is its shift from semipartner of the United States to hedging partner. Taiwan had been a semipartner of the United States from the end of the 1970s, when the United States derecognized the ROC but committed itself to Taiwan's defense in case of an assault from the mainland, through almost three ensuing decades, during which it was deadlocked in its relation with the mainland and dislodged as a US ally but still under the hegemon's protection.[21] The shift in Taiwan's status was caused by a cross-Strait rapprochement and intensified economic integration after the inauguration of President Ma Ying-jeou in 2008. As Ma took pains to reassure Washington that Taiwan would be firmly on the US side in the strategic game, and cross-Strait rapprochement did not suggest any political integration or strategic alliance with the mainland, Taiwan turned itself into a hedging partner, doing very much what all the other US allies in East Asia had been doing for decades. This shift, however, was brought about by the alignment of several critical factors that may not hold in the future. It is also more tenuous than it appears, as Taiwan did not change its basic stance toward the United States and mainland China. To understand the 2008 shift of Taiwan's mainland policy and explore its sustainability, a look at the basic structure is in order.

Conflicting forces bear on the cross-Strait relationship, some pushing the two sides together, some pulling them apart. For Taiwan, the former resulted in a "stay" strategy, and the latter in an "exit" strategy.[22] Those forces are rooted in four structural factors: divided-nation status, power asymmetry, economic integration, and Taiwanese identity.[23] They are played out in Taiwan's competitive democracy and are constrained by the external limits set primarily by the United States but also partly by Beijing.

Among the four structural factors, divided-nation status and economic integration work primarily to bind Taiwan and mainland China together. Divided-nation status provides a "one-China" constitutional structure and rallies the remnants of Chinese nationalism and ROC patriotism in defense of the status quo.[24] Economic integration of the two societies is so extensive that any serious disruption of the status quo would impose unfathomable costs on Taiwan, thus deterring the pursuit of "independence."[25] China and Taiwan's legal and economic ties also make it possible to imagine "ultimate unification" when the conditions are ripe.

Power asymmetry and rising Taiwanese identity produce forces that militate for a unilateral exit from the "one-China" status quo. The increasing power gap between Taiwan and the mainland spells misfortune for Taiwan, the smaller side, which sees its international space constricted by the much stronger opponent; hence the incentive for exiting the game.[26] Taiwanese identity has deep historical roots, but its rise has more to do with the PRC's monopoly on Chinese identity in international society and the mounting pressure that China puts on Taiwan. Hence power asymmetry and the rise of Taiwanese identity are intrinsically linked. The assertion of an exclusively Taiwanese identity drives Taiwan away from mainland China, which is considered a hostile foreign country. With a shared national identity gone, the basis for unification is undermined.[27]

The two sets of forces are embodied in the two main political camps, "Blue" (favoring more integration with the mainland) and "Green" (favoring more independence), which fight for dominance in Taiwan's competitive democracy. As the two camps advocate opposite mainland policies, power turnover at elections naturally brings about policy shifts that may disrupt cross-Strait relations.[28] Here international factors come in. The US preference to keep the status quo is a powerful force that contains actions by Taiwan's election-driven political leaders. It also of course constrains, or counters, the mainland's move to coerce the island into subjugation.[29] Given this configuration, one can picture cross-Strait relations as fluctuating along a spectrum with unification, status quo, and independence serving as main marks. Taiwan's position on the spectrum at any given time is set by the result of the last presidential election, which generally reflects the underlying forces of divided-nation status, power asymmetry, economic integration, and Taiwanese identity. The range of possible fluctuations in Taiwan's position over time, however, is set by the preference of the United States, a hegemon that tilts the balance to keep the status quo that best serves its interest. Under these constraints Taiwan's political leaders can fine-tune the island's mainland policy and adjust its position on the East Asian strategic fault line.

In the 2008 presidential campaign, Ma managed to shut down the ideological debate on the identity of the nation (a losing battle for the KMT) and instead direct popular attention to Taiwan's economy, which had considerably slowed down since 2000, when the Democratic Progressive Party (DPP) had captured power. From 2001 to 2008, Taiwan's economic growth rate averaged 3.8 percent, compared with a 6.2 percent rate in the previous decade, when the KMT was in power. The unemployment rate more than doubled from an average of 2.1 percent in the 1990s to 4.4 percent from 2001 through 2008. With the identity issue and pursuit of de jure Taiwan independence "delegitimated" in public debate and with economic issues in the ascendancy, Ma was able to win the 2008 and 2012 presidential elections by demonstrating to the people that only the KMT could smoothly handle cross-Strait relations, which were a prerequisite for the growth and development of Taiwan's economy. Even though Taiwanese identity continued to grow under Ma's watch, and power disparities across the Taiwan Strait widened rapidly, Ma was able to play the economic card effectively to win reelection, thus sustaining the party's "stay" strategy. However, the status quo was seriously shaken in 2014.

Given the framework of cross-Strait relations mentioned above, changes can be expected if the main pillars of the status quo begin to shake. Following Ma's shift to the economy, the DPP put proindependence rhetoric on the back burner and began challenging Ma's main argument that economic integration with the mainland was good for Taiwan. From 2008 to 2014, Taiwan's economy continued to grow slowly at an average of 3.8 percent, while unemployment surged to 4.7 percent. Distribution has become a serious issue, affecting particularly the young generation. The Oshima Index, which gauges the gap between the top 20 percent of households' income and the bottom 20 percent, rose from 6.03 in 2000–2007 to 6.16 in 2008–14. Part of the economic malaise was obviously caused by the international financial crisis, and part was the result of the inefficiencies of the government. The Economic Cooperation Framework Agreement (ECFA) with the mainland might have helped, but the overall economic picture was bleak. Now Ma cannot claim that cross-Strait integration can invigorate Taiwan's economy. His critics have instead pointed to the adverse effect of close economic ties with mainland China.

Under these circumstances students and young demonstrators broke into the Legislative Yuan and staged a three-week occupation of the parliament in March and April of 2014. The event was touched off by the popular uproar against a bill that would liberalize service trade across the Taiwan Strait as part of the ECFA arrangement. The bill suffered from the DPP's legislative blockade for several months, and the KMT rammed it through the committee stage. The Sunflower Movement wanted to torpedo the bill and kill future agreements that would further cross-Strait integration. The apparent rationale for the movement was to redress procedural injustices, but the bottom line was the anti-China sentiment among the most economically vulnerable and politically vocal. Ma's economic advantage was turned upside down. Since he had so successfully defused ideological debate and concentrated national attention to the economy, his administration was ill prepared to fight political opponents who equipped themselves with incisive economic arguments. With Chinese identification (and even dual Chinese-Taiwanese identification) falling precipitously under his watch, and the economy failing to deliver on his promises, Ma found his initiative to improve cross-Strait relations balked. The political wind began to blow in the other direction. The KMT suffered major losses in both the 2014 local elections and the 2016 presidential-and-parliamentary elections. The DPP's presidential candidate Tsai Ing-wen won a landslide victory in 2016, and the DPP captured for the first time a majority in the parliament. Under Tsai, Taiwan swiftly adjusted its relationship with the mainland. By refusing to recognize the "1992 Consensus" that Taiwan and the mainland make up one China while agreeing to differ on which government is its legitimate representative, Tsai at one stroke undermined the basis of cross-Strait rapprochement. Beijing began its retaliation, and Taiwan tilted further toward the maritime alliance.

With regard to the role that Taiwan plays on the East Asian strategic fault line, the crux of the matter is whether Taiwan is able, or willing, to sustain its rapprochement with mainland China. With that hedge in place, Taiwan is a hedging partner of the United States. Without it, it will simply play the role of a partner, though more a semipartner. The KMT and the DPP are representing these two roles, based on their positions on the 1992 Consensus and their willingness or unwillingness to pay lip service to the "one-China" principle that Beijing uses as a litmus test to determine amity or enmity. With the KMT or the DPP in power, a basic position on the 1992 Consensus and the one-China principle will be taken, which then determines whether the rapprochement hedge is kept in place. That puts Taiwan in the role of either a hedging partner or a semipartner of the United States on the East Asian strategic fault line.

UKRAINE: TRAGIC PIVOT

Many East European countries are like Taiwan in being situated on a strategic fault line. The lesser countries in both cases are threatened by a powerful neighbor (mainland China and Russia), yet there are very strong economic links between them and the behemoth (in the form of trade/investment and energy dependence). Both seek a security guarantee from the United States, with varying degrees of success. There have been occasions in the two cases when leaders took defiant balancing acts against the strong power (as did Chen Shui-bian and Georgia's Mikheil Saakashvili). Those acts were often followed by rapprochement gestures (as made by Ma Ying-jeou and Bidzina Ivanishvili).

Among the East European countries, Ukraine is the most comparable with Taiwan. Both have a well-developed region-based political cleavage (North vs. South in Taiwan, North and West vs. South and East in Ukraine) that harks back to the (sub)ethnic and linguistic divisions in the population and their different historical memories. Taiwan has been plagued by the identity rift between the Chinese and dual Chinese-Taiwanese identifiers on one side and exclusively Taiwanese identifiers on the other side. In Ukraine the division is between Ukrainian nationalists on one side and ethnic Russians plus Russian speakers on the other side.[30] Different camps in Ukraine hold diametrically different positions toward Russia and expect relations with Russia to evolve in opposite directions. The Chinese identifiers and dual identifiers in Taiwan accept the possibility of unification with the mainland if the conditions are ripe. The exclusively Taiwanese identifiers regard mainland Chinese as an alien nation and China as a foreign country. The same can be said of East and West Ukrainians with regard to their affinity for or antagonism toward Russia. In both cases certain industries and regions are more integrated with the strong neighbor than others, resulting in different degrees of economic vulnerability. Language is a touchy issue, starting with whether Taiwanese can be termed a southern Fukien dialect and whether Ukrainian and Russian are basically the same language. The most telling similarity between the two countries is that their different political camps took turns winning elections and governing the nation, leading to wide fluctuations in their policies toward the strong neighbor and the West.

In Ukraine, as in Taiwan, contending forces advocate diametrically opposite policies toward their great-power neighbor. Ukraine was a founding member of the Commonwealth of Independent States and kept close institutional ties with Russia after the breakup of the Soviet Union. It was part of the Russian Empire and then the Soviet Union for hundreds of years. The ethnic, cultural, and historical bonds between Ukraine and its eastern neighbor are strong, especially in the southern and eastern parts of the country. Its modern economy was created and institutionalized as an integral and complementary part of the Russian Federation's. Soviet economic plans integrated Ukraine and Russia, the two most populous Soviet republics, to an extent beyond the integration between Russia and other parts of the Soviet Union. Ukraine's market and energy dependence on Russia is overwhelming, making any disruption of those economic ties an unbearable loss to Ukraine.[31] On the other hand, ever since the independence of Ukraine Kyiv has been building a new nation by inculcating Ukrainian nationalism and targeting Russia as its main "other." Political competition in this nascent democracy necessarily intensified ethnic mobilization. Russia's rise and increasing assertiveness under Putin provided strong impetus for the advance of a Ukrainian nationalism that sees Russia as a looming threat to the identity and integrity of Ukraine. In short, legal and cultural bonds with Russia and deep-rooted economic integration act to draw Ukraine to its eastern neighbor, while rising Ukrainian nationalism and increasing power asymmetry drive the two Slav countries apart.

Since the democratic transition, Taiwan has witnessed power transfers between the Blue and Green camps, including a Blue president who changed his political hue during and after incumbency (Lee Teng-hui). The same can be said of Ukraine: the first popularly elected president Leonid Kravchuk, a vehement Ukrainian nationalist, was replaced by the pro-Russian Leonid Kuchma in 1994; Kuchma was succeeded by the pro-Western Orange Revolution leader Viktor Yushchenko in 2004; Yushchenko was defeated by Viktor Yanukovych from the East in the latter's political comeback in 2010; and Yanukovych fled the country and was succeeded by the Orange Revolutionary business tycoon Petro Poroshenko after the Russian annexation of Crimea in 2014.[32] With each power turnover, the country's policy toward its huge eastern neighbor changed dramatically.

Yanukovych was deprived of his presidency in the heyday of the Orange Revolution, being accused of vote rigging.[33] After he won the 2010 presidential election, Ukraine embarked on a policy shift toward the East. However, despite his pro-Moscow orientation Yanukovych began tilting between Russia and the EU in 2013 in an effort to elicit the best terms for Ukraine, which was on the verge of an economic crisis.[34] He showed willingness to sign an association agreement with the EU as a first step toward joining that organization. This unexpected tilt caused great concern in Putin, who then applied carrots (a pledge to purchase US$15 billion of Ukraine's government bonds and lower the price for Russian gas by one-third) and sticks (disruption of Ukrainian exports to Russia) to change

Ukraine's course. In this way, Russia and the EU found themselves in a bidding war for Ukraine.[35] Finally Yanukovych backed off from signing the association agreement with the EU on November 21 and embraced Putin's offer. In a sense, Yanukovych was successful in turning the country from a partner of Russia to a genuine pivot and taking advantage of that position.

However, the president's successful maneuvering on the international stage was not appreciated by the Ukrainian population, especially the western part of the country, who saw their rising hopes of joining the EU dashed by Yanukovych's unabashed manipulation. Hence came the Maidan Revolution, in which protracted confrontation between the demonstrators and police evolved into a semi-civil war in the heart of the capital Kyiv. After the shooting deaths of about one hundred demonstrators on February 2014, the situation spiraled out of control. Pressure from the West mounted, the Maidan revolutionaries prepared for a showdown, and Yanukovych fled for his life. Moscow swiftly declared this a Western-supported coup and moved to annex Crimea, where ethnic Russians constitute a clear majority of the population. Then came the separatists' capture of the cities and towns of a major portion of Luhanst and Donetsk, the two easternmost provinces of Ukraine that border on Russia with the highest percentage of ethnic Russian residents and Russian-speaking population. From Russia's point of view, the West and the pro-Western Ukrainians had changed the rules of game: instead of competing with the pro-Russian East in elections, they now expelled "Moscow's" president and grabbed power in a staged "revolution." As a result, Russia did not have to abide by the broken rules. Hence the annexation of Crimea and the launch of people's republics in Luhansk and Donetsk. The Ukrainian civil war has raged on, Crimea seems lost forever, and the two people's republics are becoming areas of "frozen conflict," just like Transdniestria, Nagorno-Karabakh, South Ossetia, and Abkhazia. The alternation of power holders in the past has been replaced by virtual partition of the country.

Ukraine played pivot tragically. The wide swings that Yanukovych made between Russia and the West proved too much for his countrymen and for the two giants. The result was the virtual partition of the country and chronic economic crisis. During the process, Russia paid a dear price, and so did some of the European countries, at a time of great economic difficulties in Europe. The Russian people, however, have shown their willingness to stand by their leader in a showdown with the West over Russia's core interest: strategic areas in Luhansk and Donetsk, control of Sevastopol, and protection of ethnic Russians and Russian-speaking people in East Ukraine.[36]

At the time when the crisis in Ukraine evolved, Taiwan experienced its Sunflower Movement. The two crises were not directly related, but they were rooted in similar strategic conditions: a lesser country's controversial policy amid competition between two great powers on a strategic fault line. A significant portion

of the society found the government's policy toward the huge neighbor unacceptable, and they revolted, although in different ways and with different intensity.
Yanukovych's turnabout caused greater disturbance, for it was on a fundamental
issue of Ukraine's direction and identity—join either the EU or the Russian-led
EEU—whereas the service trade liberalization agreement was merely a part of a
comprehensive economic deal between Taiwan and the mainland. The actions of
the Maidan revolutionaries and the response from Yanukovych's government were
much more violent than those of the Sunflower students and the Taipei police.
Nor did the People's Liberation Army take any actions like those of the Russian
military. Nevertheless, the root cause of the two crises is similar: the tension in
the position of a lesser power caught between competing giants. The fact that in
Taiwan and Ukraine conflicting national identities were involved added to the tension. From Taiwan's point of view, it is imperative to avoid the Ukrainian scenario.
Many lessons can be learned here.

CONCLUSION

This chapter starts with the making of a list: strategic choices of a lesser country
caught in a great-power competition. Partner, hedging partner, and pivot are identified as the choices. The list is based on traditional IR theories, the notion of power asymmetry, and the typology of the strategic triangle. A subsequent geopolitical
analysis asserts the resurgence of the conflict between the maritime alliance and
the continental alliance in the post–Cold War era. Their conflict brought about
two strategic fault lines, one cutting across East Asia and the other eastern Europe.
Taiwan sits on the East Asian fault line, and its relation with mainland China is
a case of a lesser country caught between competing great powers and choosing
from a short policy list. The grand policy shift toward rapprochement with the
Chinese mainland under Ma Ying-jeou was made possible by the president's strategy of shutting down debate on identity conflict and focusing on the economy.
Taiwan's subsequent undesirable economic performance then turned Ma's greatest
asset into a crippling liability. Taiwan's mainland policy is the key to the role it
plays on the East Asian strategic fault line: hedging partner (with rapprochement)
or semipartner (without rapprochement). In comparison, Ukraine's policy toward
Russia and the EU is presented to show how Yanukovych led the country from the
role of hedging partner of Russia to the role of pivot, with tragic consequences. The
swings that Yanukovych and his successor made went beyond the pale of acceptable maneuvers for the Ukrainians and the great powers. Ukraine's tilting caused
the country's virtual partition. This suggests that pivot is a less safe position than
hedging partner or partner for a lesser country caught between two competing
giants and that decisions on fundamental issues (such as the one of joining the

core organization of either camp) may act as catalysts for great domestic unrest and international intervention. Once the country is forced to make a decision of placing itself firmly in the camp of either great power, ambiguity is lost, causing a vehement reaction from the losing side. The result may be democratic breakdown, domestic revolution, military intervention, territorial partition, and prolonged economic crisis. Keeping away from such fundamental choices seems to be a sine qua non for a pivot player.

To put cross-Strait relations in the category of lesser powers' interactions with two competing giants on the East Asian and East European strategic fault lines serves several purposes. First, it advances IR theories in areas they overlook: small countries, asymmetrical relations, triangular interaction, and geostrategic analysis. Second, it deepens our understanding of cross-Strait relations through a theoretical perspective offered by the above analytical framework. Third, it makes structural comparison possible between Taiwan and other lesser powers along the East Asian fault line, as well as the frontline countries in eastern Europe, thus deepening our understanding of all the cases compared. The discussion and comparison of cross-Strait relations and crisis in Ukraine are thus made possible. In future research, the factors and mechanisms that affect the decisions of these lesser powers vis-à-vis two giants can be fully identified and tested in multiple case studies with a comparative perspective, thus deepening our understanding of lesser countries' strategic decisions in great-power competition more generally.

NOTES

1. Kenneth N. Waltz, *Theory of International Politics* (Reading, MA: Addison-Wesley, 1979).

2. Stephen Walt, *The Origins of Alliances* (Ithaca, NY: Cornell University Press, 1987).

3. For the concept of bandwagoning, see Stephen Walt, "Alliance Formation and the Balance of World Power," *International Security* 9, no. 4 (1985): 3–43; and Randall Schweller, "Bandwagoning for Profit: Bringing the Revisionist State Back In," *International Security* 19, no. 1 (1994): 72–107. However, bandwagoning typically is not considered a productive option in a realist world. For the limited usefulness of bandwagoning, see Walt, *Origins of Alliances*, 33; and John J. Mearsheimer, *The Tragedy of Great Power Politics* (New York: W. W. Norton, 2001), 139.

4. Take, for example, David Vital, *The Inequality of States: A Study of the Small Power in International Relations* (Oxford: Clarendon Press, 1967); Niels Amstrup, "The Perennial Problem of Small States: A Survey of Research Efforts," *Cooperation and Conflict* 11, no. 2 (1976): 163–82; Efraïm Inbar and Gabriel Sheffer, eds., *The National Security of Small States in a Changing World* (London: Frank Cass, 1997); Jeanne A. K. Hey, ed., *Small States in World Politics: Explaining Foreign Policy Behavior* (Boulder, CO: Lynne Rienner, 2003); Christine Ingebritsen et al., eds., *Small States in International Relations* (Seattle: University of Washington Press, 2006); and Clive Archer, Alyson J. K. Bailes, and Anders Wivel, eds., *Small States and International Security: Europe and Beyond* (Oxon: Routledge, 2014).

5. One example is Brantly Womack's analysis of the asymmetrical relation between China and Vietnam, from which he develops a general theory on interactions between a strong and a lesser power. See Brantly Womack, *China and Vietnam: The Politics of Asymmetry* (Cambridge: Cambridge University Press, 2006). There is also a huge literature on how China's neighbors deal with the rising hegemon; see, for example, Kokubun Ryosei and Wang Jisi, eds., *The Rise of China and a Changing East Asian Order* (Tokyo: Japan Center for International Exchange, 2004), Part III; David C. Kang, *China Rising: Peace, Power, and Order in East Asia* (New York: Columbia University Press, 2007), Part II; David M. Lampton, *The Three Faces of Chinese Power: Might, Money, and Minds* (Berkeley: University of California Press, 2008), 164–206; Li Mingjiang, ed., *China's International Relations in Asia*, vol. 4, *East Asia Responds to a Rising China* (Oxon: Routledge, 2010); Herbert S. Yee, *China's Rise: Threat or Opportunity?* (Oxon: Routledge, 2011).

6. Lowell Dittmer, "The Strategic Triangle: An Elementary Game—Theoretical Analysis," *World Politics* 33, no. 4 (1981): 485–515.

7. The strategic triangle theory, or any other analytical framework geared toward trilateral relations, cannot be directly applied to our situation here (i.e., lesser country caught between competing great powers), for it fails to address power asymmetry. A typical example is Gerald Curtis, Ryosei Kokubun, and Wang Jisi, eds., *Getting the Triangle Straight: Managing China-Japan-US Relations* (Tokyo: Japan Center for International Exchange, 2010).

8. L is still a partner in a strategic triangle in the sense that it keeps a principal security tie with another actor. However, as it hedges (engages while also balancing) against the third actor, it becomes a hedger. Since its relation with the other partner is the principal one, we shall call it a "hedging partner." The role of a hedging partner cannot be clearly shown in the traditional diagram of a marriage triangle, as hedging entails not simple amity (+) or enmity (–) in the hedger's relation with the other two players but a combination of the two in the same relationship. A hedger decisively tilts toward its partner but flirts with the outcast.

9. Thus it is more convenient for a strong nation to play pivot, as the United States did when tilting between the Soviet Union and China in the early 1970s, a role strongly advocated by Henry Kissinger. The bottom line is that a wing is more likely to court the pivot than to coerce it if the pivot is a powerful actor. When a small country plays pivot between two giants, it is more like a tail wagging two dogs. For Kissinger's advocacy of the pivot, see Henry Kissinger, *White House Years* (Boston: Little, Brown 1979), 165.

10. For a discussion of the shift in East Asia's alliance systems and Taiwan's peculiar role, see Yu-Shan Wu, "Power Shift, Strategic Triangle, and Alliances in East Asia," *Issues and Studies* 47, no. 4 (2011): 1–42.

11. Several symbolic highwater marks can be cited here: the Sino-Soviet Treaty of Friendship, Alliance and Mutual Assistance, signed in 1950, which ushered in the continental military alliance; the Sino-Russian Treaty of Good Neighborliness, Friendship, and Cooperation, signed in 2001; and the Shanghai Cooperation Organization, launched in the same year, which resumed a semialliance between the two continental countries and Sino-Russian joint naval drills presided over by the two heads of state Xi Jinping and Vladimir Putin in 2014.

12. In a triangular strategic game, it is always preferable to develop amicable relations with the other two players while guarding against their collaboration against oneself.

13. For how Japan both engaged and hedged against China, and how this was done under tight security bondage between Tokyo and Washington, see Glenn D. Hook et al., *Japan's International Relations: Politics, Economics and Security* (Oxon: Routledge, 2005), 196–202.

14. For Russia's foreign policy turnabout, see Andrei P. Tsygankov, *Russia's Foreign Policy: Change and Continuity in National Identity*, 2nd ed. (Lanham, MD: Rowman and Littlefield), 129–70.

15. Yu-Shan Wu, "Russia's Foreign Policy Surge: Causes and Implications," *Issues and Studies* 45, no. 1 (2009): 117–62.

16. In his presidential address to the Russian Parliament (Federal'noe Sobranie), heads of Russian regions, and civil society representatives in the Kremlin on March 18, 2014, Putin stated, "We are grateful to the people of China, whose leaders have always considered the situation in Ukraine and Crimea taking into account the full historical and political context." Vladimir Putin, "Address by President of the Russian Federation," March 18, 2014, http://en.kremlin.ru/events/president/news/20603.

17. For the development of Sino-Russian relations under pressure from the West, see James A. Bellacqua, ed., *The Future of China-Russia Relations* (Lexington: University Press of Kentucky, 2010); Natasha Kuhrt, *Russian Policy towards China and Japan* (New York: Routledge, 2007); Robert Legvold, ed., *Russian Foreign Policy in the Twenty-First Century and the Shadow of the Past* (New York: Columbia University Press, 2007); Bobo Lo, *Russian Foreign Policy in the Post-Soviet Era: Reality, Illusion and Mythmaking* (New York: Palgrave Macmillan, 2002); Bobo Lo, *Axis of Convenience: Moscow, Beijing and the New Geopolitics* (Washington, DC: Brookings Institution Press, 2008); Niklas Swanström, "Transformation of the Sino-Russian Relationship: From Cold War to the Putin Era," in *Eurasia's Ascent in Energy and Geopolitics: Rivalry or Partnership for China, Russia and Central Asia?*, ed. Robert Bedeski and Niklas Swanström (Oxon: Routledge, 2012); and Yu-Shan Wu, "Russia and China Security," in *Routledge Handbook of Chinese Security*, ed. Lowell Dittmer and Maochun Yu (Oxon: Routledge, 2015).

18. Lynn E. Davis et al., *U.S. Overseas Military Presence: What Are the Strategic Choices?* (Santa Monica, CA: RAND Corporation, 2012), 38.

19. David C. Kang characterizes South Korea's position on the East Asian fault line as "between balancing and bandwagoning," while Scott Snyder points out South Korea's modern-day strategic dilemma as "how to avoid circumstances that require choosing between the interests of Washington and Beijing." Both point out the pivot role that Seoul plays between the two giants. See David C. Kang, "Between Balancing and Bandwagoning: South Korea's Response to China," *Journal of East Asian Studies*, no. 9 (2009): 1–28; and Scott Snyder, "Korea, between China and United States," in *Asia's Middle Powers? The Identity and Regional Policy of South Korea and Vietnam*, ed. Joon-Woo Park, Gi-Wook Shin, and Donald W. Keyser (Stanford, CA: Walter H. Shorenstein Asia-Pacific Research Center, Stanford University, 2013).

20. There was an abrupt shift in the Philippines' position after the June 2016 inauguration of President Rodrigo Duterte, whose tirades against the United States and friendly gestures toward Beijing seem at odds with Manila's traditional role between the United States and China. Whether the Philippines will stay in that course is highly dubious, given the overwhelming influence of the United States in the country, and particularly the close ties between the two militaries and governments.

21. Yu-Shan Wu, "Under the Shadow of a Rising China: Convergence towards Hedging and the Peculiar Case of Taiwan," in *Globalization and Security Relations across the Taiwan Strait: In the Shadow of Power*, ed. Ming-chin Monique Chu and Scott L. Kastner (Oxon: Routledge, 2014).

22. "Stay" and "exit" suggest two opposite strategies by Taiwan with regard to mainland China. "Stay" means to remain in the framework of "one China" and agree to disagree with Beijing as to the meaning of that one China. Under this formula, Taipei insists that the one China is the Republic of China, while Beijing insists that it is the People's Republic of China. Neither side imposes its position on the other; both agree to "one China, differing interpretations." This compromise is embodied in the 1992 Consensus. "Exit" means to break away from the "one China" framework and to sever legal bonds with mainland China. The hard version of this advocates abolishing the ROC and launching a new and independent nation, the Republic of Taiwan. The soft version is content with severing legal bonds with mainland China without changing the name of the country. For them the ROC is Taiwan. Both versions of the "exit" strategy seek "Taiwan independence."

23. For an in-depth analysis of the four forces, see Bao Tzong-Ho and Wu Yu-Shan, eds., *Zhengbian zhongde liang'an guanxi lilun* [Contending theories on cross-Strait relations] (Taipei: Wu-nan, 1999); and Bao Tzong-Ho and Wu Yu-Shan, eds., *Chongxin jianshi zhengbian zhongde liang'an guanxi lilun* [Revisiting theories on cross-Strait relations], 2nd ed. (Taipei: Wu-nan, 2012).

24. On the recognition of divided nations and its application to cross-Strait relations, see Yung Wei, "Recognition of Divided States: Implication and Application of Concepts of 'Multi-system Nations,' 'Political Entities,' and 'Intra-National Commonwealth,'" *International Lawyer* 34, no. 3 (2000): 997–1011; and Shaocheng Tang, "A Comparison between Intra-German Relations in the 1970s and Cross-Strait Relations since 2008," *Issues and Studies* 46, no. 4 (2010): 1–36.

25. There is a large literature on economic integration and its impact on conflict mitigation and political amalgamation. For economic integration and cross-Strait relations, see Carl Clark, "Does European Integration Provide a Model for Moderating Cross-Strait Relations?" *Asian Affairs* 29, no. 4 (2003): 195–215; Mikael Mattlin, "Structural and Institutional Integration: Asymmetric Integration and Symmetricity Tendencies," *Cooperation and Conflict* 40, no. 4 (2005): 403–21; Shu Keng, "Understanding Integration and 'Spillover' across the Taiwan Strait," in *Taiwanese Identity in the Twenty-First Century*, ed. Gunter Schubert and Jens Damm (Oxon: Routledge, 2011).

26. For power asymmetry theories, see Yu-Shan Wu, *Kangheng huo hucong—liang'an guanxi xinquan: cong qian Sulian kan Taiwan yu Dalu jian de guanxi* [Balancing or bandwagoning: Cross-Straits relations in view of the former Soviet Union] (Taipei: Cheng-chung, 1997); Yu-Shan Wu, "Quanli buduicheng yu liang'an guanxi yanjiu" [Power asymmetry and the study of cross-Strait relations], in Bao Tzong-Ho and Wu Yu-Shan, *Chongxin jianshi zhengbian zhongde liang'an guanxi lilun*; Brantly Womack, "China and Southeast Asia: Asymmetry, Leadership and Normalcy," *Pacific Affairs* 76, no. 4 (2003/2004): 529–48; and Womack, *China and Vietnam*.

27. For the vast literature on the identity shift in Taiwan, see T. Y. Wang and I-Chou Liu, "Contending Identities in Taiwan: Implications for Cross-Strait Relations," *Asian Survey* 44, no. 4 (2004): 568–90; Gunter Schubert, "Towards the End of a Long Journey: Assessing the Debate on Taiwanese Nationalism and National Identity in the Democratic Era," *ASIEN*, no. 98 (2006): 26–44; Shelley Rigger, "Looking toward the Future in the Taiwan Strait: Generational Politics in Taiwan," *SAIS Review* 31, no. 2 (2011): 65–77; Rou-lan Chen, "Beyond National Identity in Taiwan: A Multidimensional and Evolutionary Conceptualization," *Asian Survey* 52, no. 5 (2012): 845–71; and Rou-lan Chen, "Taiwan's Identity in Formation: In Reaction to a Democratizing Taiwan and a Rising China," *Asian Ethnicity* 14, no. 2 (2013): 229–50.

28. For elections and Taiwan's mainland policy, see Yu-Shan Wu, "Taiwan's Domestic Politics and Cross-Strait Relations," *China Journal*, no. 53 (2005): 35–60; Yu-Shan Wu, "The Evolution of the KMT's Stance on the One China Principle," in Schubert and Damm, *Taiwanese Identity*; and Richard Bush, *Untying the Knot: Making Peace in the Taiwan Strait* (Washington, DC: Brookings Institution Press, 2005), 142–98.

29. For the role played by the United States, see Cheng-yi Lin, "A Status Quo with Different Interpretations: Taiwan, China, the United States, and Security in the Taiwan Strait," in *The Future of United States, China, and Taiwan Relations*, ed. Cheng-yi Lin and Denny Roy (New York: Palgrave Macmillan, 2011); and Nancy Tucker, "Strategic Ambiguity or Strategic Clarity?'" in *Dangerous Strait: The U.S.-Taiwan-China Crisis*, ed. Nancy Tucker (New York: Columbia University Press, 2005).

30. Although one cannot equate Russian speakers with Russophiles or Russia identifiers, Russian-speaking Ukrainians are psychologically close to Russia and view Ukrainian nationalism with suspicion. Their identity can be characterized as "East Slavonic." The cleavage between the eastern and western parts of Ukraine has deep historical roots in how the country was incorporated into the Russian Empire/Soviet Union by stages, with the eastern provinces joining Russia as early as 1654 (Treaty of Pereyaslav), and the westernmost territories falling into the Soviet hands as late as 1945. The eastern part of the country was heavily Russified, while the western part was under the influence of Poland and Austro-Hungary.

31. For a discussion of Ukraine's economic integration with Russia and its political implications, see Celeste A. Wallander and Robert Legvold, "Economics and Security in the Post-Soviet Space," in

Swords and Sustenance: The Economics of Security in Belarus and Ukraine, ed. Robert Legvold and Celeste A. Wallander (Cambridge, MA: American Academy of Arts and Sciences, 2004).

32. Both Taiwan and Ukraine adopted a semipresidential constitutional framework, in which the president typically wields ultimate power: Taiwan has remained in that constitutional framework since 1997, while Ukraine had a dominant president from 1996 to 2004, and again from 2010 to 2014. As a result, Taiwan's mainland policy and Ukraine's Russia policy are determined by their presidents, and the change of president has often brought about the most dramatic shifts of the country's policy toward its powerful neighbor. For the constitutional structure of Taiwan, see Yu-Shan Wu, "Semi-presidentialism—Easy to Choose, Difficult to Operate: The Case of Taiwan," in *Semi-presidentialism outside Europe: A Comparative Study*, ed. Robert Elgie and Sophia Moestrup (Oxon: Routledge, 2011). For Ukraine's unstable presidentialism, see Sarah Birch, "Ukraine: Presidential Power, Veto Strategies and Democratisation," in *Semi-presidentialism in Central and Eastern Europe*, ed. Robert Elgie and Sophia Moestrup (Manchester, UK: Manchester University Press, 2008); Kimitaka Matsuzato, "Disintegrated Semi-presidentialism and Parliamentary Oligarchy in Post-Orange Ukraine," in *Semi-presidentialism and Democracy*, ed. Robert Elgie, Sophia Moestrup, and Yu-Shan Wu (Basingstoke: Palgrave Macmillan). For the weak parliament of Ukraine (Verkhovna Rada), see Sarah Whitmore, *State-Building in Ukraine: The Ukrainian Parliament, 1990–2003* (London: RoutledgeCurzon, 2004).

33. The first round of the presidential election in 2004 yielded no winner. The two forerunners, Viktor Yanukovych, the incumbent prime minister and favorite of President Kuchma, and Victor Yushchenko, a former prime minister and a staunch critic of the Kuchma regime, failed to garner an absolute majority, and a runoff election was scheduled. Despite popular expectations, Yanukovych was announced winner of the second-round election on November 22 by the Central Election Commission, setting off a popular protest led by Yushchenko. This was the start of the Orange Revolution that ultimately forced the Kuchma-Yanukovych camp to agree to annul the second-round voting and do a rerun on December 26, in which Yushchenko handsomely won by an 8 percent margin. For the Orange Revolution, see Anders Åslund and Michael McFaul, eds., *Revolution Orange: The Origins of Ukraine's Democratic Breakthrough* (Washington, DC: Carnegie Endowment for International Peace, 2006). For a comparison of "color revolutions" and their aftermaths, see Yu-Shan Wu, "Yanse geming de xunuo yu juxian" [The promises and limitations of color revolutions], *Taiwan Democracy Quarterly* 4, no. 2 (2007): 67–112.

34. Yanukovych's tilts between the EU and Russia came as a surprise to Moscow, given the president's long-standing pro-Russian posture. However, a looming economic crisis prompted Yanukovych to explore the role of a pivot. Even Alexander Lukashenko of Belarus, the staunchest ally of Russia, attempted to flirt with the West by making anti-Russian statements on the crisis of Ukraine. He said that Russia's annexation of Crimea created a "dangerous precedent" and that he was "categorically opposed" to the federalization of Ukraine, the Kremlin's favored option for the country's political development. During the Maidan Revolution, Lukashenko confirmed that Minsk was "extremely interested" in mending its relations with the European Union, and he even extended a welcome to Ukraine's acting president Oleksander Turchinov, a coup plotter in the eyes of the Kremlin. Lukashenko's flirtation with the Western position on Ukraine could lead Russia to buy back Belarus's loyalty, and it could also win him favors from the West. In short, he used ambiguity as a bargaining tool to reap benefits from both Russia and the West by attempting to play pivot. Of course, this strategy did not yield any substantive gains to Belarus, a pariah regime in the eyes of the EU. For Lukashenko's moves, see Gabrielle Tétrault-Farber, "Lukashenko Plays Both Sides in Ukraine Crisis," *Moscow Times*, April 22, 2014, www.themoscowtimes.com/news/article/lukashenko-plays-both-sides-in-ukraine-crisis/498724.html.

35. The fact that the West found itself in a bidding war with Russia over Ukraine shows a lack of understanding of Moscow's bottom line. Ukraine carries more strategic, economic, cultural, and ethnic significance for Russia than any other ex-Soviet republic. The possible expansion of NATO and the

EU into Ukraine was bound to incur the most ferocious response from the leader of Russia, whoever that person might be. This point is driven home in John Mearsheimer, "Why the Ukraine Crisis Is the West's Fault: The Liberal Delusions That Provoked Putin," *Foreign Affairs* 93, no. 5 (September/October 2014): 77–89.

36. Putin's approval rating was in the low 60s when the Ukrainian crisis erupted (November 2013). It surged to 80 percent when Crimea was annexed and managed to stay at that level. In October 2016 it stood at 84 percent. See Levada-Center, "Approval of Vladimir Putin," regularly updated, www.levada.ru/eng/, accessed November 1, 2016.

12

A Farewell to Arms? US Security Relations with Taiwan and the Prospects for Stability in the Taiwan Strait

Ping-Kuei Chen, Scott L. Kastner, and William L. Reed

Continued US security ties with Taiwan, and in particular US weapons sales to the island, have long been a source of tension in the US-China relationship. The People's Republic of China (PRC) found it unacceptable that Washington insisted on selling weapons to Taiwan even after US-PRC normalization in 1979; the Taiwan Relations Act, which contained explicit references to continued US arms sales to Taiwan, further angered Chinese leaders.[1] Washington agreed in a 1982 communiqué "to reduce gradually its sale of arms to Taiwan" and promised that future arms sales to Taiwan "would not exceed, either in qualitative or quantitative terms," those of recent years,[2] but the record of US arms sales since suggests that the communiqué has had little constraining effect on US behavior.[3] US arms sales to Taiwan, in turn, often provoke an angry Chinese response, which typically includes tough rhetoric and symbolic retaliation, such as temporarily suspending US-China military-to-military dialogues.[4] US arms sales to Taiwan have continued to generate frictions in US-China relations even though relations between Taipei and Beijing improved dramatically after the 2008 election of Ma Ying-jeou as president in Taiwan. In early 2010, for instance, PRC officials were "strongly indignant" after an arms sale announcement, calling the sale a "gross intervention in China's internal affairs" that would have a "serious negative impact" on bilateral relations.[5]

As China's rapid rise as an economic and—increasingly—military power dramatically alters the security landscape in East Asia, however, prominent voices in both Washington and Beijing have in recent years advocated a shift in their respective countries' approach to the US-Taiwan relationship. In the United States, several scholars and former officials have called for a reduced US security commitment to Taiwan and in particular an end to arms sales to Taiwan. Proponents of this view suggest that a scaled-back US commitment would pay dividends in terms of an improved US-China relationship. In the PRC, meanwhile, a number of voices have called for a tougher Chinese response to US arms sales—including the imposition of economic sanctions. Advocates of a tougher approach suggest that a willingness to retaliate more strongly would force the United States to reconsider its commitment to Taiwan. This chapter critically evaluates both proposed policy shifts. In the pages that follow, we present a simple framework for thinking through the broader implications of US arms sales for the cross-Strait relationship. We use the framework, in turn, to shed light on how changes in US or PRC policy on the arms sales issue could affect the prospects for stability in cross-Strait relations and the nature of bargaining between China and Taiwan. Our key conclusion is that both proposed policy shifts—a reduction in US arms sales to Taiwan and a tougher PRC response to arms sales—carry with them significant risks (some counterintuitive) for the country that would initiate the change.

First, we show that a decision to terminate US arms sales to Taiwan could destabilize cross-Strait relations in ways not fully appreciated in existing studies. In particular, a reduced US commitment to Taiwan could help transform the basic structure of cross-Strait relations from a deterrence dynamic to a compellence dynamic. But we qualify our argument by emphasizing that ending arms sales to Taiwan could have other, stabilizing effects and that under the right circumstances such a shift in US policy could actually reduce the likelihood of military conflict in the Taiwan Strait. Second, we show that a tougher PRC response to US arms sales could reveal a stronger US commitment to Taiwan than was previously evident; Taiwan, in turn, would have more leeway to pursue nonaccommodating policies toward Beijing. In other words, both proposed policy adjustments would carry a significant risk of backfiring, as they would risk producing outcomes completely antithetical to the original intent of the policy shift. We emphasize throughout that these counterintuitive outcomes would not necessarily arise but that they are real possibilities that should induce caution in both Washington and Beijing.

The next section gives a brief overview of the recent debate in the United States concerning the US security relationship with Taiwan. We then sketch a simple model of cross-Strait relations and use the model to evaluate the likely consequences of a US decision to terminate arms sales to Taiwan. Next, we consider calls in Beijing to take a tougher stance on US arms sales to Taiwan and how such a shift in PRC policy might affect cross-Strait relations. We conclude with some brief policy recommendations.

SAYING "GOODBYE" TO TAIWAN? THE RECENT US DEBATE

Given the tensions—and the anger in Beijing—that are generated by US arms sales to Taiwan, some in the United States propose that Washington end (or at least scale back) weapons sales to the island. Doing so, proponents suggest, would remove a major irritant in the US-China relationship and would increase trust and cooperation in bilateral relations.[6] More fundamentally, proponents of a reduced US commitment to Taiwan suggest that such a policy approach would help lower the risk of armed conflict in East Asia. This argument is developed most fully by Charles Glaser,[7] who suggests that ending the US commitment to defend Taiwan would bring with it two significant benefits for the US-China relationship. First, it could improve US-China relations because such a shift in US policy would remove a key source of mistrust in Beijing concerning US motivations. Second, ending US support for Taiwan—by removing the key potential source of military conflict between China and the United States—would reduce military competition between Washington and Beijing. Glaser thus proposes a "grand bargain," in which the United States would end its commitment to Taiwan in return for Chinese willingness to "resolve its maritime disputes on 'fair' terms" and to accept a long-term US security presence in East Asia. Others argue that the US commitment to Taiwan is increasingly untenable as China's military power continues to grow. For instance, Chas Freeman warns that a continued US commitment to Taiwan is incompatible with (a) waning US relative power in the region and (b) the importance that the PRC places on the issue. A failure to accommodate US policy to new geopolitical realities, in turn, risks future military conflict over an issue about which China cares deeply.[8] John Mearsheimer argues along similar lines that China's rise as a great power, if it continues, will mean that the current US security commitment to Taiwan will be increasingly unsustainable. Taiwan will ultimately be forced to accommodate growing Chinese power.[9]

Proposals to scale back US security ties to Taiwan are controversial, however, and several scholars have written thoughtful critiques of the idea. These critiques have generally made a few key points. First, it is not self-evident that ending security ties with Taiwan would in fact transform the US-China relationship: the interests of the two countries arguably clash on many other issues (North Korea, maritime disputes in East Asia, economic issues), and it is unclear why Beijing would yield on these other issues if only the United States were to adopt a policy on arms sales that—from Beijing's vantage—the United States had already committed to follow in the 1982 joint communiqué. Second, the United States' reputation in the region could be at stake. Some worry that walking away from a commitment to Taiwan would send a troubling signal to other US allies in East Asia. Beijing might likewise view US concessions on Taiwan as a sign of weakness and conclude that Washington was unlikely to challenge the PRC on other issues in the region. Third, ending arms sales—because it would add to Taiwan's sense of insecurity—could actually make Taipei more hesitant about entering into sensitive political talks with the PRC; thus it isn't clear that a reduced US commitment to Taiwan would facilitate a peaceful resolution to the dispute. Finally, and relatedly, ending arms sales would likely undercut Taiwan's deterrent capabilities, which in turn could encourage a more coercive PRC approach to the island.[10]

While we find these counterarguments plausible, we believe the logic underpinning them needs to be teased out at greater length. This is especially so for claims about the prospects for stability in the Taiwan Strait. For instance, we believe it is likely that an end to arms sales would indeed lead Taiwanese officials to feel less confident about their bargaining power vis-à-vis the PRC. But it is not obvious why this should in itself make them less likely to negotiate with Beijing: it is also plausible that, in such a scenario, Taiwan's leaders would feel they had no other choice but to negotiate with an increasingly powerful PRC. Similarly, while a shift in the cross-Strait balance of power would indeed imply that Beijing could more easily utilize a military option, it isn't obvious that this would in turn make the relationship less stable: it is conceivable, for instance, that Taiwan would respond with more accommodating policies that would remove Beijing's incentives to consider military force. In short, how a shifting cross-Strait military balance of power would affect stability in the Taiwan Strait is not straightforward; in the following section, we consider the topic more systematically.

RETHINKING THE IMPLICATIONS OF ENDING ARMS SALES TO TAIWAN

In this section, we argue that ending the US security commitment to Taiwan—and in particular ending US arms sales to Taiwan—could be destabilizing. As others have noted, ending US arms sales would likely have a significant effect on the balance of power in the Taiwan Strait. We suggest that a sharp shift in the balance of power could alter the nature of cross-Strait bargaining, potentially transforming PRC-Taiwan relations from a deterrence relationship to a compellence relationship. This, in turn, could raise the risk of military conflict, for reasons that we detail.

We also emphasize, however, that US arms sales to Taiwan (and the broader US-Taiwan relationship) represent only one of many factors that influence Beijing's expected costs of conflict in the Taiwan Strait. If other factors cause Chinese leaders to perceive those costs of conflict to be sufficiently high, then even large shifts in the cross-Strait balance of power will not be destabilizing. Indeed, reduced arms sales could increase Beijing's expected costs of conflict. For instance, to the extent that proponents of reduced arms sales are right that such a policy shift in Washington will lead to improved relations with Beijing, it could give the PRC a greater stake in a stable US-China relationship—which would, presumably, be undermined by PRC initiation of military conflict against Taiwan.

The implications of ending arms sales to Taiwan for stability in the Taiwan Strait, in short, are not straightforward. Rather, drawing conclusions in this regard requires careful identification and analysis of the specific causal processes through which arms sales affect stability in the Taiwan Strait. We aim to undertake this sort of analysis by constructing a simple model of cross-Strait relations. We then consider how US arms sales to Taiwan affect key parameters in the model and how ending those sales would affect the likelihood of conflict.

A SIMPLE MODEL OF CROSS-STRAIT RELATIONS

The key dispute between the PRC and Taiwan concerns Taiwan's sovereign status. The PRC claims sovereignty over Taiwan and rejects the notion that the Republic of China (ROC) government on Taiwan represents an independent, sovereign state. For Beijing formal unification with the island remains an important national objective. Thus any effort on Taiwan that tries to weaken the political and historical link between Taiwan and mainland China provokes opposition in Beijing; the PRC refuses to renounce the use of force against Taiwan and has vowed to fight a war to prevent Taiwan's formal separation from China. Taiwan's position on the sovereignty issue, meanwhile, has evolved considerably over time. For several decades following the Nationalist retreat to Taiwan, the ROC government continued to view itself as the legitimate government of all of China; the PRC, in turn, was a "bandit" regime that lacked legitimacy. As Taiwan democratized in the 1980s and 1990s, however, its government began to distance itself from the notion that both sides of the Taiwan Strait were parts of "one China." Under President Lee Teng-hui's "pragmatic diplomacy," Taiwan sought greater participation in international society as a political entity separated from PRC. Lee floated concepts such as "one China, two political entities," and in 1999 described the cross-Strait relationship as "state-to-state, or at least special state-to-state relations." President Chen Shui-bian (2000–2008) later took numerous symbolic steps to highlight Taiwan's separateness from China. Chen often described Taiwan as an "independent, sovereign country," and during his presidency he advocated a new constitution more "suitable" to the needs of Taiwan than the ROC constitution (which predated the Nationalist retreat to the island). Cross-Strait relations were often tense during the Lee and Chen presidencies, and Beijing frequently warned that it was willing to use force to prevent Taiwan from formalizing its independent status.

The relationship between China and Taiwan stabilized considerably after the election of Ma Ying-jeou as Taiwan's president in 2008. Ma articulated a "three nos policy" of no independence, no unification, and no use of force while he was president, and he pursued (with considerable success) cooperation with the PRC in functional areas such as trade, investment, tourism, and extradition. But whereas Ma was more accommodating than his predecessors on sovereignty issues, the fundamental question of Taiwan's status remained unresolved. Progress on this front appears unlikely in the foreseeable future: Ma's successor, Tsai Ing-wen of the

Democratic Progressive Party, has been less accommodating on sovereignty issues than Ma, and the post-2008 détente in cross-Strait relations has largely evaporated. The relationship across the Taiwan Strait, in short, remains untransformed at its core, reflecting continuing disagreement over Taiwan's sovereign status.

We assume, then, that Taiwan's sovereign status is the principal issue over which the PRC and Taiwan are (explicitly or implicitly) bargaining. For simplicity, we assume that Taiwan's status can be represented on a single dimension ranging from formal unification with China (U) at one extreme to a formally independent Taiwan (I) on the other (see figure 11).[11] Assume further that Taiwan's leadership prefers an outcome closer to I and China's prefers an outcome closer to U, and assume that China's utilities range from 0 for formal independence to 1 for unification.[12] The preferences of the PRC and Taiwan for unification or independence are strictly opposed and linear. In our model, we assume a status quo point lying somewhere between U and I, and we assume that Taiwan may at any given time propose a different status quo. The PRC can either tolerate the new status quo as defined by Taiwan or try to impose its most preferred outcome (U) through force. Assume that if the two sides were to fight a war, China would prevail with probability p and that victory would enable Beijing to impose its preferred outcome of unification on Taiwan.[13] Finally, assume that the expected utility each side would reap from the war outcome would be reduced by the costs of actually fighting the war, represented by c_c for China. China's expected utility for war thus is $p - c_c$, which is represented by point R in figure 11. R represents the PRC's reversion point: so long as Taiwan chooses a level of sovereign status to the right of R, then the PRC prefers to tolerate that status. But if Taiwan chooses a status to the left of R, then the PRC prefers to initiate military conflict. War, of course, would be tremendously costly for Taiwan, so Taiwanese leaders have strong incentives to choose a level of sovereign status to the right of R. R, in other words, defines the best outcome Taiwan can hope to achieve.

Regarding the prospects for instability in the Taiwan Strait, the most likely scenario for a cross-Strait conflict typically given by analysts of the China-Taiwan relationship has involved a "revisionist" Taiwan trying to formalize its independent status (or taking steps in that direction), thus triggering a PRC military response.[14] A president strongly committed to formalizing Taiwan's status as an independent country might, for instance, engineer a change in the island's official name (to the Republic of Taiwan) or push through a new constitution written specifically for Taiwan. In terms of figure 11, war could arise in this scenario if the new status quo lay to the left of China's reversion point, R. Why would Taiwan cross such a red line, given the high costs it would undoubtedly pay if war were to erupt with the PRC? If Taiwan could know with certainty where R actually lay, it would choose a level of sovereign status just to the right of R and leave it at that. Unfortunately, Taiwan cannot know with certainty where R actually sits because it cannot know

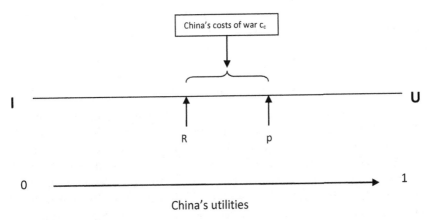

FIGURE 11. A model of cross-Strait relations.

with certainty how China assesses p and c_c. Moreover, it is difficult for Beijing to reveal this information credibly to Taiwan, since the PRC has clear incentives to overstate its power and resolve so as to convince Taiwan's leadership that R lies farther left than might truly be the case. Taiwan, in turn, surely knows that Beijing has incentives to bluff.[15]

In recent decades, then, the cross-Strait relationship has been characterized primarily by a problem of deterrence, where the PRC tries to deter Taiwan from taking steps toward formal independence but where there may be some uncertainty in Taiwan concerning how credible these deterrent threats are. The centrality of deterrence was most clear under the Lee and Chen administrations: both presidents aimed to redefine Taiwan's relationship with the PRC in a way that was antithetical to Beijing's ideal point of ultimate reunification. The PRC, in turn, sought to deter Taiwan from pushing too far on sovereignty issues by signaling its willingness to use force to stop Taiwan independence. Examples here include the PRC's escalating series of military exercises conducted after Lee Teng-hui visited Cornell University in 1995, its 2000 white paper warning that it would not wait indefinitely on national unification, frequent assertions during the Chen administration that the PRC was prepared to "pay any costs" to prevent Taiwan independence, and the passage of the 2005 antisecession law. After the election of Ma Ying-jeou in 2008, the relationship stabilized greatly: Ma did not push sovereignty issues to the same degree as his predecessors, and Chinese leaders consequently did not need to signal opposition to Taiwan independence as forcefully as before. But deterrence remains central to the relationship. Indeed, the PRC threat to use force appears to be the primary reason support for independence is not more widespread among Taiwan's voters in the first place.[16] And now that the Democratic Progressive Party has returned to power in Taiwan, it is quite likely that the PRC deterrent threats will again become more frequent and pronounced.

WHY ENDING US ARMS SALES TO TAIWAN COULD BE DESTABILIZING

How would a reduced US security commitment to Taiwan affect the likelihood of cross-Strait conflict? More concretely, what would happen if the United States were to terminate arms sales to the island? Remember that in our simple model conflict occurs if Taiwan claims a level of sovereign status to the left of point R on the I-U continuum. How, then, might an end to arms sales affect the probability that Taiwan's claimed status would lie to the left of point R? Here, we begin by considering the most intuitive, direct ways that changing levels of arms sales to Taiwan could affect the parameters of the model and the associated implications. In the following subsection, we consider more indirect and nonintuitive effects of ending arms sales, which in turn serve to qualify points made in this subsection.

Intuitively, it would seem that US arms sales to Taiwan directly affect both the costs (c_c) that China would expect to pay in a cross-Strait military conflict and the probability (p) that China would win such a conflict. On the margins at least, arms sales should improve Taiwan's military capabilities relative to those of the PRC, thereby reducing p and increasing c_c. Of course, p and c_c are determined not simply by the balance of power between China and Taiwan but also by likely US behavior in the event of a cross-Strait war: US intervention would at a minimum greatly complicate the PRC's ability to prevail in a cross-Strait war and would certainly increase China's expected costs of such a conflict. Thus a higher likelihood of US intervention implies a smaller p and a larger c_c. Arms sales to Taiwan, in turn, may signal some level of US commitment to the island. To the extent that arms sales to Taiwan do in fact increase confidence in Beijing and Taipei that the United States is likely to intervene in a cross-Strait conflict, continued US arms sales to Taiwan imply a smaller p and larger c_c than would be the case in the counterfactual world where the United States did not sell weapons to Taiwan.

These direct effects suggest, then, that ending arms sales should reduce China's expected costs of war and increase the probability of PRC victory; R, in turn, should shift to the right. This makes intuitive sense: to the extent that the balance of power in the Taiwan Strait favors the PRC, we might expect Beijing to be more demanding on sovereignty issues (and less tolerant of outcomes that diverge sharply from its ideal point of unification). Were R to shift to the right of Taiwan's actual status, the model suggests that the PRC would prefer to fight a war rather than to accept a continuation of that status quo; military conflict would ensue if Taiwan failed to accommodate this new reality by redefining its sovereign status (i.e., to push the status quo back to the right of R). Given the obviously high costs of war for Taiwan—costs that would presumably be especially high in the absence of any US security commitment to the island—leaders in Taipei would have strong incentives to avoid this outcome by bowing to new power realities and accommodating the PRC on sovereignty issues to some degree.

Yet there are some reasons to think that accommodation in this regard would be difficult. Recall that in recent decades the primary strategic challenge in cross-Strait relations can be characterized as a problem of deterrence, with the PRC trying to deter Taiwan efforts to redefine its sovereign status in a way that conflicts with PRC hopes for unification. But if R were to shift right of the status quo, the model suggests that the cross-Strait relationship would instead be characterized by a problem of compellence. Here, a war could occur, not because the PRC fails to deter unilateral Taiwan changes to the status quo, but rather because the PRC fails to compel Taiwan to alter the status quo in a way that is more to Beijing's liking (remember that once R shifts right of the status quo, Beijing's expected war payoff exceeds its utility for a continuation of the status quo). Nevertheless, commitment problems could complicate the search for a peaceful accommodation even if Taiwan recognized that R had moved to the right of the status quo and even if Taiwan was in principle willing to bargain away some of its sovereignty.[17] The reason is that the issue being bargained over, Taiwan's sovereign status, could affect future bargaining power between the two sides: that is, bargaining some of its sovereign status to avoid war in the short term could further diminish Taiwan's future bargaining power vis-à-vis Beijing.

Even if the United States were to stop selling arms to Taiwan and renounce any security commitment to the island, Taiwan would remain qualitatively different from areas under direct PRC control. It would continue to be self-governing and democratic, it would continue to maintain armed forces, and it would—for all intents and purposes—continue to resemble an independent country on all dimensions except international legal recognition. But Taiwan's continued otherness in this regard opens the door to possible US intervention in a cross-Strait conflict even after a US decision to end its security commitment to Taiwan. Leaders in Washington, for instance, might revise their view of the PRC, especially in the aftermath of an attack on Taiwan, and particularly if renouncing the security commitment entailed a quid pro quo PRC pledge. Thus, even after the United States ended arms sales to Taiwan and renounced a security commitment to the island, the probability of US intervention in a cross-Strait conflict would not drop to zero—in contrast to the likelihood of US intervention in other areas of China such as Tibet (or, for that matter, Hong Kong). But the more Taiwan accommodated PRC demands by allowing itself to become something more resembling Hong Kong or Tibet than an independent country, then the more the probability of US intervention would begin to approach zero as it does for other areas under direct

PRC control. Such intervention would increasingly, and unambiguously, represent intervention in a civil, rather than an international, conflict.[18]

Thus any bargain involving a reduction in Taiwan's sovereignty should independently reduce Beijing's expected costs of war, thus pushing R even further to the right. The credibility of Beijing's commitment to such a bargain would therefore be suspect, as once it was implemented Beijing would have incentives to demand an even more favorable bargain (and Taiwan would not be in a position where it could refuse). Fearon develops a similar model where states bargain over strategic territory and the outcome of the negotiations explicitly shifts the balance of power.[19] This change in the balance of power happens because the outcome of the negotiation transfers territory to a rival state and thereby improves that rival's fighting capacity. When this type of dynamic is at work, reaching a settlement becomes difficult because the consequence of the shift in power caused by a settlement may be less desirable than fighting and forgoing any negotiations. Although a hypothetical bargain between the PRC and Taiwan is not over strategic territory, it is certainly possible that a similar dynamic is at work as the PRC and Taiwan negotiate over Taiwan's sovereignty. Inasmuch as giving up sovereignty to the PRC strengthens the PRC's bargaining leverage, Taiwan may come to the conclusion that risking war is preferable to any negotiated settlement with the PRC over unification. In other words, Taiwan may conclude that it would be better to roll the dice in a war with China today than to accept the terms of an obsolescing bargain likely to result in a progressively more subordinate status within a unified China. Therefore, in the same way that bargaining over strategic territory is complicated by the strategic consequences of any deal that might be struck, bargaining over unification can be dangerous because it has implications for the future bargaining power of the PRC and Taiwan.

In summary, ending arms sales to Taiwan would have the potential to increase instability in the Taiwan Strait. Such a shift in US policy could alter the balance of power in the Taiwan Strait, which in turn could shift the strategic dynamic from deterrence to compellence. In turn, there are reasons to believe that a China-Taiwan relationship in which China tried to compel steps toward unification would be more conflict prone than one where the PRC tried to deter Taiwan steps toward independence, as credible commitment problems could make it difficult for Taiwan to accommodate new power realities.

WHY ENDING US ARMS SALES TO TAIWAN WOULD NOT NECESSARILY BE DESTABILIZING

The analysis above suggests that ending arms sales to Taiwan would be destabilizing if doing so had enough of an effect on p and c_c to push R to the right of the status quo. However, there are reasons to question whether ending sales would indeed have such a large effect. On the one hand, as the balance of power in the Taiwan Strait continues to shift in China's favor, it is not obvious that the arms themselves have a large impact on that shifting power balance. Whether the sales do in fact have a significant effect in this regard, moreover, will likely depend heavily on the types of weapons the United States would be willing to sell to Taiwan (and which weapons Taiwan would be willing to buy). For instance, some have suggested that Taiwan's efforts to purchase high-profile and expensive packages such as the F-16C/D fighter are counterproductive given their high cost and the PRC's growing air capabilities; according to these analysts, more mundane (and cheaper) systems are likely to be more effective at countering PRC capabilities.[20] Whether ending arms sales has a significant effect on p and c_j, then, will hinge in part on what types of weapons the United States would sell Taiwan if arms sales were to continue.

Likewise, it is not self-evident how large of a signaling effect arms sales have. As we show in the next section, US arms sales send the clearest signal of US support for Taiwan when the sales are costly for the United States to undertake. Yet it is quite clear not only that the sales do not appear to be especially costly for Washington but also that many in the United States actually benefit economically and politically from the sales. When the Obama administration was considering the F-16C/D package in 2011, for instance, a large number of US senators signed a letter to the president urging the sale to go forward; often, the signatories represented states that stood to benefit economically from increased demand for the fighter jets.[21] In other words, so long as Chinese retaliation against the United States for selling weapons remains limited, the costs of the policy to Washington do not appear especially high. Thus it would not appear to us that arms sales represent an especially strong signal of US commitment to Taiwan, meaning that ending the sales would not necessarily lead Taiwan and China to dramatically alter their assessments of likely US behavior in the event of a cross-Strait conflict.

It is also worth emphasizing that many factors besides US arms sales to Taiwan determine the value of p and c_j, including Taiwan's indigenous military capabilities, the PRC's capabilities, the level of economic integration across the Taiwan Strait, and so forth. The rapid growth in cross-Strait economic integration and cooperation in recent decades, combined with China's general integration into global markets, for instance, suggests that the costs for China of a cross-Strait military confrontation are probably quite high—even if the PRC would likely win such a confrontation. Compared to these costs, the dent to c_c caused by reduced arms sales could actually be quite small.

Finally, and perhaps most importantly, ending arms sales to Taiwan could actually increase c_c in some ways. While critics sometimes suggest that ending arms sales might simply whet the appetite of China and encourage further demands on the United States, it is also conceivable—as proponents such as Glaser argue—that ending arms sales would lead to significant improvement in the US-China relationship.[22] Furthermore, whether the United States sells weapons to Taiwan or not, it is hard to imagine a strong and cooperative US-China relationship withstanding PRC coercion against the island. Therefore, if the PRC values a stable US-China relationship, and if ending arms sales to Taiwan does in fact lead to an improved Sino-American relationship, then ending arms sales to Taiwan will also mean that the PRC will have more to lose (in terms of a strong US-China relationship) by initiating conflict in the Taiwan Strait. If this sort of effect outweighs the direct effect of ending arms sales on China's costs of war, then ending arms sales could help to reinforce a stable status quo.

SUMMARY

In sum, even in the context of our highly stylized and simplified model of cross-Strait relations, changes in US policy have complex and uncertain net implications for stability in the Taiwan Strait. Analysts should recognize that ending arms sales to Taiwan could be highly destabilizing: such a change in US policy could help to tip cross-Strait relations from a relatively stable deterrence relationship to an unstable compellence relationship. But ending arms sales will not necessarily have this effect and could actually contribute to stability in the Taiwan Strait by reinforcing China's stake in a stable status quo. It is our hope that our model will help to organize thinking around this important topic, by showing how different types of effects fit together.

WHY A TOUGHER PRC POLICY ON ARMS SALES COULD BACKFIRE

Just as there have been calls in the United States for a changed US policy on Taiwan arms sales, so have there been calls in Beijing for a changed PRC policy on the issue.[23] As noted earlier, arms sales to Taiwan provoke an angry response from Beijing. When the United States confirmed a US$5.8 billion weapons package to Taiwan in 2011, official Chinese media referred to the sale as a "despicable breach of faith in international relations," while one general wrote that the United States was "cheating and making a fool of the Chinese people."[24] This type of response is not new; in 1992, for instance, the Standing Committee of the National People's Congress issued a statement expressing "extreme indignation over US wanton interference in China's internal affairs" after the Bush administration announced it would sell 150 F-16 fighter jets to Taiwan.[25]

Despite the anger that US arms sales to Taiwan typically generate in China, the actual policy response to these sales has typically been muted. Beyond the tough rhetoric, retaliation has been mostly symbolic. For instance, the PRC often responds to arms sales by halting dialogue between the two countries. In recent years, the PRC has temporarily frozen military-to-military dialogues after arms sales decisions.[26] In 1992, the PRC suspended human rights discussions in response to the F-16 sale.[27] The PRC has at times hinted at the possibility of a stronger response: in both 1992 and 2010, Chinese officials suggested that the PRC might retaliate with economic sanctions.[28] Nevertheless, there is little evidence that China has—to date—followed through on these sorts of threats.[29]

China's unwillingness to react more vigorously to US arms sales has led to some frustrations among Chinese analysts and military officials, who have at times advocated a tougher, tit-for-tat response. In early January 2010, Rear Admiral Yang Yi (retired), a prominent defense analyst, called for tougher sanctions against US companies involved in arms sales, and high-profile scholar Shi Yinhong emphasized that China should impose more significant costs on the United States in response to arms sales.[30] Shortly thereafter, when the US government announced a new weapons sale package for Taiwan in late January, PRC government officials did in fact issue a threat of sanctions (noted above)—warning that China would retaliate against Taiwan arms sales by sanctioning US companies involved in the sales. Chinese media quoted several well-known scholars and analysts expressing support for such a policy, including Yang Yi and Beijing University's Wang Yong.[31] Media reports also suggested widespread support for such a tougher policy among Chinese "netizens."[32] To be clear, these sorts of sentiments are not new; there have long been voices in China advocating for a tougher PRC response to Taiwan arms sales. John Garver notes, for instance, that military leaders wanted to see a strong response to the 1992 F-16 sale, with some advocating economic sanctions on US exports to China (including agricultural products like wheat). Garver writes that these voices were ultimately overruled by Deng Xiaoping himself.[33]

The rationale for a tougher approach is ultimately twofold. First, a tougher approach would impose higher costs on the United States for pursuing the status quo policy of arms sales to Taiwan. These increased costs could, in turn, lead Washington to reevaluate the utility of the status quo and to conclude that the benefits associated with arms sales no longer justified the costs. Sanctions, in short, have the potential to improve PRC bargaining power in the Taiwan Strait by making it more likely that the United States will scale back its commitment to Taiwan. Second, even if the United States failed to change policy, a tougher approach would at least enable the PRC to signal more clearly—to both domestic and international audiences—its own dissatisfaction with the status quo. As Peking University's Jia

Qingguo has written, facing "mounting domestic pressure, the [Chinese Communist Party] is finding it increasingly difficult to justify its 'weak' responses, such as verbal protests, to U.S. weapons sales and believes it needs to demonstrate its courage with concrete acts of retaliation."[34]

But a tougher approach to arms sales also entails significant risks for China. Obviously, threatening or imposing sanctions on US companies could further harm the Sino-American relationship and perhaps trigger a trade war. But more fundamentally, consider what happens if the United States continues to sell the weapons even in the face of PRC retaliation. In this case, the weapons sales would become more unambiguously costly for Washington to carry out. By continuing with the sales despite these increased costs, the United States would essentially be signaling a sincere interest in Taiwan's security; it would be much harder to make the argument that US arms sales to Taiwan were motivated by a cynical desire to further the interests of US companies and create a few US jobs. Thus the PRC faces a significant trade-off in responding to US arms sales. To the extent that Chinese policy makers believe that the United States is motivated primarily by cynical economic and political motivations in selling weapons to Taiwan, it makes sense to get tough: the United States would be more likely to back down in such a scenario, and the door would thus open to an end to US arms sales. But to the extent the PRC believes that sincere concerns over Taiwan security enter into US calculations in selling weapons, a tougher policy response could backfire. The United States would be unlikely to back down, and by standing firm in the face of PRC sanctions would signal—to both the PRC and Taiwan—a stronger commitment to the island than was previously evident. The tougher response, moreover, would likely lead to further turbulence in the bilateral Sino-American relationship.

CONCLUSION

The continuing US commitment to Taiwan's security, and in particular continued US arms sales to Taiwan, represents one of the key sources of tension in the broader Sino-American relationship. In recent years, analysts in both Washington and Beijing have proposed new approaches to the issue. In the United States, some have suggested that the United States end weapons sales to Taiwan and consider backing away from its commitment to the island more broadly. In the PRC, some have suggested that a rising China take a tougher line in response to US arms sales. We have argued that both proposed policy alterations carry with them significant risks. In the US case, ending arms sales to Taiwan could contribute to an increase in the likelihood of conflict in the Taiwan Strait by helping to shift cross-Strait relations from a deterrence dynamic to a compellence dynamic. In the Chinese case, a tougher approach to US arms sales could backfire by revealing a stronger US commitment to Taiwan's security than might be currently assumed. A revealed stronger US commitment, in turn, could make Taiwan less willing to accommodate the PRC on sovereignty issues.

NOTES

1. The act stipulated that the United States would provide Taiwan with "such defense and defense services in such quantity as may be necessary to maintain a sufficient self-defense capability" and that the specific nature of these weapons would be determined by the president and Congress "based solely upon their judgment of the needs of Taiwan, in accordance with procedures established by law." For a discussion of the act and its consequences, see Steven M. Goldstein and Randall Schriver, "An Uncertain Relationship: The United States, Taiwan and the Taiwan Relations Act," *China Quarterly*, no. 165 (2001): 147–72.

2. For the full text of the communiqué, see "Joint Communiqué on Arms Sales to Taiwan," August 17, 1982, Taiwan Documents Project, www.taiwandocuments.org/communique03.htm. The Reagan administration subsequently interpreted the commitments made by the United States in loose terms, emphasizing that dollars would be inflation adjusted, that quality would be assessed in relative terms, and that the restrictions on arms sales would apply only to weapons and not to technology transfer. See Harry Harding, *A Fragile Relationship: The United States and China since 1972* (Washington, DC: Brookings, 1992), 116–17. For a good description of the communiqué, see also Richard C. Bush, *At Cross Purposes: U.S.-Taiwan Relations since 1942* (Armonk, NY: M. E. Sharpe, 2004).

3. In 1992, for instance, the United States announced a sale of 150 F-16 fighter jets to Taiwan; the sale exceeded—in quality and quantity—previous weapons sales by a substantial margin. Beijing has frequently protested such perceived US violations of the 1982 communiqué. For detailed discussion, see Zhang Qingmin, "Zhongmei guanxizhong de meiguo shou tai wuqi wenti" [The question of US arms sales to Taiwan in US-China relations], *Waijiao Xueyuan Xuebao*, no. 1 (1994): 84–92. For a detailed summary and discussion of US arms sales to Taiwan since 1990, see Shirley A. Kan, "Taiwan: Major U.S. Arms Sales since 1990," in *Taiwan-U.S. Relations*, ed. Samantha E. Marshall (New York: Nova, 2010), 1–75.

4. Despite the tough rhetoric and symbolic retaliation, the PRC has generally been restrained in its response to US arms sales and has not allowed the issue to derail the broader US-China relationship despite the anger US sales generate in Beijing. See Michael S. Chase, "'Strong Indignation,' but Limited Retribution: China's Response to U.S. Arms Sales to Taiwan," *China Brief* 11, no. 19 (2011): 3–7. See also the report prepared by the US-Taiwan Business Council and Project 2049 Institute, *Chinese Reactions to Taiwan Arms Sales* (Arlington, VA: US-Taiwan Business Council and Project 2049 Institute, 2012, https://project2049.net/documents/2012_chinese_reactions_to_taiwan_arms_sales.pdf.

5. "US Sells Weapons to Taiwan, Angering China," *Washington Post*, January 30, 2010, www.washingtonpost.com/wp-dyn/content/article/2010/01/29/AR2010012904113.html. For a discussion of the role of emotion in China's Taiwan policy (focusing specifically on anger during the 1995-96 Taiwan Strait crisis), see Todd H. Hall, "We Will Not Swallow This Bitter Fruit: Theorizing a Diplomacy of Anger," *Security Studies* 20, no. 4 (2011): 521–55.

6. Bill Owens, "America Must Start Treating China as a Friend," *Financial Times*, November 17, 2009, www.ft.com/intl/cms/s/0/69241506-d3b2-11de-8caf-00144feabdco.html#axzz2REBX57hW.

7. Charles L. Glaser, "A U.S.-China Grand Bargain? The Hard Choice between Military Competition and Accommodation," *International Security* 39, no. 4 (2015): 49–90. See also Charles L. Glaser, "Will China's Rise Lead to War? Why Realism Does Not Mean Pessimism," *Foreign Affairs* 90, no. 2 (2011): 80–91.

8. Chas W. Freeman Jr., "Beijing, Washington and the Shifting Balance of Prestige," speech delivered at China Maritime Institute, Newport, RI, May 10, 2011, http://chasfreeman.net/576/.

9. John J. Mearsheimer, "Say Goodbye to Taiwan," *National Interest*, March-April 2014, http://nationalinterest.org/article/say-goodbye-taiwan-9931. See also Bruce Gilley, "Not So Dire Straits: How the Finlandization of Taiwan Benefits US Security," *Foreign Affairs* 89, no. 1 (2010): 44–60; Robert Sutter, "Taiwan's Future: Narrowing Straits," National Bureau of Asian Research Analysis, 2011; Ted Galen Carpenter, "Walking a Tightrope: U.S. Arms Sales to Taiwan," Cato Institute, 2011, www.cato.org/publications/commentary/walking-tightrope-us-arms-sales-taiwan. For an excellent summary (and critique) of these arguments, see Richard C. Bush, *Uncharted Strait: The Future of China-Taiwan Relations* (Washington, DC: Brookings Institute, 2013), chap. 10.

10. See especially Nancy Bernkopf Tucker and Bonnie Glaser, "Should the United States Abandon Taiwan?," *Washington Quarterly* 34, no. 4 (2011): 23–37; Shelley Rigger, "Why Giving Up Taiwan Will Not Help Us with China," American Enterprise Institute, November 29, 2011, www.aei.org/publication/why-giving-up-taiwan-will-not-help-us-with-china/; Bush, *Uncharted Strait*; Douglas H. Paal, "China: Reaction to Taiwan Arms Sales," Carnegie Endowment for International Peace Web Commentary, January 31, 2010, http://carnegieendowment.org/2010/01/31/china-reaction-to-taiwan-arms-sales; T. Y. Wang, "Analyzing the 'Abandoning Taiwan' Argument," paper presented at the American Association for Chinese Studies Annual Meeting, University of Pennsylvania, Philadelphia, 2011. Glaser ("Grand Bargain") himself highlights some of the risks associated with walking away from a commitment to Taiwan.

11. A similar model is developed in Scott L. Kastner, *Political Conflict and Economic Interdependence across the Taiwan Strait and Beyond* (Stanford, CA: Stanford University Press, 2009); and Scott L. Kastner, "US Rebalancing: Implications for Taiwan's Security and Stability across the Taiwan Strait," in *The US Strategic Pivot to Asia and Cross-Strait Relations: Economic and Security Dynamics*, ed. Peter C. Y. Chow (New York: Palgrave, 2014), 97–112.

12. We don't assume that the Taiwan leadership's ideal point necessarily lies at I. The current Ma government, for instance, appears to prefer a status quo that leaves open the door to eventual unification over a fully and formally independent Taiwan. It is worth noting, however, that Ma does view the ROC as fully independent and sovereign.

13. The logic of this framework does not hinge on the exact value of p. We assume p to be exogenous, as to do otherwise would greatly complicate the model. For works that endogenize the probability of victory within a bargaining framework, see, for instance, James D. Fearon, "Bargaining over Objects That Influence Future Bargaining Power," paper presented at the annual meeting of the American Political Science Association, Washington, DC, August 1996; and Carmen Beviá and Luis C. Corchó, "Endogenous Strength in Conflicts," *International Journal of Industrial Organization* 31, no. 3 (2013): 297–306.

14. See, for instance, Richard C. Bush and Michael E. O'Hanlon, *A War Like No Other: The Truth about China's Challenge to America* (Hoboken, NJ: John Wiley and Sons, 2007); Ted Galen Carpenter, *America's Coming War with China: A Collision Course over Taiwan* (New York: Palgrave, 2005); and Gabe T. Wang, *China and the Taiwan Issue: Impending War at the Taiwan Strait* (Lanham, MD: University Press of America, 2006). For a more detailed discussion of this and other Taiwan Strait conflict scenarios, see Scott L. Kastner, "Is the Taiwan Strait Still a Flash Point? Rethinking the Prospects for Armed Conflict between China and Taiwan," *International Security* 40, no. 3 (Winter 2015/16): 54–92. The discussion that follows draws in part from this article.

15. Incentives to misrepresent bargaining power are at the center of Fearon's seminal paper on bargaining failure as a cause of war. Even when there are bargains that both sides prefer to war, incentives to misrepresent one's bargaining leverage make war possible. And even if a state is able to communicate its bargaining leverage to its rival, it is possible for this communication to reduce the probability of bargaining failure only if the act of communication changes the actors' payoffs (e.g., is a costly signal). James D. Fearon, "Rationalist Explanations for War," *International Organization* 49, no. 3 (1995): 379–414.

16. Emerson Niou, for instance, shows that a significant majority of Taiwanese would support Taiwan independence if the outcome could be achieved peacefully. See Emerson M.S. Niou, "Understanding Taiwan Independence and Its Policy Implications," *Asian Survey* 44, no. 4 (2004): 555–67. Recent polls conducted through Taiwan's Election and Democratization Study (TEDS) show that this basic pattern persists. See results online at www.tedsnet.org/.

17. And these, of course, are "big ifs" given the lack of support for unification among Taiwan's citizens. On this lack of support, see for instance polling data from the Election Study Center at National Chengchi University, which can be found online at http://esc.nccu.edu.tw/main.php.

18. For a more extensive discussion along these lines, see Scott L. Kastner and Chad Rector, "Bargaining Power and Mistrust: Credible Commitments and the Prospects for a PRC/Taiwan Agreement," *Security Studies* 17, no. 1 (2008): 39–71. The discussion here draws in part from that article. For a broader discussion of the dangers of a shift from deterrence to a compellence dynamic in the Taiwan Strait, see Kastner, "Is the Taiwan Strait Still a Flash Point?"

19. Fearon, "Rationalist Explanations."

20. See, for instance, William S. Murray, "Asymmetric Options for Taiwan's Deterrence and Defense," in *Globalization and Security Relations across the Taiwan Strait: In the Shadow of China*, ed. Ming-chin Monique Chu and Scott L. Kastner (London: Routledge, 2015), 61–79.

21. The text of the letter is available on the webpage of US senator Robert Menendez: "Menendez Urges President Obama to Expedite Sale of Military Aircraft to Taiwan," May 27, 2011, www.menendez.senate.gov/news-and-events/press/menendez-urges-president-obama-to-expedite-sale-of-military-aircraft-to-taiwan.

22. Glaser, "Grand Bargain."

23. This section draws from Scott L. Kastner, William L. Reed, and Ping-Kuei Chen, "Mostly Bark, Little Bite? Modeling US Arms Sales to Taiwan and the Chinese Response," *Issues and Studies* 49, no. 3 (2013): 111–50.

24. "Taiwan Arms Sale Draws Angry, but Familiar, Reaction," *New York Times*, September 22, 2011, www.nytimes.com/2011/09/23/world/asia/china-expresses-anger-over-latest-us-arms-sales-to-taiwan.html.

25. "US Government 'Angrily Condemned' for Taiwan Arms Deal," *BBC Summary of World Broadcasts*, September 9, 1992 (original source, Xinhua, September 4, 1992).

26. US-Taiwan Business Council, *Chinese Reactions*; Alastair Iain Johnston, "How New and Assertive Is China's New Assertiveness?" *International Security* 37, no. 4 (2013): 7–48.

27. "China Apparently Halts Rights Talks with U.S.," *New York Times*, November 25, 1992, A12.

28. On the 1992 episode, see "China Threatens Tariff Retaliation on U.S. Goods," *Washington Post* September 10, 1992, A9. The article notes that although China's threats were in direct response to punitive tariffs the United States was at the time considering, (unnamed) analysts believed the threats might also have been tied to the recent F-16 decision. On the 2010 episode, see US-Taiwan Business Council, *Chinese Reactions*.

29. US-Taiwan Business Council, *Chinese Reactions*.

30. "Zhuanjia: Rang mei geng tongkude ganshoudao sunhai zhongguo liyide daijia" [Expert: Make America more painfully feel the costs of harming China's interests], Xinhua Net, January 8, 2010, http://news.xinhuanet.com/mil/2010–01/08/content_12776204.htm; "Jiefangjun shaojiang jianyi zhicai meiguo dui tai junshou qiye" [PLA major general recommends sanctioning American companies that sell weapons to Taiwan], Xinhua Net, January 7, 2010, http://big5.xinhuanet.com/gate/big5/news.xinhuanet.com/mil/2010–01/07/content_12767991.htm.

31. "Sanctions against U.S. Firms Selling Arms to Taiwan Not Violating WTO Rules: Chinese Experts," *Xinhua*, February 5, 2010.

32. "PRC Public Support Sanctioning US Companies Involved in Arms Sales to Taiwan," Xinhua, February 6, 2010.

33. John W. Garver, *Face Off: China, The United States, and Taiwan's Democratization* (Seattle: University of Washington Press, 1997).

34. Jia Qingguo and Alan D. Romberg, "Taiwan and Tibet," in *Debating China: The U.S.-China Relationship in Ten Conversations*, ed. Nina Hatchigian (New York: Oxford University Press, 2014), 179.

13

Xi Jinping's Taiwan Policy

Boxing Taiwan In with the One-China Framework

Jing Huang

Cross-Strait relations under Xi Jinping's leadership remain stable and progressive in general, despite growing anti-Beijing sentiment in Taiwan, as highlighted by the Sunflower Movement, which protested the passing of the Cross-Strait Service Trade Agreement between Taiwan and the mainland, and the embarrassing failure of the ruling Kuomintang (KMT) party, which had emphasized a platform of strengthening Taiwan-China economic ties in the 2014 election. Both sides have been prevented from making any substantial progress in cross-Strait relations since Xi came to power in 2012 (coinciding with Ma's second term)—Taiwan by growing anti-Beijing sentiment, especially among young people, and a drop in President Ma Ying-jeou's popularity,[1] and China by Xi Jinping's preoccupation with fighting corruption and restructuring the economy amid a substantial economic slowdown. But peaceful development across the Taiwan Strait has remained the trend since 2008, when Ma Ying-jeou came to power. The 1992 Consensus that there is only one China and that Taipei and Beijing agree to disagree on which government is its legitimate representative is still the foundation of cross-Strait relations. Moreover, the two sides have a better understanding and growing tolerance of each other's differing views of the implications, at home and abroad, of the assertion that there is only "one China." Meanwhile, economic, social, and political exchanges between the two sides of the Taiwan Strait continue to increase.

With this background, this chapter seeks to address the following questions: What is China's strategy toward Taiwan under Xi Jinping's leadership? Have there been any changes to China's Taiwan policy since Xi Jinping came to power? Is there a departure from Hu Jintao's Taiwan policy? If there is a departure, to what extent will such a change affect cross-Strait relations?

This chapter will start with a brief review of developments in cross-Strait relations since Ma Ying-jeou came to power in 2008. It will then argue that despite substantial developments the status quo remains intact. However, this status quo in the long run is in favor of Beijing's policy goal to eventually reunify the two sides of the Taiwan Strait into the People's Republic of China (PRC). In this regard, while Xi Jinping's Taiwan policy continues to follow the fundamental approach adopted by Hu Jintao, namely to prioritize prevention of Taiwan's de jure independence over promotion of reunification, Xi has increasingly emphasized strengthening the strategic framework of the "one-China principle" in cross-Strait relations. The aim is to box Taiwan in toward the goal of eventual reunification, which has been incorporated into Xi's grand goals for China that are expressed in his "Chinese Dream." Although Taiwanese people seem to be less and less identifying with mainland China nationally and politically, Taiwan has been deeply drawn into China's economic orbit, while its international status, in terms of both legitimacy and influence, continues to decline. Thus Taiwan sees increasing difficulty in moving away from mainland China's influence both economically and politically. The dilemma faced by Taiwan is that it will either be drawn deeper into China's orbit or be marginalized in international affairs as well as regional economic integration. Taiwan does not have much choice but to accept the fact that it will have greater interdependence with the mainland. I conclude that although there may be a bounce or reaction against mainland China's Taiwan policy after the presidential election in 2016, this will only be a storm in the teacup, which will not alter the overall direction of the development.

FROM PREVENTION OF DE JURE INDEPENDENCE TO PROMOTION OF "POLITICAL AGREEMENTS"

The turning point of cross-Strait relations took place in 2004 with the May 17 Statement issued by the Taiwan Affairs Office of the State Council of the PRC. In this statement, for the first time Beijing made it clear that prevention of Taiwan's de jure independence was the top priority of Beijing's Taiwan policy.[2] With growing concern and suspicion from the international community over China's rise and a potential "China threat," Beijing had realized that a policy aimed at reunification was unrealistic under the current circumstances and would conflict with its efforts to build up the image of a peaceful rising power. On March 14, 2005, this policy was formalized by the Anti-Secession Law passed by the third conference of the Tenth National People's Congress. After that, joint efforts by Beijing and Washington kept Taiwan's then president Chen Shui-bian from going too far in his relentless pushing of the envelope for Taiwan's independence, which peaked when Chen won his second term in 2004. The de facto co-management between Washington and Beijing to check the movement for Taiwan's de jure independence has helped advance Beijing's strategic vision for "one China" in cross-Strait relations despite some fundamental differences between the one-China policy that the United States espouses (which agrees to the existence of only one China but allows different interpretations as to which government is the legitimate representative of it) and the one-China principle that mainland China insists on (which stresses that the government of PRC is the sole legitimate government representing China and consequently entails eventual reunification).[3] The two sides seem to have reached a temporary but fundamental consensus on the Taiwan issue, namely that the movement toward Taiwan's independence does not serve the interests of either China or the United States, although the latter is by no means supportive of the former's policy of eventual reunification. Since then, both the Bush and Obama administrations have endorsed the policy of "peaceful development across the Taiwan Strait" adopted by the Hu Jintao leadership, although a "peaceful resolution"—not necessarily reunification—has been the US policy goal versus China's goal for eventual reunification. Together with this newly clarified US position, China's policy shift from proreunification to anti-independence enabled President Ma Ying-jeou to accept the 1992 Consensus as the foundation for cross-Strait relations immediately after he assumed the office.

As a result, during Ma's first term, the two sides achieved a long-overdue breakthrough in cross-Strait relations, the "three links," or commencement of direct flights, shipping, and postal service across the Taiwan Strait in 2008, which has in turn brought about an irrevocable economic integration between the two sides of the Taiwan Strait through direct transportation, trade, and communications. Furthermore, the establishment of the Economic Cooperation Framework Agreement (ECFA) has institutionalized economic interdependence across the Taiwan Strait. It is expected that ECFA will further boost cross-Strait trade and economic exchanges, leading to the "one-China market" advocated by Ma Ying-jeou's first vice-president, Vincent Siew Wan-chang.[4] Thus, in terms of economic development, the two sides of the Taiwan Strait have already been moving toward reunification.

Since President Xi Jinping came to power in 2012, cross-Strait relations have remained stable, although there have not been many major achievements so far, largely because of Taipei's reluctance to approve any political agreement or any formal or informal measures to build trust between PRC and ROC militaries, despite the push from Beijing. Xi Jinping, on the sidelines of the Asia-Pacific Economic Cooperation (APEC) forum in Indonesia in Bali in October 2013, told Vincent Siew that "increasing mutual political trust across the Taiwan Straits and jointly building political foundations are crucial for ensuring the peaceful development of relations";[5] he also hinted broadly about the importance of a cross-Strait framework for mutual military confidence and trust.[6] But there has been little response from Ma Ying-jeou's administration to Xi's requests. Several reasons account for the two sides' failure to reach any political deals. Ma Ying-jeou's rapidly decreasing popularity in Taiwan and his inept management of internal strife within the KMT have greatly constrained Taipei's ability to handle cross-Strait relations. Given the leadership transition in China and the US policy of pivoting toward Asia, it has become unrealistic for Beijing to push any further in cross-Strait relations.

However, as Xi Jinping told Lien Chan, the honorary chair of the KMT, Beijing has patience and confidence.[7] Given the overall situation, especially China's focus on developing, with the United States, a "new type of great-power relations" and on t promoting the "One Belt, One Road" initiative that would build overland and maritime economic corridors linking China and Europe through central, West, and South Asia, Taiwan is no longer a priority for Beijing at the moment. Xi Jinping may not necessarily want to push any further in the cross-Strait relations and may wish merely to maintain the stability of the status quo. This is clearly suggested by Xi's speech at the Chinese People's Political Consultative Conference (CPPCC) in March 2015, during which he emphasized that maintaining the 1992 Consensus as a foundation for cross-Strait relations was indispensable for peace and stability between the two sides of the Strait,[8] while reunification was a long-term goal that could be achieved only after substantial development took place across the Taiwan Strait.

XI JINPING TRIES TO BOX TAIWAN IN WITH THE ONE-CHINA FRAMEWORK

Xi Jinping has rich experience in handling cross-Strait affairs, for he has been the provincial party secretary in Fujian, Zhejiang, and Shanghai, where the local governments have established substantial connections with Taiwan. These provinces not only are agents of the central government in Beijing but also have developed their own close social, economic, and political ties with their counterparts in Taiwan.[9] Thus, after Xi became a designated successor at the Seventeenth Party Congress in October 2007, he played an increasing role in cross-Strait relations. In December 2007 and January 2009, he met visiting former US president Jimmy Carter twice as China's vice-president. Besides emphasizing Hu Jintao's six proposals for peaceful development of cross-Strait relations, Xi expressed China's willingness to cooperate with the United States against Taiwan's de jure independence, which as he said would not only serve mutual interests but also help to maintain regional peace and development.[10] Among all of his talks on Taiwan during this period, the most impressive one is the speech he gave at the opening ceremony of the 2010 Chinese Roots-Seeking Tour summer camp in Beijing on July 25, 2010. He claimed that for Chinese people inside and outside of China the solidarity and unity of the Chinese nation constituted their common root, and Chinese culture their soul. On this basis, he claimed that it was the common dream for all Chinese to revitalize the great Chinese nation.[11]

After Xi came to power, he continued Hu Jintao's Taiwan policy and prioritized the prevention of de jure independence rather than promoting immediate reunification. In April 2013, Xi met Vincent Siew at the Twelfth Boao Forum. Xi called on compatriots from both sides of the Strait to work hard to rejuvenate the Chinese nation. He also called for closer economic cooperation between the Chinese mainland and Taiwan.[12] There was no mention of any development of the political relationship in his remarks. Two months later, however, when he met Wu Po-hsiung, the honorary chair of the (KMT), he made four new proposals to further cross-Strait relations: "First, the two sides should take the overall interests of the Chinese nation into consideration when assessing the overall situation of cross-Strait ties"; "Second, the two sides should clearly recognize development trends throughout history in order to gain a better understanding of the future prospects for cross-Strait ties"; Third, "The mainland and Taiwan should enhance mutual trust, engage in favorable interactions, seek common ground and shelve differences, and be pragmatic and enterprising"; and finally, "The two sides should steadily promote the overall development of cross-Strait ties."[13] Compared to his previous talks on the Taiwan issue, this one more clearly articulated how to promote political trust between the two sides of the Strait based on peaceful economic development. Xi emphasized that the two sides "share the same destiny" and called for efforts to inspire them to "strengthen their pride in the Chinese nation as well as their shared goal of its rejuvenation." He also noted that "though the mainland and Taiwan are yet to be reunified, they belong to one China and are inseparable parts of the country." Xi added that "safeguarding national territorial integrity and sovereignty is at the core of this goal" Xi said, and emphasized that the two sides should uphold the one-China framework.[14]

Now Xi Jinping has put forward some specific political requirements for interactions with Taiwan, including reinforcing confidence building, promoting positive interactions, optimizing common interests, and being pragmatic. The essence, he emphasizes, is to consolidate and protect Beijing's strategic advancement of the "one-China" principle, which should be agreed on in cross-Strait relations. In October 2013, when meeting Vincent Siew in Bali ahead of the APEC gathering, Xi brought up the notion that "both sides of the Strait are of one family." As he emphasized, the two sides should treasure this historical opportunity, maintain the momentum of peaceful development of relations across the Taiwan Strait, and strengthen political mutual trust, so as to lay a political foundation. He expressed for the first time that in the long term disputes across the Taiwan Strait could and should be gradually resolved—"We cannot hand those problems down from generation to generation." This remark reflects Xi's resolve to make substantial progress under his leadership in pushing cross-Strait relations toward reunification.

Xi urged heads of departments in charge of cross-Strait ties to meet and exchange views in order to build up cross-Strait political mutual trust.[15]

Xi's position on cross-Strait relations was further clarified in February 2014, when he met a Taiwanese delegation led by Lien Chan. He made it clear that reunification was an essential part of the Chinese Dream. Again he made four points in explaining China's Taiwan policy, but these four points included more political elements than the previous four. Reunification, he said, was the common wish of compatriots from both sides, and he affirmed that "no power can separate us."[16] His speech closely linked the Chinese Dream to Taiwan's future and again emphasized the importance of retaining a one-China framework. He expressed optimism over the eventual resolution of disputes across the Strait, even though he acknowledged that it might take a long time to achieve. Xi asked "the two sides across the Strait to consolidate the basis for adhering to the 1992 Consensus and opposing 'Taiwan independence' and to foster the common understanding of One China." He stated that "compatriots from both sides have chosen the path of peaceful development of cross-Strait relations, a correct choice that safeguards cross-Strait peace, promotes common development, helps realize the rejuvenation of the Chinese nation, and brings benefits to people on both sides." Despite a general trend of peaceful development and increasing exchanges and communication, currently there are disturbances such as the Sunflower Movement, Xi noted. "We will try to do our best, as long as what we do can contribute to the well-being of our Taiwan compatriots, to the peaceful development of cross-Strait relations, and to the overall interest of the Chinese nation."[17]

After carrying forward Hu Jintao's Taiwan policy, Xi shifted his emphasis more to establishing and consolidating a strategic framework under the "one China" principle. The aim is to box Taiwan in for eventual reunification. In September 2014, Xi Jinping told a visiting Taiwanese delegation that the basic guideline to solve the Taiwan issue is "peaceful reunification; One Country, Two Systems." He added, "No secessionist act will be tolerated. The path of 'Taiwan independence' is unfeasible."[18] The concept of "one country, two systems" has not been part of mainland China's official language toward Taiwan for quite a while. With Ma Ying-jeou's government being discredited by the Sunflower Movement, and with unrest in Hong Kong, Xi seemed to have come to a conclusion that certain principles needed to be reemphasized. This idea is reflected in Xi's remarks while he was joining a panel discussion with members of the National Committee of the CPPCC in March 2015. He proclaimed, "We should unswervingly pursue peaceful development, unswervingly adhere to the common political basis, unswervingly bring benefits to the people across the Strait and unswervingly join hands to realize the national revitalization." It is worth noting that on the same occasion he called on compatriots to be vigilant against the "Taiwan independence" forces.[19] It is a good indication that Xi Jinping is fully taking a no-nonsense approach to cross-Strait relations in response to new factors in Taiwan that are unfavorable to mainland China.

Since Deng Xiaoping, Chinese leaders have realized that the United States plays an essential role in cross-Strait relations. On the basis of the political heritage from his predecessors, Xi Jinping has developed a new strategy. Even before he became the top leader in China, he emphasized that the Taiwan issue should not interfere with Sino-U.S. bilateral relations.[20] Since he came into power, he has been trying to isolate the Taiwan issue from the Sino-U.S. bilateral relationship while at the same time trying to build up what he calls a "new type of great-power relationship." That is why in all of his discussions, communications, and joint statements with President Obama one can hardly find any mention of the Taiwan issue, at least not in published statements. This clearly indicates Xi's position on Taiwan when he is dealing with the United States: since Taiwan is a core interest of China, China will not allow Taiwan to become a bargaining chip while it is making efforts to develop a new type of relationships between major powers. The aim is to isolate the Taiwan issue from the Sino-US bilateral relationship and cut out any US involvement in cross-Strait relations, or at least to make sure there is no direct US involvement. Thus it is not surprising that with regard to the US rebalancing policy in Asia, Taiwan has been absent from discussion.

Overall, Xi's strategy can be summarized as follows. First, he has not made any dramatic departure from Hu Jintao's Taiwan policy, which focused on the prevention of Taiwan's de jure independence. Second, he is most concerned to consolidate the strategic fulfillment of the "one China" principle in order to box Taiwan in. Consequently, he has placed more emphasis on developing a political relationship between the mainland and Taiwan, based on a solid economic foundation in cross-Strait relations. Last but not the least, Xi is obviously a tough player on the Taiwan issue. His response toward any opposition in Taiwan against eventual reunification can be summarized as "If you move one step forwards, I will move two steps." Xi Jinping's revival of the slogan "One country, two systems," which has not been mentioned since 2005, when the Anti-secession Law was passed, is only one example. His tough stance may continue because of domestic and external situations. This doesn't necessarily mean that Xi wants to copy a Hong Kong model for cross-Strait relations. Rather, it reflects his determinations not to allow any setback in cross-Strait relations under his leadership. Xi Jinping believes that as long as he can keep institutionalizing the one-China framework in cross-Strait relations, Taiwan will eventually come back to the embrace of the mother country.

CONCLUSION

Though in general Xi Jinping's Taiwan policy has followed that of Hu Jintao in prioritizing the prevention of Taiwan's de jure independence over the promotion of reunification, Xi, apparently in response to the stability and enhanced development of relations across the Taiwan Strait after Ma Ying-jeou came to power, has tried to push forward some political agreements between Beijing and Taipei. However, this effort has hardly been fruitful, not only because of Ma Ying-jeou's decreasing popularity in Taiwan, but also because Xi's priority has been the anti-corruption campaign at home and the crises in East and South China Seas against the background of US rebalancing abroad.

As discussed in the previous sections, there are some emerging trends under Xi's leadership. First of all, as China has become increasingly capable of managing the situation on its Asian borders, Xi Jinping has tried to insulate the Taiwan issue from US-China relations in order to decrease US leverage on this issue in the bilateral relationship. Xi's policy has resulted in an obvious decrease in the influence of the United States on cross-Strait relations, to the point that the United States no longer plays a decisive role.[21]

Second, because of the rapid development of economic interdependence across the Taiwan Strait and both sides' acceptance of the 1992 Consensus as a foundation for cross-Strait relations, the topic of reunification is no longer an untouchable third rail in Taiwan politics. Despite seemingly growing indifference from Beijing, there are increasing discussions on the issue, not only among scholars but also in the media and in political discourse. Meanwhile, the issue of Taiwan independence has become increasingly difficult to discuss in Taiwanese political affairs. Even Democratic Progressive Party (DPP; more proindependence) leaders nowadays try to avoid giving an opinion on the issue, not because of any change in the DPP's guidelines or ideology, but because it will deprive them of political support at home and abroad that is necessary for them to prevail in Taiwan politics.

Third, as Xi Jinping's leadership is expected to further consolidate, it is inevitable that he will put more pressure on achieving "political progress" in cross-Strait relations. This is clearly indicated by his recent remarks on Taiwan. While emphasizing that the two sides will have to forgo political agreements in the foreseeable future, Xi unambiguously included the eventual reunification of Taiwan and mainland China in his "Chinese dream," which is centered on the revitalization of a great Chinese nation. This shows that Xi Jinping aims to make some achievements on the Taiwan issue a part of his political legacy.

Given the defeat of the KMT in the midterm election of 2014 and President Ma Ying-jeou's rapidly declining popularity, the DPP entered the 2016 presidential and legislative electoral campaign in an advantageous position and indeed won a convincing victory. This cannot but amount to a substantial challenge to Xi's leadership on the Taiwan issue. Given Xi's position and public statements, it will not be surprising if Beijing imposes more pressure on Taiwan. From Xi's perspective, it is unacceptable for cross-Strait relations to go back to the situation under President Chen Shui-bian in the first eight years of the twenty-first century. Given the increasing economic interdependence of the mainland and Taiwan, and more importantly the deep interdependence of the United States and China, it is inevitable that the focus of Xi Jinping's Taiwan policy will shift toward political issues. The aim of reaching political agreements across the Taiwan Strait is to institutionalize not only the interdependence of the two sides of the Taiwan Strait but also the strategic framework of the one-China principle. Thus the victory of the DPP in the 2016 presidential campaign may only provoke a stronger reaction from mainland China on the Taiwan issue. After all, pushing for political agreements was already part of Xi's policy toward Taiwan. So there will be more challenges in cross-Strait relations in the coming years, not just because the proindependence DPP has come into power again after eight years since their defeat in the 2008 presidential election, but also because Xi has invested much of his political capital in this issue.

NOTES

1. Ma Ying-jeou's approval rate plunged to 11 percent, according to a poll conducted by TVBS in December 2014, and he was listed as the least popular of twelve politicians. TVBS Public Opinion Poll, "Guónèi zhǔyào zhèngzhì rénwù shēngwàng diàochá" [Survey on the main political figures in China], TVBS Poll Center, December 23, 2014, www.tvbs.com.tw/static/FILE_DB/PCH/201412/20141226172450208.pdf.

2. For the full context, see PRC Embassy in the United States, "Taiwan Affairs Office Issues Statement on Current Cross-Straits Relations (17/05/04)," May 17, 2004, www.china-embassy.org/eng/zt/twwt/t111117.htm. Also see Jing Huang with Xiaoting Li, *Inseparable Separation: The Making of China's Taiwan Policy* (Singapore: World Scientific Publishing, 2010), 281–86.

3. Huang with Li, *Inseparable Separation*, 272–95.

4. Scott L. Kastner, "Drinking Poison to Quench a Thirst? The Security Consequences of China-Taiwan Economic Integration," in *The Economy-Security Nexus in Northeast Asia*, ed. T. J. Pempel (London: Routledge, 2013), 33.

5. "Xi Meets Taiwan Politician Ahead of APEC Gathering," Xinhuanet, October 6, 2013, http://news.xinhuanet.com/english/china/2013–10/06/c_132775470.htm.

6. "Xíjìnpíng shuō 'liǎng'àn zhèngzhì fēnqí wèntí zhōngguī yào jiějué' shìfàng shà xìnhào," *News of the Communist Party of China*, October 9, 2013, http://cpc.people.com.cn/n/2013/1009/c241220–23138541.html.

7. "Mainland Respects Taiwan's Social System: Xi," Xinhuanet, February 18, 2014, http://news.xinhuanet.com/english/china/2014–02/18/c_133125207.htm.

8. "Jùjiāo liǎnghuì: Sān niánjiān xíjìnpíng qīnlín de shǒu gè tuán zǔ," *News of the Communist Party of China*, March 5, 2015, http://cpc.people.com.cn/n/2015/0305/c385474–26641415.html. Whether Xi continues to insist on this prerequisite if Tsai Ing-wen, the winner of the 2016 Taiwan presidential election, maintains her denial of the 1992 Consensus remains to be seen but seems likely.

9. Back in 2006, when Xi Jinping was the party secretary in Zhejiang Province, he hosted Lien Chan, the honorary chair of the KMT in Hangzhou. Their talks focused on historical ties and social and economic exchanges between Zhejiang Province and Taiwan. See "Xíjìnpíng zài hángzhōu huìjiàn bìng yànqǐng liánzhàn yìxíng," Xinhua News Agency, April 22, 2006, www.gwytb.gov.cn/zt/xijinpingzhuanti/201401/t20140115_5531536.htm.

10. "Xíjìnpíng huìjiàn měiguó qián zǒngtǒng kètè," Xinhuanet, December 6, 2007, www.gwytb.gov.cn/zt/xijinpingzhuanti/201401/t20140115_5531538.htm; "Xíjìnpíng chūxí zhōng měi jiànjiāo 30 zhōunián

jìnián wǎnyàn bìng huìjiàn kǎtè yīxíng" [Xi Jinping attended the thirtieth anniversary of the establishment of diplomatic relations between China and the United States and met with Carter and his party], Xinhuanet, January 12, 2009, www.gwytb.gov.cn/zt/xijinpingzhuanti/201401/t20140115_5531539.htm.

11. "2010 nián hǎiwài huáyì jí gǎng'ào tái dìqū qīngshàonián 'zhōngguó xúngēn zhī lǚ' xiàlìngyíng kāi yíng, xíjìnpíng chūxí bìng jiǎnghuà," Xinhuanet, July 25, 2010, www.gwytb.gov.cn/zt/xijinpingzhuanti/201401/t20140115_5531543.htm.

12. "12th Boao Forum for Asia Concludes," CCTV, April 8, 2013, http://english.cntv.cn/program/china24/20130408/106818.shtml.

13. "Xi Meets with KMT Honorary Chairman, Calling National Rejuvenation a 'Common Goal,'" Xinhuanet, June 13, 2013, http://news.xinhuanet.com/english/china/2013-06/13/c_132453077.htm.

14. Ibid.

15. "Xi Meets Taiwan Politician."

16. "Xi Proposes Equal Consultations on Cross-Strait Political Differences," Taiwan Affairs Office of the State Council PRC, February 18, 2014, www.gwytb.gov.cn/en/Headline/201402/t20140220_5705694.htm.

17. Ibid.

18. "Xinhua Insight: Xi Steadfast on Reunification," Xinhuanet, September 29, 2014, http://news.xinhuanet.com/english/china/2014-09/26/c_133675240.htm.

19. "Xi Stresses Cross-Strait Peaceful Development, Urges Vigilance against Taiwan Independence," Xinhuanet, March 4, 2015, http://news.xinhuanet.com/english/2015-03/04/c_134037908.htm.

20. In February 2012, during his Washington, D.C., visit, as China's then vice-president, Xi Jinping raised the prospect of "a new type of relationship between major countries in the 21st century," emphasizing the importance of the bilateral relationship. See David M. Lampton, "A New Type of Major-Power Relationship: Seeking a Durable Foundation for U.S.-China Ties," Asia Policy 16, no. 1 (2013): 51–68.

21. I argue that with the power shifting among major countries, it is inevitable that the two sides of the Taiwan Strait will play a more and more decisive role in cross-Strait relations. See more details in Huang Jing, "Hépíng jiāoliú, gòngtóng fāzhǎn: Jìnián wǎng gū huìtán èrshí zhōunián" [Developing cross-Straits relations: Commemorating the twentieth anniversary of the Wang-Koo dialogue], Jiāoliú Zázhì [Exchange magazine] (Straits Exchange Foundation), June 2013.

14

Strategies of China's Expansion and Taiwan's Survival in Southeast Asia

A Comparative Perspective

Samuel C. Y. Ku

In October 1949, the People's Republic of China (PRC) was established and China was politically divided into two parts. This was because in December 1949, because of the civil war, the government of the Republic of China (ROC) retreated to Taiwan. Over the past six decades, cross-Straits relations have undergone tremendous transformations. These changes can be categorized into four stages, which have greatly influenced China and Taiwan's relations throughout Southeast Asia.

The first stage, December 1949 to October 1971, was when the PRC had not yet been admitted to the United Nations (UN). There was a military standoff across the Taiwan Straits and political confrontation between the PRC and ROC, who each maintained to the international community that they were the true Chinese representatives. Because of its alliance with the United States, the ROC was able to maintain its formal diplomatic relations with Thailand, the Philippines, and the former Republic of Vietnam,[1] whereas, because of its extensive support for the communist movements in Southeast Asia, the PRC was relatively isolated in the region.

The second stage, from October 1971 to July 1987, was marked by the admission of the PRC into the United Nations and the beginning of Taiwan's political isolation. However, the island's economy continued to grow, branding it as one of the four Asian dragons. Under a "one-China" policy that countries could officially recognize the PRC or the ROC but not both, the PRC was able to block Taiwan from increasing its diplomatic ties. As a result, in 1975, the ROC lost all of its diplomatic relationships in Southeast Asia. Although, by the mid-1980s, the ROC's official diplomatic partners worldwide had been reduced to only twenty-three, the number of Taiwan's representative offices in foreign countries continued to increase. Because of so-called "pragmatic diplomacy," by 1987 the number of international representative offices had increased to eighty-five.[2]

The third stage was from 1987 to 1997. In July 1987, martial law was lifted in the ROC, which resulted in great progress for cross-Strait relations. In May 1991, the period of mobilization for the suppression of communist rebellion was abolished, officially ending the civil war with the communists on the Chinese mainland.[3] Governmental institutions were recognized, and more interactions between Taiwan and China were slowly initiated, such as the Straits Exchange Foundation (SEF), which was established in Taipei in March 1991, and the Association for Relations Across the Taiwan Straits (ARATS), which was established in Beijing in December 1991. However, both sides were unwavering when it came to diplomacy. Taiwan's economic ties with Southeast Asia continued to grow, while China continued to expand its political influence on the region.

In 1997, the Asian financial crisis marked the beginning of the fourth phase of cross-Strait relations. China's economic power increased, whereas Taiwan's remained relatively unchanged. China was now not only generating its own capital but sending financial aid to economies in the region, making it an economic giant. This trend continues today and has granted China its increasing regional power. China continues to expand its political and economic influence on Southeast Asia, with the intentions of replacing the United States as the regional superpower.[4] This has put Taiwan in the position of no longer competing with China but instead having to struggle to survive, not only in Southeast Asia but also around the world.

China has developed its expansion goals to build up its political economy in Southeast Asia and in doing so has implemented a comprehensive framework for expanded political and economic relations with countries throughout the region. Meanwhile, Taiwan's survival strategy is to continue to prosper economically and to try to build an environment that will allow for political and economic linkages with Southeast Asian countries.

This chapter takes a comparative perspective in examining China's expansion strategy and Taiwan's Southeast Asian survival strategy that have been unfolding since the turn of the century. It argues that China's expansion strategy has established a relatively solid relationship with most Southeast Asian countries. However, it faces challenges that could impede further expansion in the region. And although Taiwan continues to face the challenges of political isolation and economic marginalization, its political resilience may allow for its continued survival in the international community: given the recent democratic shift in Southeast Asia, Taiwan has won more support and friendship across the region than China has been able to keep up with.

CHINA'S EXPANSION STRATEGY IN SOUTHEAST ASIA: BUILDING A CHINA-DOMINATED POLITICAL ECONOMY IN THE REGION

China's Political Expansion: Building a China-Dominated Political Environment

During the Cold War era, China was not influential in Southeast Asia, even though by 1991 it had formalized diplomatic relations with all the countries in the region.[5] In 1990, through the implementation of the Good Neighbor Policy, China began to make changes regarding its regional diplomatic relations. After the brutal Tiananmen Square massacre of June 4, 1989, it tried to reshape its image.[6] In August 1990, Chinese premier Li Peng (at that time) visited Indonesia, Singapore, and Thailand. In December 1990, he visited Malaysia and the Philippines. This was the first time that a Chinese leader had, within four months, visited five major countries in Southeast Asia. In 1991, the previously isolated Asian giant was then invited to attend the annual Association of Southeast Asian Nations (ASEAN) meeting, and in July 1996 it was accepted as a full dialogue partner. This laid a sound foundation for the further development of China's diplomatic relations throughout Southeast Asia.

In 1997, because of its strong currency, the Asian financial crisis gave China greater opportunity to expand its engagement with Southeast Asia. While most currencies in Southeast Asia depreciated after the financial crisis, China's currency, the renminbi (RMB), maintained its value. This helped keep other Southeast Asian currencies from depreciating further. The United States and Western-dominated international financial bodies such as the World Bank and the International Monetary Fund (IMF) gave the Southeast Asian countries a hard time when they came to them for help. China, on the contrary, was quick to assist by issuing huge loans and economic assistance to suffering countries in the region.

Since the turn of the century, China has further expanded its political and economic relations with Southeast Asia and attempted to replace the United States as a dominant power in the region by establishing a China-dominated political economy there. Therefore, over the coming century, China's Southeast Asian expansion strategy is designed to bring the region completely under its dominance. The strategy has three elements:(1) getting more involved in regional political affairs; (2) resolving security issues with Southeast Asian countries; (3) establishing a new mechanism over regional affairs.

Getting More Involved in Regional Political Affairs.   Before 1990, China had limited involvement in regional affairs, despite its cordial relations with Burma and Laos during the Cold War era. However, things changed for the Asian giant in 1991, when it was invited to attend the Twenty-Fourth ASEAN Ministerial Meeting in Kuala Lumpur and then in July 1996, when it was invited to the Twenty-Ninth

ASEAN Ministerial Meeting in Jakarta and accorded the full status of a dialogue partner.

Since the turn of the century, China has continued to strengthen its political relationships with the region's countries. This can be evidenced in the numerous agreements and meetings that have occurred between China and the ASEAN countries. In October 2003, one of the most significant of these was the joint declaration on strategic partnership for peace and prosperity that was signed at the Seventh ASEAN-China Summit in Bali, Indonesia. Around the same time, China signed the Treaty of Amity and Cooperation in Southeast Asia (TAC), making it the first ASEAN dialogue partner to be included in the agreement.[7] China's entry into TAC marked a closer relationship with its southern neighbors.

In October 2010, at the Thirteenth ASEAN-China Summit in Ho Noi, China, ASEAN adopted a four-year partnership plan for 2011–15, which again elevated its bilateral political and strategic cooperation with the organization. In November 2011, China established the ASEAN-China Center (ACC) in Beijing, the first and only intergovernmental organization between China and ASEAN. The ACC is a one-stop information center, designated to promote cooperation in a number of areas, such as trade, investment, tourism, education, and culture. In September 2012, the PRC appointed its first resident ASEAN ambassador to Jakarta and established an official mission statement for its role in ASEAN. This again strengthened its ties with the regional members.

In October 2013, at the Sixteenth ASEAN-China Summit and tenth anniversary of the ASEAN-China strategic partnership, China and ASEAN issued a joint statement on expanding bilateral cooperation in eleven priority areas: agriculture, information technology, human resources development, Mekong Basin development, investment, energy, transport, culture, public health, tourism, and the environment. The statement truly exemplified China's comprehensive cooperation with Southeast Asia.

Resolving Security Issues with Southeast Asian Countries.   China has a long history of territorial disputes with its Southeast Asian neighbors, most notably a dispute over a number of islands and reefs in the South China Seas that has been ongoing with Vietnam and the Philippines. Previously, China insisted on bilateralism with individual Southeast Asian countries over these territorial and security disputes.[8] However, China now seems to be showing a willingness to join multilateral platforms to manage territorial and security issues. In November 2002, after a series of discussions and meetings, China and the ASEAN countries signed a Declaration on the Conduct of Parties in the South China Sea (DOC). In July 2011, at the Fourteenth ASEAN-China Summit in Bali, Indonesia, guidelines for implementing the DOC were adopted. At the summit, China's then premier Wen Jiabao announced that China would provide RMB 3 billion to establish the China-ASEAN Maritime

Cooperation Fund, in order to assist ASEAN members in areas such as maritime scientific research, connectivity, and navigation safety.

At the Sixteenth ASEAN-China Summit of October 2013, China and ASEAN discussed drafting a Code of Conduct (COC). In 2014, two meetings were held, in order to discuss the implementation of the DOC and further consult on how to develop the COC. These meetings were in March, at the Tenth ASEAN-China Joint Working Groups on the DOC, in Singapore and in April, at the Seventh ASEAN-China Senior Officials' Meeting on the DOC, in Thailand. In May 2014, at the Conference on Interaction and Confidence Building Measures in Asia, Chinese leader Xi Jinping stated, "Matters in Asia ultimately must be taken care of by Asians, Asia's problems ultimately must be resolved by Asians, and Asia's security ultimately must be protected by Asians."[9] This demonstrated China's attempt to engage in closer ties with Asian countries on security issues in the region and to strain relations with the United States and its Southeast Asian partners.

Although the DOC and progress on the COC have been criticized for their inefficiency and slow progress, a multilateral platform has been established for China and ASEAN to discuss and manage its long-standing disputes in the South China Seas. The DOC's signatories have ten points to be carried out, including respect for each other's positions and the promotion of a peaceful, friendly, and harmonious environment in the South China Seas.[10] However, it has become questionable if the DOC and the COC are considered official documents or if all dispute resolution signatories are required to carry them out. Since January 1974, China and Vietnam have been engaging in military confrontation over the Paracel Islands (a group of islands and reefs). In January 1995, Chinese troops also detained a Filipino fishing vessel on Mischief Reef in the East Vietnam Seas. Though tensions in the South China Seas have improved a little since the DOC was signed in 2002, in late March 2014 there were renewed confrontations between China and the Philippines, and in May 2014 there were confrontations with Vietnam.

Along with the DOC and the COC, China and ASEAN have made progress regarding nontraditional security issues that have become prevalent since the turn of the century. In November 2002, at the Sixth ASEAN-China Summit, China and ASEAN leaders signed the Joint Declaration of ASEAN and China on Cooperation in the Field of Non-traditional Security Issues.[11] Since then, Chinese leaders have reiterated China's intention to cooperate with Southeast Asia on nontraditional security issues. This was exemplified on October 30, 2006, when at the Tenth ASEAN-China Summit China's premier at that time, Wen Jiabao, stated that China and ASEAN should expand their already thriving economic networks and deepen cooperation on cross-border issues concerning counterterrorism, transnational crimes, maritime security, rescue operations, and disaster relief.

In 2009, China and ASEAN signed a renewed five-year (2010 to 2014) Memorandum of Understanding on Cooperation in the Field of Non-traditional Security

Issues.12 Since then, China has provided a series of training workshops for ASEAN members to implement a plan of action on such issues, and their scope has expanded to include illegal trafficking of drugs and narcotics.

Establishing a New Mechanism over Regional Affairs. The United States has for decades been a dominant power in world politics. Since the turn of the century, China has risen as Asia's economic and political giant. It has been developing new mechanisms on international affairs, particularly with regard to the Asia-Pacific region. In February 2001, the Boao Forum for Asia (BFA) was formally inaugurated. This exemplified China's intention to establish a platform for handling affairs in the Asia-Pacific region. The forum consists of twenty-six Asian countries and Australasian states, and the PRC is not only a founding member but also a driving force in the international nongovernmental, nonprofit organization.

Permanent headquarters are located in Boao, Hainan, in southern China. According to Article 3 of the BFA Charter, the BFA was designed to promote and strengthen economic exchanges, interaction, and cooperation within the region and between the region and other parts of the world. Article 3 also stipulates that the BFA is to "provide high-level venues for dialogues between government leaders, private enterprises, academia, and regional associations, in order to discuss, exchange, and develop ideas in the scope of economic, social, environmental and related issues." The most significant issues are discussed at its annual general meetings, and the BFA sponsors other meetings and forums that address other Asian-related concerns and issues, such as the Youth Forum in 2010, the International Capital Conference in 2011, the Asia Financial Cooperation Conference in 2012, the SME Conference (for small and medium-sized enterprises) in 2013, and the Energy, Resources and Sustainable Development Conference in 2014.[13] Clearly, the BFA has become a significant platform for Asian leaders, influential enterprises, and academics to engage in comprehensive dialogue over a wide range of issues.

Chinese leaders and government officials regularly participate in BFA annual meetings, and numerous other political leaders, business tycoons, and prestigious academics are invited as well. In 2008, when the BFA was also celebrating the thirtieth anniversary of China's open-door policy, the twentieth anniversary of Hainan Province's Special Economic Area, and the opening of the 2008 Olympics in Beijing, the ROC's then vice-president Vincent Siew was invited to attend.[14] This resulted in a historic meeting between the ROC vice-president and the then PRC president Hu Jintao. It was indeed a significant year for China. Meanwhile the number of BFA participants kept increasing: at BFA 2003 there were 1,000 delegates; at BFA 2008, there were 1,700; and at BFA 2015 there were 2,800. International participants have included business tycoons, such as Bill Gates at BFA 2013 and 2015 and Indian tycoon Ratan Tata at BFA 2014. Tata was the first Indian citizen to be appointed as a BFA board member. This was a unique appointment considering the strained relationship between China and India at the time.

Since the BFA's founding in 2001, it has become quite clear that China intends to use it to expand its dominance in Asian-related affairs and to further alienate the United States by blocking it from participating. According to Indonesian political analyst Bambang Suryono, "The Boao Forum will strongly push for the integration of Asia, as well as the development of a common destiny for a more closely-knit Asian community."[15]

A China-Dominated Economic Expansion

Throughout the twentieth century, China was not as economically influential in Asia as Japan, the United States, or even the four Asian "Dragons" (Hong Kong, Singapore, South Korea, Taiwan). In 2002, however, China implemented its "go global" policy, which has transformed its economic relations in the region. China's economic expansion goals are to establish a China-dominated economy throughout Southeast Asia by (1) increasing trade with Southeast Asia; (2) expanding investment in the Southeast Asian region; (3) becoming a major source for tourism revenue in the Southeast Asian region; and (4) developing an agenda for increasing geo-economic development.

Increasing Trade with Southeast Asia.   The volume of international trade reflects a country's capacity to increase its economic strength. The higher the volume of foreign trade a country engages in, the more powerful the economy of that country. Usually the bigger and more powerful countries, such as China and the United States, can engage in more international trade. Before the outbreak of the Asian financial crisis, China's economic role in Southeast Asia was insignificant because of its relatively small trade volume with other countries in the region. In 1997, China was ranked as ASEAN's eighth-largest trading partner, after Japan, the United States, Hong Kong, Taiwan, South Korea, the United Kingdom, and Germany.[16]

However, because of the sustained growth of the Chinese economy during the Asian financial crisis, in 2000 China became ASEAN's sixth-largest export market, taking 3.5 percent of the market share and becoming its fourth-largest importer with 5.2 percent of its imports.[17] In 2010, China exceeded Japan, the United States, and the Europe Union to become ASEAN's largest export market (12.1 percent market share) and import market (15.9 percent market share) (see tables 10 and 11). In 2011, Japan exceeded China as ASEAN's largest export market, but China sustained its leading position as ASEAN's largest importer in that year and was ASEAN's largest export market. In 2012, China further increased its trade with Southeast Asia, taking a 12.2 percent share of ASEAN's total exports and 16.2 percent of its total imports These trends were generally maintained throughout 2015 are predicted to continue in the coming years. A burgeoning trade with

TABLE 10 ASEAN's leading export markets (% of market share), 2010–15

	2010	2011	2012	2013	2014	2015
ASEAN	25.0	26.4	25.8	26.0	25.5	25.9
China	12.1	11.4	12.2	11.8	9.2	11.3
Japan	9.8	11.7	10	9.7	9.3	9.6
USA	9.5	8.6	8.6	9.0	9.5	10.9
EU	10.9	10.2	10	9.8	10.3	–

SOURCES: Figures for 2010 and 2011 come from ASEAN, *ASEAN Statistical Yearbook 2012* (Jakarta: ASEAN Secretariat, 2013), 78; figures for 2012 from the *ASEAN Economic Community Chart Book 2013* (Jakarta, ASEAN Secretariat, 2013), 22; and figures for 2013 to 2015 from ASEAN Statistics, http://asean.org/storage/2016/06/table21_as-of-30-Aug-2016-2.pdf, accessed October 10, 2016.

TABLE 11 Leading ASEAN importers (% of market share), 2010–15

	2010	2011	2012	2013	2014	2015
ASEAN	25.9	23.6	22.8	22.4	22.5	21.9
China	15.9	15.5	16.2	17.4.0	17.5	19.4
Japan	10.8	11.2	11.2	9.5	8.8	11.4
USA	9.0	8.1	7.5	7.4	7.3	7.6
EU	9.8	9.4	9.6	9.8	9.4	–

SOURCES: Figures for 2010 and 2011 come from ASEAN, *ASEAN Statistical Yearbook 2012* (Jakarta: ASEAN Secretariat, 2012), 78; figures for 2012 from ASEAN, *ASEAN Economic Community Chart Book 2013* (Jakarta: ASEAN Secretariat, 2013), 22; and figures for 2013 to 2015 from ASEAN Statistics, http://asean.org/storage/2016/06/table21_as-of-30-Aug-2016-2.pdf, accessed October 10, 2016.

Southeast Asia has given China a faster growth rate in international trade volume than its other leading trading partners. As the PRC's imports have increased throughout Southeast Asia, these countries have suffered greater trade deficits and have become more economically dependent on the Asian superpower. The PRC has become Southeast Asia's largest trading partner, with a share of exports now exceeding, and a share of imports far exceeding, those of Japan, the EU, and the United States. With increasing economic integration and regionalization, China will continue to maintain its trade dominance in the region.

Expanding Investment in Southeast Asia.   Foreign direct investment (FDI) is another indicator of the strength of a country's economy. The stronger a country's economy, the more foreign investment a country is able to deliver. Countries like Japan, the United States, and China all exemplify this.

Throughout the twentieth century, because of its weak economy, China invested only an insignificant amount in Southeast Asia. According to ASEAN's statistics, before the year 2000 China's share of FDI in Southeast Asia was less than 1 percent (table 12).[18] From 1995 to 2003, it was at an average of 0.29 percent per annum,

TABLE 12 China's FDI share in ASEAN (%)

	1995	2000	2005	2011	2012	2013	2014	2015
China	0.49	0.19	1.4	8.1	4.7	5.1	5.4	6.8
Japan	20.12	4.03	15.5	10.0	20.8	19.8	12.1	14.5
USA	15.38	22.79	7.7	9.4	9.7	5.7	11.3	10.2
EU	17.98	35.83	27.5	30.4	15.8	19.6	19.2	16.4

SOURCES: Figures for 1995 and 2000 come from ASEAN, *ASEAN Statistical Yearbook 2004* (Jakarta: ASEAN Secretariat, 2004), 146; figures for 2005 from *ASEAN Statistical Yearbook 2012* (Jakarta: ASEAN Secretariat, 2012); figures for 2011, 2012, and 2013 from ASEAN Statistics table 27, "Top ten sources of foreign direct investment inflows in ASEAN," www.asean.org/wp-content/uploads/images/2015/January/foreign_direct_investment_statistic/Table%20 27.pdf, accessed February 10, 2015; and figures for 2013–15 from ASEAN Statistics, http://asean.org/storage/2015/09/Table-272.pdf, accessed October 10, 2016.

whereas the United States had an average of 16.47 percent at that time and Japan came second with 12.90 percent of Southeast Asia's FDI.[19]

Since 2010, China has begun to expand its investment in ASEAN. As a result its total FDI gradually expanded from 1.4 percent in 2005 to 8.1 percent in 2011. It did decline in 2012 to 4.7 percent, but in 2014 it went up to 5.4 percent, and in 2015 it increased again to 6.8 percent (table 12). Since 2011, China has become the third-largest foreign investor in Southeast Asia, a dramatic change from its status in the late twentieth century. Given a growing national economy, China will without a doubt continue to increase its regional economic significance and investment in Southeast Asia.

Becoming a Major Source for Tourism Revenue in Southeast Asia.   Tourism is another indicator that can exemplify a country's economic strength. The stronger a country's economy, the more tourists it will attract, both domestically and internationally. The more one country promotes another country's tourism, the more important that country becomes to the country that is hosting the tourists. Throughout the twentieth century, Europeans, Americans, Japanese, and residents of the four Asian Dragon countries were the largest contributors to the Southeast Asian tourist industry. At that time, China was insignificant in ASEAN's tourism. In 1995, Chinese visitors to Southeast Asian countries were only 2.8 percent of the market share in the region, compared with Japan's 11.1 percent, Taiwan's 7.2 percent, and America's 4.9 percent.[20]

Since the turn of the century, the numbers of Chinese tourists have increased greatly throughout Southeast Asia. In 2000, China had a market share of 5.9 percent, which increased to 6.3 percent in 2007, 10.4 percent in 2012, and 12.4 percent in 2014 (table 13). However, it should be noted that even in 2000 the 5.9 percent share meaning that of individual countries it was the second-largest source, after Japan, of tourists arriving in Southeast Asia. Since 2007, it has achieved a 6.3 percent share and become the individual country constituting the largest source of

TABLE 13　Percent share in visitor arrivals to ASEAN countries, by country of origin

	1995	2000	2005	2007	2011	2012	2013	2014
China	2.8	5.9	5.9	6.3	9.0	10.4	12.4	12.4
Japan	11.1	9.9	5.9	5.9	4.5	4.8	4.8	4.8
USA	4.9	5.0	4.4	4.1	3.5	3.3	3.1	3.1
EU	14.5	13.6	11.3	12.5	12.1	9.1	8.5	8.8

SOURCES: Figures for 1995 and 2000 are from ASEAN, *ASEAN Statistical Yearbook, 2004* (Jakarta: ASEAN Secretariat, 2004), 228–29; figures for 2005 and 2007 from ASEAN, *ASEAN Statistical Yearbook, 2012* (Jakarta: ASEAN Secretariat, 2012), 168; figures for 2011 and 2012 from ASEAN Statistics, table 30, "Top Ten Country/Regional Sources of Visitors to ASEAN," www.asean.org/wp-content/uploads/images/resources/2014/Jan/StatisticUpdate28Jan/Tourism%20Update/Table%2030.pdf, accessed February 10, 2015; and figures for 2012 to 2014 from ASEAN Statistics, www.asean.org/storage/2015/11/tourism/Table_30.pdf, accessed October 10, 2016.

international tourist arrivals in Southeast Asia (ASEAN tourist industry). Since 2007, the percentage of Chinese tourists in Southeast Asia has increased significantly and continues to grow, whereas the percentages of Japanese and American tourists in the region have been in decline. This trend, which is expected to continue for years to come, illustrates another way that China is exerting dominance in the region.

Developing an Agenda for Geo-Economic Development.　In 1989, the Asia-Pacific Economic Cooperation (APEC) forum began. The United States at first dominated this forum. But between 2000 and 2008, because of President Bush's involvement in antiterrorism diplomacy, American leadership was often absent from APEC meetings. Not until July 2009, at the annual ASEAN Regional Forum, when former US secretary of state Hillary Clinton announced implementation of the "Returning to Asia Policy," did the United States resume taking interest in Asia-Pacific affairs. Since then, high-level officials from the United States have reiterated this policy at various international events. In January 2012, US president Barack Obama announced that by 2020 the United States would be reconsidering its global military strategy by deploying 60 percent of its military in the Asia-Pacific.[21]

During the Bush administration, when American presence in Asia was in decline, China was expanding its economic relations and political influence in Southeast Asia. In November 2000, at the Fourth ASEAN-China Summit, Chinese premier Zhu Rongji proposed a free trade area with ASEAN. In November 2001, it was officially announced, and on November 4, 2002, it was enacted at the Sixth ASEAN-China Summit. In 2010, ASEAN laid the foundation for its senior members to participate in the ASEAN-China Free Trade Area (AFTA), and in 2015 newer members gained membership.[22] Although AFTA is essentially an economically oriented agreement, political influence in the region came with it. The geo-economic platform allowed China to build a closer relationship with ASEAN countries.

In November 2012, Xi Jinping became the secretary general of the Chinese Communist Party (CCP), and in March 2013 he became the PRC's president.[23] As president he continued China's expansion policy in neighboring Southeast Asia. In September 2013, during his visit to Kazakhstan, he proposed the New Silk Road Economic Belt, the land-based component of his "One Belt, One Road" development strategy to link China through central and western Asia to Europe. In October 2013, in a speech at the Indonesian parliament, he proposed the maritime component of this strategy, the Twenty-First Century Maritime Silk Road, and declared his intention to draw on the China-ASEAN Maritime Cooperation Fund in order to accomplish China's grand development plan.

Xi reiterated this aggressive geo-economic strategy in November 2014 at the APEC Summit and then again in 2015 at the BFA. According to him, China would be investing US$50 billion into the Asian Infrastructure Investment Bank (AIIB) and US$40 billion into the Silk Road Fund—signaling Xi's intentions of making rising China the "center of a new Asian order."[24] Despite resistance from the United States, the AIIB got a resounding positive response from Southeast Asian countries and major European countries, including the United Kingdom, Germany, France, and Italy.[25] On April 15, 2015, China announced that fifty-seven countries were founding members of the AIIB.

Around the same time, Chinese premier Li Keqiang was also expanding China's financial diplomacy in Southeast Asia. In November 2014, when Li visited Myanmar for the Twenty-Fifth ASEAN Summit, the announced that China would provide ten ASEAN members US$20 billion in soft loans for infrastructure projects.[26] In December 2014, Li attended the fifth summit of the Greater Mekong Subregion (GMS) in Bangkok, where he pledged another huge amount, US$11.5 billion, to the five GMS neighboring countries,[27] including US$1 billion in funding for interconnected infrastructure, US$490 million in aid to alleviate poverty, and US$10 billion in special loans.[28] Li also announced that China would help Thailand build its first eight-hundred-kilometer standard-gauge railway line, which would cost an estimated US$10.6 billion.[29] In addition to rail cooperation, the Chinese premier pledged to help prevent flooding in the area by investing US$16.4 million to dredge waterways along the Mekong River.[30]

In addition to the "One Belt, One Road" geo-economic strategy and increasing financial assistance to Southeast Asian countries, there are reports that China is proposing to undertake the ambitious strategy of building a megatransportation system that will link up China and Southeast Asia.[31] This will help the Southeast Asian countries improve their local infrastructures and economies and will also expand China's economic and political influence in the region.

Challenges for China's Expansion Strategy in Southeast Asia

Yet even as China is aggressively increasing its expansion strategy in Southeast Asia, it is facing four major challenges.

Southeast Asian Perceptions of a Chinese Threat.   China's expansionist policy to Southeast Asia has won friends throughout the region, but the rising hegemonic power does not seem to be winning great respect from its southern neighbors. This is mainly because of the escalation of China's territorial disputes with Southeast Asian countries in the South China Sea. Unlike the United States, which is generally considered to be a stabilizing power in Southeast Asia, China is often regarded as a threat to the countries throughout the region. This is the first challenge that China must face.

Despite the DOC and the COC that were signed between China and ASEAN, conflict continues with Vietnam and the Philippines over the sovereignty of disputed islands and reefs in the South China Seas. On May 2, 2014, China unilaterally placed a HD-981 oil rig in Block 143 of Vietnam's Exclusive Economic Zone. China then protected itself by moving in almost eighty ships, including People's Liberation Army navy warships. The situation worsened when Vietnam dispatched its Coast Guard to defend its territorial jurisdiction and the Chinese commander ordered its ships to use water cannons to deliberately damage the Vietnamese vessels. In this case Chinese aggression also caused several injuries to the Vietnamese crew.

China and Vietnam held a series of meetings after the incident. However, in June 2014, during a press conference, Chinese foreign minister spokesman Hong Lei maintained China's firm position that they had deployed the oil rig within China's traditional territory. ASEAN foreign ministers also issued public statements expressing serious concerns over China's actions in the South China Seas and urged all parties to abide by international laws and regulations, including the DOC, the COC, and the United Nations Convention on the Law of the Sea. Although the statement did not mention China by name, it implicitly expressed support for Vietnam.[32] Japan and the United States extended their support to Vietnam by characterizing China's actions as provocative.

The Vietnamese initiated a nationwide anti-China movement, protesting against the Chinese "invasion" of Vietnam's territorial waters. In southern Vietnam, violent protesters even took over a number of foreign factories and shops and destroyed their doors, windows, and internal equipment.[33] Unfortunately, the majority of businesses damaged were Taiwanese-owned factories and shops, because protesters mistakenly regarded them as Chinese owned. One Taiwanese manager working in Vietnam said in an interview that the Vietnamese protests were actually aimed at Chinese staff working in Taiwanese-owned factories, making the Taiwanese and their properties scapegoats in the incidents.[34] Vietnam had held anti-China campaigns earlier in 2012 and again in 2013 over a similar sovereignty dispute in the South China Seas. But the May 2014 protest was the largest to ever be held in typically Buddhist Vietnam and coincided with the escalation of tremendous anti-Chinese sentiment.

China has threatened not only Vietnam but also the Philippines. During their annual security talks in 2015, the Philippines' foreign undersecretary Evan Garcia and top US diplomat for East Asia Daniel Russel made a joint statement in a press conference that China's land reclamation in the disputed South China Seas was "massive" and "a clear violation" of the 2002 accord. They did however support the freedom to navigate seas that were not under any country's jurisdiction.[35] In early July 2016, when the Permanent Court of Arbitration in the Hague made the ruling in favor of the Philippines and against China's South China Seas claims, Filipino activists held a protest rally in front of the Chinese Consulate in Manila, calling for a "Chexit" and demanding that China pull out of Philippine territorial waters.[36]

In July 2016, the Philippines' position changed when President Rodrigo Duterte came to power. In late September 2016 in Hanoi he stated that he wanted to suspend ongoing joint military maneuvers with the United States, the Philippines' long-standing ally, in the disputed South China Seas. From his inauguration on, he took an aggressive attitude toward then president Barak Obama and US policies in Asia.[37] In September 2016, as a result of these aggressions, Obama, while attending the ASEAN Summit in Vientiane, canceled meetings with Duterte.[38] This move may change the political relationship between the Philippines and the United States and between the Philippines and China. In any case, many Southeast Asian countries seem to be very concerned about the revival of an aggressive Chinese Empire.

Confrontation with Major Powers in the Region.   China's second challenge is to confront the increasing involvement of other major powers in Southeast Asia, such as Japan and the United States. Japan has also recently been engaging in territorial disputes with China over the Diaoyu Islands (in Chinese) or Senkaku Islands (in Japanese) in the East China Seas. In December 2012, when Japanese prime minister Shinzo Abe took office, he began a counter-China policy, which quickly escalated tensions between Japan and China. Over the last three years, Mr. Abe has visited most Southeast Asian countries and promised more assistance to the countries in the region. After the prime minister's successful visit to the United States in late April 2015, Japan also strengthened its military ties with the United States.[39] In early February 2015, Japan's defense minister, General Nakatani, also stated that Japan was "deepening its cooperation with the US" and that the situation in the South China Seas had had an impact on their national security.[40] General Nakatani also indicated that Japan was committed to enhancing Vietnam's and the Philippines' surveillance capabilities.

Since July 2009, the United States has taken an even stronger position in Southeast Asia, particularly since Secretary of State Hillary Clinton announced the Asia rebalancing policy. In July 2010, at the Forty-Third ASEAN Foreign Ministers' Meeting, Secretary Clinton stressed that the United States would stay in Asia because of its "national interest in freedom of navigation, the maintenance of peace and stability, and respect for international law in the South China Sea. . . . The US shares these interests not only with ASEAN members but with other maritime nations and the broader international community."[41]

In November 2011, during his participation in the Sixth East Asia Summit (EAS), together with most Southeast Asian leaders, US president Barack Obama directly confronted Chinese premier Wen Jiabao over China's recent expansion in the South China Seas. Barack Obama was the first US president to attend the EAS.[42] In January 2012, President Obama further announced that by 2020 the United States would be deploying 60 percent of its military to the Asia-Pacific area, a measure that was directly aimed at increased Chinese aggression in the region. In April 2014, on his Asian trip, in a discussion of the Philippines' issues involving the resource-rich Spratly Islands, President Obama said, "Our commitment to defend the Philippines is ironclad and the United States will keep its commitment, because allies never stand alone. . . . International law must be upheld. Freedom of navigation must be preserved. . . . Disputes must be resolved peacefully and not by intimidation or by force."[43] In early April 2015, President Obama also declared that "where we get concerned with China is when it is not necessarily abiding by international norms and rules and is using its sheer size and muscle to force countries into subordinate positions."[44]

Members of the US congress also expressed a strong opposition toward China's recent land reclamation and expansion in the Spratly Islands. In mid-March 2015, four leading US senators (John McCain, Bob Corker, Jack Reed, and Bob Menendez) wrote letters to US secretary of state John Kerry and US secretary of defense Ash Carter, indicating that China's recent actions in the South China Sea were "a direct challenge, not only to the interests of the United States and the region, but to the entire international community."[45] They also claimed that the United States should take "specific actions" to slow down or stop China's land reclamation activities.[46]

Given the recent stance of Japan and the United States, speculation has risen that the partners are developing a containment policy toward China, thus escalating the possibility of a confrontation between China and major powers in Southeast Asia. This is a true challenge that China has to seriously face.

The Widening Economic Gap between China and Southeast Asia. Since the beginning of the century, China has improved its economic relations with Southeast Asian countries. It has also exhibited a more accelerated economic development than its southern neighbors. This has widened the economic gap between China and most countries in Southeast Asia. In 2000, as exhibited in table 14, China's GDP per capita was US$949, only slightly higher than that of the four least developed countries in Southeast Asia, Cambodia, Laos, Myanmar, and Vietnam. But as China's economy has continued to grow, its GDP per capita has risen. In 2015, China's GDP per capita reached US$7,925, falling behind only that of the three most modern nations in Southeast Asia, Singapore, Brunei, and Malaysia. Given China's huge population of 1.3 billion, it is clear that China's economic strength and potential far exceeds that of the entire Southeast Asian region, whose population totals only six hundred million people. As the table shows, in 2013, compared with all the other Southeast Asian countries, China enjoyed the second-highest economic growth rate. Its economy is projected to increase in the near future as the economic gap between China and Southeast Asia continues to widen.

Table 14 also shows that while China widens its gap with the economically weaker countries, it is narrowing its gap with Malaysia, Brunei, and Singapore, which are still ahead of the hegemonic power. In 2015, for example, China's GDP per capita was US$7,925, only a little less than Malaysia's (US$9,657). This greatly contrasts with China's GDP in 2000, which was only US$949, whereas Malaysia's was US$3,844 that same year. Thailand's GDP per capita in 1996 was US$3,134, much higher than China's US$703 in that same year. However, in 2011, for the first time, China's GDP per capita (US$5,447) exceeded Thailand's (US$5,116). Since then, the GDP per capita gap between the two countries has continued to widen. In 2015, China's GDP per capita was US$7,925, compared with Thailand's US$5,737 for the same year. Given China's massive economy and growth rate, compared with that of its neighbors in the South, a feeling of unfairness has been growing in the region.

Rising Tensions between New Chinese Immigrants and Local People.   Finally, tensions between new Chinese immigrants and native people in Southeast Asian countries have increasingly become a challenge that the Chinese must face. At the turn of the century, when China began expanding its trade and investment into Southeast Asia, Chinese immigrants began moving into most of the countries, bringing with them Chinese products, shops, restaurants, hotels, and casinos. Some of these Chinese investments have been very controversial, considering the massive environmental problems that construction projects such as dams and highways have caused. These investments have also caused local people to lose their land and jobs.

China's recent increasing investments in Laos exemplify this. One Laotian businessman from the Lao People's Democratic Republic stated he was afraid his people were gradually losing their autonomy, since they were gradually losing their land and wealth to Chinese expansion in their countries.[47] One Hong

TABLE 14 Economic gaps between China and Southeast Asian countries, 1996–2011
(GDP per capita in US$ and GDP growth rates)

	China	Brunei	Cambodia	Indonesia	Laos	Malaysia	Myanmar	Philippines	Singapore	Thailand	Vietnam
1996	703	17,096	312	1,167	393	4,766	109	1,184	25,127	3,134	337
1998	821	11,961	268	488	244	3,257	144	896	20,892	1,900	361
2000	949	18,469	288	807	375	3,844	192	978	23,007	1,976	403
2002	1,135	17,158	309	932	369	3,884	136	956	21,098	2,001	440
2004	1,490	21,863	392	1,105	487	4,877	191	1,039	25,791	2,501	555
2006	2,069	29,922	515	1,636	645	5,902	233	1,351	30,053	3,164	725
2009	3,744	28,454	735	2,362	913	7,215	538	1,828	37,960	3,946	1,128
2011	5,447	42,431	881	3,497	1,262	9,962	868	2,339	51,247	5,116	1,404
	6,808	39,678	1,046	3,466	1,505	10,420	916	2,706	55,183	5,678	1,908
2013	(7.7%)	(-1.8%)	(7.0%)	(5.8%)	(8.2%)	(4.7%)	(7.5%)	7.2%)	(3.9%)	(2.9%)	(5.4%)
2014	7,587	41,505	1,105	3,526	1,741	11,153	1,277	2,854	55,904	5,892	2,053
	7,925	30,942	1,198	3,357	1,831	9,657	1,246	2,850	52,744	5,737	2,109
2015	(5.9)	(-0.6)	(7.1)	(4.8)	(7.6)	(5.0)	(7.1)	(5.8)	(2.0)	(2.8)	(6.7)

SOURCES: China's figures are from World Bank, "GDP per Capita (Current $US)," http://data.worldbank.org/indicator/NY.GDP.PCAP.CD, and "GDP Growth (Annual %)," accessed March 12, 2015, http://data.worldbank.org/indicator/NY.GDP.MKTP.KD.ZG. Figures for the 1996 to 2006 ASEAN countries statistics come from ASEAN, *ASEAN Statistical Yearbook 2003* (Jakarta: ASEAN Secretariat, 2003) and *ASEAN Statistical Yearbook 2008* (Jakarta: ASEAN Secretariat, 2008); figures for 2009 to 2013 ASEAN GDP per capita figures are from ASEAN, table 7, "Gross Domestic Product per Capita in ASEAN, at Current Prices (Nominal), in US Dollars as of December 2014," www.asean.org/storage/2015/01/macroeconomics/T7-dec14.pdf; ASEAN's 2013 economic growth rates are from ASEAN, table 2, "Selected Key ASEAN Macroeconomic Indicators as of December 2014," www.asean.org/storage/images/2015/January/ selected_key_indicators/table2_as%20of%20December%202014_R2.pdf; 2015 growth rates are from World Bank, "GDP Growth, Annual Percent," http://data.worldbank.org/indicator/ NY.GDP.MKTP.KD.ZG, accessed February 12, 2015.

Kong media outlet described China's recent economic expansion in Laos and subsequent tensions between Chinese immigrants and the Laotian people as "reckless nationalism."[48]

Different lifestyles and cultures have also caused clashes between new Chinese immigrants and local people. For example, since the turn of the century, roughly one million Chinese have relocated in Singapore, making it the country that has taken on the largest number of Chinese immigrants. However, there is a great gap between them and local Singaporeans, mainly because of their ignorance regarding the local culture and the strict Singaporean legal system. In the May 2011 general election, the ruling People's Action Party (PAP) suffered a loss in one of its group's representative constituencies.[49] This was mainly because many Singaporeans were not satisfied with the perennial PAP government's immigration policy. When asked about the new Chinese immigrants, one local Singaporean said, "Singaporeans look down on mainlanders as country bumpkins and they look down on us because we don't speak proper Chinese."[50]

Two decades of firsthand field study data collection in all of the Southeast Asian countries except East Timor clearly show rising tensions between new Chinese immigrants and locals in Singapore, Thailand, Malaysia, Indonesia, and the Philippines. Recently anti-immigration sentiment has been increasing in Thailand as well. However, currently this seems to be aimed more at cheap migrant labor from neighboring Myanmar, Laos, and Cambodia than at the Chinese.[51]

TAIWAN'S SURVIVAL STRATEGY IN SOUTHEAST ASIA: MAINTAINING TAIWAN'S POLITICAL ECONOMY IN THE REGION

Taiwan's Political Survival: Sustaining Substantial Relations with Southeast Asia

In contrast to China, with its aggressive Southeast Asian expansion strategy, the comparatively smaller and diplomatically weaker Taiwan has had to develop a survival strategy in order to maintain its political economy in the region and to develop partnerships with its Southeast Asian neighbors. In the political arena, Taiwan's goal is to sustain the substantial relationships that it already maintains with major countries in Southeast Asia. This entails (1) rejecting an antagonistic "scorched-earth diplomacy" such as that practiced by former president Chiu Shuibian, and adopting the "diplomatic truce" approach developed by President Ma Ying-jeou, and (2) increasing Taiwan's political interactions with major countries throughout Southeast Asia.

Transforming "Scorched-Earth Diplomacy" into a "Diplomatic Truce". Since the turn of the century, Taiwan has experienced several transfers of political power.

The Democratic Progressive Party (DPP) was elected for two terms from 2000 to 2008, and the Chinese Nationalist Party (the Kuomintang, or KMT) was elected to serve for the next two terms, from 2008 to 2016. DPP president Chen Shui-bian and KMT president Ma Ying-jeou took very different approaches to dealing with China. The DPP administration took a more antagonistic political approach that negatively affected Taiwan's relations throughout Southeast Asia.

During his presidency, President Chen initiated his "scorched-earth diplomacy," a zero-sum game in which Taiwan went to great lengths to induce China's diplomatic partners to defect in the hopes of increasing Taiwan's number of diplomatic partners at China's expense. This strategy was developed with the intention of gaining more political-economic ground for Taiwan. Some scholars, such as Yasuhiro Matsuda, contend that Chen's diplomacy was mainly instigated by a change in DPP internal politics, while others such as Elizabeth Larus argue that Taiwan was using a soft-power approach to win more international recognition.[52] In any event it backfired, causing contention and deterioration in cross-Straits and Southeast Asian relations—and irritating the US government to the point that when Chen was on a May 2006 diplomatic visit to Latin America, it refused to allow his aircraft a refueling stop in San Francisco.[53] China already mistrusted President Chen because of his promotion of "Taiwanization" policies, which China perceived as controversial and as a possible move toward Taiwanese claims of independence, so it ramped up its own competitive maneuvers by blocking Taiwan in many international arenas and made aggressive diplomatic strides, causing Taiwan to lose nine of its diplomatic partnerships and thereby reducing the number of countries with which it had official diplomatic relations from thirty to twenty-one.

In 2002, despite his continuing implementation of Taiwan's "southward policy" of cultivating relations with Southeast Asia, Chen's confrontations with China destabilized Taiwan's relations with its Southeast Asian allies.[54] During the 1990s, Taiwan had had frequent exchanges with its Southeast Asian neighbors, with several visits from high-level government officials, including former president Lee Teng-hui's visits to three Southeast Asian countries in February 1994. Also from 1991 to 1996, Indonesia's former state minister for research and technology, Mr. Habibie, visited Taiwan three times. During Chen's administration, these types of exchanges were greatly reduced. In mid-August 2002, when vice-president Annett Lu paid an unexpected visit to Indonesia, under duress from China, the Indonesian government publicly announced that Taiwan was an integral part of the PRC.

In May 2008, when President Ma Ying-jeou took office, he initiated a diplomatic truce with China. This improved relations not only across the Taiwan Straits but also with one of Taiwan's longest political and economic allies, the United States. His rationale was that given China's rising influence around the world, it was better to show goodwill toward the mainland, since this would result in a more stable and peaceful environment for Taiwan. Ma's approach greatly reduced

Chinese obstruction and allowed Taiwan to operate more freely in international arenas. During his administration from 2008 to 2016, Taiwan maintained all but one of its diplomatic partnerships and made great strides with its diplomacy in Southeast Asia.

On May 20, 2016, President Tsai Ing-wen was sworn into office. She immediately initiated a "new southward policy" aimed at strengthening Taiwan's overall relations in Southeast Asia to an even greater extent than her predecessors had done. This may benefit Taiwan's international relationships, but since the president is unwilling to accept the 1992 Consensus, the success of this policy is in a very tenuous position. Since her inauguration, relations across the Taiwan Straits have deteriorated. Over coming years, China may seriously obstruct Taiwan's political and economic activities in Southeast Asia.

Engaging in More Political Interactions with Southeast Asia. Throughout President Ma's administration, cross-Strait relations were more peaceful, so Taiwan was able to engage in more political interactions with countries of Southeast Asia. Taiwan received visits from high-level government officials from Southeast Asia's most significant countries and engaged in high-level bilateral talks and meetings. However, these were usually not publicized in the media.

In 2010, for instance, Taiwan and Singapore entered talks on a bilateral economic partnership agreement. On November 7, 2013, both parties signed the Agreement between Singapore and the Separate Customs Territory of Taiwan, Penghu, Kinmen and Matsu on Economic Partnership (ASTEP).[55] Then on March 25, 2015, after receiving notice of the death of Singapore's former prime minister Lee Kuan Yew, under a status of special circumstances, President Ma Ying-jeou made a private trip to pay his last respects to the Singaporean leader and founding father of the city-state. In early November 2015, Singapore hosted a historical meeting between President Ma Ying-jeou and his Chinese counterpart, President Xi Jinping. However, it did not result in any agreements being signed between the two leaders.[56] Singapore has been the only country so far to win the trust of both of these hostile governments, which indeed exemplifies the special relationship they have.

Vietnam has been the Southeast Asian country that has received the largest investment from Taiwan. After President Ma came to office, Taiwan's relationship with Vietnam also greatly improved. In January 2009, Taiwan and Vietnam signed the Scientific and Technological Cooperation Agreement. In September 2011, Minister of Finance Lee Sush-der visited Vietnam and witnessed the signing of Taiwan and Vietnam's Memorandum of Understanding on Financial Cooperation; and in May 2012, Taiwan and Vietnam signed the Memorandum of Understanding on Tourism Cooperation.[57] In November 2012 the first Taiwan-Vietnam Conference on Tourism Cooperation was held in Taipei. According to Vietnam's statistics, 409,385 Taiwanese visited Vietnam in 2013, an increase of 13.39 percent from 2012, making Taiwan Vietnam's fifth-largest source of international tourists. In 2013, more than ninety thousand Vietnamese visited Taiwan, a 40 percent increase from 2012.[58] In 2014, Taiwan held approximately 150,000 Vietnamese migrant workers, ninety thousand Vietnamese wives, and five thousand Vietnamese students.[59] The two countries are expected to continue building close ties in the years to come.

Taiwan's political relationship with Indonesia is also noteworthy. From 2009 to 2013 there were several high-level exchanges between the two countries, including visits from Indonesia's minister of education and minister of economics in 2010; in 2011 the minister of economics returned to Indonesia. In 2013, the minister of finance, the minister of the Economic Development Council, and the minister of education visited.[60] The chair of the Overseas Chinese Affairs Council visited in 2009 and 2012, and the chair of the Mainland Affairs Council visited in 2009 and 2013. Over the same years, high-level Indonesian officials who visited Taiwan included the minister of fisheries, Fadel Muhammad, in 2010 and 2011; the minister of labor, Muhaimin Iskandar, in 2011; the deputy minister for coordinating economic affairs, Rizal Lukman, in 2013; and the deputy minister of agriculture, Rusman Heriawan, in 2013. In 2010 Indonesia and Taiwan signed the "One Village, One Product, and Agri-Business Cooperation Plan," and in 2012 they signed a memorandum of understanding on cooperation with regard to immigration affairs, human trafficking, and smuggling prevention, along with an agreement on agricultural and technical cooperation .

Because of President Ma's improvement of political relations, most Southeast Asian countries granted Taiwanese citizens either visa-free privileges, as in Singapore and Malaysia, or arrival visas, as in Thailand, Indonesia, Cambodia, Laos, Brunei, and Timor Leste.[61] In 2011, Malaysia was the last major country in Southeast Asia to grant a visa-free status to Taiwanese citizens. On account of these privileges, the Taiwanese now enjoy easier access, not only to trade and invest in Southeast Asia, but also to engage in more social and cultural interactions across the region.

Since May 2016, President Tsai Ing-wen hopes to promote a much stronger relationship between Taiwan and its Southeast Asian allies. Taiwan expects to engage in more political interactions with its southern neighbors, despite possible obstruction from China.

Taiwan's Economic Survival: Strengthening Taiwan's Economic Links with Southeast Asia

By the 1990s, Taiwan had already established a sound economic foundation in Southeast Asia. If Taiwan's was to continue its economic success in the region was to continue, it would need to develop stronger economic links with its southern neighbors and continue signing economically oriented agreements and memo-randums. In September 2011 Taiwan and Vietnam signed an agreement on cus-toms administrative cooperation, and in October 2014 Taiwan and the Philippines signed a memorandum of understanding on the promotion of trade and invest-ment. With the signing of these official documents, politically isolated Taiwan could possibly do three things to strengthen its economic relations in Southeast Asia: (1) strengthen Taiwan's economic relations with Southeast Asian countries; (2) build a platform for regional economic interactions; (3) continue attempts at joining regional economic blocs.

Strengthening Taiwan's Economic Relations in Southeast Asia.   As indicated ear-lier, foreign investment and the volume of foreign trade are two important indica-tors of a country's economic strength and relationships with other countries. The more foreign trade and investment one country engages in with another country, the closer the economic relations of the two countries.

Prior to 1980, Taiwan did not engage much in trade and investment in Southeast Asia because of its comparatively low level of economic development. However, from the mid-1980s on, Taiwan began strengthening its economic relations with Southeast Asia, partly because of the appreciation of Taiwan's currency against the American dollar and partly because of Taiwan's rapid economic development that began in the early 1980s.[62]

In 1990 Taiwan's trade with Southeast Asia's ten ASEAN countries totaled only US$11.02 billion, but in 1995 this increased to US$25.54 billion, and in 2000 it in-creased to US$38.71 billion.[63] With the implementation of its southward policy, Taiwan has continued to augment its trade throughout Southeast Asia. In 2005, its total trade volume was US$48.53 billion. In 2010 it increased to US$70.84 billion and in 2014 to US$93.64 billion. However in 2015, there was a noticeable decline to US$79.3 billion (table 15). Taiwan's trade share with Southeast Asia greatly ex-panded in from 9 percent in 1990 to 13.4 percent in 2000 and 15.6 percent in 2015 (table 15). Another significant point is that since 2010 Southeast Asia is Taiwan's second-largest trading partner, exceeded only by China.

In September 2014, at the opening ceremony of the 2014 Asian MICE (Meet-ings, Incentives, Conferences, and Events) Forum, W. S. Chiang (Taiwan's deputy director of the Bureau of International Trade) pointed out that Southeast Asia was gradually becoming a great exhibition platform for global enterprises and manu-facturing industries and that the Taiwanese government would continue to make efforts to develop the economy in this part of the world.[64] This statement exempli-fies how Taiwan has been sustaining efforts to strengthen its economic relations with countries throughout Southeast Asia.

The concentration of Taiwan's foreign investment also shows how the island is strengthening economic relations with Southeast Asia. Since the early 1990s,

TABLE 15 Taiwan's Southeast Asian trade totals (in US$ billion) and trade share (%), 1988–2015

Year	1990	1995	2000	2005	2008	2010	2012	2013	2014	2015
Trade volume	11.02	25.54	38.71	48.53	64.60	70.84	88.07	91.37	93.64	79.3
Share of total trade	9.0	11.8	13.4	12.7	12.9	13.4	15.3	15.8	15.9	15.6

Source: Taiwan's trade share and totals with Southeast Asia calculated at Bureau of Foreign Trade, Ministry of Economics, Republic of China, http://cus93.trade.gov.tw/FSCI/, accessed October 10, 2016.

Taiwan has gone from not having much foreign investment in Southeast Asia to greatly expanding investment throughout the region.[65] In 1994, Taiwan's investment in Southeast Asia peaked to US$5.1 billion, but after 1998 and the Asian financial crisis it went into decline. The 1990s were actually Taiwan's golden age of investment in Southeast Asia, and at that time Taiwan was one of the leading foreign investors in the region—especially in Vietnam, where for more than two decades Taiwan was been either its largest or its second-largest source of foreign investment.

Since the beginning of the century, Taiwan's investment in Southeast Asia has seen many ups and downs (as exemplified in table 16). It peaked in 2008, when Taiwan made a combined regional investment of US$12.4 billion. Three years after the global financial meltdown in 2008, Taiwan's investment in Southeast Asia went into decline, but in 2012 it again expanded to US$5.8 billion. However, from 2013 to 2015, investment totals fluctuated (table 16). Despite these fluctuations over the last two decades, the table demonstrates Taiwan's continued interest in investing in Southeast Asia.

Building a Platform to Connect Taiwan with Southeast Asia.   Over the last three decades, Taiwan has initiated a series of policies to stimulate economic growth and strengthen economic relations with countries in the Asia-Pacific region. During the 1990s, the then ruling KMT government proposed the establishment of an Asia-Pacific Regional Operations Center (APROC) to make Taiwan a hub for regional economic activities. This proposal, however, was not successful because of the democratic transfer of power to the DPP in May 2000, when President Chen Shui-bian assumed office. The new government then proposed the "Green Silicon Island" as the new plan for Taiwan's future economic development. Unfortunately, in May 2008, when KMT president Ma Ying-jeou took office, the plan was discontinued.

At first President Ma tried to revive the APROC, but in 2012 he proposed the Free Economic Pilot Zones (FEPZs). Its main goal was to make Taiwan a free economic zone so that it could strengthen economic relations with countries throughout the Asia-Pacific region. The main FEPZ directives were to implement deregulation, open markets, internationalization, institutional reform, and international

TABLE 16 Taiwan's 1990–2015 investment in Southeast Asia (in US$ billion)

1959–89	1990	1994	1997	2000	2004	2008	2010	2012	2013	2014	2015
5.1	4.1	5.1	4.8	1.6	1.9	12.4	2.3	5.8	1.3	2.7	2.1

SOURCE: "Wǒguó zài dōng xié gèguó tóuzī tǒngjì biǎo" [China's investment statistics in the ASEAN countries], http://twbusiness.nat.gov.tw/old/pdf/inv_3.pdf.

alignment in order to allow the free movement of money, people, and goods. Ma claimed that FEPZs would align Taiwan's open market with other regional economies, provide tax incentives for land acquisition, promote cross-border industrial cooperation, and build a high-quality environment for business. August 2013 marked the beginning of the FEPZs' first stage, which included six of Taiwan's harbors. The second stage required several laws to get passed, but a series of disputes between the KMT and its DPP opposition stopped the proposal from going any further.

Now President Tsai Ing-wen's administration is implementing the new southward policy, making an even stronger attempt to expand Taiwan's overall relations throughout Southeast Asia. Although Taiwan's internal political disputes occasionally affect the implementation of economic development initiatives, Taiwan has no other choice but to go forward.

Continuing Attempts to Join Regional Economic Blocs.   Southeast Asian countries are represented by the ten members of ASEAN.[66] This organization has successfully accomplished a number of free trade agreements with major neighboring countries, including its 10 Plus 1, 10 Plus 3, and 10 Plus 6, and it continues to expand its economic cooperation and integration.

Recently, the emergence of two more regional economic blocs has attracted a great deal of international attention. These are the Regional Comprehensive Economic Partnership (RCEP) and the Trans-Pacific Partnership (TPP). The RCEP was introduced in November 2011 at the Nineteenth ASEAN Summit and was composed of members from the 10 Plus 6[67]. In November 2012, at the Twenty-First ASEAN Summit in Cambodia, it was endorsed by all sixteen leaders of its member countries. Its goal is to build an open trade and investment environment to boost economic growth, enhance economic cooperation, and deepen economic integration throughout the region. In June 2016, the sixteen participating states completed its thirteenth round of negotiations over related issues, including stipulations regarding goods and services, investment, intellectual property, and dispute settlement. Although talks are behind schedule, progress has been going smoothly and a final draft is expected soon.

The TPP is essentially an extension of the Pacific Three Closer Economic Partnership (P3 CEP), which includes Chile, Singapore and New Zealand. In 2005 it was renamed the Trans-Pacific Strategic Economic Partnership (TPSEP, or P4) in order to include Brunei. In January 2008, The United States showed an interest in talking with the P4 countries, and when President Barack Obama assumed office in January 2009 he too reaffirmed America's commitment to the TPP. Since the end of 2014, participating countries have held nineteen formal rounds of negotiations over TPP-related issues, such as cooperation and capacity development, cross-border services, e-commerce, financial services, government procurement, intellectual property, and elimination of tariffs and other trade and investment barriers.

Although Taiwan is part of the Asia-Pacific region, it is politically isolated and therefore faces a multitude of challenges in joining these regional economic blocs. There are at least four ways a country can participate in ASEAN: as a full member, an observer, a candidate member, or a dialogue member. Over the past three decades, Taiwan has made great efforts to establish a connection with ASEAN.[68] However these have been derailed by China's ongoing political and economic obstruction,[69] which continues to threaten Taiwan's economic development.

In September 2013 the Taiwan government officially announced its interest in joining the RECP and the TPP. On February 17, 2014, at an international conference in Taipei, President Ma Ying-jeou stated that Taiwan had made it an "unshakable goal" to join the RCEP and TPP and would be "simultaneously carrying forth" a bid to join the two trade blocs as expeditiously as possible.[70] Ma also stated that in 2013 Taiwan already had a 34.4 percent total trade share with the twelve nations that were participating in TPP trade negotiations and a 56.6 percent trade share with the sixteen states negotiating the RCEP.[71] On March 29, 2015, at the Boao Forum 2015, Taiwan's vice-president Vincent Siew met with China's president Xi Jinping. The then ROC vice-president expressed Taiwan's willingness to also join the AIIB.[72] Two days later, on March 31, Taiwan's government sent an official application to join the AIIB, seeking to become a founding member of the PRC-led financial body.[73]

Although Taiwan has encountered many obstacles to gaining entrance into regional economic blocs, it has successfully accomplished free trade–like agreements with China, Singapore, and New Zealand. These include the Cross-Straits Economic Cooperation Framework Agreement (ECFA), which became effective in August 2010; the Agreement between New Zealand and the Separate Customs Territory of Taiwan, Penghu, Kinmen and Matsu on Economic Cooperation (ANZTEC), which went into effect on December 1, 2013; and ASTEP, which became effective on March 19, 2014. In March 2013, Taiwan resumed negotiations with the United States over a Trade and Investment Framework Agreement.

One study estimates that about 23 percent to 27 percent of foreign enterprises would increase their investment in Taiwan if the island was able to join these emerging economic groups in East Asia.[74] Without a doubt, Taiwan must continue striving to joining regional economic groups.

Challenges for Taiwan's Survival

Political Isolation and an Uncertain Future.   As previously evidenced, Taiwan has successfully established a substantial, stable relationship with major Southeast Asian countries. However, a substantial relationship is not equivalent to a formal diplomatic relationship. Although for more than three decades Taiwan has coped well with this awkward situation, there is still little possibility that it will change in the foreseeable future.

In the past, Taiwan's international survival was primarily due to US support and China's political and economic weaknesses. However, as China develops an increasingly robust political economy, its powerful influence over international politics, its strategic relationship with the United States, and a possible US alliance with China in international affairs make the continued survival of diplomatically isolated Taiwan questionable.

Since July 1987, when the ROC government lifted martial law, there has been an ongoing debate over whether Taiwan should unify with China, maintain the status quo, or seek independence. For decades, China has maintained that it will use military force if necessary to "liberate" Taiwan. In 1992, only 17.6 percent of the population identified exclusively as Taiwanese. However, this percentage has been steadily on the rise, increasing from 36.9 percent in 2000 to 52.7 percent in 2010 and 60.6 percent in 2014. There was a slight decline in June 2016 to 59.3 percent.[75] The percentage of Taiwan's population who identify as exclusively Chinese has also been in decline from 25.5 percent in 1992 to 3.5 percent in 2014 and 3.0 percent in June 2016. The proportion of people who identify as both Taiwanese and Chinese has also been in decline, from 46.4 percent in 1992 to 32.5 percent in 2014, but with a slight increase to 33.6 percent in June 2016.[76]

According to Chengchi University's Election Study Center, the percentage of Taiwanese in favor of maintaining the status quo but eventually moving toward independence has been steadily rising, from 8.0 percent in 1994 to 18.0 percent in 2014 and to 19 percent in June 2016, whereas the percentage of those in favor of maintaining the status quo but moving toward unification has declined from 15.6 percent in 1994 to 7.9 percent in 2014 and to 8.0 percent in June 2016.[77] Therefore, despite China's growing political and economic influence and its diplomatic and economic developments, an increase in the numbers of those claiming a Taiwanese identity has psychologically kept the island distant from the mainland.[78]

China is now Taiwan's largest economic partner, making up roughly 50 percent of its global trade and 70 percent of its FDI. On the basis of ECFA, which Taiwan and China signed in June 2010, it is likely that Taiwan will become increasingly economically dependent on China in the coming years. China intends to use economic means to accomplish its political goal of unification with Taiwan, but politically isolated Taiwan continues to focus on achieving economic growth without losing its political sovereignty.

Given the changing political economy between Taiwan and China, Taiwan's politicians and citizens face unavoidable serious challenges with regard to Taiwan's future.

Economic Marginalization and Future Development.   During the Cold War, Taiwan was branded one of the four Asian Dragons because of its great economic achievements and its early openness to the world. This chapter has demonstrated numerous examples of how the island's deepening economic relations with Southeast Asia have transcended diplomacy. During a speech at the annual dinner of the Asia Society in mid-June 2002, with regard to Taiwan's dynamic economy and vibrant democracy, former US secretary of state Colin Powell stated, "I call Taiwan a problem of a success story." Taiwan's economic achievements have brought it international prestige and have contributed to its democratization.

Since the end of the Cold War in the early 1980s, China and most Southeast Asian countries have also begun to open up to the world. These Asian countries have been actively engaging in the development of economic regionalization. But although Taiwan continues to work toward joining regional economic groups, the PRC's political obstruction keeps it marginalized. Previously, Taiwan's economic achievement was mostly due to the island's liberalness and openness, but now economic marginalization is keeping it from getting fair participation in the increasingly free and integrated Asia-Pacific market. Time will tell what survival mechanisms Taiwan will use in order to survive despite this economic marginalization.

Since the turn of the century, a number of Taiwan's macroeconomic indicators have revealed a decline in its economic development. In 2000, Taiwan's economic growth declined from 6.42 percent to 5.62 percent in 2006, to 2.23 percent in 2013. Since 2011, Taiwan's economic growth has been less than 5 percent, which is particularly striking given that by 2013 most Southeast Asian countries were enjoying growth rates of above 5 percent. Another concern with regard to Taiwan's declining economic development is that public enterprise contribution to the GDP has been below 2 percent since 2004 and government capital contribution to the GDP has steadily been in decline from 2000, when it was at 5.44 percent, to 4.13 percent in 2008 and 2.86 percent in 2014.[79] These figures show that since the turn of the century a weakness in Taiwan's public investment has seriously impeded the island's economic development. This decline has coincided with Southeast Asian economic regionalization while Taiwan remains isolated. If Taiwan continues to be economically marginalized, sustaining future economic development will be a tremendous challenge.

CONCLUSION

Taiwan's economic development has made it an international sensation and has certainly been instrumental in improving its diplomatic relations with Southeast Asian countries. Although it has enjoyed an improved political economy in the region, it continues to face serious challenges of diplomatic isolation and economic marginalization. This chapter has explored Taiwan's efforts in developing relations with its neighbors to the south. President Tsai Ing-wen's administration will need to continue to expand relations with Southeast Asia. While the new southward policy may appear promising, political isolation, economic marginalization, and China's intervention and obstruction are major barriers that Taiwan will have to face in furthering its relations with Southeast Asia. Although Taiwan does not compete against China in the international community, it cannot keep China from imposing the one-China policy that affects Taiwan's future development politically and economically.

Another noteworthy potential influence on Taiwan's relations with Southeast Asia and its relationship with China is that from the 1950s to the 1980s Asian values were practiced, promoted, and used to support political authoritarianism. This was in stark contrast to Western values, which seem to have become more universally accepted today. However, China continues to promote a culture and value system that advocates Asian values.

Since the late 1980s, many Asian countries have transitioned into democracy. In February 1986, when the People's Power Revolution overthrew former dictator Ferdinand Marcos, the Philippines was the first Asian country to adopt a democratic political system. In July 1987, after an extensive period of martial law was lifted, Taiwan also began to transition into democracy. In February 1988, President Roh Tae-woo was democratically elected as the leader of the Republic of Korea, which signified great political change. Although Thailand has theoretically been a democracy since 1932, in 1997 it revised its constitution. However, with the riots of May 1992, Thailand's democracy is still facing some challenges. Since May 1998 and the downfall of former President Suharto, Indonesia has also implemented democracy.

During the past two to three decades, Asia has demonstrated tremendous democratization. This seems to have become a universal value in the region and includes the Muslim country of Indonesia, the Catholic state of the Philippines, and Buddhist nations such as Taiwan and South Korea. Taiwan may face the difficulty of diplomatic isolation, but the island's democratic transformation has been a role model for countries in the region. This is something China and its leaders will also have to face in the future.

NOTES

1. The Republic of Vietnam (South Vietnam) was taken over in April 1975 by Communist-led North Vietnam, which ultimately unified Vietnam into one country.

2. *Pragmatic diplomacy* means that despite its diplomatic isolation the ROC government was able to establish semigovernmental offices in friendly countries in order to promote greater economic relationships.

3. On May 20, 1990, President Lee Teng-hui denounced the period of mobilization for the suppression of communist rebellion during a news conference. It occurred within a year of his inauguration as the seventh president of the ROC.

4. One expert contends that China has crafted a strategy using various nonkinetic actions to recast an overall balance of power in Asia that displaces the United States as the dominant force in the region. See Harry J. Kazianis, "Superpower Showdown: America Can Stop Chinese Aggression in Asia," *National Interest*, March 6, 2015, http://nationalinterest.org/feature/superpower-showdown-america-can-stop-chinese-aggression-asia-12368.

5. By the mid-1970s, most of Southeast Asia had switched formal diplomatic recognition to China. In August 1990, Indonesia was the first major country in the region to do so, followed by Singapore in October 1990 and Negara Brunei Darussalam in October 1991. Vietnam suspended its relations with China in the late 1970s, but in October 1991 it too restored formal relations.

6. Four of the seven elements of the Good Neighbor Policy have to do with Southeast Asia. See S. D. Muni, *China's Strategic Engagement with the New ASEAN*, IDSS Monograph No. 2 (Singapore: Institute of Defense and Strategic Studies, 2002), 16.

7. TAC was originally signed in February 1976 by ASEAN's original founding members. In December 1987 it began to include other states outside of Southeast Asia.

8. The key reason why China developed bilateralism was that it perceived the territorial disputes to be internal matters between only itself and the other clamant.

9. "China President Speaks Out on Security Ties in Asia," BBC News, May 21, 2014, www.bbc.com/news/world-asia-china-27498266.

10. Leszek Buszynski, "ASEAN, the Declaration on Conduct, and the South China Sea," *Contemporary Southeast Asia* 25, no. 3 (December 2003): 343–61.

11. Nontraditional security issues include the human trafficking of women and children, piracy on the high seas, terrorism, arms smuggling, money smuggling, money laundering, international economic crime, and cybercrime. See "Joint Declaration of ASEAN and China on Cooperation in the Field of Non-Traditional Security Issues 6th ASEAN-China Summit Phnom Penh," November 4, 2002, http://asean.org/?static_post=joint-declaration-of-asean-and-china-on-cooperation-in-the-field-of-non-traditional-security-issues-6th-asean-china-summit-phnom-penh-4-november-2002-2.

12. The first memorandum of understanding was signed in 2004 and expired in 2009.

13. The theme of the 2012 BFA was "Asia in the Changing World: Moving towards Sound and Sustainable Development"; in 2015 it was "Asia's New Future: Towards a Community of Common Destiny."

14. Vincent Siew was also the first high-level government official from Taiwan to attend a BFA meeting.

15. See "2015 Boao Forum to Unite Asia-Pacific Nations, Promote All-Win Aspiration," *Aysor*, March 27, 2015, www.aysor.am/en/news/2015/03/27/2015-Boao-Forum-to-unite-Asia-Pacific-nations-promote-all-win-aspiration/926202.

16. ASEAN, *ASEAN Statistical Yearbook 2004*, http://asean.org/?static_post=asean-statistical-yearbook-2004, 70.

17. Ibid., 78.

18. Ibid., 46.

19. Ibid.

20. Ibid., 228.

21. On June 2, 2012, at the IISS Eleventh Asian Security Summit, the US secretary of defense Leon Panetta reiterated this policy in his speech. See "The US Rebalance towards the Asia-Pacific: Leon

Panetta," June 2, 2012, https://www.iiss.org/en/events/shangri-la-dialogue/archive/sld12–43d9/first-plenary-session-2749/leon-panetta-d67b, accessed March 7, 2015.

22. The older, more senior members of ASEAN include Thailand, Malaysia, Singapore, Indonesia, the Philippines, and Brunei, whereas newer members include Vietnam, Cambodia, Laos, and Myanmar.

23. In November 2012, at the Eighteenth Central Committee of the CPC, Xi Jinping was appointed both general secretary of the CPC and chair of the CPC Central Military Commission at the same time. These posts are two of the most important positions in China's political system. In March 2013, Secretary/Chair Xi became president of the PRC.

24. Jeremy Page, "China Sees Itself at Center of New Asian Order," *Wall Street Journal*, November 9, 2014, www.wsj.com/articles/chinas-new-trade-routes-center-it-on-geopolitical-map-1415559290. The AIIB is expected to collect US$100 billion.

25. One major factor that contributed to the creation of AIIB was that the US Congress suspended a resolution to expand the voting weight of member countries in the International Monetary Fund (IMF). In 2010 China decided to establish an international financial body that it could control.

26. "China Plans to Give Loans, Aid to Mekong Neighbors," *Taipei Times*, December 22, 2014, www.taipeitimes.com/News/world/archives/2014/12/22/2003607336.

27. The five GMS neighboring countries are Vietnam, Laos, Cambodia, Thailand, and Myanmar.

28. Zheng Limin, "China to Boost Infrastructure of Neighbors with New Aid Offer," CCTV.com, December 21, 2014, http://english.cntv.cn/2014/12/21/ARTI1419129751664937.

29. Ibid.

30. Ibid.

31. See David Arase, "China's Two Silk Roads: Implications for Southeast Asia," *ISEAS Perspective*, no. 2, January 22, 2015.

32. Carl Thayer, "China's Oil Rig Gambit: South China Sea Game-Changer?," *Diplomat*, May 12, 2014, http://thediplomat.com/2014/05/chinas-oil-rig-gambit-south-china-sea-game-changer/.

33. One Vietnamese scholar presented a more patriotic interpretation of the anti-China riots by saying that some Vietnamese workers had even formed a human shield to avoid further destruction by the violent protesters. See Huong Le Thu, "The Anti-Chinese Riots in Vietnam: Responses from the Ground," *ISEAS Perspective*, no. 32, May 27, 2014.

34. Taiwanese manager working in southern Vietnam, interview, May 2014.

35. Jim Gomez, "Beijing's South China Sea Reclamation 'Massive': Manila," *China Post*, January 22, 2015, www.chinapost.com.tw/asia/regional-news/2015/01/22/427131/Beijings-South.htm.

36. Karlo Mikhail Mongaya, "Filipino Call on China to Do a 'Chexit' in the South China Sea," *Hong Kong Free Press*, July 14, 2016, https://www.hongkongfp.com/2016/07/14/filipinos-call-china-chexit-south-china-sea/.

37. "Rodrigo Duterte to End Joint US and Philippine Military Drills," *Guardian*, September 29, 2016, https://www.theguardian.com/world/2016/sep/29/rodrigo-duterte-to-end-joint-us-and-philippine-military-drills.

38. "Obama Cancels Meeting with Philippines President after Duterte Calls US Leader 'Son of a B****,'" CNBC, September 6, 2016, www.cnbc.com/2016/09/05/obama-cancels-meeting-with-philippines-president-after-duterte-calls-us-leader-son-of-a-b.html.

39. Toko Sekiguchi and Yuka Hayashi, "Shinzo Abe's Speech to Congress Brings Military Alliance Closer," *Wall Street Journal*, April 30, 2015, www.wsj.com/articles/shinzo-abes-speech-to-congress-brings-military-alliance-closer-1430367466?tesla=y.

40. Mark J. Valencia, "The US, Japan and the South China Sea," *Diplomat*, February 8, 2015, http://thediplomat.com/2015/02/the-us-japan-and-the-south-china-sea/.

41. Hilary Clinton, July 23, 2010, "Remarks at Press Availability," US Department of State," https://2009–2017.state.gov/secretary/20092013clinton/rm/2010/07/145095.htm.

42. President Obama and most Asian leaders advocated multilateralism over sovereignty disputes in the South China Sea, in contrast with the bilateralism insisted on by the Chinese premier. Jackie Calmes, "Obama and Asian Leaders Confront China's Premier," *New York Times*, November 19, 2011, www.nytimes.com/2011/11/20/world/asia/wen-jiabao-chinese-leader-shows-flexibility-after-meeting-obama.html.

43. Mark Felsenthal and Matt Spetalnick, "Obama Says U.S. Commitment to Defend Philippines 'Ironclad,'" Reuters, April 29, 2014, www.reuters.com/article/2014/04/29/us-philippines-usa-obama-idUSBREA3S02T20140429.

44. "US, China Spar over 'Bullying' in the South China Sea," *Taipei Times*, April 11, 2015, www.taipeitimes.com/News/front/archives/2015/04/11/2003615647.

45. "US Senators Speak Out against China's Territorial Moves," *Taipei Times*, March 21, 2015, www.taipeitimes.com/News/front/archives/2015/03/21/2003614040.

46. Ibid.

47. See Samuel C. Y. Ku, "Laos in 2014: Deepening Chinese Influence," *Asian Survey* 55, no. 1 (January/February 2015): 214–19.

48. Having visited Laos in both September 2002 and September 2014, I share this viewpoint.

49. This is the first time ever that the PAP has lost one of its group representative constituencies.

50. Andrew Jacobs, "In Singapore, Vitriol against Chinese Newcomers," *New York Times*, July 26, 2012, www.nytimes.com/2012/07/27/world/asia/in-singapore-vitriol-against-newcomers-from-mainland-china.html?_r=o.

51. Amy Sawitta Lefevre and Panarat Thepgumpanat, "Thailand Cracks Down on Migrant Workers as Anti-immigration Feelings Rise," Reuters, September 29, 2016, in.reuters.com/article/thailand-migrants-idINKCN11ZoCJ.

52. Yasuhiro Matsuda, "PRC-Taiwan Relations under Chen Shui-bian's Government: Continuity and Change between the First and Second Terms," paper presented at the Brookings-FICS Conference, Taipei, May 23, 2004; Elizabeth Freund Larus, "Taiwan's Quest for International Recognition," *Issues and Studies* 42, no. 2 (June 2006): 23–52.

53. President Chen, however, reluctantly continued without a US stopover on his trip to visit Taiwan's diplomatic partners in Latin America.

54. This is the third term of the southward policy. The first southward policy was implemented from 1994 to 1996, and the second from 1997 to 1999.

55. ASTEP was enacted on April 19, 2014.

56. For more about this historic meeting, see Charlie Campbell, "Leaders of China and Taiwan Meet for the First Time," *Time*, November 11, 2015, http://time.com/4103732/china-taiwan-xi-jinping-ma-ying-jeou/.

57. These agreements were drawn up by the Taipei Economic and Cultural Office in Hanoi and the Vietnam Economic and Cultural Office in Taipei.

58. "Taiwanese Arrive in Hanoi to Attend Promotional Event," *Taipei Times*, April 18, 2013, www.taipeitimes.com/News/taiwan/archives/2013/04/18/2003560040.

59. Taiwan opened its doors to Vietnamese migrant workers in 1999. The number of Vietnamese workers had reached 150,000 by the end of 2014. Taiwan has more migrant workers from Vietnam than any other country that employs many Southeast Asian workers.

Since 1987, Vietnamese women have been marrying Taiwanese men. By the end of 2014, Vietnamese wives were the largest group of foreign wives in Taiwan.

Because of the December 2006 signing of the Education Cooperation Agreement between Taiwan and Vietnam, Vietnamese students make up the largest group of foreign students studying in Taiwan.

60. In January 2014, the Economic Development Council was renamed the National Development Council, after it merged with the Research and Evaluation Council of the Executive Yuan.

61. By the end of 2014, ROC passport holders could enter 135 countries, either without a visa or with an arrival visa.

62. Before 1985, one US dollar was the equivalent of forty Taiwan dollars. However from 1986 to 1988, after its appreciation, one US dollar was equivalent to twenty-five to twenty-six Taiwan dollars.

63. Bureau of Foreign Trade, Ministry of Economics, Republic of China.

64. "Asian Conference Industry Forum 2014," b8efa1ee-91b2–4c6c-8624–4aed8e9b8370.pdf, accessed March 17, 2015.

65. Regarding Taiwan's early investment in China and Southeast Asia, see Xiang Ming Chen, "Taiwan Investments in China and Southeast Asia: 'Go West, but Also Go South,'" *Asian Survey* 36, no. 5 (May 1996): 447–67; Rong Yung King, "Taiwan and ASEAN: Another Approach to Economic Cooperation," *Issues and Studies* 34, no. 11/12 (November/December 1998): 181–201.

66. ASEAN consists of ten countries; East Timor is the only country in Southeast Asia that is not included.

67. The members of the RECP include the ten ASEAN countries plus China, Japan, South Korea, India, Australia, and New Zealand.

68. For Taiwan's economic relations with ASEAN, see Hong Zhao, "Taiwan-ASEAN Economic Relations in the Context of East Asian Regional Integration," *International Journal of China Studies* 2, no. 1 (April 2011): 39–54.

69. China continues to obstruct Taiwan from joining these types of economic groups because of its so-called one-China policy. See, for example, Christopher M. Dent, "Taiwan and the New Regional Political Economy of East Asia," *China Quarterly* 182 (June 2005): 385–86.

70. Ministry of Foreign Affairs, ROC, "President Ma Ying-jeou Attends Seminar on Taiwan's Bid to Participate in TPP and RCEP," press release, February 17, 2014, www.mofa.gov.tw/EnMobile/News_Content.aspx?s=812442E092DF7B2B.

71. Ibid.

72. See "Siew Delivers Message to Xi as Boao Forum Opens," *Taipei Times*, March 29, 2015, www.taipeitimes.com/News/front/archives/2015/03/29/2003614643.

73. Taiwan's last-minute bid to join AIIB came just before the application deadline. See Lawrence Chung, "Taiwan in Last-Minute Bid to Join AIIB as Founding Member," *South China Morning Post*, March 31, 2015, www.scmp.com/news/china/article/1751994/taiwan-last-minute-bid-join-aiib-founding-member.

74. Tung Chen-Yuan, "The East Asian Economic Integration Regime and Taiwan," *Asian Perspective* 34, no. 2 (April/June 2010): 83–112.

75. Election Study Center, National Chengchi University, Taiwan, "Trends in Core Political Attitudes among Taiwanesses [sic]," August 24, 2016, http://esc.nccu.edu.tw/course/news.php?class=203.

76. Ibid.

77. Ibid.

78. Since the early 1990s, the issue of Taiwanese identity has surged. For early work on Taiwanese identity, see Lowell Dittmer, "Taiwan and the Issue of National Identity," *Asian Survey* 44, no. 4 (July/August 2004): 475–83; Yun-Han Chu, "Taiwan's National Identity Politics and the Prospect of Cross-Strait Relations," *Asian Survey* 44, no. 4 (July/August 2004): 484–512; Chi Huang, "Dimensions of Taiwanese/Chinese Identity and National Identity in Taiwan," *Journal of Asian and African Studies* 40, nos. 1/2 (February/April 2005): 51–70.

79. Directorate General of Budget, Accounting and Statistics, Executive Yuan, ROC.

IV

Conclusion

15

Taiwan and the Waning Dream of Reunification

Lowell Dittmer

China and Taiwan constitute one of the four nations divided by the Cold War.[1] This division was originally intended to be only temporary, but reunification soon became impossible as the Cold War polarized in the late 1940s and each "half" became embedded in the front lines of its side. This division has proved especially intractable because the international ideological cleavage overlay embittered civil wars—in China, the revolutionary civil war. Yet reunification has been incorporated into the founding visions of national self-realization in China and to some extent in Taiwan.

This concluding chapter focuses on why, after the dream was revived along with the KMT (Kuomintang, or Nationalist Party) victory in 2008, it now seems to be fading. The first part of the chapter outlines the original legitimacy basis for reunification as a national goal. The second critically reviews vicissitudes in the reunification narrative since 1949. The third attempts to explain the current turn away from reunification.

WHY REUNIFICATION?

The appeal of national unification is the quest for collective roots, which are to some extent primordial. The Chinese claim to Taiwan is both historical and ethnolinguistic. Some mainland historians claim that Taiwan has been part of China since the beginning of the Sui dynasty (598–618), though official dynastic histories as late as the Ming (1368–1644) make no reference to Taiwan in the section on administrative geography (the *dilizhi*, which comprehensively lists all provinces, prefectures, subprefectures, and counties of the Ming state), so we may infer it was then no more than an outlying frontier region. By the thirteenth century, however, there were a significant number of Chinese settlements on the island, where fertile virgin land and mild climate drew economic migrants. The island also attracted early imperialist interests. (In 1622 the Dutch drove out Spanish settlers and established a colony.) A rebel named Cheng Chenggong (known in the West as Koxinga) established a "pirate" garrison near Tainan in the name of the recently defeated Ming, but the Qing dispatched their navy under Admiral Shi Lang to destroy the Zheng fleet in the Battle of Penghu (1683), thereafter annexing the island as a prefecture of Fujian Province. In 1887 Taiwan finally became an imperial province, only to be annexed by Japan only eight years later, following China's defeat in the Sino-Japanese War. It remained a colony from 1895 to 1945. The Nationalists, having brutally reestablished Chinese control in 1945–47, retreated to the island upon losing the civil war on the mainland in 1949 with the declared intention of reversing that outcome at the first opportunity.

For its part, the People's Republic of China (PRC) fully expected to "liberate" the island as soon as they consolidated control of southern China, thereby completing their revolution and ending "one hundred years of humiliation" (*bainian guochi*) by overthrowing the "unequal treaty" of Shimonoseki that ceded Taiwan to Japan. But Chinese intervention on behalf of the Democratic People's Republic of Korea in the Korean War in November 1950 precipitated US intervention in support of the Nationalists, indefinitely postponing plans to bring the civil war to a conclusion. Ethnically, all but some 2 percent of the populace, both natives (*benshengren*) and migrants from the mainland (*waishengren*), are Han Chinese, speak a local dialect of Mandarin, and observe Chinese ceremonial rituals.

Since the unfinished Second Civil War, the goal of unification has been deeply embedded in national identity symbolism on both sides of the Strait. The Chiangs both believed to their dying days in "one China," notoriously declining the chance to retain international diplomatic recognition and membership in the UN General Assembly as an independent Taiwan if that meant renouncing the claim to be part of one China. That claim is written into the constitutions of both the PRC and the Republic of China (ROC), and it endures in the flags, coinage, postage stamps, and history texts of both sides. Taiwan throughout the Chiang dictatorship continued to represent all mainland provinces in the (largely symbolic) National Assembly, just as both the Chinese People's Political Consultative Congress and the National People's Congress included (and still include) delegates nominally representing Taiwan. Taiwanese, whether native *benshengren* or *waishengren*, are distinguished from foreigners (*waiguoren*) on the mainland as "compatriots" (*tongbao*). Despite recent disenchantment with the dream of reunification, there is a persisting legacy that insistently, recurrently raises the question. Indeed, the spirit of nationalism cannot be evoked on either side without reopening that issue. Ambition for enhanced national power is also relevant:

a freely united China would be an even more powerful and prestigious presence on the world stage than it already is.

From an international perspective the Taiwan question is a painful diplomatic anomaly. During the Cold War it was an unstable point in the structure of global bipolarity, as exhibited by refugee flows, inflammatory rhetoric, unilateral threats, and red line crossings. And since the Cold War it remains a perennial international flash point that could still spark war between two nuclear powers and suck in surrounding states. Thus the international community (such as it is) would in principle welcome its orderly, peaceful resolution. Since 172 sovereign states (including the United States) have formally acknowledged China's claim that there is one China and that Taiwan is part of China, any objection to such reunification would technically involve them in self-contradiction. Some American allies (e.g., Australia) have even expressed the wish to opt out of their alliance commitments should they involve the China-Taiwan dispute. And, as Ping-Kuei Chen, Scott Kastner, and William Reed note above (chapter 12), some analysts urge the United States to abandon Taiwan in order to facilitate reunification and improve relations with the more strategically relevant PRC. A survey conducted by the Chicago Council on Global Affairs in 2014 showed that only 26 percent of Americans agree with the idea of sending troops to help Taiwan, compared to 47 percent who support South Korea. This result has been very consistent over time with other surveys since 1982. While no one agrees with China's threats to use force in the last resort to achieve reunification, few are prepared to fight if it does.

The fact that the interest in unification is fundamental on both sides of the Strait does not mean that there is agreement on how to get there, who should rule the reunified state, or how it should be organized. Nor does it mean that this interest is evenly distributed. The pattern has been for the side that is more powerful to have the greatest interest in reunification and to be willing to use more forcible means to get it, under the premise that it will continue to dominate the unified state. The weaker side, drawing on the same premise, in contrast has a propensity to demur or procrastinate and to try to prohibit the use of force to achieve unification.

THE PURSUIT OF UNITY

If the historical legacy and the international balance of power are so overwhelmingly in favor of reunification, what is holding it back? There have been two Taiwanese counterarguments. The first, championed mainly by the Democratic Progressive Party (DPP), is that Taiwan has not been part of China for well over a century, that the democratic government of Taiwan fulfills all the requirements of statehood, and that its independence should consequently be recognized by a name change and a revision of the constitution. The second argument, made mainly by the Nationalist Party or KMT, is that the ROC was established and internationally recognized after the Xinhai rebellion in 1911 and that it was never defeated (there has been no armistice or peace treaty) but was driven to take refuge in Taiwan, where it continues to claim sovereignty over the Chinese mainland. Since the late 1990s the first argument has proved more electorally persuasive on the island but is denounced on the mainland as "splittism." The second argument, reaffirmed by the Ma Ying-jeou regime in 2008, is implicitly accepted by Beijing in the form of the "1992 Consensus," in which each side defines "one China" in its own way.

But this is to get ahead of our story. During the Cold War both "Chinas" expressed a commitment to reunification, and the means by which this was to be achieved were coercive. For the first three decades of Taiwan's existence, while the two respective leaders of the civil war remained at the helm, warlike conditions essentially continued: the Nationalists imposed martial law, invoked anticommunism to legitimate their authoritarian rule and the prosecution of political dissent, and promised to "recover the mainland" (*huifu dalu*), presumably by force, supplemented (as in the Bay of Pigs) by a popular anticommunist uprising. Beijing precipitated two cross-Strait crises in 1954–55 and 1958 by threatening an invasion of the offshore islands still occupied by Taiwan and bombarding the islands with deadly artillery, continuing desultory bombardments (mostly propaganda leaflets) until January 1979. Yet neither a Chinese invasion of Taiwan nor a Nationalist invasion of the mainland ever took place. The balance of forces was too strong for the People's Liberation Army (PLA) after formation of the Sino-American security alliance in 1954, and the United States refused to "unleash" a Nationalist invasion of the mainland during the disastrous aftermath of the Great Leap or during the Cultural Revolution. But each side's plans for reunification were zero-sum, premised on elimination of the opposing government. The ROC government represented "China" in the United Nations (including the Security Council) and in most foreign embassies, enforcing a "one-China policy" by breaking diplomatic relations with any country that recognized the PRC. Since replacing Taiwan in the UN in 1971 the PRC has turned the tables, refusing to recognize any state that recognizes Taiwan.

The end of the Cold War, which occurred about two decades earlier in Asia than in Europe thanks to the Nixon-initiated Sino-American détente, opened opportunities for innovative approaches untrammeled by the ideological frameworks and internal alliance networks that had previously anchored the issue to bloc solidarity. Beginning with the advent of "reform and opening" in China and the onset of democracy in Taiwan a decade later, both sides explored new ideas for breaking the deadlock. Promptly after gaining US diplomatic recognition (and derecognition of Taiwan and termination of the Sino-American Alliance), Beijing introduced proposals for "three direct links" across the Strait (travel, trade, and postal) and the slogan "One country, two systems" to describe a form of reunification that would grant a "high degree of autonomy" to Taiwan for a period of fifty years. This was Beijing's most generous offer to date, for the first time offering a reasonably attractive option for peaceful unification. The immediate response from Chiang Ching-kuo was "three nos" ("no contact, no compromise, no negotiation"), but the mainland persisted, and before his death Chiang initiated a reciprocal opening to the mainland by permitting retired soldiers to visit their home villages on the mainland. The succeeding Lee Teng-hui regime established a cabinet-level National Unification Council, which in 1991 issued "National Unification Guidelines" that affirmed the ultimate goal of national unification premised on prior agreement to preserve Chinese culture and the achievement of political democracy, economic liberalization, and social pluralism in the PRC.

These offers were mutually incompatible: the Chinese package educed no reason for Taiwan to believe that an otherwise totalitarian government would grant full autonomy to a former enemy, while the Taiwan package imposed demands for transformation of the mainland regime and none for Taiwan. But both offers envisaged peaceful reunification and positive-sum postunification governing arrangements for the first time, opening the way to further discussion. First Taipei and then Beijing set up quasi-official diplomatic organs, the Straits Exchange Foundation (SEF) and the Association for Relations Across the Taiwan Straits (ARATS) respectively, and after secret negotiations in Hong Kong (where what became known as the 1992 Consensus was agreed upon) engaged in a series of meetings in Singapore to discuss further steps to facilitate trade, postal, and other exchanges. Although the "three direct links" remained off the table, trade, indirect investment, and travel grew steadily via Hong Kong.

Meanwhile politics—the intended dependent variable of socioeconomic integration—proceeded erratically, refusing to follow neofunctionalist (or Marxist) logic. Both sides hedged, reflecting continuing distrust: Taiwan engaged in rapprochement with China but tried to match this with equivalent diplomatic steps to the West via "flexible diplomacy" (e.g., dollar diplomacy, vacation diplomacy, and other expedients, none having lasting results); Beijing's hedge was to accompany its pledges of peaceful reunification with a refusal to renounce the use of force and a continuing military buildup on the Fujian coast. Roughly speaking, the period from 1988 to 1995 was one of political "thaw," followed by the 1995–96 missile crisis, which resulted in a "freeze" from 1995 to 2005, followed by another, warmer "thaw" from 2005 to 2015. The pattern was initiated by the PRC, which placed national reunification at the top of its twentieth-century agenda and established a politburo-level Taiwan Affairs Leading Small Group in 1979 to coordinate the effort.

Trade took off dramatically and investment followed, drawing in still more trade; some industries were attracted by promised access to the China market, while others used China's cheap labor pool to manufacture for export, exploiting the price advantage afforded by China's cheap currency. The Taiwan Strait crisis of 1995–96 had a temporary dampening effect (some capital flight and, between July 1995 and March 1996, a loss to Taiwan's stock market of nearly 30 percent of its value), but trade continued to thrive, a trend Lee's government sought to counter with his "go south" and "go slow" (*jieji yongren*) initiatives. But economic headwinds elsewhere (the 1997–99 Asian financial crisis, followed in 2000 by the global high-tech recession) propelled Taiwan capitalists (*taishang*) back to the mainland. Not even the election of former "Taiwan independence" (*taidu*) firebrand Chen Shui-bian of the DPP in 2000 had a noticeable adverse impact on cross-Strait relations. The mainland of course did not attempt to discourage trade or investment, but it did try to extort political concessions by demanding a halt to "splittist" tendencies, most forcibly in 1995–96 but again in 2000 and 2004. There were also some Chinese attempts to blackmail prominent proindependence Taiwanese investors like Hsu Wen-long into disavowing DPP support. But for the most part China avoided politicizing an economic relationship from which it also benefited.

Business thus continued to grow in politically good times and bad. By 2014, over 40 percent of Taiwan's trade was with the mainland, and some 80 percent of its foreign direct investment (FDI) went there; Taiwanese businesses operated more than one hundred thousand enterprises on the mainland. The trade balance has consistently been in Taiwan's favor. The upshot after a decade of anti-China Taiwanese political leadership was a widening gulf between economic and political trajectories. The DPP, deprived of official contacts with the mainland, proceeded to "de-Sinify" official political culture and build Taiwanese nationalism by invoking Chinese threats and utilizing "soft power"—reorienting educational curricula, renaming holidays, constructing museums and monuments—and the percentage of Taiwanese who favored reunification either immediately or eventually reached a historical nadir of around 10 percent in 2012. But meanwhile, Beijing demonstrated the power to choke the island's economic and diplomatic lifelines and deter other countries from offering military support. Economic interdependence continued to grow despite official DPP disfavor.

Beijing learned from its experience. After the narrow reelection of Chen in March 2004, Beijing revised its blanket no-contact policy by mixing "harder sticks and sweeter carrots." In his May 17, 2004, statement, Hu Jintao made overtures to Taipei on resuming negotiations for the "three links," reducing misunderstandings, and increasing consultation. In March 2005, the Anti- Secession Law (ASL) was unanimously passed by the National People's Congress, authorizing "nonpeaceful means" in response to a declaration of formal independence in Taiwan. Yet the ASL prohibited "secession" rather than demanding reunification and set no deadline for talks. It also for the first time authoritatively committed Beijing to negotiations on the basis of equal status between the two sides and revised its demand for "one China" as a precondition for talks (quietly disclosing that the 1992 Consensus would be an acceptable interpretation of "one China"). The Chinese

Communist Party (CCP) also initiated contacts on a party-to-party basis with the opposition, welcoming "pan-Blue" (KMT and People First Party) leaders to the mainland in 2005 and convoking the CCP-KMT Forum, an obvious revival of the United Front, which had historically worked to facilitate cooperation despite ideological contradictions. And when Chen Shui-bian resumed his drive for independence by "freezing" the National Unification Council and National Unification Guidelines in early 2006, Beijing expressed opposition but avoided threats of force, inducing the United States to rebuke Chen for violating the "five nos" that he had promised after his election in 2000 and again in 2004 (no declaration of independence; no change in the ROC's name; no "state-to-state description in the constitution"; no referendum to change the status quo; no abolition of the National Unification Council or the Guidelines for National Unification). By thus lowering the temperature of cross-Strait relations and depriving the DPP of a mainland threat to inveigh against, Beijing contributed to the KMT's landslide victory in both legislative and presidential elections in 2008.

Ma Ying-jeou's response to Beijing's new Taiwan policy was diplomatically positive but domestically more low-key, cognizant of the drift since the early 1990s of domestic public opinion away from reunification. Ma sought to halt the identity battle and shift popular attention to the government's economic performance. His strategy was to skirt "future nation preference" issues, court the middle-of-the-road voter who cared less about the name of the country than concrete performance, and count on the pan-Blues as captive voters. Thus Ma attempted to redefine Taiwan's politics by shifting its main cleavage from national identity to the economy. The corruption case against Chen Shui-bian was a late-breaking windfall for the KMT that underscored its accusations of DPP managerial incompetence.

After the KMT's 2008 landslide victory in both legislative and executive elections, the new Ma administration lost no time pursuing reconciliation with the mainland along the lines already anticipated in the 2005 pan-Blue visits to the mainland, justifying this departure from his campaign rhetoric by arguing that improved cross-Strait relations would dramatically improve the island's economy. In his inaugural speech, Ma issued "three nos"—no unification, no independence, no war (butong, budu, buwu)—to reassure the electorate, maintaining a discreet silence about the ultimate destination of cross-Strait rapprochement beyond a peaceful and prosperous working relationship. He would move from the easy to the hard, from economic issues to political issues, anticipating a future (repeatedly postponed) discussion of a cross-Strait peace treaty. The cap was lifted on Taiwanese trade and investment with the mainland, and Chinese investment on Taiwan was for the first time permitted. The SEF-ARATS negotiating forum was reconvened, alternating visits between Beijing and Taipei, and by December 15, 2008, the two sides had formally institutionalized "three direct links," facilitating Chinese tourist visits of nearly two million people in the first two years. The SEF and ARATS were reconvened and held many sessions, resulting in some twenty-three cross-Strait agreements, culminating in the summer of 2010 in an Economic Cooperation Framework Agreement (ECFA), which reduced bilateral trade barriers and cleared the way for Taiwan to negotiate preferential trade agreements with various Southeast Asian countries.

After winning a second term in 2012 by a comfortable if less impressive margin, the Ma administration launched a "re-Sinification" campaign to revive domestic support for the ROC and associated Nationalist symbolism, as Jean-Pierre Cabestan describes in chapter 3. Foreign policy continued to prioritize cross-Strait relations: Ma negotiated the next stage of economic integration, the Cross-Strait Service Trade Agreement (CSTA), while distancing himself from earlier discussion of a peace treaty or political talks. The CSTA was waylaid by procedural opposition and apparent intraparty factional opposition to Ma in Taiwan's legislature, and was finally in effect blocked by the student-led Sunflower Movement, which occupied the legislature in March 2014. Political talks, Ma stipulated, would be contingent on Chinese confidence-building steps, which were not forthcoming. By the end of 2014, the PLA had over 1,500 ballistic and cruise missiles targeting Taiwan, ten times more than in 2000, more accurate and destructive than those launched in the Strait crisis. Ma repeatedly called on the PRC to dismantle this arsenal, most recently at the December 2015 Singapore summit, to no avail. Meanwhile Taiwan's own arms spending lagged, and Ma's election promise to boost it to 3 percent of GDP remained unfulfilled—defense expenditures have continued to decline as a percentage of Taiwan's budget. The United States remained the only actor with a strategic commitment to defend Taiwan, but that commitment was made more "ambiguous" by China's weapons acquisition program, which focused on advanced A2AD (Anti-Access Area Denial) weapons designed to deter US forces from approaching the Strait. Beijing also objected to other countries' sales to Taiwan of weapons designed to redress the defense gap as interference in China's internal affairs. And US arms sales to Taiwan have declined over time. Meanwhile, though Ma had attempted to change the subject domestically from cross-Strait relations to economic growth, the underlying assumption that the former was sure to spur the latter proved overoptimistic. After a spectacular growth spurt in 2010, Taiwan's economy stagnated.

In the presidential and legislative elections in 2016, the KMT suffered a comprehensive defeat. President Tsai Ing-wen took 56 percent of the vote, and her DPP won 68 of 113 seats in the legislature, its first-ever majority. The CSTA and the subsequent Trade in Goods Agreement languished, with only a faint chance of passing in the now DPP-controlled legislature. While President Tsai Ing-wen has promised to preserve mutually beneficial relations with the mainland, she has refused to endorse the 1992 Consensus that Beijing stipulates as prerequisite to talks. Beijing is deeply suspicious of Tsai as the rumored author of the "two states" formula that

Lee Teng-hui articulated in 1999 (the framing of PRC-ROC relations as "state-to-state relations") and as chair of the Mainland Affairs Commission (MAC) at the time of Chen's 2001 formulation of "one country on each side" (of the Strait; that is, the idea that Taiwan and mainland China are two different countries rather than two political entities within the larger nation of China). Since Tsai's May 2016 inauguration diplomatic contacts have been cut and tourist trade has declined drastically. But the Chinese leadership has refrained from threats of violence, and economic integration continues without political interference.

HEADWAY AND BLOWBACK

Beijing has always preferred reunification on its terms, of course, either by continuing a civil war to military victory (before Korea) or by making a deal with Taiwan's presumably homesick mainland-exiled KMT elite. When those prospects disappeared with the passing of Taiwan's first-generation leadership, Beijing constructed a path-dependent strategy to assimilate the island peaceably. Taiwan would gradually be enveloped in a web of socioeconomic ties; meanwhile Beijing would cut off its lifelines to the rest of the world by preconditioning all diplomatic relations on denial of the island's legal existence except as part of "China." Trade relations are less amenable to political control than diplomatic, but by entering the expanding regulatory tangle, or "noodle bowl," of Asian free trade agreements and making its own trade contingent on denial of Taiwan's membership China could place Taiwan at an economic disadvantage as well. The three essential components of the strategy were (1) contingent use of force, (2) socioeconomic convergence, and (3) asymmetry in political power. Why has this strategy failed?

First of all, the division between China and Taiwan was born in war, and force has remained an inescapable contingency for resolving the impasse. For many years the mainland threatened "armed liberation" (*wuli jiefang*) of the island, and it has never renounced the option of force, while the Nationalist regime has launched U-2 surveillance flights and occasional raids in pursuit of its dream to "recover the mainland." In the early 1990s Taiwan renounced the use of force to recover the mainland with a statement that it did not actively challenge Chinese sovereignty over the mainland but only over Taiwan and adjoining offshore islands. The mainland never reciprocated this acknowledgment, insisting on sovereignty over Taiwan under a one-China principle (that there is only one China, that only the PRC represents China, and that Taiwan is a part of that China) and on the "right" to use force (including nuclear weapons) to uphold it, ironically even persuading Taipei to rescind its own disclaimer of mainland sovereignty in 2008 to accord with China's "one-China principle." Beijing has focused its contingency planning with regard to force on a swift and decapitating fait accompli precluding escalation or outside intervention.[2] To achieve this would require both amphibious superiority to win a local offensive war and sufficient regional naval and air capability to deter great-power intervention. China believes it has progressed with the former, making US intervention much more costly than in 1996, and with the acquisition of mobile intercontinental ballistic missiles (ICBMs) and MIRV (multiple independently retargeted vehicle) capability and with submarine-launched missiles (SLBMs), China boasts a credible deterrent against US nuclear blackmail. Though Beijing has not been engaged in military operations since 1979, it is quite aware of the costs of war, which it would certainly prefer to avoid with the United States, but Beijing has a stronger commitment to unification than the US commitment to prevent it and could use this to deter US intervention. If it comes to a second missile crisis, will the United States send aircraft carriers to the Strait if they can be knocked out by Chinese antiship ballistic missiles? If the United States calculates that Taiwan's autonomy is not worth the cost, and if Taiwan's military forces are clearly inferior to those arrayed against them, China can impose its will on the island without firing a shot.

Yet this scenario, premised on unquestioned local superiority, contains risks China is not yet willing to run. Until then, Beijing's use of force via coercive diplomacy is apt to prove counterproductive because of the democratic blowback to the use of insufficient force. Force can be a successful means of reunification if it is decisive, as in the 1975 Vietnamese reunification. If force is not decisive, as in the Korean War or the 1995–96 Taiwan Strait crisis, it merely antagonizes the opponent and forfeits credibility. Yet Beijing still deems threats of force essential to deter movement toward formal independence and to signal its continuing commitment to reunification. Otherwise Beijing seems to have erased force from its public repertoire, shifting from sticks to carrots and the "boxing in" strategy described by Jing Huang in chapter 13 of this book. But Taiwan realizes that the public downplaying of threats that might discredit Beijing's charm offensive does not mean the weapons are no longer there. This is a dilemma for Beijing: force cannot be used, yet Beijing cannot give up the threat to use it.

Reunification necessarily involves more than the two parts of the divided nation. Even after the end of the Cold War, "great powers" have tended to see their interests at stake in any alteration of the status quo and to intervene. Great-power intervention by the United States has since 1950 been a perennial obstacle to reunification efforts. The United States abandoned Taiwan to embrace China in the early 1970s in a "strategic triangular" move against the USSR. Since the latter's dissolution in 1991, Washington, hoping to retain leverage with both sides, has attempted to shift its role from supporter to impartial referee, stipulating that the two decide the issue either way so long as they disavow the use of force. Hegemonic intervention, as the United States construes the post–Cold War rules of the game, contains two contradictory imperatives. One has been to maintain the peace, and the other has been to block changes in the territorial status quo that are adverse to the hegemon's strategic interests. Preserving the peace is necessary in an era of globalization because wars are unpredictable and at best disrupt gainful economic intercourse. On this objective both sides can agree. But unification under Beijing's auspices, even if peaceful, may shift the regional power balance against American strategic interests.[3] American China policy has striven to resolve this contradiction. Having declared its principled commitment to neutrality in the three Sino-American communiqués that it signed with the PRC, the United States becomes actively engaged in the reunification issue only when the two sides are on the verge of hostilities—because if war breaks out it is informally committed to fight China, something it would prefer not to do. Thus in the early Strait crises it limited its involvement to defensive moves, not following up after blocking China's moves against the offshore islands and refusing to authorize Chiang's proposal to invade the mainland during the post-Leap disaster.

The continuing counterbalancing role of the United States, as symbolized after derecognition by arms sales to Taiwan, has nonetheless deeply aggrieved the PRC, which is convinced that reunification on terms favorable to the mainland would otherwise be quickly achieved. Beijing prefers to define the issue in purely "domestic" (i.e., bilateral) terms, defining the United States out of the equation. Though the US "one-China" policy formally constrains the United States to accept peaceful reunification even if that is against the US national interest, Beijing has a reasonable suspicion that US support emboldens advocates of the "China threat theory" in Taiwan to resist reunification. As Chen, Kastner, and Reed have pointed out in this volume, this may well be mistaken, and it would in any event be risky to act on such assumptions. Nevertheless, if Beijing and Taiwan both believe that US arms sales have this steeling effect they will tend to inhibit reunification based on force—at least until the balance of power shifts.

In sum, when it comes to force, China is for the time being powerful but frustrated. The PLA at long last is gaining local military superiority over Taiwan. But if it tries to use force to take Taiwan or threatens to do so, it risks triggering US intervention. Unless China can prevent such intervention, a confrontation would result either in asymmetric war or in an embarrassing climb-down and would tend to discredit Chinese threats, as in 1996. Thus the United States is key: China must have local superiority over intervening US forces, plus a sufficiently robust deterrent to inhibit nuclear blackmail if it chooses to use that local capability (for example, by sinking an American aircraft carrier). Chinese objections to US weapons sales are hence somewhat misplaced. What China really needs from the United States is a promise not to intervene in case it uses force across the Strait, but for China to request that would discredit its peaceful reunification intentions and would incur blowback from Taiwan.

Second, under Mao, China represented a revolutionary rejection of both Chinese traditional culture and Western bourgeois values, sharply divergent from a Taiwan that viewed itself as the last bastion of Confucian civilization. After the advent of "reform and opening," the CCP leadership under Deng Xiaoping espoused "emancipation of the mind," a more pragmatic attitude to the capitalist world that involved attempting to introduce more efficient economic, techno-scientific, and cultural practices from more advanced countries. These innovations were successful in accelerating economic modernization but were socially and environmentally disruptive. Tiananmen was just the largest and most celebrated of the demonstrations that roiled China through the 1980s. China emerged from the Tiananmen incident and the collapse of the communist bloc with its ideological confidence severely shaken. The leadership was in a quandary for the next two years, as some rose to the defense of prereform ideological formulas blaming the Western bourgeoisie for "peaceful evolution," while surviving reformers came under a cloud for having licensed the protests.

Not until Deng's 1992 "voyage to the south" in defense of continuing economic reform was the impasse broken: China would quietly shelve further political experimentation and adopt the Singapore compact of political authoritarianism and economic eclecticism, bringing Zhu Rongji up from Shanghai (initially as vice-premier) to staunch inflation, prepare China for entry into the World Trade Organization, and restructure banks and state-owned enterprises in accord with international "best practices." This proved to be a winning formula, and for the next two decades China experienced a sustained economic boom rarely seen in world history, unavoidably accompanied by a modernizing urban middle-class subculture increasingly convergent with that of other emerging industrial economies—including Taiwan.

Meanwhile Taiwan emerged from the Cold War to dismantle the Nationalist martial law regime and organize democratic capitalism. Economically export-oriented growth was sustained while pushing manufacturing up the value chain into computer peripherals and information technology in collaboration with Silicon Valley. When Taiwanese entrepreneurs ventured across the Strait in the early 1990s, they were welcomed by growth-obsessed local elites, a cheap and capable labor force that spoke the same language (even the same dialect), and a receptive domestic market and/or export opportunities. Taiwan did not join in the post-Tiananmen sanctions imposed by the Organisation for Economic Co-operation and Development countries after Tiananmen; it even lobbied the United States to end them. As economic growth boomed on both sides of the Strait, the mutual advantages of economic and cultural complementarity became obvious, and Taiwan's economic elites began to set up factories and resettle on the mainland. China became Taiwan's largest trade and investment partner. Over two million Taiwanese have settled on the mainland, where they have careers, families, business associations, schools, and comfortable lifestyles. A recent survey reported that nearly one-third of Taiwanese under age forty hoped to find a job in China because of potentially higher salaries and greater room for career advancement. Under ECFA, millions of Chinese tourists, thousands of Chinese permanent residents (mostly spouses of Taiwanese), and some Chinese business ventures have been established on the island. With the mainland's revival of traditional values ("harmonious society"), even cultures have begun to converge.

But social assimilation has had only limited political impact, Shu Keng and Emmy Ruihua Lin report (chapter 4), increasing "Blue" and decreasing "Green" (DPP coalition) votes and compatible business practices but exerting no noticeable effect on Taiwanese national identity, which has become firmly established on both sides of the Strait. Voting is one thing, but there is as yet no sign of prounification advocacy by *taishang* among the island's ruling elites. And the ideological convergence witnessed under the pragmatic Deng Xiaoping has clearly diminished under Xi Jinping.

Why does politics remain an outlier? The basic motive force of convergence has been economic. For twenty years China's double-digit growth was irresistible to Taiwan business. The global financial crisis that struck in 2008 made Taiwan more economically dependent on China by cutting export demand elsewhere, which seemed fortuitous at the time, as China introduced a huge stimulus package in 2009 that helped salvage Taiwan as well. But after a big GDP upsurge to 10.8 percent in 2010, Taiwan's growth declined.[4] Though there is a widespread impression in Taiwan that inequality also increased, careful examination of available statistics shows this claim to be ill-founded.[5] Over 60 percent of Taiwan's economy is dependent on exports, and China and Hong Kong are Taiwan's biggest trade partners, but Taiwan's exports have been very choppy since plunging deeply in 2009, sinking into negative territory again in 2015. Part of this can be attributed to the steady annual decline of China's GDP growth since 2010. But why has the drop been more precipitous in Taiwan? At least one reason is the effort since 2009 to move Chinese industry up to a higher value-added, technology-intensive niche, in effect squeezing out Taiwan industries (whether in Taiwan or on the mainland) in favor of a "red supply chain" of Chinese manufacturers, as Tse-Kang Leng makes clear in chapter 9.

Meanwhile the cumulative impact of outsourcing has been a decline of employment opportunities in Taiwan. Aggregate employment statistics actually show an upswing, from 5.2 percent unemployment in 2010 to 3.79 in 2015. But youth unemployment has been hovering at around 12 to 13 percent, reaching a high of 14.02 percent in August 2014. Taiwan's youth thus backed the 2014 Sunflower Movement and voted overwhelmingly DPP in 2016. Taiwan has entertained only a fraction of Hong Kong's mainland tourists (3.4 million in 2015 vs. Hong Kong's 47 million), but the sudden influx has been felt: they have high per capita incomes and have injected some US$200 billion per annum into the economy. But they arouse familiar complaints: they are described as a loud, uncouth lot whose spendthrift ways drive up prices. The KMT's attempt in the CSTA to open Taiwan's economy to mainland investment, though a potential economic boom, excited fears of a "Trojan Horse" in the form of Chinese purchase of mass media and high-tech firms.

In sum, economic convergence has indeed brought the two sides closer together, but it has also driven up expectations faster than they could realistically be fulfilled and has included unanticipated externalities. Meanwhile, the decisive economic variable is not convergence but growth, which has declined on both sides of the Strait for the first sustained period since détente took off in the early 1990s. It turns out to be risky to base reunification so narrowly on an everlasting economic boom.

Third, power symmetry across the Strait has changed over time, and this has affected the reunification dynamic. The stronger side has greater incentive (and resources) to assume a leadership role in the reunification process, assuming it will dominate the reunified state. One big problem is that the response of the weaker side to asymmetry has been to lose interest in political unification. Thus Ma Ying-jeou retreated from his early proposal for a cross-Strait peace treaty and repeatedly postponed initiation of political talks. The logic of asymmetry implies that the stronger state must be exceedingly gentle in order to build the confidence of a weaker counterpart facing greater risks. Yet this runs counter to the human tendency for the strong to exploit their advantage and humble the weak. Given this human propensity and suspicions of what Mao called "sugar-coated bullets" even when terms seem more generous, the best time for plausible reunification proposals has been during periods of relative symmetry. The most auspicious of these was in the early 1990s, viewed retrospectively by KMT elites as a golden era (*dianfeng shiqi*). On both sides there was a spirit of emancipation: Taiwan from the Chiangs' dictatorship, China from Mao's fitful tyranny and the Cultural Revolution. The Cold War structures had collapsed; it was a new world. On both sides there was greater willingness to open-mindedly experiment. "China fever" (*dalu re*) brought renewed human contact and the informal realization of Beijing's "three links." Despite its small size and population, at the time Taiwan's economy was nearly half as big as China's and more technologically advanced; from a security perspective the island still had a qualitative edge sufficient to deter any threat of invasion without US intervention.

Today the power balance has changed momentously. While in 1990 China's GDP was only 2.4 times that of Taiwan, by 2010 it was 13.7 times as large. Trade interdependency has become asymmetrical in the sense that Taiwan has proportionately more to lose than the mainland. China is Taiwan's biggest trade partner, but Taiwan is only China's fifth-largest trade partner. While 80 percent of Taiwan's FDI goes to the mainland (up from 50 percent in 2003), only a tiny fraction of China's FDI goes to Taiwan, because of the latter's reservations.

In terms of military power the asymmetry is even more striking, partly because even a small proportion of the world's second-largest economy is a very substantial arms budget, partly because the PRC has successfully dissuaded many other countries from selling arms to Taiwan. Beijing's military budget has risen eight-fold in the last twenty years, according to the Stockholm International Peace Research Institute, reaching 10 percent of global arms spending in 2012. Beijing has grown confident of its ability to defeat Taiwan quickly in a bilateral war. Diplomatically Beijing officially granted Taipei equal status in 2005, but this is valid only bilaterally; internationally Beijing colludes with others to ostracize Taiwan except as "Taipei, China," or "Chinese Taipei."

Notwithstanding its growing superiority, the PRC has attempted to maintain bilateral noblesse oblige, offering not only a high degree of autonomy in future reunification arrangements but generous trade packages and fostering many exchange arrangements. During the period of rapprochement Beijing's generosity extended to a sincere (if very limited) diplomatic truce. None of these are more than time-bound accommodations, however, as Taiwan's narrowing diplomatic space in the Tsai era has since demonstrated. And the gap between generous bilateral policy and continuing international ostracism, not to mention tightening domestic constraints on civic freedom amid a crackdown on dissent, tends to inspire skepticism about purpose-rational bilateral concessions. China's economic miracle, taking it far past Taiwan economically and promising to overtake it with regard to technology and eventually living standards as well, has made it a proud giant reluctant to expand upon the generous "one country, two systems" formula offered under Deng in the early 1980s. The only concession since has been the "differing interpretations" addendum to "one China" granted in 1992, which Xi Jinping would now like to take away. Hong Kong's recent experience has not encouraged faith in Taiwan's future as part of China.

CONCLUSION

The China-Taiwan relationship, highly volatile from the beginning, has changed greatly since the advent of democracy in Taiwan and reform and opening in China, but it remains volatile just the same. For a time it seemed that a troubled relationship that has resisted all military and diplomatic solutions might be resolved by mutual interests. But that bubble of hope has now also popped. Whether economic interests could have continued to integrate the two sides of the Strait is doubtful in any case, but now the economic engine is decelerating. Although it has failed to bring about reunion, there is little space for reaction in the other direction. Beijing still clings to the dream. Even on the (highly unlikely) chance that Beijing will overlook a declaration of formal independence, geographic, sociocultural, and economic ties are now too tightly bound to permit the island to go far from Beijing's embrace.

What are the main reasons for the waning of the dream? Surely the threatened use of force remains among them. This is now more or less exclusively wielded by Beijing, though reciprocal military exercises and an arms race continue. China reserves its right to use force and may in due course feel strong and bold enough to do so. Yet some progress has been made. Both sides have agreed that peaceful reunification, preceded by economic integration, is a better solution for both than the use of force. Beijing has learned that the use of force is politically counterproductive unless wielded in a decisive blow, making that option less likely and more risky. Great-power intervention has diminished over time as the absence of crises has made it unnecessary. Neither arms sales to Taiwan nor the military buildup on the Fujian coast has ceased, but there seems to have been a tacit understanding since the Strait Crisis that as Chinese threats and crises diminish, American arms sales will avoid destabilizing the balance: hence no submarines, no fifth-generation stealth fighters. It would be better if the threat of force could be completely removed from the picture, but that would require more trust than is currently at hand. Even without trust, given a protracted hiatus in the actual use of force (i.e., no crises), the probability of its invocation may tacitly diminish over time.

One of the biggest changes has been socioeconomic convergence. Though to some extent inhibited by Taiwanese "self-ghettoization" in homogeneous communities and mainlander discrimination, there is no language barrier, and there has been considerable intermixing on both sides of the Strait. Mutual understanding does not necessarily entail mutual affinity or political agreement, and socioeconomic convergence has not yet led to perceptible progress toward changes of national identity. This may have to await future generations, assuming continuing intermarriage between Taiwanese and Chinese. National identity may be last to change. Before that may come voting patterns, the buildup of vested interests, and finally some political concessions on both sides. For attitudes truly to change it would also be useful to have honest political discussions, which is difficult at present, particularly on the mainland. It will be a long process.

There is also the problem of relative gains. While reunification would be good (an absolute gain) for both sides and beneficial to the international community, it might be better for one side than the other. Specifically, it is better for the stronger power than for the weaker. A rational stronger power tends to minimize concessions and push for simple annexation while making minimal changes in the domestic status quo (as in the German case). This enhances domestic support for the process but motivates the weaker power to resist. The Taiwan-China relationship has become steeply asymmetrical, and to extrapolate current growth rates this is apt to increase, heightening Taiwan's disincentive to move toward unification. It will require great sensitivity on the part of the dominant party to reassure the weaker. Hence China offers "early harvest" and other concessions to Taiwan as "loss leaders" to encourage economic integration. The *taishang* respond as "free riders," gladly accepting all concessions. This leads to increasing economic integration, but whether the Taiwanese become more politically committed to the PRC is unclear. This is frustrating to the giver of the concession, who cannot however accuse the receiver of bad faith because the political quid pro quo was never explicit. To make it explicit would encumber Beijing's "no-strings-attached" and "win-win" trust-building model with political quid pro quos. Thus we have fragile sociocultural integration without much political payoff, at least in the short run.

Growing asymmetry has become perhaps the most unexpected obstacle to reunification. In itself the Chinese economic miracle is an epochal achievement. One of its motives was to surpass Taiwan, on the assumption that once China was in a position of undisputed superiority all resistance would surely collapse. Economic growth also incentivized "win-win" cross-Strait socioeconomic integration. Yet the same economic miracle that boosted the Chinese (aggregate) economy well past that of Taiwan and made the PLA Asia's largest military has also constructed a party-state juggernaut that has become a threat to any who stand in its way. To be fair, Beijing has since 2005 leaned over backward to court Taiwan with sundry concessions. But all this is not enough. The world's second-largest economy, which now aspires to become a global "pole" commanding its own strategic periphery and integrating Eurasia with ports and high-speed rail, sees no need to restructure its party-state to reassure a reincorporated Taiwan of any real influence in governing greater China. Taiwan is small and China is big, to parody Yang Jiechi. The Taiwanese have been able to descry the difference between economic convergence and political assimilation and to accept the former while evading the latter. The Xi Jinping leadership looks askance at this and is disinclined to let it continue. What they can do to stop it without unacceptable damage to their own economy and international reputation remains to be seen.

In sum, in view of recent developments the route to a mutually acceptable arrangement for divided sovereignty may yet be a long and bumpy one. Taiwan may never fully break out of Beijing's comprehensive geo-economic "boxing in" strategy. But Beijing may also not succeed in peacefully integrating the long-separate island nation into its vision of an ideologically homogeneous "one China."

NOTES

1. Actually, Germany and Korea were divided by the victors in the aftermath of World War II, and China was divided by a civil war immediately after World War II; only Vietnam was divided during the Cold War. But in all cases the basis of cleavage was the ideological split between capitalism and communism that defined the Cold War.

2. See Steve Tsang, *If China Attacks Taiwan: Military Strategy, Politics and Economics* (New York: Routledge, 2006).

3. There is an interesting ambiguity about this. On the one hand, the United States no longer recognizes or has an alliance with Taiwan, and its declaratory policy is neutral about peaceful reunification. China has promised as part of its "one country, two systems" approach not to station troops and to permit the island's continued strategic autonomy. On the other hand, the Chinese have never spelled out how Taiwan's military would continue to function autonomously or what its future relation to the PLA would be, and they clearly consider Taiwan a key link in the "first island chain." See Alan M. Wachman, *Why Taiwan? Geostrategic Rationales for China's Territorial Integrity* (Stanford, CA: Stanford University Press, 2007), 208n119.

4. In 2008 Taiwan's GDP was 1.8 percent, plunging to -1.9 percent in the aftermath of the global financial crisis in 2009, resurging to 10.8 percent in 2010, then declining to 4 percent in 2011, 1.5 percent in 2012, 2.1 percent in 2013, 3.5 percent in 2014, 0.7 percent in 2015, and 1.5 percent in 2016. The average annual growth rate from 1962 to 2015 was 7.01 percent, so this obviously represented a decline from the perceived "normal" and was lower than Taiwan's "Small Tiger" reference group (South Korea, Hong Kong, and Singapore).

5. Taiwan's Gini index of inequality is relatively low among developed economies (and far lower than China's). It has indeed increased along with globalization, from .28 in 2008 to .34 in 2015, but the rate of increase is no higher than in previous decades and is not statistically significant.

CONTRIBUTORS

JEAN-PIERRE CABESTAN is Professor and Head of the Department of Government and International Studies at Hong Kong Baptist University. He is also Associate Researcher at the Centre for Asia and the Pacific at Sciences Po International, Paris, and at the French Centre for Research on Contemporary China, Hong Kong. His main themes of research are Chinese politics and law, China's foreign and security policies, China-Taiwan relations, and Taiwanese politics.

PING-KUEI CHEN is an Assistant Professor in the Department of Diplomacy, National Chengchi University, Taiwan. He received his PhD from the Department of Government and Politics, University of Maryland, College Park, in 2016. He is interested in interstate conflict, security institutions, alliance cohesion, East Asia affairs, and cross-Strait relations.

ROU-LAN CHEN is an Assistant Professor in the Department of Political Economy at National Sun Yat-sen University, Taiwan. She received her PhD in political science from the University of California at Berkeley. Her research interests include political methodology and nationalism, with a specific focus on hierarchical linear modeling and Taiwan's identity politics. Her recent research on China encompasses Internet nationalism, youth identity, and antiglobalization movements.

LOWELL DITTMER is Professor of Political Science at the University of California at Berkeley, where he teaches Chinese and Asian comparative politics, and editor of *Asian Survey*. He is currently working on an analysis of China's recent Asia policy. Recent works include *Sino-Soviet Normalization and Its International Implications* (University of Washington Press, 1992); *China's Quest for National Identity* (with Samuel Kim, Cornell University Press, 1993); *China under Reform* (Westview, 1994); *Liu Shaoqi and the Chinese Cultural Revolution* (rev. ed., M. E. Sharpe, 1998); *Informal Politics in East Asia* (with Haruhiro Fukui and Peter N. S. Lee, eds., Cambridge, 2000); *South Asia's Nuclear Security Dilemma: India,*

Pakistan, and China (M. E. Sharpe, 2005); *China's Deep Reform: Domestic Politics in Transition* (with Guoli Liu, eds., Rowman and Littlefield, 2006); *China, the Developing World, and the New Global Dynamic* (Lynne Rienner, 2010); *Burma or Myanmar? The Struggle for National Identity* (2010); and many scholarly articles. His most recent book is *Routledge Handbook of Chinese Security* (with Maochun Yu, eds., 2015).

YOU-TIEN HSING is Professor of Geography and Chair of the Center for Chinese Studies at the University of California at Berkeley. She is the author of *Making Capitalism in China: The Taiwan Connection* (Oxford University Press, 1998) and *The Great Urban Transformation: Politics of Land and Property in China* (Oxford University Press, 2010). She is currently completing her third monograph, tentatively entitled *Projectizing Nature and Culture in China's Northwest.*

JING HUANG is a Lee Foundation Professor on US-China Relations and Director of Centre on Asia and Globalization at the Lee Kuan Yew School of Public Policy. Huang was a Residential Fellow at the Rockefeller Foundation Bellagio Center in 2012 and is a Richard von Weizsäcker Fellow at the Robert Bosch Academy.

YI-HUAH JIANG is a Professor of the College of Liberal Arts and Social Sciences at City University of Hong Kong. His academic interests lie in political philosophy, liberalism, democratic theory, national identity, and Taiwanese politics. He is the author of *Liberalism, Nationalism and National Identity* (Yang-Chih Book, 1998), *Essays on Liberalism and Democracy* (Linking, 2000), and *Nationalism and Democracy* (National Taiwan University Press, 2003). He also served as Minister and Premier of Taiwan from 2008 to 1014.

SCOTT L. KASTNER is an Associate Professor in the Department of Government and Politics at the University of Maryland, College Park. His book *Political Conflict and Economic Interdependence across the Taiwan Strait and Beyond* was published by Stanford University Press (2009).

SHU KENG, Research Fellow in the School of Public Affairs and Associate Chair of the Department of Sociology, Zhejiang University, received his PhD from the University of Texas at Austin. His specializations include comparative politics, comparative political economy, and cross-Strait relations.

SAMUEL C. Y. KU was a Professor at National Sun Yat-sen University for twenty-seven years and since August 2016 has been Vice-President for International Affairs at Wenzao Ursuline University of Languages. His major research interests include Southeast Asia's political development and China's and Taiwan's relations with Southeast Asia. His publications are mostly in Chinese, but his English articles have appeared in such international journals as *Asian Survey, Asian Perspective, Contemporary Southeast Asia, Issues and Studies, Journal of Contemporary China,* and *Journal of Asian and African Studies.*

TSE-KANG LENG is a Research Fellow at the Institute of Political Science of Academia Sinica (IPSAS) and Professor of Political Science at National Chengchi University. His research interests focus on the political economy of globalization, local governance in China, and cross–Taiwan Strait relations. His academic works have appeared in *Asian Survey, China Journal, Pacific Focus, Journal of Contemporary China, Journal of Contemporary China Studies,* and edited volumes.

EMMY RUIHUA LIN is an Assistant Professor in the School of Public Economics and Administration, Shanghai University of Finance and Economics. Her research interests include immigration studies, *taishang* studies, and cross-Strait relations.

GANG LIN is a Distinguished Professor and the Chair of the Academic Committee at the Shanghai Jiao Tong University's School of International and Public Affairs, Director of Center for Taiwan Studies, Vice-President of the Shanghai Society for Taiwan Studies, and Senior Fellow of the Collaborative Innovation Center for Peaceful Development of Across-Strait Relations.

CHIH-SHIAN LIOU is an Associate Professor of the Graduate Institute of East Asian Studies at National Chengchi University, Taiwan. She specializes in comparative politics, political economy, and Chinese politics. Her research has appeared in *Asian Survey, Taiwanese Political Science Review, World Development*, and other journals.

WILLIAM L. REED is an Associate Professor in the Department of Government and Politics and a Research Fellow of the Center for International Development and Conflict Management (CIDCM) at the University of Maryland. His research interests include mathematical and statistical models of international conflict and cooperation, Asian security politics, disputes over natural resources/territory, and experimental studies of conflict bargaining.

CHUNG-MIN TSAI is an Associate Professor of Political Science at National Chengchi University in Taiwan. He obtained his doctoral degree in political science from the University of California at Berkeley. His academic interests include comparative politics, political economy, and China studies. He has published articles in the *China Quarterly, Asian Survey, Issues and Studies, Taiwanese Political Science, Chinese Political Science*, and edited volumes.

WEIXU WU is currently a postdoctoral fellow of the Institute for Taiwan Studies at Tsinghua University. He received his PhD in public administration from Shanghai Jiao Tong University (2015). He was a visiting PhD student of College of Social Science at Taiwan University from February to July 2014. His current research projects include Taiwan issues, the executive-legislature relationship, and public opinion polls.

YU-SHAN WU is a Distinguished Research Fellow at the Institute of Political Science, Academia Sinica, and Professor of Political Science at National Taiwan University. He is an Academician of Academia Sinica. His major interests are political and economic transitions in former socialist countries, constitutional engineering in nascent democracies, and theories of international relations and cross–Taiwan Strait relations. He has written and edited twenty books and published more than 130 journal articles and book chapters.

INDEX

CPSIA information can be obtained
at www.ICGtesting.com
Printed in the USA
LVOW05s2237091017
551751LV00016B/1178/P

9 780520 295988